Communications in Computer and Information Science 2339

Rationale

The CCIS series is devoted to the publication of proceedings of computer science conferences. Its aim is to efficiently disseminate original research results in informatics in printed and electronic form. While the focus is on publication of peer-reviewed full papers presenting mature work, inclusion of reviewed short papers reporting on work in progress is welcome, too. Besides globally relevant meetings with internationally representative program committees guaranteeing a strict peer-reviewing and paper selection process, conferences run by societies or of high regional or national relevance are also considered for publication.

Topics

The topical scope of CCIS spans the entire spectrum of informatics ranging from foundational topics in the theory of computing to information and communications science and technology and a broad variety of interdisciplinary application fields.

Information for Volume Editors and Authors

Publication in CCIS is free of charge. No royalties are paid, however, we offer registered conference participants temporary free access to the online version of the conference proceedings on SpringerLink (http://link.springer.com) by means of an http referrer from the conference website and/or a number of complimentary printed copies, as specified in the official acceptance email of the event.

CCIS proceedings can be published in time for distribution at conferences or as post-proceedings, and delivered in the form of printed books and/or electronically as USBs and/or e-content licenses for accessing proceedings at SpringerLink. Furthermore, CCIS proceedings are included in the CCIS electronic book series hosted in the SpringerLink digital library at http://link.springer.com/bookseries/7899. Conferences publishing in CCIS are allowed to use Online Conference Service (OCS) for managing the whole proceedings lifecycle (from submission and reviewing to preparing for publication) free of charge.

Publication process

The language of publication is exclusively English. Authors publishing in CCIS have to sign the Springer CCIS copyright transfer form, however, they are free to use their material published in CCIS for substantially changed, more elaborate subsequent publications elsewhere. For the preparation of the camera-ready papers/files, authors have to strictly adhere to the Springer CCIS Authors' Instructions and are strongly encouraged to use the CCIS LaTeX style files or templates.

Abstracting/Indexing

CCIS is abstracted/indexed in DBLP, Google Scholar, EI-Compendex, Mathematical Reviews, SCImago, Scopus. CCIS volumes are also submitted for the inclusion in ISI Proceedings.

How to start

To start the evaluation of your proposal for inclusion in the CCIS series, please send an e-mail to ccis@springer.com.

Boutaina Hdioud · Si Lhoussain Aouragh
Editors

Arabic Language Processing

From Theory to Practice

8th International Conference, ICALP 2023
Rabat, Morocco, April 19–20, 2024
Proceedings, Part I

Editors
Boutaina Hdioud
ENSIAS, Mohammed V University
Rabat, Morocco

Si Lhoussain Aouragh
ENSIAS, Mohammed V University
Rabat, Morocco

ISSN 1865-0929 ISSN 1865-0937 (electronic)
Communications in Computer and Information Science
ISBN 978-3-031-79163-5 ISBN 978-3-031-79164-2 (eBook)
https://doi.org/10.1007/978-3-031-79164-2

This Springer imprint is published by the registered company Springer Nature Switzerland AG
The registered company address is: Gewerbestrasse 11, 6330 Cham, Switzerland

Preface

This volume constitutes the refereed proceedings of the 8th International Conference on Arabic Language Processing (ICALP 2023), formerly known as CITALA. The conference, initially scheduled for 2023, was postponed due to organizational constraints and was ultimately held in April 2024 in Rabat, Morocco; it was organized by the National Higher School of Computer Science and Systems Analysis (ENSIAS) in collaboration with the Arabic Language Engineering Society of Morocco (ALESM).

The ICALP 2023 conference brought together experts, scholars, and professionals from academia and industry to exchange ideas, share insights, and explore the latest advancements in all branches of Arabic Natural Language Processing.

The ICALP 2023 conference provided an exceptional opportunity for participants to present their research and achievements and to engage in the exchange of experiences and insights. Additionally, it facilitated the creation of valuable new collaborations and partnerships with leading experts in the field.

For this notable edition, we received 107 submissions from different countries. Over 71 technical experts participated in the peer-review process. Each paper was assigned to at least three reviewers, ensuring thorough evaluation. The 41 papers selected for presentation were all reviewed under a rigorous double-blind process.

The conference highlighted new approaches related to the Arabic language, from theoretical models to industrial applications. All branches of natural language processing (NLP) related to Arabic spoken or text language processing constituted the core focus of ICALP 2023. The papers covered a wide range of very interesting topics including Learning Arabic and Dialects, Learning Arabic and Translation, Deep Learning for Arabic, and other aspects of NLP. The volume is structured into four sections: The first part contains papers focused on learning Arabic, including dialectal variation and sentiment analysis. The second part is dedicated to advancements in deep learning for Arabic language processing, covering tasks such as text generation, translation, and question answering—an area with numerous challenges. The third part emphasizes resources essential for natural language processing (NLP), while the final part presents papers that explore various aspects of Arabic language analysis.

This achievement is the result of the hard work and dedication of many people, and we would like to express our heartfelt gratitude to everyone involved.

First and foremost, we would like to thank all the authors who have contributed their research papers to this proceedings volume. Their dedication and expertise have greatly enriched the content of this volume. We also extend our appreciation to the Scientific Committee members for their thorough evaluation and constructive feedback, which ensured the quality and rigor of the papers included. Additionally, we extend our appreciation to the Publicity, Organizing, and all Committee members for their assistance in making this conference a success.

We are particularly grateful to our distinguished keynote speakers for agreeing to address the conference attendees. Their insights and contributions were essential to the success of this conference.

Furthermore, we would like to acknowledge the efforts of the Organizing Committee members and session chairs for their invaluable contributions in organizing and coordinating the conference. Their meticulous planning and execution were instrumental in creating a successful and enriching conference experience for all attendees.

We would also like to express our gratitude to Springer for their assistance in publishing the ICALP 2023 proceedings in the CCIS series for their technical support and endorsement of the conference.

Lastly, we extend our heartfelt appreciation to all the sponsors.

Thank you for your participation, support, and contributions to ICALP 2023. We sincerely hope that you find this conference proceedings volume informative and inspiring.

April 2024

Boutaina Hdioud
Si Lhoussain Aouragh

Organization

General Chair

Si Lhoussain Aouragh	ENSIAS, Mohammed V University of Rabat, Morocco

Program Committee Chairs

Si Lhoussain Aouragh	ENSIAS, Mohammed V University of Rabat, Morocco
Yasser El Madani El Alami	ENSIAS, Mohammed V University of Rabat, Morocco
Hatim Guermah	ENSIAS, Mohammed V University of Rabat, Morocco
Boutaina Hdioud	ENSIAS, Mohammed V University of Rabat, Morocco
Mohamed Naoum	ENSIAS, Mohammed V University of Rabat, Morocco

Steering Committee

Si Lhoussain Aouragh	ENSIAS, Mohammed V University of Rabat, Morocco
Boutaina Hdioud	ENSIAS, Mohammed V University of Rabat, Morocco

Program Committee

Siham Aouad	ENSIAS, Mohammed V University of Rabat, Morocco
Si Lhoussain Aouragh	ENSIAS, Mohammed V University of Rabat, Morocco
Yasser El Madani El Alami	ENSIAS, Mohammed V University of Rabat, Morocco
Hatim Guermah	ENSIAS, Mohammed V University of Rabat, Morocco

Boutaina Hdioud ENSIAS, Mohammed V University of Rabat, Morocco
Hakima Khamar EMI, Mohammed V University of Rabat, Morocco
Mohamed Lazaar ENSIAS, Mohammed V University of Rabat, Morocco
Mohamed Naoum ENSIAS, Mohammed V University of Rabat, Morocco
Adnan Souri Abdelmalek Essaâdi University, Morocco
Tajmout Rachida FLSH, Mohammed V University of Rabat, Morocco

Additional Reviewers

Nabil Ababou
Yousfi Abdellah
Arfat Ahmad Khan
Abdelmoula Abouhilal
Hassina Aliane
Husni Al-Muhtaseb
Chafik Aloulou
Abdulaziz AlQabbany
Abdulmalik AlSalman
Rym Ammar
Ibrahim Amrani
Siham Aouad
Mohamed Aouaj
Si Lhoussain Aouragh
Ouiame Azzaoui
Mohamed Badr Benboubker
Abdelmajid Ben Hamadou
Karim Bouzoubaa
Naoual Chaouni Benabdellah
Violetta Cavalli-Sforza
Gaël de Chalendar
Marwa Dridi
Mohamed El Ammari
Mahmoud El-Haj
Anoual El kah
Yasser El Madani El Alami
Ismail El Bazi
Widad Ettazi
Rdouan Faizi
Hatim Guermah
Brahim Habibi
Kais Haddar
Abdelfattah Hamdani
Aboubekeur Hamdi-Cherif
Jaafar Hamid
Mohamed Hedi Riahi
Boutaina Hdioud
Mohamed Jmaiel
Mohammed Kasbi
Hakima Khamar
Mohamed Khenchouch
Abdelhak Lakhouaja
Mohamed Lazaar
Hajar Makhoukhi
Alaf Makke
Meryem Manessouri
Azzeddine Mazroui
Anis Mohamed
Khalid Nafil
Mohamed Naoum
Omar Ouhejjou
Youssef Ouguengay
Taoufik Rachad
Mohamed Radouane
Majda Rami
Salim Rami
Imen Rassas
Azeddine Rhazi

Paolo Rosso
Khalid Sami
Younes Samih
Khaled Shaalan
Kamel Smaïli
Adnan Souri
Ibtissam Touahri
Abderrahim Tragha
Adnan Yahya
Randa Zarnoufi
Imad Zeroual
Iman Zubeiri

Sponsors

ALESM: The Arabic Language Engineering Society in Morocco
CNRST: The National Center for Scientific and Technical Research
ENSIAS: High National School for Computer Science and Systems Analysis

Contents – Part I

Advancements in Deep Learning for Arabic Language Processing: Generation, Translation, and QA

Contents – Part II

Various Analysis of Arabic

Learning Arabic and dialectal and Sentiment Analysis

Sentiment Analysis on Moroccan Dialect of Arabic Combining NLP and ML Methods

Khalil Ladrham[1(✉)] and Hicham Gueddah[2]

[1] Intelligent Processing and Security of Systems, Faculty of Sciences, Mohammed V University, B.P:8007, Av. Nations Unies, Agdal, Rabat, Morocco
khalil_ladrham@um5.ac.ma

[2] Intelligent Processing and Security of Systems Team, E.N.S, Mohammed V University, B.P:8007, Av. Nations Unies, Agdal, Rabat, Morocco

Abstract. In recent years, machine learning and websites have developed rapidly. This resulted in continual and explosive growth in the sharing of ideas and views on products and services over the worldwide web in an array of sectors. As a result, there is an enormous flow of internet data attainable for analytical research. Sentiment analysis (SA) is a part of Natural Language Processing (NLP) that requires to process enormous amounts of data in order to identify people's opinions and sentiments. Several studies have been conducted to deal with the negative effects of social networks. This field of research is increasing popularity in both the public and private sectors, leading to the creation of several challenges. However, the majority of the available datasets were in English. Whereas the Arabic Moroccan dialect (Darija) ones were not. Following that, we created models combining NLP and Marching learning techniques to detect and classify sentiments. We evaluated the models using the most used metrics: accuracy, loss, F1-score, precision, and recall. The results of the experiment revealed modest scores between 87% and 89%.These findings imply that the models require to be upgraded due to a lack of accessible datasets and pre-processing techniques to handle the Moroccan dialect of Arabic (Darija).

Keywords: Sentiment analysis · Arabic Moroccan dialect · Natural Language Processing NLP · Maching Learning ML · pre-processing · datasets

1 Introduction

Social media has become a widely used communication tool for exchanging opinions, thoughts, and feelings in recent years. People use it to voice their opinions on a wide range of topics, including news, sports, movies, and items and locations. Thanks to the hundreds of reviews that active users publish on a daily basis, this information has become must reading for many. Nowadays, more than 2 billion people use social media to participate in online conversations, research subjects, and express their opinions [1], Social media platforms such as Facebook and Instagram have transformed global communication by linking individuals from all over the globe. These platforms are largely aimed towards

B. Hdioud and S. L. Aouragh (Eds.): ICALP 2024, CCIS 2339, pp. 3–16, 2025.
https://doi.org/10.1007/978-3-031-79164-2_1

young people with the goal of creating relationships [2], They enable quick content production and social engagement, and have become an essential component of the lives of numerous teenagers today [3]. Many users have become addicted to social media sites, dragging through their cell phones over the day [4], This behavior often leads to losing valuable time and delaying on important jobs or occupations. Social media addiction and weariness have become widespread problems, hurting users' productivity and general health [5].

Natural Language Processing (NLP) aims to teach robots how to read and produce human language, whether written or spoken [8]. One of the most vital and sophisticated aspects of computational intelligence, including a wide range of issues [9], especially when working with the Arabic language, which we shall discuss more in this article. Sentiment Analysis frequently referred by the term opinion mining [6], it is the statistical analysis of the views of individuals on an array of subjects [7], including products, enterprises, personalities, events, ideas, and qualities [10]. SA has become one of the most well-known Natural Language Processing (NLP) applications.

Machine Learning (ML) approaches have been extensively used in recent years to solve different categorization and prediction challenges, such as handwriting recognition [11, 12]. Sentiment analysis makes it possible to extract from tweets the opinions of the general public on one or more issues [14, 15], the use of social media has had a major influence on the efficacy of Arabic SA techniques [16, 17].

The current research presents an effort to perform sentiment analysis using Moroccan individual's comments to find responses by utilizing local phrases and idioms in their original dialect as a basis. With Social media, sites like Youtube are being used more often in Morocco and are becoming a significant information source for citizens. Our objective intends to develop an emotional analysis model that can correctly classify Arabian Moroccan comments as positive or negative. To achieve this, we grabbed a large database of Moroccan Dialect in Arabic from Youtube. However, the process of gathering this data was not without difficulty. Moroccan Arabic, a complicated dialect that varies greatly from area to region, has no uniform written form.

We used a variety of pre-processing approaches on the gathered comments before building our SA model, comprising stop word, removal, url removal, HTML removal, emoji's removal, tokenization. We also used two feature extraction methods, one-hot encoding and TF IDF, in conjunction with machine learning algorithms such as SVM, KNN, and NB. To record the semantic relationships between words and sentences and classify comments based on their sentiment.

To evaluate the accuracy of these algorithms, a portion of the dataset was utilized for training and a separate set of comments was used for testing. Our model is distinctive in that it focuses exclusively on sentiments using Arabic spoken in the Moroccan Dialect and integrates regional accents and vocabulary to improve accuracy. Our study results are promising since our system correctly categorized comments as positive, or negative.

2 Related Works

We have observed that the sentiments's investigation is mostly focused on English. As a result, there are now numerous good tools and structures for english content available.

However, further study is needed to develop sophisticated approaches for other languages, such as Arabic [18]. They used bi-grams as features in their model to represent the content. Researchers utilized both the term frequency (TF) or term frequency inverse document frequency (TF-IDF) grading methodologies to evaluate the performance of numerous classifiers, including Support Vector Machine (SVM), Naive Bayes (NB), and K-Nearest Neighbor (KNN). [19] Used three machine-learning methods: support vector machine (SVM), Naive Bayes (NB), and MultiLayer-Perceptron (MLP). All tests took place in Python using Scikit Learn for categorization & gensim for vector representational learning.

The authors of [20] analyze several ensemble approach types. In terms of sentiment analysis using arabic, it was clear SVM algorithm performed far more effectively than other classifiers, and by an important proportion. However, no one classifier scored anywhere close to as excellent as the efficiency of a combination of many classifiers [16] applied the SVM technique to extract basic features. They had a poor accuracy of 64.1%, which could have been attributed to the too basic treatment of features according to rates.

It Used a variety of classifiers on balanced and unbalanced datasets, including SVM, Logistic Regression (LR), Binomial NB (BNB), and other techniques. The authors extracted features using n-grams and TF-IDF [21]. Their imbalanced corpus test yielded a highest accuracy of up to 69.1% when they used TF-IDF and SVM classifiers. To assess several lexicons, a nonlinear SVM using a radial basis function (RBF) kernel. The SVM classifier was trained using sentence vectors, which are composed from three numerical attributes that represent the emotions (i.e., positive, negative, or neutral) referred to in each expression. By matching the lemmas in each phrase to each of the lexicons, the value of each characteristic is determined. Results proved that the combination of the two lexicon creation methods provides better results, gaining an F1-score of up to 64.5% [17].

In [12] authors extracted features using both the Bag Of Words (BOW) or Doc2vec approaches. They used several algorithms for classification, like SVM, NB, LR, and furthermore, with LR surpassing other classifiers by reaching an F1-score of up to 78%. Despite the fact that the F1- score for Arabizi categorization reached 68%, these writers worked with both Arabic and Arabizi.

Multinomial Naïve Bayes (MNB) is a popular sentiment analysis classifier because of its short training time and ease of usage. In text classification, support vector machines (SVMs) are a popular machine learning algorithm that outperform a variety of other methods. SVMs are quicker and often provide better results than the Naïve Bayes algorithm while maintaining the same level of accuracy [19].

3 Materials and Methods

3.1 Short Description of the Desired Framework

The first stage in creating a comprehensive dataset is to acquire raw information from various sources. Pre-processing is the process of cleaning, organizing, and structuring data to remove noise and manage missing information. Classification entails classifying data into discrete categories based on certain criteria, while the outcome reflects the insights, trends, or predictions obtained from the analysis, which may be used to influence decision-making and future study.

While preprocessing, cleaning, and preparing the data for the following essential steps is critical. It has a direct influence on the performance of classification models. Preprocessing activities are required before building a predictive model. The key ones are: reduction to lowercase, tokenization, punctuation removal, stopwords removal, and stemming. The work of sentence or comment categorization comprises the token level rather than the document level, which is unusual. The purpose is to categorize the phrase itself, not the symbol. The goal is to label the comment with the proper class rather than the tokens with the class, thus keep the context in mind. Each comment's punctuation is removed and then tagged with the correct class to display the most specific tokens for determining the layout of emotive charge or for detecting emotional activation or intensification.

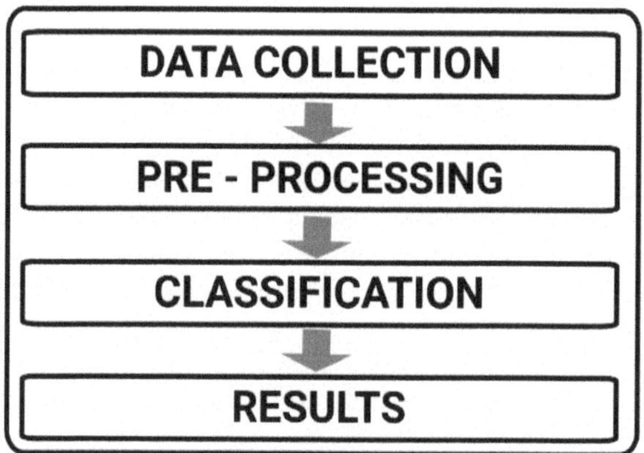

Fig. 1. Short Description of the Desired Framework

3.2 Difficulties Recognizing Moroccan Dialect

Moroccans are among the most chosen individuals in the world for design sentiment evaluations, especially the younger generation. Sentiment analyses based on the MSA have been produced for Arabic, and in some situations, Darija, one of Morocco's primary national languages, as well [20]. Sentiment analysis in Moroccan Dialect (MD) is a challenging and comparatively understudied area of Natural Language Processing (NLP) for a number of reasons, including pronunciation variances, colloquial phrases, and the incorporation of vocabulary from other languages into MD [21]. The increasing degree of linguistic variation seen in Moroccan internet material is illuminated by the lack of MD sentiment analysis. Texts that are accessible on the internet provide a number of difficulties for MD sentiment analysis.

Daija, an Arabic dialect unique to Morocco, enjoys widespread usage among Moroccans, as well as in the content of brand websites on social media, television shows, and advertisements targeting the public. It bears the influence of several tongues Darija keeps its individuality with respect to spelling, syntax, vocabulary, and pronunciation [17]. Recently, there has been a notable surge in the written use of Darija across various platforms. Yet, some challenges persist in the processing of Darija, including: ion -Code Switching and Mixing-Romanized Arabic-Informal Language Use Limited Language Resources-Text classification and sentiment analysis.

The term "Moroccan Dialect" (MD) refers to a group of mutually understandable dialects [22]. Written dialect Arabic (WDA) is a key component of MSA technology and is used on a variety of digital platforms. Dialectal Arabic presents challenges for orthographic representation since transcriptions vary widely and digraphs and trigraphs occur often. Despite 150 years of effort in Standard Arabic (MSA) to standardize grammatical and orthographical rules, Dialectal Arabic lacks consensus on linguistic norms. Additionally, since it is one of the most widely spoken dialects in the nation and for historical reasons, we look at Morocco's most varied and urban-centered MD variant here: Among the biggest and most significant cities.

A set of French structural conjunctions that directly translate average French linking expressions, extensive lexical borrowing from French, Spanish, and Berber languages, extensive code-switching with French (North African Code-Switching), the use of French words when no dialect word exists, the maintenance of French identities through loan translation of phonetic approximations of French clusters, and finally Sabir words are characteristics of the MD of MCMC. There are a great deal of phrases that are restricted by area and a few historical borrowings that are approved by region [23]. It will be challenging for people from various Moroccan areas to converse with one another in Darija. There are six primary of Darija, which are sufficiently different from one another to impede mutual comprehension and prevent local dialects from normalizing or receiving formal recognition.

3.3 Moroccan Arabic Dialect Using Sentiment Analysis

We describe a Maching Learning (ML) technique for SA based on sentiment analysis comments written in MDA in this part. This procedure begins with data cleaning, preprocessing, and features selection before classification, with the goal of reducing complexity and improving the reliability of our models for categorization. Furthermore, the performance of our model is measured in the evaluation stage. The suggested ML system for Arabic sentiment analysis is shown in Fig. 2

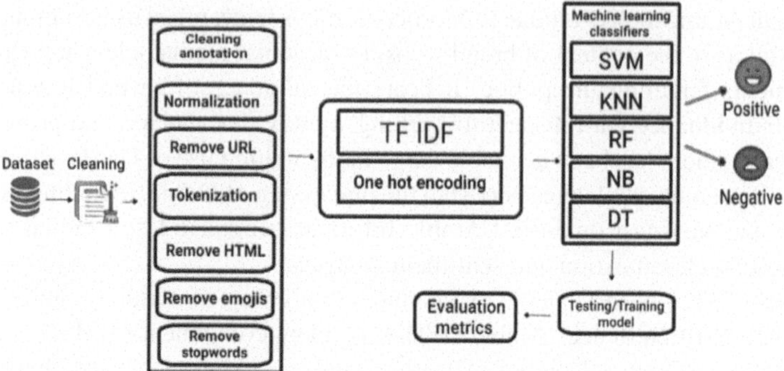

Fig. 2. ML Approaches and Features Extraction

3.4 Description of the Dataset

Within our research, we utilized a sentiment analysis (SA) dataset comprising comments posting within Arabic dialect, which is open to the public via the Simulation and Analysis of Data platform. The initial dataset comprised of sentiments obtained from active users residing in specific Moroccan cities. The resulting dataset encompasses 2900 positive comments, 1490 negative comments, For illustrative purposes, we provide a selection of sample entries in Table 1 and Table 2.

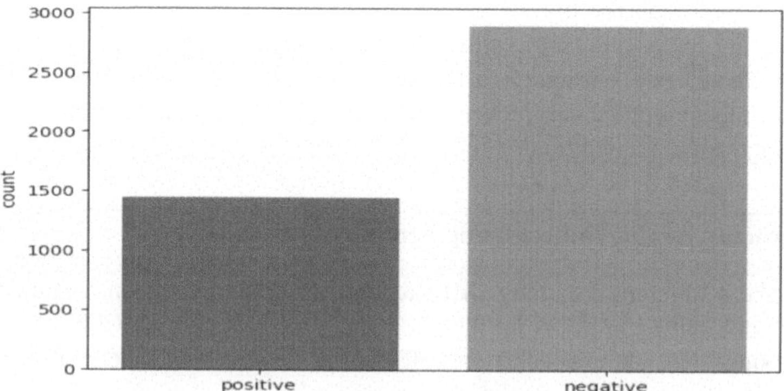

Fig. 3. Sentiment polarity

Table 1. Sample Annotating

Text	The opposite text in English	Emotion
دبا فهاد الوضع اللي عندو شي روندیفو مع طبيب ديالو بال ما يمشي والايقدر اتصل بيه فالهاتف اصلا بحال هاد الناس معرضين اكثر لخطر الاصابة اللهم يبقا فدار	In this situation where someone has an appointment with their doctor without being able to go or even contact them by phone, they are more exposed to the risk of getting infected.	Negative
الحمد لله على أن ڤيروس كورونا لا يعيش في ما فوق 22 درجة حرارية . وما كون بقا الطايح كتر من الواقف . وخير ذليل على هذا الكلام وزير النقل وشحال من مسؤول سلم عليه وشحال من واحد سلم على كل واح	Thank God that the coronavirus does not survive at temperatures above 22 degrees Celsius. It seems that the fallen are more numerous than those standing are. And the best to confirm this statement is the Minister of Transport. How many officials have followed him, and how many people have followed each one."	Positive

Table 2. An illustration of process tasks based on a comment

Task	Outcome	The opposite text in English
Original text	أنا تنحتارم اصحاااب الاختصاص وتندخل لهاد الصفحة باش نقرا التعاليق ☺وتبارك الله شحال ديال العلماء عندنا فالبلاد	I respect the specialiiiists, and I come to this paage to reaad the comments. God blesse the many scientiiists we have in our country! ☺
Cleaning	نا تنحتارم اصحاااب الاختصاص وتندخل لهاد الصفحة باش نقرا التعاليق وتبارك الله شحال ديال العلماء عندنا	I respect the specialiiiists, and I come to this paage to reaad the comments. God blesse the many scientiiists we have in our country
Normalization	نا تنحتارم اصحاب الاختصاص وتندخل لهاد الصفحة باش نقرا التعاليق وتبارك الله شحال ديال العلماء عندنا فالبلاد	I respect the specialists, and I come to this page to read the comments. God bless the many scientists we have in our country
Tokenization	نا‘,‘تنحتارم‘,‘اصحاب‘,‘الاختصاص‘‘,‘و‘,‘تندخل‘,‘,‘لهاد‘,ال صفحة‘,‘باش‘,‘نقرا‘,‘التعاليق‘,‘تبارك‘,‘الله‘,‘شحال‘,‘ديال‘,‘ا لعلماء‘,‘عندنا‘,‘فالبلاد	‘I’ ,‘respect’ ,’the’,’specialists’,’and’,’I’,’come’ ,’to’,’this’, ’page’,’to’, ,’read’,’the’’comments’,’god’,’bless,’the’,’many’ ,’scientists’,’we’,’have’,’in ’,’our’, ’country’
Stopwords removal	‘تنحتارم‘,‘ اصحاب‘,‘ الاختصاص‘,‘,‘تندخل‘,‘,الصفحة نقرا‘ ,‘التعاليق‘,‘تبارك‘,‘الله‘,,‘العلماء‘,,‘فالبلاد‘	respect’,’specialists’,’come’ ’page’,’read’,’comments’,’god’,’bless’, ,’scientists’,’have’,’country’

3.5 Features Extraction

Feature extraction is the process of reducing a text to its most significant words and keywords, which are retrieved using various methods. It is a machine learning strategy that selects just the words with the greatest influence on the categorization process. Feature extraction entails removing stop words, stemming, and generating n-grams. This strategy starts by removing words that have no importance. This strategy increases processing speed, improves accuracy, and removes ambiguity in categorization, especially for short strings with low context. In general, just maintain terms from the text that have NLP meanings.

Here, we used a different feature extraction technique called “one-hot encoding” in machine learning for a number of significant reasons: Categorical data is represented using one-hot encoding so that machine learning algorithms can analyze and comprehend it efficiently. It is appropriate for a variety of machine learning models since it converts categorical data into binary vectors, where each category is given a distinct binary value. This method is selected because it works with a variety of algorithms and can avoid ordinal data from being misinterpreted. Additionally, it enhances model performance by making precise categorical data handling possible, which is crucial for several real-world applications.

We have opted to use TF-IDF (Term Frequency-Inverse Document Frequency) as a substitute feature extraction technique in machine learning in this part. This choice is driven by a number of significant benefits. With its ability to efficiently reduce dimensionality, emphasize the significance of features, improve model performance, and provide adaptability across a broad variety of natural language processing applications, TF-IDF is particularly well suited for text data. By incorporating it, we want to improve the accuracy and efficiency of our machine learning models, which are crucial for managing categorical data in many real-world applications.

4 Outcomes and Discussion

4.1 Configuring Efficient Algorithms and Building up Experiments

In this section, we discuss the study's findings and assess the result concerning sentiments. The Google Colab open cloud environment, which provides the Tesla K80 Processor GPU and 12GB in GDDR5 virtual memory is used to implement the experimental models. Tensor Flow, Scikit-learn, and Python 3.7 are among the technologies used to generate the models. The experiments were conducted using grid search to identify the optimal hyper-parameters for the proposed model

4.2 Evaluation Metrics

Sentiment Analysis (SA) has received a lot of interest in the Natural Language Processing (NLP) industry. It is a method for determining if a text expresses positive, negative sentiments. Several theories and analytical frameworks have been created in recent years to help determine this. Because the consequences of the accepted method for SA are diverse, a variety of performance indicators are being used to assess them. For binary classification, such as Positive/Negative, accuracy, precision, recall, F1-score, Area under the curve (AUC) are often used to assess the classifier's effectiveness [24].

4.3 Testing Findings

When Maching Learning models are trained, a prediction-ready simulation containing the suitable sizes for the given target is produced. A summary of the model metrics' accuracy and recall and F1-score overall precision are given for features extraction, both one hot encoding and TF- IDF as shown in Table 3 and Table 4 and Area under the curve (AUC) in Fig. 4 and Fig. 5.

The best results were obtained using TF-IDF feature extraction when looking at both accuracy (87%) and then precision (89%) in support matching vector (rbf) model. With an accuracy of (86%) and a precision of (87%), the Random Forest model is the model that ranks second. The Decision Tree model, which has an accuracy of (81%) and a precision of (78%), comes in last. Conversely, in the best scenario, the One-Hot feature extraction in the Random Forest model achieves an accuracy of (69%) and a precision of (71%). When using TF-IDF feature extraction, our model continues to perform better in terms of accuracy and precision when compared to previous researches [12–15, 17–19].

Table 3. Models performmance with One Hot Feature Extraction

Feature Extraction	Model	Accuracy	Precision	Recall	F1-score
One hot encoding	SVM	64%	82%	50%	39%
	KNN	61%	54%	53%	52%
	RF	69%	71%	59%	57%
	NB	50%	55%	50%	50%
	DT	60%	57%	56%	56%

Table 4. Models performmance with TF-IDF Feature Extraction

Feature Extraction	Model	Accuracy	Precision	Recall	F1-score
TF-IDF	SVM	87%	89%	81%	83%
	KNN	79%	76%	73%	74%
	RF	86%	87%	81%	83%
	NB	85%	90%	77%	80%
	DT	81%	78%	78%	78%

4.4 Discussion

In this article, we proposed five Maching Learning models using two features extraction to identify feelings based on polarity. 2900 positive and 1490 negative entries make up the dataset we utilized from the twitter platform. This dataset adheres to the principles and guidelines for generating precise sentiments. There are two properties in the dataset: sentiment and text.

A zero denotes a favorable feeling and a one denotes a negative sentiment for each component. We started with the initial phase by preparing the unprocessed data using a number of different methods. Among these procedures are the removal of punctuation and alphanumeric characters as well as the deletion of pointless repetitions.

With the goal to examine the impact of features extraction techniques on the suggested model, we provided two methodologies for encoding words in the proposed

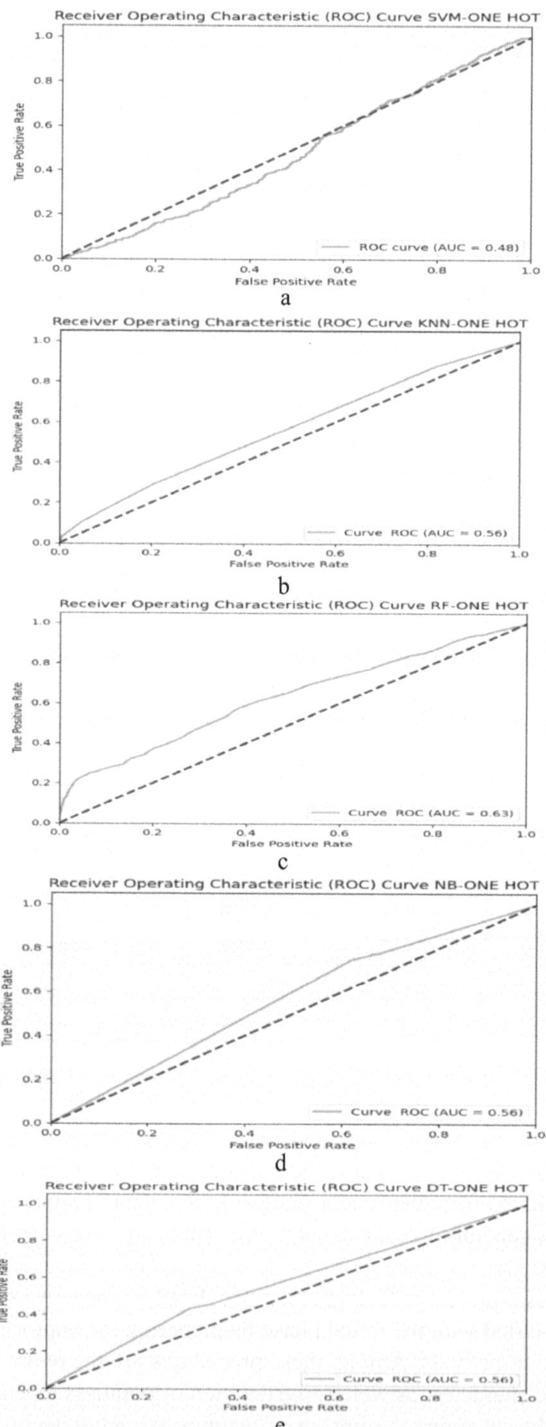

Fig. 4. a. ROC SVM-ONE-HOT, b. ROC KNN-ONE-HOT, c. ROC RF-ONE-HOT, d. ROC NB-ONE-HOT, e. ROC DT-ONE-HOT

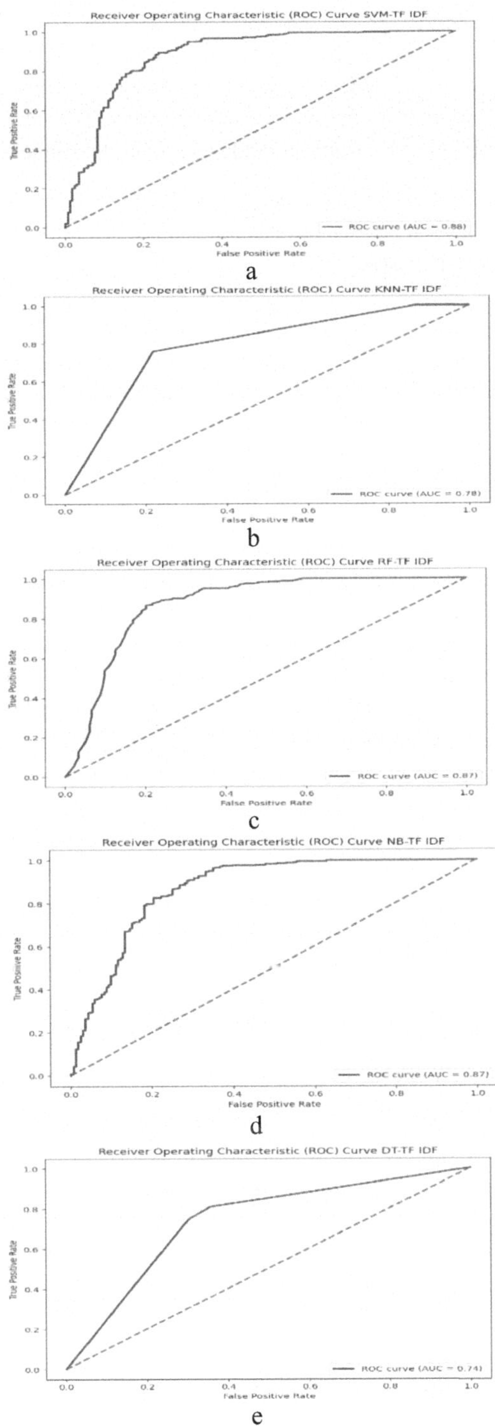

Fig. 5. a. ROC SVM-TF IDF, b. ROC KNN-TF IDF, c. ROC RF-TF IDF, d. ROC NB-TF IDF, e. ROC DT-TF IDF

system architecture. Using one hot encoding and TF-IDF combine the learnt word representation vector.

The purpose of integrating Maching Learning models within the model topology intended to collect sentiment components from opinions. The tests showed using TF-IDF coupled of our Maching Learning models provided the highest levels of precision and accuracy.

5 Conclusion and Perspectives

In this research, we explored various steps and techniques that allowed us to evaluate the performance and efficiency of several approaches to sentiment analysis. Our dataset, comprises 4390 sentiment per comments categorized into two balance groups of negative, and positive sentiments, the major goal concerning this type of study was to get a satisfactory result and improve the performance of the suggested identification sentiments system. The primary aim of this strategy was to convert words into intelligible numerical vectors by using features extraction. The second challenge was to train our models using Maching learning topologies. When contrasted to typical machine learning methods and related work results, the acquired findings demonstrate a boost in the level of precision and accuracy. We plan to enhance our model significantly by employing sophisticated ML and DL methods that include BERT and studying various features extraction approaches which could offer higher accuracy.

In addition, we want to extend the data collection to incorporate a greater number of sources of Moroccan Arabic language as well as additional topics in order to boost the model's performance over a wider range of problems. Furthermore, we seek to expand on our research to include additional Arabic dialects in order to provide a more comprehensive evaluation of emotions on the dialect of Arabic. Furthermore, we want to collaborate with other academics in the area to develop an acknowledged structure in Arabic emotion analysis that would allow for the comparison and evaluation of various methodologies and models.

References

1. Freund, L.E., Cellary, W.: Advances in the Human Side of Service Engineering. San Jose, CA, USA: Springer, vol. 266, pp. 3–17 (2014). https://doi.org/10.1007/978-3-030-80840-2_1
2. Vichare, M., Thorat, S., Uberoi, C.S., Khedekar, S., Jaikar, S.: Toxic comment analysis for online learning. In: 2021 2nd International Conference on Advances in Computing, Communication, Embedded and Secure Systems (ACCESS), pp. 130–135. IEEE (2021). https://doi.org/10.1109/ACCESS51619.2021.9563344
3. Mihalcea, H.L., Lieberman, H.: NLP (Natural Language Processing) for NLP (Natural Language Programming). In: Computational Linguistics and Intelligent Text Processing, vol. 3878, A. Gelbukh, Ed. Berlin, Heidelberg: Springer Berlin Heidelberg, pp. 319–330 (2006). https://doi.org/10.1007/11671299_34
4. Fan, H., et al.: Social media toxicity classification using deep learning: real-world application UK Brexit. Electronics **10**(11), 1332 (2021). https://doi.org/10.3390/electronics10111332
5. Elkateb, S., Black, W., Farwell, D.: Arabic WordNet and the challenges of Arabic, p. 10. https://aclanthology.org/2006.bcs-1.2

6. Yue, L., Chen, W., Li, X., Zuo, W., Yin, M.: A survey of sentiment analysis in social media. Knowl. Inf. Syst. **60**(2), 617–663 (2019). https://doi.org/10.1007/s10115-018-1236-4
7. Hamida, S., Cherradi, B., El Gannour, O., Terrada, O., Raihani, A., Ouajji, H.: New database of French computer science words handwritten vocabulary. In: 2021 International Congress of Advanced Technology and Engineering (ICOTEN), Taiz, Yemen, pp. 1–5 (2021). https://doi.org/10.1109/ICOTEN52080.2021.9493438
8. Aqab, S., Usman, M.: Handwriting Recognition using Artificial Intelligence Neural Network and Image Processing. IJACSA, vol. 11, no. 7 (2020). https://doi.org/10.14569/IJACSA.2020.0110719
9. Maghfour, M., Elouardighi, A.: Standard and dialectal Arabic text classification for sentiment analysis. In: Abdelwahed, E.H., Bellatreche, L., Golfarelli, M., Méry, D., Ordonez, C. (eds.) Model and Data Engineering, vol. 11163, Cham: Springer International Publishing, pp. 282–291 (2018). https://doi.org/10.1007/978-3-030-00856-7_18
10. Duwairi, R.M., Qarqaz, I.: Arabic sentiment analysis using supervised classification. In: 2014 International Conference on Future Internet of Things and Cloud, Barcelona, Spain, pp. 579–583 (2014). https://doi.org/10.1109/FiCloud.2014.100
11. Malmasi, S., Refaee, E., Dras, M.: Arabic dialect identification using a parallel multidialectal corpus. In: Hasida, K., Purwarianti, A. (eds.) Computational Linguistics - 14th International Conference of the Pacific Association for Computaitonal Linguistics, PACLING 2015, Revised Selected Papers. Vol. 593. Singapore: Springer, Springer Nature, pp. 35–53 (2016). (Communications in Computer and Information Science). https://doi.org/10.1007/978-981-10-0515-2_3
12. Oussous, A., Lahcen, A.A., Belfkih, S.: Improving sentiment analysis of Moroccan tweets using ensemble learning. In: Tabii, Y., Lazaar, M., Al Achhab, M., Enneya, N. (eds.) Big Data, Cloud and Applications, vol. 872, Cham: Springer International Publishing, pp. 91–104 (2018). https://doi.org/10.1007/978-3-319-96292-4_8
13. Nabil, M., Aly, M., Atiya, A.: ASTD: Arabic sentiment tweets dataset. In: Proceedings of the 2015 Conference on Empirical Methods in Natural Language Processing, pp 2515–2519 (2015). https://doi.org/10.18653/v1/D15-1299
14. Badaro, G., Baly, R., Hajj, H., Habash, N., El-Hajj, W.: A large scale Arabic sentiment lexicon for Arabic opinion mining. In: Proceedings of the EMNLP 2014 Workshop on Arabic Natural Language Processing (ANLP), pp 165–173 (2014). https://doi.org/10.3115/v1/W14-3623
15. Guellil, I., Adeel, A., Azouaou, F., Hussain, A.: SentiALG: automated corpus annotation for Algerian sentiment analysis. In: 9th International Conference, BICS 2018, Xi'an, China, July 7–8, 2018, Proceedings (2018). https://doi.org/10.1007/978-3-030-00563-4_54
16. Abdulla, N.A., Al-Ayyoub, M., Al-Kabi, M.N.: An extended analytical study of Arabic sentiments. Int. J. Big Data Intell. **1**(1-2), 103–113 (2014). https://doi.org/10.1504/IJBDI.2014.063845
17. Harrat, S., Meftouh, K., Smaïli, K.: Maghrebi Arabic dialect processing: an overview. vol. 1, no. 1, p. 8 (2018). https://doi.org/10.1007/s10579-020-09490
18. Mouaad, E., Ouassil, M.A., Rachidi, R., Cherradi, B., Hamida, S., Raihani, A.: Sentiment analysis on Moroccan dialect based on ML and social media content detection. Int. J. Adv. Comput. Sci. Appl. **14**, 315–325 (2023). https://doi.org/10.14569/IJACSA.2023.0140347
19. Medhafar, S., Bougares, F., Esteve, Y., Hadrich-Belguith, L.: Sentiment analysis of Tunisian dialects: Linguistic resources and experiments. In: Proceedings of the Third Arabic Natural Language Processing Workshop, pp. 55–61 (2017). https://doi.org/10.18653/v1/W17-1307
20. Alrefai, M., Faris, H., Aljarah, I.: Sentiment analysis for Arabic language: a brief survey of approaches and techniques. Vol. 119 International Journal of Advanced Science and Technology, pp.13–24 (2018). https://doi.org/10.14257/ijast.2018.119.02
21. Jbel, M., Hafidi, I., Metrane, A.: Sentiment Analysis Dataset in Moroccan Dialect: Bridging the Gap Between Arabic and Latin Scripted dialect. (2023). https://arxiv.org/abs/2303.15987

22. Nawaf Ghanem, A., et al.: Real-time infoveillance of Moroccan social media users' sentiments towards the COVID-19 pandemic and its management. Int. J. Environ. Res. Public Health **18**(22), 12172 (2021). https://doi.org/10.3390/ijerph182212172.PMID:34831927; PMCID:PMC8624830
23. Touileb, S., Barnes, J.: The interplay between language similarity and script on a novel multi-layer Algerian dialect corpus (2021). ArXiv, abs/2105.07400
24. Rahab, H., Haouassi, H., Laouid, A.: Rule-based Arabic sentiment analysis using binary equilibrium optimization algorithm. Arab. J. Sci. Eng. **48**(2), 2359–2374 (2023). https://doi.org/10.1007/s13369-022-07198-2. Epub 2022 Sep 26. PMID: 36185591; PMCID: PMC9513016

Enhancing Arabic Sentiment Analysis Using Arabic LLMs

Ghizlane Bourahouat(✉), Manar Abourezq, and Najima Daoudi

LyRICA Laboratory, ESI, ITQAN Team, Rabat, Morocco
{ghizlane.bourahouat,mabourezq,ndaoudi}@esi.ac.ma

Abstract. Considering Sentiment Analysis's importance, the Natural Language Processing (NLP) field has seen a surge in studies dedicated to this task. However, research efforts in Arabic Natural Language Processing haven't reached the same prominence as those in non-Latin alphabet languages. This discrepancy can be attributed to the specificity of the Arabic language and the limited availability of freely accessible lexical resources.

Considering these challenges, our paper focuses on Sentiment Analysis in Modern Standard Arabic. We achieve this using pre-trained Arabic BERT models, specifically AraBERT, ALBERT, CAMeLBERT, AraELECTRA, and QARIB. Our approach was tested on the 100k reviews dataset and Arabic Moroccan Arabic corpus (MAC) dataset. Notably, with the MAC dataset, our proposed system at-attains an accuracy of 96% when using the QARIB model, 93% when using AraBERT and 26% with CAMeLBERT. Regarding the 100k reviews dataset, the best accuracy of 93% was achieved when using AraBERT, followed by QARIB with an accuracy of 89% and lower accuracy was when using ALBERT with 39%.

We compared the research results obtained through our approach with those of other leading methods, demonstrating the effectiveness of our methodology. These findings provide valuable insights for future enhancements in this field.

Keywords: ANLP · Arabic Sentiment Analysis · Standard Arabic · Transformers · LLM

1 Introduction

Examining individuals' emotions and viewpoints has emerged as a pivotal area of focus in research. Over the past few years, there has been a substantial surge in research efforts to develop techniques for evaluating and recording the sentiment analysis process across various languages. In the same context, additional studies have elevated the examination and categorisation of individuals' perspectives to a heightened level of precision [1]. These endeavours involve delving more profoundly into the emotional dimensions, introducing innovative models for classifying emotions and gaining a more comprehensive understanding of both the sentiment and emotions experienced.

Numerous obstacles must be tackled when addressing sentiment analysis (SA), including informal writing styles and language-specific difficulties. Moreover, numerous words in different languages possess diverse meanings and orientations. Consequently,

B. Hdioud and S. L. Aouragh (Eds.): ICALP 2024, CCIS 2339, pp. 17–27, 2025.
https://doi.org/10.1007/978-3-031-79164-2_2

there is a need for more tools and resources that are available to all languages [1]. The Arabic language belongs to this category, so researchers need help conducting Arabic Sentiment Analysis (ASA).

Arabic is the globe's fifth most spoken language, with a community of billions of individuals. It has a unique set of characteristics that present difficulties in NLP. The latter is carried out by following a series of steps, beginning with data collection, and ending with the performed task in our research SA

Our article intends to test various combinations of Arabic pre-trained BERT models, namely AraBERT, QARIB, ALBERT, AraELECTRA, and CAMeLBERT, as both embedding layers and a baseline model to investigate the impact of their structure. Data collection is also an investigated challenge, especially with the scarcity of datasets suited for ASA.

The rest of this paper is organised as follows: Sect. 2 presents the context and problem statement, which deals with ASA techniques and the transformers' architecture based on the BERT model. Section 3 focuses on the related work in the field of ASA using Arabic pre-trained BERT models, Machine Learning (ML), and Deep Learning (DL). Section 4 presents the proposed approach with a focus on techniques used in data collection and embedding. Finally, Sect. 5 discusses the findings and some areas for further research.

2 Context and Problem Statement

2.1 Sentiment Analysis

Sentiment analysis, also called opinion mining, is a technique to ascertain whether a user's stance on a subject is positive or negative. This process involves extracting meaningful information and semantics from text through natural language processing techniques, thereby discerning the writer's attitude, which can be categorised as positive, negative, or neutral [2].

Arabic sentiment analysis (ASA) encounters numerous challenges specific to the nature and structure of the Arabic language, setting it apart from other languages like English. In addition to its distinct structure, the Arabic language comprises three primary variations: Classical Arabic (CA), Standard Arabic (MSA), and Arabic dialect (AD).

The research conducted in Arabic sentiment analysis (ASA) is comparatively less extensive than in other languages because of the challenging syntax of the language. Therefore, researchers turned to ML and DL algorithms as they provide enhanced processing and analysis [1].

2.2 Arabic LLMs and Transformers

Arabic Language Models (LLMs) and transformers have become instrumental in advancing natural language processing capabilities for Arabic text. These specialized models are designed to understand, process, and generate text in Arabic, catering to the unique linguistic nuances of the language. LLMs, particularly those based on transformer architectures, have demonstrated remarkable proficiency in sentiment analysis, machine translation, and text summarization for Arabic content. They leverage deep learning techniques to capture contextual relationships within sentences, enabling them to generate more contextually accurate and coherent responses [3]. As a result, Arabic LLMs and transformers are pivotal in bridging the gap between natural language processing research and practical applications for Arabic-speaking communities worldwide.

Pioneering models like AraBERT, QARIB, ALBERT, CAMeLBERT, and AraELECTRA have played instrumental roles in this evolution. AraBERT [4], for instance, stands out for its exceptional proficiency in understanding Arabic text across various domains and dialects, making it a cornerstone in sentiment analysis, question-answering, and other language-understanding tasks. QARIB [2], on the other hand, demonstrates remarkable versatility in question-answering, particularly in complex contexts. ALBERT, a model known for its efficiency and performance gains, has also made notable strides in Arabic language processing. CAMeLBERT excels in capturing the nuances of informal Arabic expressions with its unique adaptation for social media text. Lastly, AraELECTRA [5], leveraging the power of Electra pre-training, has contributed to achieving state-of-the-art results in multiple Arabic NLP benchmarks. To- Together, these models represent a quantum leap in the capabilities of Arabic language processing, empowering applications across a broad spectrum of fields, including sentiment analysis, machine translation, and information retrieval in the Arabic-speaking world.

3 Related Work

This study investigates SA in MSA when used with Arabic Transformers models. Based on this objective, we have focused on BERT models used for MSA SA and compared the models based on their effectiveness.

In [6], they proposed a modified switch transformer, which uses probabilistic projections and Variational Enmesh Experts routing. The proposed approach results with Accuracy = 66,81%, Recall = 89,67% and F1-Score = 59,17%. [7] aims to implement a multi-classification sentiment analyser for Arabic text while using four recently published contextualized embedding models and came out with ARABERT as one of the best models for ASA. [8]

In [8], a Discriminative Multinomial Bayes (DMNB) approach was formulated and assessed in comparison to other models including NB, SVM, K-Nearest Neighbor (KNN), and Decision Trees using an Arabic dataset. Notably, DMNB demonstrated the highest accuracy 87.50%.

[9] utilised a combination of CNN and LSTM on an Arabic Dataset. The best result was 88.10%. To create vector representations, they used a CNN with two word embedding models, CBOW and Skip-Gram. In [10], they employed CNN, LSTM, and CNN-LSTM techniques to analyse datasets from ArTwitter. Interestingly, they found that utilizing LSTM with dynamic CBOW yielded the most promising outcome, achieving an accuracy of 87.27%.

In [2], the researchers incorporated the pre-trained Arabic BERT models AraBERT and QARIB- throughout the process with various combinations such as SVM and CNN. The proposed system achieved the highest accuracy of 93% while using the QARIB model.

In the realm of Arabic Language Models (LLMs), it is evident that there has been relatively limited research compared to other languages. Hence, in our methodology, we intend to collectively leverage the capabilities of AraBERT, CAMeLBERT, ALBERT, AraELECTRA, and QARIB to conduct Sentiment Analysis (SA).

4 Proposed Method

As illustrated in Fig. 1, our methodology relies on pre-trained Arabic BERT models, specifically AraBERT, ALBERT, CAMeLBERT, AraELECTRA, and QARIB. This entails employing the entirety of the model's architecture to conduct Sentiment Analysis (SA).

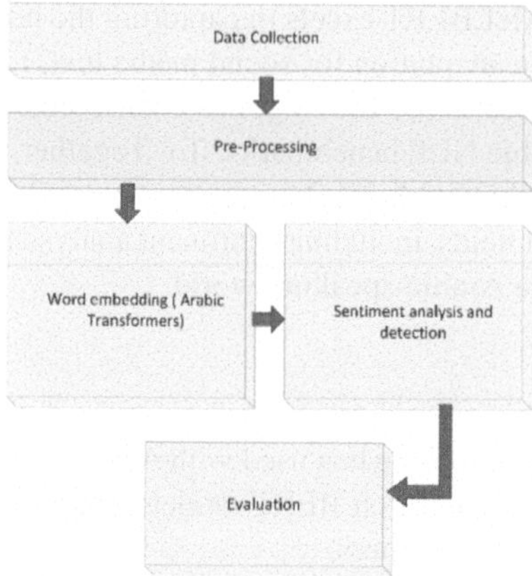

Fig. 1. Proposed Approach for ASA.

4.1 Data Collection

The choice of dataset is pivotal in any research on natural language processing (NLP). Our study encountered a challenge in selecting an appropriate dataset, as we sought a Modern Standard Arabic (MSA) dataset meticulously designed for sentiment analysis (SA) with a substantial volume of data. Our investigation uncovered a need for more readily available open-source MSA datasets. As a result, we decided to overcome this limitation by employing two carefully curated datasets in our research: the Moroccan Arabic corpus (MAC) dataset [11] and the Arabic 100k Reviews [12].

Mac Dataset

The MAC dataset comprises 18,000 manually labelled tweets, offering a sizable and freely accessible Modern Standard Arabic (MSA) corpus. This dataset contains 30,000 words classified into positive, negative, and neutral labels as shown in Fig. 2.

It also contains 12611 rows classified as standard Arabic towards 5476 classified as dialectal as illustrated in Fig. 3.

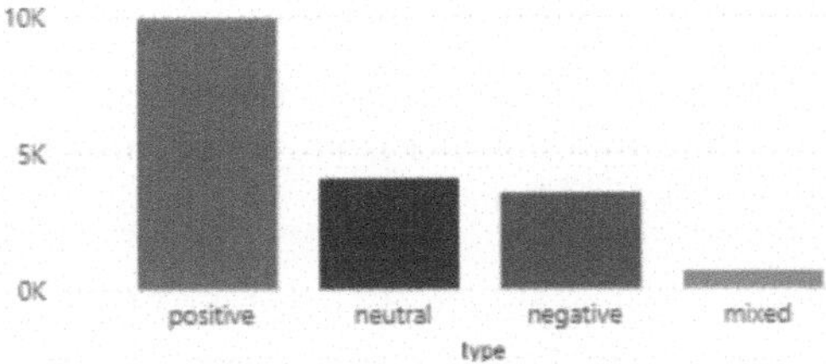

Fig. 2. Distribution of Mac dataset types

class	Count of tweets
dialectal	5476
standard	12611
Total	**18087**

Fig. 3. Distribution of the Mac dataset class

Arabic 100k Reviews

This dataset combines reviews from various domains, including hotels, books, movies, products, and a limited number of airline reviews. This dataset mainly compiles several available datasets and a selection of 100k rows. The reviews are a subset of the HARD and BRAD datasets.

It is structured into three distinct classes: Mixed, Negative, and Positive. All the classes are balanced with 33333 for each class as depicted in Fig. 4.

Count of text	label
33333	Mixed
33333	Negative
33333	Positive
99999	

Fig. 4. Arabic 100K reviews classes' distribution

4.2 Pre-processing

The pre-processing step typically involves several sub-steps such as tokenization, stop word removal, stemming or lemmatization, and normalisation.

4.3 Word Embedding and Sentiment Detection

Our research objective revolves around examining the impact of the structure of various Arabic pre-trained BERT models by exploring different combinations. To achieve this, we implemented several models including AraBERT, QARIB, ALBERT, AraELECTRA, and CAMeLBERT. Each model was utilised to perform SA, leveraging the comprehensive architecture of the respective model.

- AraBERT
  AraBERT, derived from the BERT model, is a multi-layer bidirectional transformer encoder. This Arabic BERT model is pre-trained using MSA data, which restricts its suitability for tasks involving dialects.
- QARiB
  QARiB is a BERT model explicitly designed for dialectal Arabic. Unlike AraBERT, QARiB is trained on a large dataset comprising 420 million tweets and 180 million sentences of text. This extensive training data includes a wide range of dialectal Arabic content, enabling QARiB to effectively handle and understand the nuances of dialects in its language representations. [13].
- ALBERT
  ALBERT is an optimized version of BERT, as indicated by its name. Compared to BERT, the largest ALBERT model consists of approximately 70% of BERT-large parameters. Despite having fewer parameters, ALBERT achieves notable improvements in performance across various natural language processing (NLP) tasks [14].
- CAMeLBERT
  CAMeLBERT is a comprehensive set of pre-trained BERT models using Arabic texts of various sizes and variants, as outlined in the study by [15]. This collection includes pre-trained language models tailored explicitly for MSA, DA, and CA.
- AraELECTRA

AraELECTRA, which stands for Arabic ELECTRA, is a language representation model designed explicitly for Arabic text. It has undergone pre-training on extensive MSA corpora [5].

Given the adaptability of Arabic BERT-based models to various downstream tasks, we will leverage them for SA targeting the MSA. The central part of the architecture has been trained on extensive text corpora, resulting in frozen parameters within the internal layers. On the other hand, the outermost layers, responsible for task adaptation, will undergo fine-tuning (Fig. 5).

Next, we delve into the outcomes of the applied approach, as outlined in the following section.

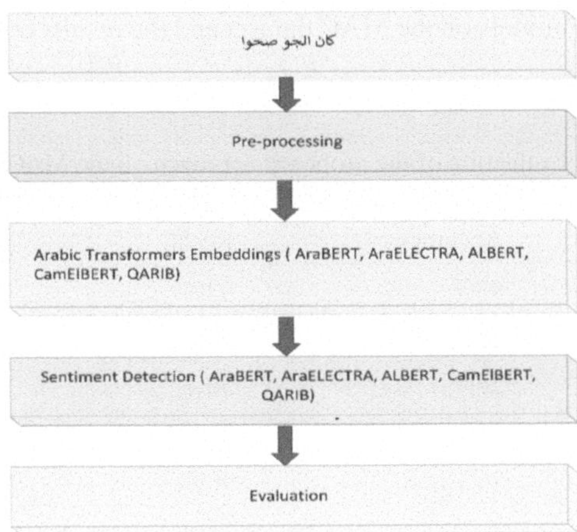

Fig. 5. Sentiment Analysis using AraBERT, QARIB, ALBERT, AraElECTRA and CAMeLBERT

5 Experiments and Results

In this section, we compare the performance of the different models we tested: AraBERT, QARIB, ALBERT, AraElECTRA and CAMeLBERT.

5.1 Experiments Settings

We set the maximum sequence length at 140, the batch size used is 6 and the learning rate was fixed to 1e-6 as illustrated in Table 1.

Table 1. Models training setting

Model	Epochs	Maximum sequence length	Learning rate	Metric
AraBERT				
ALBERT				Accuracy Recall F1-score
CAMeLBERT	10	140	1e-6	
AraELECTRA				
QARIB				

The implemented approach in this study is evaluated using standard metrics, namely, accuracy, recall, and f1-score.

5.2 Results and Discussion

In this section, we compare the performance of the different models we tested, namely AraBERT, QARIB, ALBERT, AraElECTRA and CAMeLBERT.

We first tested the models on the MAC dataset and the results obtained are illustrated in Table 2.

Table 2. Evaluation of the proposed approach on the MAC dataset.

Model	Accuracy	Recall	F1-score
AraBERT	93%	92%	92%
ALBERT	57%	55%	52%
CAMeLBERT	26%	50%	34%
AraELECTRA	83%	82%	82%
QARIB	96%	96%	96%

From the results detailed in Table 2, we can see that the highest performance is obtained while using QARIB and its embedded pre-processing technique with an accuracy of 96%, followed by AraBERT with 93%. CAMeLBERT achieved the lowest accuracy of 26% but a recall of 50% and an F1-score of 34%.

Then, we tested our approach on the 100k Arabic reviews dataset to carry the following results (Table 3).

Table 3. Evaluation of the proposed approach on the Arabic 100k reviews.

Model	Accuracy	Recall	F1-score
AraBERT	93%	92%	92%
ALBERT	39%	50%	44%
CAMeLBERT	53%	51%	49%
AraELECTRA	84%	84%	84%
QARIB	89%	89%	89%

The findings presented in Table 3 show that the most impressive performance is achieved when employing AraBERT in conjunction with its integrated pre-processing technique, yielding an accuracy of 93%, followed closely by QARIB with 93% and AraELECTRA with 84%. On the other hand, ALBERT recorded the lowest accuracy at 39%, yet it demonstrated a recall of 50% and an F1-score of 44%.

Regarding the MSA SA, it was expected to get the AraBERT model as the best model in both datasets, which was different. The difference between the two datasets is the source of the extracted dataset and the phrases and reviews syntax. The MAC dataset was extracted from Moroccan tweets and then annotated to dialectal or standard. However, some reviews are closer to being dialectal as standard but were considered standard. Therefore, QARIB, one of the best models for dialects, achieved the highest accuracy, followed by AraBERT.

Then, we selected an MSA dataset extracted from Arabic sources. In this case, the first model was AraBERT and then QARIB. Overall, we can say that AraBERT and QARIB are the best models for MSA sentiment detection as depicted in Fig. 6.

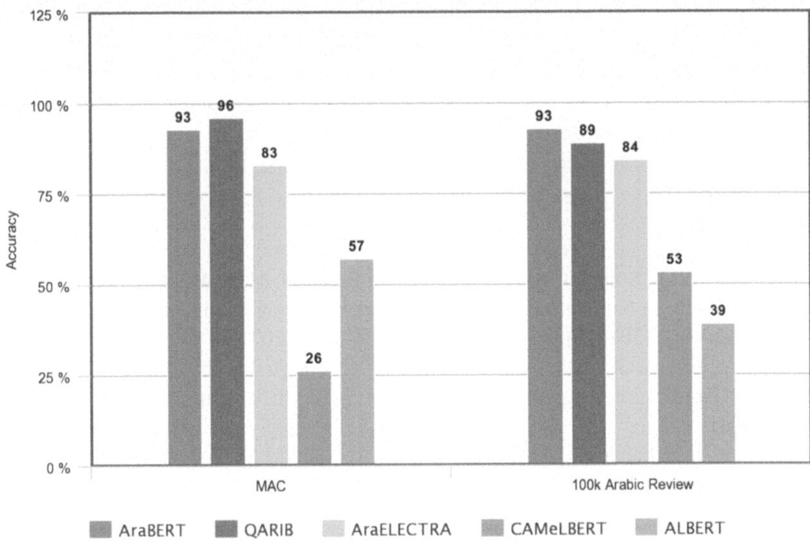

Fig. 6. Proposed approach experimentation results

We can also highlight the importance of the dataset used, its quality, and the annotation quality.

The results in Tables 1 and 2 demonstrate that utilising Transformer-based models trained on MSA as classifiers and embedding models consistently outperforms other models trained on DA. This superior performance can be attributed to several factors, including the extensive language knowledge acquired by Transformers through training on diverse language modelling objectives.

6 Conclusion

Sentiment analysis and detection of the Arabic language remains a complex task and an ongoing challenge for researchers in NLP. In this study, we have introduced our approach, which leverages multiple Arabic BERT-based models, including AraBERT, QARIB, ALBERT, AraELECTRA, and CAMeLBERT. These models were chosen to address the specific nuances and complexities of sentiment analysis in Arabic, aiming to improve the accuracy and effectiveness of sentiment classification in this language. The approach starts with inputting our model into a pre-processed text from the MSA dataset. Then, we implement the forenamed BERT-based models to perform sentiment analysis, after which we use the generated embeddings and classify them using the BERT-based models.

Moreover, our evaluation is based on the MAC and 100k Arabic reviews datasets. With well-tuned parameters of the QARIB model, we obtained the best accuracy in the MAC, reaching 96% followed by AraBERT with 93%. For the 100k Arabic reviews dataset, AraBERT achieved the best accuracy of 93% followed by QARIB with 89%. The lowest accuracy was carried out with ALBERT and CAMeLBERT in both datasets. These BERT-based models gave better results when implemented as embedding models and classifiers. Our work is still in progress. For future research directions, we aim to investigate other Arabic Transformer-based models for SA and detection while adapting our approach for other tasks.

References

1. Abdelgwad, M.M., Soliman, T.H.A, Taloba, A.I., Farghaly, M.F.: Arabic aspect-based sentiment analysis using bidirectional GRU based models. J. King Saud Univ. - Comput. Inf. Sci. **34**(9), 6652–6662 (2022). https://doi.org/10.1016/j.jksuci.2021.08.030
2. Alsayat, A., Elmitwally, N.: A comprehensive study for Arabic Sentiment Analysis (Challenges and Applications). Egypt. Inform. J. **21**(1), 7–12 (2020). https://doi.org/10.1016/j.eij.2019.06.001
3. Al-Ayyoub, M., Khamaiseh, A.A., Jararweh, Y., Al-Kabi, M.N.: A comprehensive survey of Arabic sentiment analysis. Inf. Process. Manag. **56**(2), 320–342 (2019). https://doi.org/10.1016/j.ipm.2018.07.006
4. Bourahouat, G., Abourezq, M., Daoudi, N.: Leveraging Moroccan Arabic sentiment analysis using AraBERT and QARIB. In: Innovations in Smart Cities Applications Volume 6, vol. 629, M. Ben Ahmed, A. A. Boudhir, D. Santos, R. Dionisio, and N. Benaya, Eds., in Lecture Notes in Networks and Systems, vol. 629. , Cham: Springer International Publishing, pp. 299–310 (2023). https://doi.org/10.1007/978-3-031-26852-6_29
5. Zhao, W.X., et al.: A Survey of Large Language Models (2023). https://doi.org/10.48550/ARXIV.2303.18223
6. El-Alami, F., Ouatik El Alaoui, S., En Nahnahi, N.: Contextual semantic embeddings based on fine-tuned AraBERT model for Arabic text multi-class categorization. J. King Saud Univ. - Comput. Inf. Sci. **34**(10), 8422–8428 (2022). https://doi.org/10.1016/j.jksuci.2021.02.005
7. Antoun, W., Baly, F., Hajj, H.: AraELECTRA: Pre-Training Text Discriminators for Arabic Language Understanding (2020). https://doi.org/10.48550/ARXIV.2012.15516
8. Shah, S.M.A.H., Shah, S.F.H., Ullah, A., Rizwan, A., Atteia, G., Alabdulhafith, M.: Arabic sentiment analysis and sarcasm detection using probabilistic projections-based variational switch transformer. IEEE Access **11**, 67865–67881 (2023). https://doi.org/10.1109/ACCESS.2023.3289715
9. Dakalbab, F., Elnagar, A.: Performance evaluation of contextualized Arabic embeddings: the Arabic sentiment analysis task. In: Proceedings of Data Analytics and Management, vol. 572, A. Khanna, Z. Polkowski, and O. Castillo, Eds., in Lecture Notes in Networks and Systems, vol. 572. , Singapore: Springer Nature Singapore, pp. 733–747 (2023). https://doi.org/10.1007/978-981-19-7615-5_60
10. AlSalman, H.: An improved approach for sentiment analysis of Arabic tweets in twitter social media. In: 2020 3rd International Conference on Computer Applications & Information Security (ICCAIS), Riyadh, Saudi Arabia: IEEE, pp. 1–4 (2020). https://doi.org/10.1109/ICCAIS48893.2020.9096850
11. Alayba, A.M., Palade, V., England, M., Iqbal, R.: A combined CNN and LSTM model for Arabic sentiment analysis. In: Machine Learning and Knowledge Extraction, vol. 11015, A.

Holzinger, P. Kieseberg, A. M. Tjoa, and E. Weippl, Eds., in Lecture Notes in Computer Science, vol. 11015, Cham: Springer International Publishing, pp. 179–191 (2018). https://doi.org/10.1007/978-3-319-99740-7_12

12. Al-Azani, S., El-Alfy, E.-S.M.: Hybrid deep learning for sentiment polarity determination of Arabic microblogs. In: Neural Information Processing, vol. 10635, D. Liu, S. Xie, Y. Li, D. Zhao, and E.-S. M. El-Alfy, Eds., in Lecture Notes in Computer Science, vol. 10635, Cham: Springer International Publishing, pp. 491–500 (2017). https://doi.org/10.1007/978-3-319-70096-0_51
13. Garouani, M., Kharroubi, J.: MAC: an open and free Moroccan Arabic corpus for sentiment analysis. In: Innovations in Smart Cities Applications Volume 5, vol. 393, M. Ben Ahmed, A. A. Boudhir, İ. R. Karaş, V. Jain, and S. Mellouli, Eds., in Lecture Notes in Net- works and Systems, vol. 393. , Cham: Springer International Publishing, pp. 849–858 (2022). https://doi.org/10.1007/978-3-030-94191-8_68
14. Arabic 100k Reviews. https://www.kaggle.com/datasets/abedkhooli/arabic-100k-reviews. Accessed 12 Oct 2023
15. Abdelali, A., Hassan, S., Mubarak, H., Darwish, K., Samih, Y.: Pre-Training BERT on Arabic Tweets: Practical Considerations (2021). https://doi.org/10.48550/ARXIV.2102.10684
16. Lan, Z., Chen, M., Goodman, S., Gimpel, K., Sharma, P., Soricut, R.: ALBERT: A Lite BERT for Self-supervised Learning of Language Representations (2019). https://doi.org/10.48550/ARXIV.1909.11942
17. Inoue, G., Alhafni, B., Baimukan, N., Bouamor, H., Habash, N.: The Interplay of Variant, Size, and Task Type in Arabic Pre-trained Language Models (2021). https://doi.org/10.48550/ARXIV.2103.06678

Sentiment Analysis of Texts Written in Arabic: Addressing the Issue of Negation

Mohamed El Ammari(✉), Azeddine Rhazi, and Salim Rami

Caddy Ayyad University, Marrakech, Morocco
elammari1212@gmail.com

Abstract. Negation is a crucial issue in sentiment analysis and opinion extraction as it can fundamentally alter the meaning and polarity of an opinionated statement. How-ever, numerous opinion-mining tools (lexicons, models, and classifiers) which are currently in use to identify and classify sentiment in texts written in Arabic language often fall short of expectations to account for negation structures, resulting in inaccurate classifications. To address this issue, this research proposes a linguistic approach using the Nooj platform to formalize recognition rules for negation in Arabic text and apply them with an opinion lexicon to a manually collected corpus of opinionated data obtained from websites and social media posts. The method utilizes sets of local grammars specifically designed to identify negation structures in subjective Arabic texts and assign the appropriate polarity to the sentence. Through the application of these recognition rules and the use of an opinion lexicon, the proposed method yields encouraging results and demonstrates the ability to accurately identify and classify negation sentences in text written in Arabic. This research aims to improve the overall accuracy of sentiment analysis in the Arabic language by incorporating the proper handling of negation into the classification process.

Keywords: Sentiment Analysis · Negation · Nooj · Arabic · NLP

1 Introduction and Background

The internet has become a vast repository of user-generated content, including large and varied volume of opinions expressed through social media, blogs, forums, and review websites. This large amount of opinionated data left by users on the internet offers a wealth of information for businesses, researchers, and individuals to gain insights and make data-driven decisions. However, dealing with such a large and diverse data can be challenging. The volume, the diversity and the unstructured nature of user-generated content can make it difficult to manually process, analyze, and identify patterns and trends to extract meaningful insights. Sentiment analysis, also known as opinion mining, is a subfield of natural language processing that deals with identifying and extracting subjective information from large amounts of textual data, such as social media posts, customer reviews, and news articles. The final goal of sentiment analysis is to automate the process of identifying and extracting/classifying subjective information from text

B. Hdioud and S. L. Aouragh (Eds.): ICALP 2024, CCIS 2339, pp. 28–37, 2025.
https://doi.org/10.1007/978-3-031-79164-2_3

data. Sentiment analysis makes it possible via using natural language processing (NLP), text analysis and computation-al techniques-to gain insights into the attitudes and perceptions of internet users from the sentiment or opinion expressed in a tweet, a review, or a news article. Sentiment analysis enables businesses, researchers, and individuals to easily gain insights for various applications such as monitoring brand perception, measuring customer satisfaction, and gauging public opinion on a particular topic. However, dealing with large textual data presents several challenges for sentiment analysis. One of the challenges that makes the analysis more difficult in opinion mining is negation, which refers to words or phrases that alter the meaning of the sentence; thus, the sentiment ex-pressed in a sentence since opinion words are completely modified by negation words and expressions.

In this paper, we introduce a method to recognize negation structures in texts writ-ten in Modern Standard Arabic based on Nooj platform. NooJ is a linguistic development environment based on dictionaries and local grammars that can be utilized to perform several NLP applications.

This paper is divided into four parts, the first part deals with the related work in sentiment analysis, Arabic language, negation, and negation markers in Arabic. The second part of the paper is devoted to the implementation phase discussing the corpus, Nooj linguistic resources used in the form of an electronic dictionary and a local grammar. The third part describes the experimentation stage and the evaluation of the method, and the challenges faced. Finally, results are presented and perspectives for futures studies are discussed.

2 Related Work

This section seeks to provide an account of the issue of negation and covers the different notions which are related to the title of this study from a theoretical perspective.

2.1 Sentiment Analysis and Arabic Language

The inception of Web 2.0 has allowed for websites to provide interactive content and for users to post their opinions, comments, and reviews. This massive textual data generated by users were thought to contain useful information that need to be extracted, but their immense size makes it difficult to analyze manually. The computational treatment of opinion, sentiment and subjectivity in text is the focus of Sentiment Analysis as an emerging field [1]. This field of study employs computational techniques to extract valuable information from these textual data automatically [2]. The process of extracting and classifying sentiments is widely utilized across numerous domains, such as marketing, social media analyses, customer service and tracking political opinions.

It has been traditionally thought that sentiment analysis is a simple binary classification of opinion [3]. In fact, it involves several subtasks like recognizing subjective information, determining the polarity, determining its intensity if not more [4]. Cambria et al., (2017) describes sentiment analysis as a "large suitcase of sub-tasks and sub-problems", involving grammatical and se-mantic problems [5]. Research in this field has been shaped by two major approaches: (1) machine learning and (2) lexicon-based methods. The first approach involves the development of classifiers by identifying key features and algorithms while the latter relies solely on lexical resources such as sentiment lexicons or dictionaries to identify opinionated words and their corresponding polarity [1]. Sentiment analysis has been carried out at three distinct levels: the document level, the sentence level, and the aspect level [1]; [6].

In NLP, Arabic Language is considered a low-resourced language and numerous studies have targeted Arabic Sentiment Analysis (ASA). Poria et al. [7] conducted a study in which the researchers concluded that some languages, including Arabic, French and Hindi, do not have good and reliable lexicons for sentiment analysis and opinion extraction. Ahmed et al. (2013) identified in their study several challenges in conducting subjectivity and sentiment analysis on Arabic text and presented several solutions [8]. Likewise, El-Masri et al. (2017) conducted an exhaustive study on all the problems and challenges of Arabic sentiment analysis systems on texts written in Arabic [9]. The researchers found that these challenges are several and related to multi levels, negation phrases handling is one of problems.

2.2 Sentiment Analysis and Arabic Language

Negation is a language-universal found in all human languages [10, 11]. It is a necessity in human communication, for "the capacity to negate is the capacity to refuse, to contradict, to lie, to speak ironically, to distinguish truth from falsity – in short, the capacity to be human" [12]. It is a complex phenomenon that has been studied for a long time and from diverse perspectives, including logic, cognition, philosophy, and linguistics. The debate surrounding the nature of negation has been ongoing since the time of Plato, Aristotle, and the Stoics and it has persisted for centuries, as discussed in [12]. Aristotle is widely regarded as the primary scholar to study negation from a philosophical perspective [13]. Since then, thousands of studies have been carried out as cataloged by the Basic Bibliography of Negation in Natural Language [14]. Over the last few years, several researchers [15–17]; and [18] have investigated the topic of negation from different perspectives.

As far as sentiment analysis is concerned, Negation is a polarity shifter that can change the polarity of an expression; that is why it is considered a significant area of investigation, and numerous research works investigated the topic. Although several studies have been performed to address the issue of negation in Arabic Sentiment Analysis [19–21] these studies were limited and none of them was comprehensive. It is found that the way of expressing negation varies significantly between languages, indicating a language-specific nature to this linguistic phenomenon.

Compared to English, Modern Standard Arabic (MSA) has a negation system that is characterized by a high level of metalinguistic complexity in the sense that negation markers in Arabic language carry a multitude of referential, metalinguistic, modal, and aspectual meanings. Thus, addressing negation in a way that accounts for the peculiarities of the Arabic language system is primordial. It is worth of noting that studies of Arabic negation system have been predominantly characterized by a temporal perspective in the sense that negation particles have been widely perceived as having temporal values, such as those that indicate negation in the past, present, and future, as exemplified in [22]. Additionally, classical studies of Arabic negation system by Arab grammarians such as

Sibaweihi, Al Mubarrad, Al Zamakhshari, Ibn Hisham, Ibn Al Sarraj, Ibn Ya'iish, and Ibn Jinni have been dominated by a temporal perspective [22]. Addressing the matter of negation in research is expected to have a positive impact on the improvement of performance in various Natural Language Processing (NLP) tasks and applications, including Sentiment Analysis, Machine Translation, and Information Extraction.

The typology of negation in Arabic language. Let us study the following Arabic negative examples:

1. لم تحضر سارة إلى العمل اليوم. (Sara did not come to work today.)
2. لنْ تصل إلى حل لمشكلتك وأنتَ غاضب. (You will not reach a solution to your problem when you are angry.)
3. أقبل فصل الشتاء ولمّا تمطر السماءُ. (Winter came and it didn't rain.)
4. ليس أحمد متكاسلا. (Ahmed is not lazy.)
5. ليس يقول هذا إلا جاهل. (Only an ignorant person would say this.)
6. لا تفوق بدون اجتهاد. (No excellence without diligence.)
7. شكرا، لا أدخن. (Thanks, I don't smoke.)
8. ما خالدٌ حاضرا اليوم. (Khalid isn't present today.)
9. أنتم ما تنجزون واجباتكم المنزلية. (You do not do your homework.)

As we can notice, negation in Standard Arabic is found to be characterized by some features:

- Negation in Arabic is associated with tense, it indicates not only negation but also time [17].
- Particle negation is the most common type of negation in Arabic.
- Negation can be expressed using some negation markers, especially particles (لم"lam", ما"maa", لما"lammaa", لا"laa", لن"lan" in addition to verb: ليس"laysa") that negate whatever comes after them. These particles (Lam, maa, leisa, lammaa, laa, and lan) constitute the nucleus of the Arabic negation system and behave as a micro-system.
- Laa لا is the most common Arabic negative particle.
- Laysa ليس, unlike other Arabic negative particles, is considered a verb and has an agreement feature with the subject in terms of number, gender and person while negating a nominal sentence.

Here is a summary of Arabic negation particles in the following table (Table 1):

Table. 1. Arabic negation particles

Particle	Example	Tense	Usage
Laa = لا	*لا تتهاون في دراستك. Do not neglect your) (studies = imperative لا يلعب خالد في الشارع. Khalid doesn't play in) (the street. لا أحد في المنزل. (No one is in the house)	Present Tense	- Pre-nominal and pre-verbal negator (precedes a verb or noun) - Used for categorical negation before an indefinite noun. - Can be a negating particle and a forbidding particle as well.
Maa = ما	ما لعب خالد في الشارع. Khalid didn't play in) (the street.	Past Tense	- Used to negate present states. - No Adjacency between particle and verb is required
Lam = لم	لم يلعب عمر في الشارع Omar didn't play in the) (street.	Past Tense	- Used with verbal sentences. - Adjacency is required between particle and verb. - Affects verbs in the imperfective and puts them in the past
lan = لن	لن يلعب محمد في الشارع. Omar won't play in the) (street.	Future tense	- Used with verbal sentences. - Adjacency is required. - It expresses negation and futurity.
Laysa = ليس	ليس البيت كبيرا. (The house isn't big.) ليس يعلم الغيب أحد. No one knows the) (unseen.	Present tense	- Used mostly in nominal sentences - Negates present states and sometimes future ones

3 Implementation

3.1 Corpus

Studying linguistic phenomena requires collecting linguistic data to be analyzed to gain a full understanding of the linguistic topic and to make data-based in-sights. Thus, building a corpus of linguistic data is phase number one in this research. In this respect, our corpus in this study consists of texts written in MSA. These texts constitute the opinions of users on multiple topics (government policies, Moroccan football national team, rising prices…). These textual data was collected manually from a number of internet websites. Then, the corpus is cleaned and preprocessed manually, to remove irrelevant or noisy information (date and time, user's name, post title, additional punctuation, special characters, as well as correcting misspellings and normalizing the text to a standard format) to improve the accuracy of the results (Fig. 1 and 2).

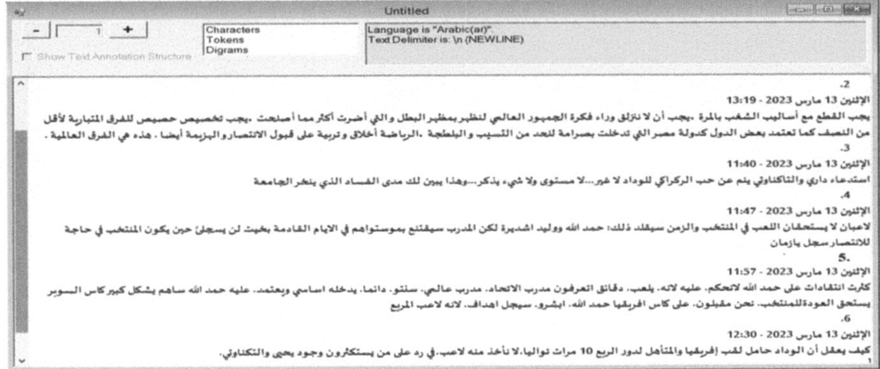

Fig. 1. Screen shows samples of our corpus before cleaning.

Fig. 2. Screen shows samples of our corpus after cleaning

3.2 Linguistic Resources

Our adopted approach utilizes linguistic resources as Nooj platform requires [23]. In this respect, an electronic dictionary containing entries with the necessary lexical rules is built as well as a local grammar is composed to apply on the corpus.

Lexical Rules. Electronic dictionaries are an essential component in Nooj approach NLP analysis [24]. They are the building block of analyzing and processing natural language text by recognizing and providing information about the words in the text.

Our sample dictionary is composed of a limited number of entries (particles, prepositions, verbs, nouns, pronouns). Each entry is accompanied with the linguistic and semantic information necessary, for instance the grammatical category and the syntactic information (Fig. 3).

```
[Modified] C:\Users\Mohamed\Documents\NooJ\ar\Lexical Analysis\Negationdictionary.dic
#
# Special Characters: '\' '"' ' ' ',' '+' '-' '#'
#Use Negationdictionary.nof

لا,PART+Negation;
ما,PART+Negation;
لم,PART+Negation;
لن,PART+Negation;
غير,Prep;
ليس,V+Tr+Negation+FLX=V_laysa:Flexion;
قعد,V+Intr+FLX=V_qa3ada+DRV=N_qa3ada:FlxDRV;
حضر,V+Tr+FLX=V_hadara+DRV=N_hadara:FlxDRV;
وصل,V+Tr+FLX=V_wassala+DRV=N_waàatha46:FlxDRV;
أقبل,V+Tr+FLX=V_aqbala+DRV=N_aqbala:FlxDRV;
دخن,V+Tr+FLX=V_dakhana+DRV=N_dakhana:Flx1;
صدق,V+Tr+FLX=V_saddaka+DRV=N_saddaka:Flx1;
أنجز,V+Tr+FLX=V_anjaza+DRV=N_anjaza:FlxDRV;
أعطى,V+Tr+FLX=V_aata+DRV=N_aata:FlxDRV;
خير,N+m+FLX=Khair+DRV=Koutoubon:FlexionPL;
شيء,N+m+FLX=Chay+DRV=Achiaa:FlexionPL;
خبر,N+FLX=KitAb+DRV=Akhbar:FlexionPL
أحمد,ENAMEX+PERS;
```

Fig. 3. Screen shows samples of the entries of the Nooj dictionary

Local Grammar. After building the dictionary, we built the local grammar that accounts for negative structures in Modern Standard Arabic using Nooj graphs (Fig. 4).

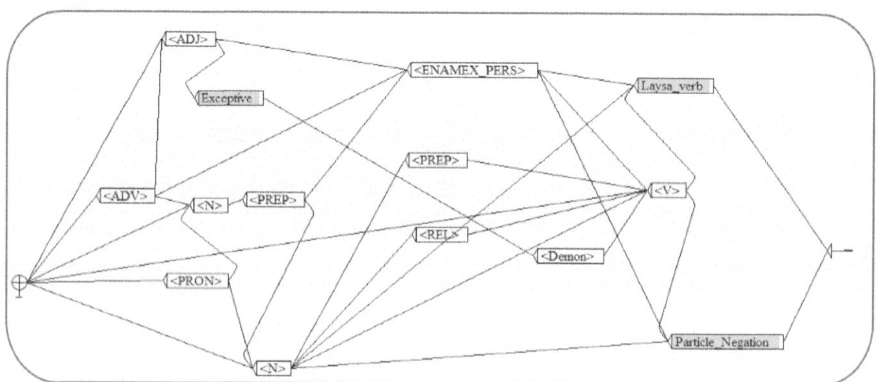

Fig. 4. Screen shows samples of the entries of the Nooj dictionary

4 Experimentation

After building the dictionary and the local grammar, we tested our local grammar first on the example sentences we started with in this paper, and we found that the local grammar recognized all the negative structures (Fig. 5).

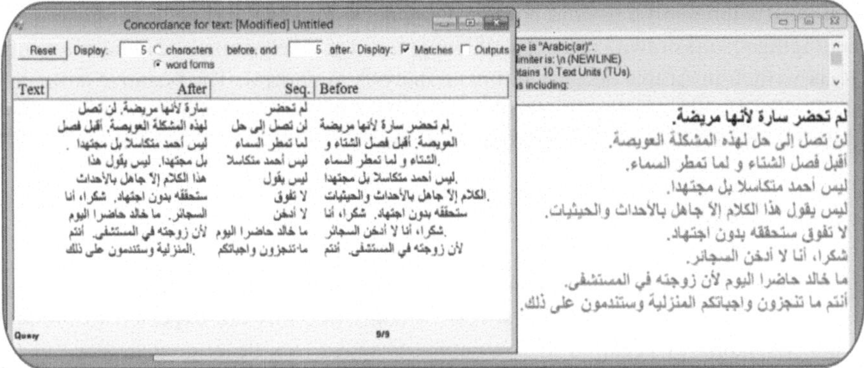

Fig. 5. Screen shows the testing the local grammar on example sentences

Then, we applied the same local grammar on our corpus to see if it recognizes the negative structures expressed in the opinions and we got the following results (Fig. 6):

Concordance for text: [Modified] Untitled

Reset | Display: 5 characters before, and 5 after. Display: ☑ Matches ☐ Outputs
word forms

Text	After	Seq.	Before
	مدارس او مستشفيات أو غيرها	لم نشاهد افتتاح	المدونة مع الأسف
	مسمى دولة اذا كان اعتمادها	لا يوجد	،والعنف والانهيار في أي لحظة
	بالنفاق بل تتعامل الند بالند	لا تتعامل	شيء آخر. المملكة المغربية الشريفة
	وإنما تطاول متعمد ومستفز يستوجب	ليست زلة لسان	مواضيعه وظروف وطريقة تناولها. فهذه
	هذه اللجنة أستعمال القضية الفلسطينية	لم تستنكر	إلى حجمه الطبيعي. و لماذا
	سبتة و مليلية فاي علاقة	لم يسترجع	المنتخبة من أجلها . اذا المغرب
	بتحرير المدينتين الاستراجيتين.فكيف سيتقدم	لا يطالب	او اتفاق سينهار. المغرب صامت
	كلنا معرضين للافات، اللهم نجي	لا شماتة	لله وإنا إليه راجعون. اللهم
	فرحتنا حتى يتم الإفراج عن	لن تكتمل	و أبعد البلاء عن الأبرياء
	الى اگادير ومن تواجد فهم	لم يتنقل	بين الجماهير ولكن الجمهور الرجاوي
	وراء فكرة الجمهور العالمي لنظهر	لا ننزلق	أساليب الشغب بالمرة .يجب أن
	اللعب في المنتخب والزمن سيؤكد	لا يستحقان	الفساد الذي ينخر الجامعة لاعبان
	حين يكون المنتخب في حاجة	لن يسجل	بموستواهم في الأيام القادمة بحيث
	عليه لأنه يلعب دقائق. حمد	لا نحكم	.كثرت انتقادات على حمد الله
	اتركوه يشتغل كما فعل في،	لا يحتاج آراءكم	للسيد الركراكي الدروس الخصوصية، المدرب
	التي هي عبارة عن لعبة	لا كرة القدم	العالم المغاربة البسطاء تهمهم الأسعار
	لمن تنادي ومستشفيات المغرب تشكو	لا حياة	.المتخصص في التسجيل ضد مرماه
	لها بالانتخابات. فهي مسؤلية الجميع	لا علاقة	.بنايات بلا روح قضية فلسطين
	أن تقسم والا فليس هنالك	لا يمكن	باحزاب صورية ومسرحية الانتخابات !!فالديمقراطية
	أن اتفق مع هذا الحزب	لا أستطيع	مرجعية الحزب جعلتني أشعر انني
	أن ليس له الحق في	لا يعني	هذا الحزب نهائيا. لكن هذا

Fig. 6. Screen shows the results after applying the local grammar on the corpus

We see that the local grammar recognizes the negative structures in the corpus. We got 32 sequences in our corpus. These sequences are the structures containing Arabic particle negation in verbal and nominal sentences. We also noticed that some negative structures were not recognized especially when the particle is attached to a preposition as well as other types of negation using lexical negators like غير"ghair" which means "non-" and also دون"douna" which means "without" because the paper doesn't take them into account.

To sum up, the adopted linguistic approach demonstrates a high level of accuracy in recognizing negation structures which are correctly identified in the corpus. We notice also that 32 sequences (out of 34) were identified in our corpus, approximately 94.12% that is a precision rate reaching 0.94. The extracted sequences are structures containing negation structures in verbal and nominal sentences. This highlights the promising and encouraging results drawn via the use of Nooj platform to recognize and handle negation in texts written in Arabic and in sentiment analysis in general. The negative structures that were not recognized were due to the fact that the particle is attached to another word and the incompleteness of the electronic dictionary.

5 Conclusion

Negation is a complex linguistic phenomenon, which needs further studies from different perspective to account for it exhaustively. Studies like this are expected to broaden our understanding of negation in Arabic and to make significant contributions to the enhancement of the accuracy of sentiment analysis results carried out on Arabic texts. This paper contributes to clarify some aspects of the Arabic negation system and display how Nooj platform can be utilized in recognizing negative sentiment in posts written in Arabic. Further research on Arabic sentiment analysis using Nooj should be conducted to explore new avenues – other lexical negators, semantic and implicit negation – to handle challenges and problems in the field. Likewise, efforts can be made to expand the electronic dictionary and to refine the local gram-mar rules for more large-scale sentiment analysis.

References

1. Pang, B., Lee, L.: Opinion Mining and Sentiment Analysis. Now Publishers, Boston (2008)
2. Liu, B.: Sentiment Analysis: Mining Opinions, Sentiments, and Emotions, 2nd edn. Cambridge University Press, New York (2020)
3. Pang, B., Lee, L., Vaithyanathan, S.: Thumbs up? Sentiment classification using machine learning techniques. In Proceedings of the 2002 Conference on Empirical Methods in Natural Language Processing (EMNLP 2002), pp. 79–86. Association for Computational Linguistics, (2002)
4. Esuli, A., Sebastiani, F.: Determining the semantic orientation of terms through gloss classification. In: Proceedings of the 14th ACM International Conference on Information and Knowledge Management October 2005. pp. 617–624. Association for Computing Machinery, Germany (2005). https://doi.org/10.1145/1099554.1099713
5. Cambria, E., et al.: A Practical Guide to Sentiment Analysis. Springer, Switzerland (2017)
6. Bing Liu.: Sentiment Analysis and Opinion Mining. Morgan and Claypool, San Rafael (2012)
7. Poria, S., et al.: Multimodal Sentiment Analysis. Springer, Switzerland (2018). https://doi.org/10.1007/978-3-319-95020-4
8. Ahmed, S., Pasquier, M., Qadah, G.: Key issues in conducting sentiment analysis on Arabic social media text. In: 2013 9th International Conference on Innovations in Information Technology (IIT), pp. 72–77. IEEE (2013)
9. El-Masri, M., Altrabsheh, N., Mansour, H.: Successes and challenges of Arabic sentiment analysis research: a literature review. Soc. Netw. Anal. Min. **7**(1) (2017). https://doi.org/10.1007/s13278-017-0474-x
10. Lindstad, A.M.: Analyses of Negation: Structure and Interpretation. Faculty of Humanities. University of Oslo, Oslo (2007)
11. Dudschig, C., Kaup, B., Liu, M., et al.: The processing of negation and polarity: an overview. J. Psycholinguist. Res. **50**, 1199–1213 (2021). https://doi.org/10.1007/s10936-021-09817-9

12. Horn, L.R.: A Natural History of Negation. CSLI Publications, USA (2001)
13. Morante, R., Sporleder, C.: Modality and negation: an introduction to the special issue. Comput. Linguist. **38**(2), 223–260 (2012). https://doi.org/10.1162/COLI_a_00095
14. Seifert, S., Welte, W.: A Basic Bibliography on Negation in Natural Language. G. Narr, Tübingen (1987)
15. Pollock, J.: Verb movement, universal grammar, and the structure of IP. Linguistic Inquiry, vol. 20, no. 3, pp. 365–424. The MIT Press (1989)
16. Brustad, K.: The Syntax of Spoken Arabic: A Comparative Study of Moroccan, Egyptian Syrian and Kuwaiti Dialects. Georgetown University Press, Washington (2000)
17. Benmamoun, E.: The Feature Structure of Functional Categories: A comparative study of Arabic dialects. Oxford University Press, Oxford (2000)
18. Ouhalla, J., Shlonsky, U.: The structure and logical form of negative sentence in Arabic. In: Ouhalla, J., Shlonsky, U. (eds.) Themes in Arabic and Hebrew Syntax, pp. 299–320. Kluwer, Dordrecht (2002)
19. Elhawary, M., Elfeky, M.: Mining Arabic business reviews. In: Data Mining Workshops (ICDMW), 2010 IEEE International Conference, pp. 1108–1113 (2010)
20. Farra, et al.: Sentence-level and document-level sentiment mining for Arabic texts. In: Data Mining Workshops (ICDMW), 2010 IEEE International Conference on, pp. 1114–1119 (2010)
21. Hamouda, A., El-taher, F.: Sentiment analyzer for arabic comments system. Int. J. Adv. Comput. Sci. Appl. (IJACSA) **4**(3) (2013). https://doi.org/10.14569/IJACSA.2013.040317
22. Kahlaoui, M.H.: Negation in standard arabic revisited: a corpus-based metaoperational approach. In: Smaïli, K. (ed.) Arabic Language Processing: From Theory to Practice. ICALP 2019. Communications in Computer and Information Science, vol. 1108. Springer, Cham (2019). https://doi.org/10.1007/978-3-030-32959-4_12
23. Silberztein, M.: Formalizing Natural Languages: The NooJ Approach. Wiley (2016)
24. Silberztein, M.: NooJ Manual (2003). https://atishs.univ-fcomte.fr/nooj/downloads.html

Automatic Arabic Essays Scoring: A Scoping Review

Chima Elhaddadi[1](✉), Imad Zeroual[1], and Anoual El Kah[2]

[1] L-STI, T-IDMS, FST Errachidia, Moulay Ismail University, Meknes, Morocco
elhddadi.chaima@gmail.com

[2] Polydisciplinary Faculty, Sultan Moulay Slimane University, Beni Mellal, Morocco

Abstract. As the call for efficient assessment tools in Arabic language education grows, releasing an automatic scoring system to mark students' dissertations has attracted the scholars' attention. Such tools can considerably reduce teachers' time and effort spent on the scoring task due to the growing number of students in different schools and universities. Therefore, research in this field has been started since the second decade of the twenty-first century while various works of Automatic Essay Scoring (AES) have been done. However, most of these works have focused on languages like English and German, while working on other languages such as Arabic is still limited. This scoping review provides a comprehensive overview of automatic Arabic essay scoring following the PRISMA-ScR guidelines while using the most relevant online bibliographic databases, namely ScienceDirect, Google Scholar, Scopus, and Web of science.

Keywords: Automatic Scoring · Arabic Essay · PRISMA-ScR guidelines

1 Introduction

The COVID-19 pandemic has shed light on distance education and finding online solutions to continue study normally without unfairly marking students [1]. In the education system, writing assessments is the most used method to determine or evaluate the level of students' linguistic.

Writing a dissertation has mainly two different forms. It can be an essay scoring for long answers that primarily includes an introduction section, a body part, and final conclusion. Besides, it can be a short answer scoring for define, what, and why questions, to name a few. We could also score Multi-choice, True or False and Matching questions [2].

Manually assessing long answers (i.e., Essays) requires considerable effort and time from teachers, and sometimes it is unfair because the corrector's view can vary depending on the correction time and conditions. Automatic Scoring Essay (AES) appears to solve this issue, which is a computer-based technology that automatically scores a written assess.

The history of the Automatic Scoring System (AGS), particularly in English, dates back to 1966 with Ellis Battan Page [3] when he discussed the importance of using a

B. Hdioud and S. L. Aouragh (Eds.): ICALP 2024, CCIS 2339, pp. 38–48, 2025.
https://doi.org/10.1007/978-3-031-79164-2_4

computer to grade essays during conceptualization and development of Project Essay Grading (PEG). Since then, many researchers have developed AES tools to evaluate English essays, such as E-rater, C-rater, and IntelliMetric [3]. On the other hand, works dealing with Arabic essays are still limited due to the rich and complex characteristics of the language at all linguistic levels (phonological, lexical, morphological, syntactic and semantic) [4].

The rest of the paper is structured into seven main sections. In Sect. 2, we delve into the challenges associated with Arabic language characteristics that significantly impact the task of automatic essay scoring. Section 3 outlines the methodology employed for conducting our review. The subsequent sections focus on the key findings of the review. Section 4 presents relevant Arabic datasets available for Arabic automatic essay scoring, while Sect. 5 introduces commonly utilized text pre-processing techniques to enhance evaluating essay performance. Section 6 compiles a list of popular text representation and vectorization methods employed in the features selection phase. Section 7 overviews the text similarity algorithms commonly implemented to assess the resemblance between two or more pieces of text. The paper concludes in Sect. 8.

2 Arabic Language and Natural Language Processing

Natural Language Processing (NLP) is an area of intersection between artificial intelligence and linguistics that allows machines to understand human language. This is not new since the intelligence of a machine has historically been assessed by its ability to hold a credible human conversation, as happened with the Turing test proposed as early as 1950. The complexity and diversity of human language is staggering. There are countless methods by which we can communicate verbally and in writing. There are hundreds of languages and dialects, not to mention that every language has its specific vocabulary, slang, and rules for grammar and syntax. We often lack punctuation or use incorrect spelling or acronyms when writing. We mumble, stutter, adopt vocabulary from other languages, and talk with regional accents.

The Arabic language has over 400 million speakers around the world [5]. Arabic in its standard form, known as Modern Standard Arabic (MSA), is one of the six official languages of the United Nations, poses many challenges to Arabic NLP, given its complexity when considered with its dialects, the language pushes the boundaries of NLP and necessitates serious researchers to create solutions posed by the inherent nature of the language especially if the aim is to integrate NLP into Arabic learning and teaching [6].

In Arabic morphology, there is a derivational morphology and inflectional morphology. For instance, the root word "درس"(en. Study) many phrases can be formed such as "هو يَدْرُسُ"(en. he is studying) or "هي تَدْرُسُ"(en. She is studying). Semantically, we can generate some words like "مَدْرَسَة"(en. School), "تَدْرِيس"(en. Education). This richness of the Arabic language makes it difficult for machine learning-based algorithm to deal with. However, Arabic NLP has seen an interesting advancement in the last years, availability of robust Arabic Pre-trained models (e.g., AraBERT [7] and AraGPT2 [8]) and language resources (e.g., Masader[1]).

[1] https://arbml.github.io/masader/

3 Automatic Essay Scoring

Generally, an automatic scoring system is composed of four main phases [9, 10]. Firstly, the data pre-processing phase prepares the input using different techniques including tokenization, stop words removal, stemming, and lemmatization. The next step consists of filtering or selecting the key features in which an initial set of data is reduced by identifying these key features to be fitted later to a machine learning algorithm. These extracted features are used in the model construction to train it for scoring student's essays before evaluating the model that gives a mark for each input dissertation in the last phase as the figure Fig. 1 illustrates.

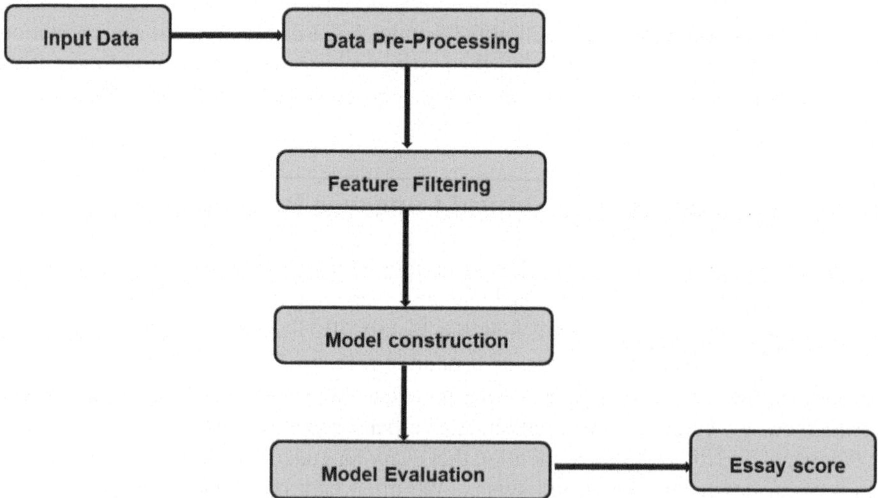

Fig. 1. An illustrative schema of an automatic essay scoring system.

A scoping review is a type of knowledge synthesis that aims to provide a descriptive overview without critically appraising individual studies or synthesizing evidence from different studies. On the contrary, systematic reviews aim to provide a synthesis of evidence from studies assessed for risk of bias [11]. Figure 2 indicates the flow diagram adopted in this PRISMA-ScR review.

As a start, we found 71 records by searching in the following well-known databases (ScienceDirect, Google Scholar, Scopus, Web of Science, and IEEE Xplore) using several search queries. Here is an example of the search queries performed: ("Automatic" OR "Automated") AND ("Scoring system" OR "Grading system") AND ("Arabic" OR "Arab") AND ("Essays" OR "Dissertations" OR "Assessments"). In addition, we also had to carry out searches in Arabic, notably in certain Arabic databases like Shamaa[2], which is an educational information network that aims to document studies of education in Arab countries. Following the PRISMA-ScR guidelines we excluded many records

[2] https://shamaa.org/eng/.

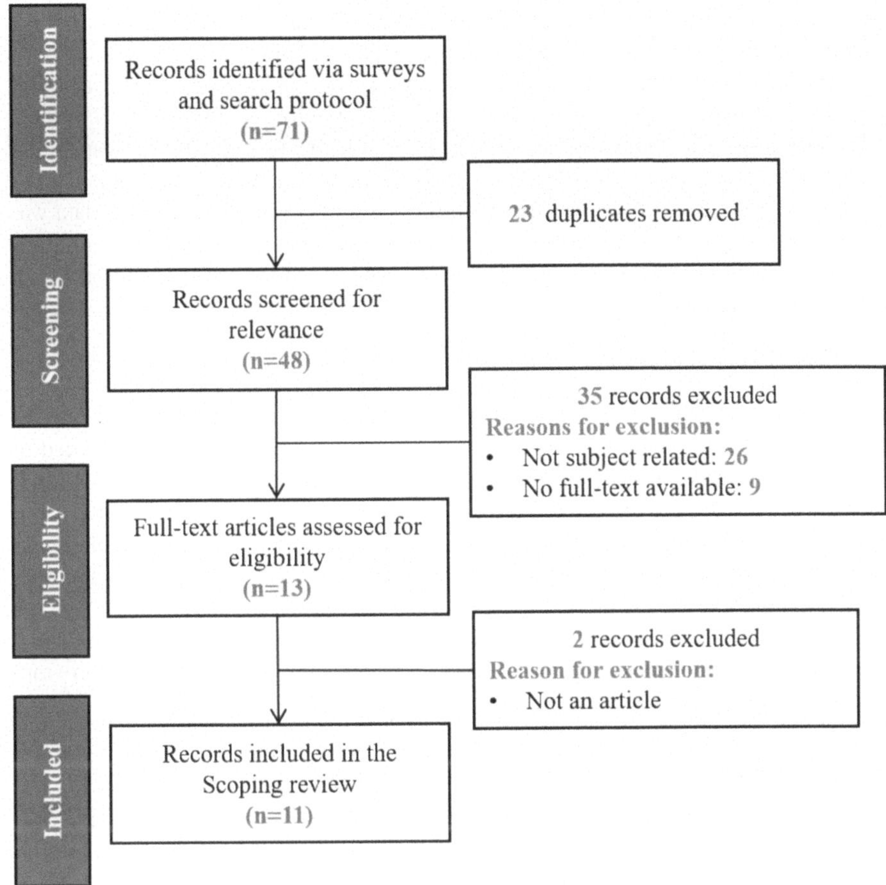

Fig. 2. PRISMA-ScR flow diagram.

according to different criteria, in the end, we were left with only 11 records to be included in this review.

4 Datasets

The number of Arabic datasets was increasing in the last years, covering several NLP tasks such as topic classification and sentiment analysis. Unfortunately, Arabic corpora that can be used in automatic scoring essays task are limited and not freely available. To the best of our knowledge, there are two datasets publicly available:

- **ARA-ASAG**[3]: Three distinct tests, along with sample responses and student responses from three different classes, are included in this corpus [12], which was obtained from an exam for a cybercrime course. 16 short answer questions constitute

[3] https://data.mendeley.com/datasets/dj95jh332j/1.

each exam, and the amount of student responses fluctuates for each question. For a total of 48 questions, 2133 student responses are included in this dataset.
- **AraScore**[4]: This dataset was created through several steps [13]. There are thirty graded tests in all, with five questions covering geography and history on each exam. The responses were manually entered into a CSV file together with the corresponding grades. Additionally, a scale from 0 to 3 was used to normalize all grades. Then, thirty responses per question were insufficient. Increasing the size of the current data was the second stage. Back-translation was used for text augmentation by translating the source text into any language and then converting the translated material back into the source language.

5 Essay Pre-processing

Morphological analysis of Arabic words presents a number of challenges that need to be taken into account. The first challenge is that some root letters may be deleted or modified when deriving words from roots. The second challenge is that many affixes can be affected to the beginning of the word (prefixes) and to the end of the word (suffixes). These affixes can be formed from one or more letters. The third challenge is that Arabic words are written without short vowels. Various diacritical marks are used to replace short vowels.

According to the most publications covered in this review, there are 4 essential text pre-processing techniques used in Arabic essay scoring, namely tokenization, stop-word removal, stemming and lemmatizing.

5.1 Tokenization

Tokenization is the first step in any NLP process. A tokenizer divides a sequence of text into small unit that can be considered discrete elements. However, the Arabic tokenization task is complicated [14] due to the difference between written and spoken forms of the language.

5.2 Stop Words Removal

Stop words are those words that are repeated in every essay, so they're considered weak. Removing words requires determining a stop word list to calculate the frequency of appearance of each word. This method is for general applications. The second method is statistical and relies on the frequency feature within a specific dataset [15].

5.3 Stemming

Stemming an Arabic word is a technique for finding the lexical root or radical of words in a natural language, by removing the affixes attached to its root. As an Arabic word can have a more complicated form with these affixes, the objective of stemming is to find the representative indexing form of a word by truncating these affixes. Fortunately, there are many Arabic stemmers that are used frequently in Arabic NLP tasks [16]. Furthermore, in this review, the most used stemmers are Farassa [17] and ISRI stemmer [18].

[4] https://github.com/guc-research/AraScore-Dataset.

5.4 Lemmatization

Lemmatization is a critical pre-processing step that is indispensable in many applications using natural language processing. The process of determining the word's dictionary look-up form is called a lemma. Free Tools that are available for Arabic lemmatization are Farassa [17] and Madamira [19].

6 Features Selection Methods

The goal of feature extraction techniques is to filter and keep the most significant features from redundant or unnecessary data. To transform the raw data into a set of useful features, these approaches may include statistical procedures, domain-specific expertise, or mathematical transformations. To facilitate algorithm analysis and prediction or classification, the extracted features should ideally capture the key elements of the data.

Our review indicates that the following methods are most frequently used for vectorization and text representation in Arabic AES:

- **ArabicWordNet:** WordNet is a lexical database that classifies synonyms with the same meaning into groups called synsets without regard to word form or linguistic similarity. It is a knowledge-based technique for measuring semantic similarity [20]. 2006 saw the creation of Arabic WordNet, which was expanded in 2016. The Arabic WordNet tool is used to evaluate every synonym before calculating the Cosine similarity between the two phrases to determine their semantic similarity.
- **Word2vec:** An NLP approach called Word2vec is used to produce vector representations of words. The context and meaning of words are captured by these vectors [21]. Word2vec uses two fundamental models namely Continuous Bag-of-Words and the Skip-grams. After each word has been defined as a vector, Word2vec computes the angles between the vectors using similarity metrics.
- **Continuous Bag-of-Words (CBOW):** It is a common method in natural language processing for producing word embeddings. The CBOW model predicts the target term that is positioned in the middle of a context window of nearby words by using this window as input [22]. The model refines its capacity to predict the target word by identifying patterns in the input data after being trained on a large text corpus.

7 Text Similarity Algorithms

Text similarity algorithms are computational techniques designed to assess the resemblance between two or more pieces of text. These algorithms play a crucial role in various NLP tasks [23], such as document clustering, plagiarism detection, and information retrieval. Figure 3 from [23]exhibits the arborescent that contains each type of these algorithms. In this paper we will focus in Arabic language as the demand for efficient text processing continues to grow in this language, the development and refinement of text similarity algorithms become essential for enhancing the accuracy and effectiveness of diverse applications across the realm of natural language understanding. In general, essays assessment used two approaches [24]: String-Based Text Similarity, Corpus-Based Text Similarity.

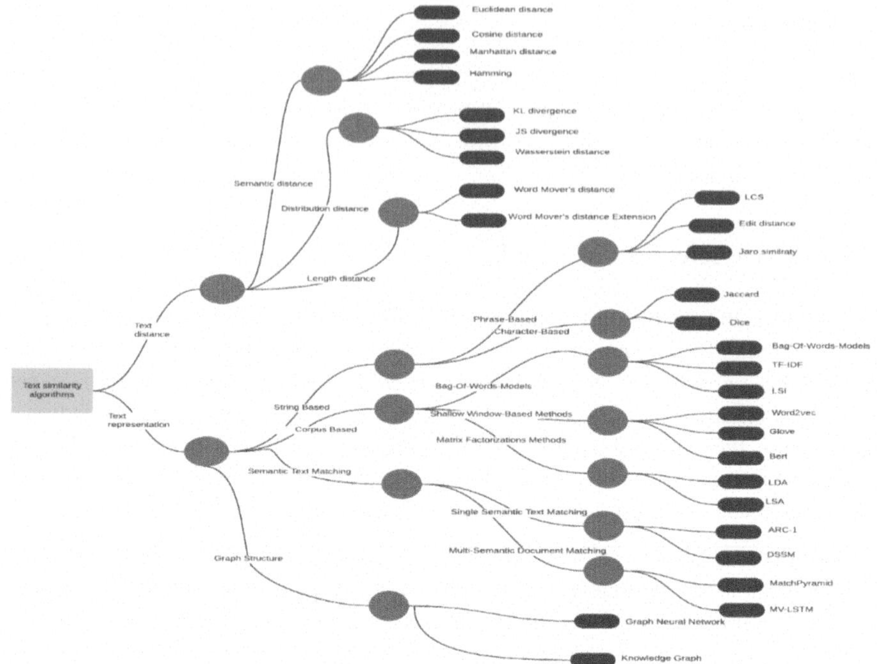

Fig. 3. Text similarity algorithms arborescent

7.1 String-Based Text Similarity

String-based text similarity algorithms focus on comparing and measuring the similarity between two text strings based on their characters, substrings, or sequences. These algorithms are fundamental for tasks like spell checking, plagiarism detection, and information retrieval. The following are the common techniques we found in our review in this category [25]:

- **Levenshtein Distance (Edit Distance):** This algorithm calculates the minimum number of single-character edits required to transform one string into another. There are two main definitions of editing distance: L-distance and D-distance [23]. The operations of D-distance comprise delete, insert, replace, and adjacent exchange operations, whereas L-distance only involves delete, insert, and replace operations. Due to the inclusion of adjacent exchange operation, D-distance is limited to handling single editing errors, whereas L-distance is capable of managing multiple editing errors.
- **Jaccard Similarity:** This method compares sets of words (w_a, w_b) or characters in two texts by calculating the intersection divided by the union of the sets as illustrated in Eq. (1). Jaccard Similarity is particularly useful when the order of words is not significant.

$$\mathrm{J}(w_a, w_b) = \frac{w_a \cap w_b}{w_a \cup w_b} \tag{1}$$

- **Cosine Similarity:** Cosine similarity is a frequently employed metric for measuring similarity, which assesses the cosine of the angle between two non-zero vectors within a multi-dimensional space. It finds widespread application in comparing documents, texts, or other data points existing in high-dimensional spaces. Unlike measures focusing on vector magnitudes, cosine similarity emphasizes the orientation or direction of the vectors. The cosine similarity formula between two vectors A and B can be expressed as follows:

$$C(a, b) := \cos(\theta) = \frac{a.b}{\|a\| \|b\|} = \frac{\sum_{i=0}^{n} a_i.b_i}{\sqrt{\sum_{i=1}^{n} a_i{}^2 . \sum_{i=1}^{n} b_i{}^2 .}} \quad (2)$$

- **Longest Common Subsequence (LCS):** LCfinds the longest subsequence (not necessarily contiguous) that is present in two strings (S_a, S_b). It is valuable for applications like version control systems and DNA sequence comparison. In this context, the LCS refers to the maximum length of identical substrings shared by S_a and S_b. This concept is particularly useful when analyzing lengthy texts. The LCS similarity of two given strings (S_a, S_b) is calculated as follows:

$$LCS(S_a, S_b) = \left\{ \begin{array}{c} 0, ifS_a = 0orS_b = 0 \\ 1 + LCS(S_a - 1, S_b - 1), ifxS_a == y[S_b] \\ max \left\{ \begin{array}{l} LCS(S_a, S_b - 1) \\ \qquad\qquad\qquad ifxS_a \neq y[S_b] \\ LCS(S_a - 1, S_b) \end{array} \right\} \end{array} \right\} \quad (3)$$

- **N-gram:** The n-gram comparison algorithm assesses the similarity between two strings by examining their subsequences of n consecutive characters, known as n-grams. These n-grams are essentially substrings of length n derived from the original strings. Widely applied in text analysis, natural language processing, and similarity comparison tasks, this algorithm follows a series of steps to execute its comparison process:
  - N-gram Extraction: Begin by partitioning each input string into overlapping sequences of n characters.
  - Counting N-grams: Proceed to tally the occurrences of every distinct n-gram in both strings.
  - Calculating Similarity: Compare the n-gram counts across the two strings and generate a similarity score. This score can be computed using different metrics, with Jaccard similarity and cosine similarity being popular choices.

7.2 Corpus-Based Text Similarity

Corpus-based text similarity algorithms focus on comparing and measuring the similarity between entire texts or documents based on the content of a larger body of text, known as a corpus. These algorithms are particularly useful for tasks such as document clustering, topic modeling, and information retrieval. Here are some common approaches of corpus-based text similarity [22]:

- **Latent Semantic Analysis (LSA) / Latent Semantic Indexing (LSI):** LSA is a technique that uses singular value decomposition to reduce the dimensionality of the term-document matrix. It captures the latent semantic structure in the data, allowing for the identification of semantic similarity between documents. LSA involves three primary steps. The initial step entails representing the document collection as a matrix of co-occurrences. The second step involves applying Singular Value Decomposition (SVD) to the matrix obtained in the first step, resulting in a multidimensional space. The final step entails reducing the dimensionality by eliminating certain dimensions obtained from the second step, deemed irrelevant for the analysis.
- **DISCO:** DISCO operates by assessing distributional similarity, a principle asserting that synonyms typically occur in similar contexts. The calculation of distributional similarity involves statistical analysis applied to extensive text collections. Initially, the corpus undergoes pre-processing, involving tokenization and the removal of stop words. In the primary step, a straightforward context window, with a size of $\pm$ 3 words, identifies occurrences of words that coincide. DISCO offers two variants: DISCO1, which aligns words based on their sets of co-occurring words, and DISCO2, which aligns words using their sets of distributional similarity.
- **TF-IDF:** operates effectively due to its consideration of a term frequency within a document $tf(w, d)$ and its occurrence across the whole corpus $idf(w, D)$. However, while words may frequently occur within a document, their presence alone may not necessarily signify their significance or relevance to that document. The computation of the TF-IDF is as follows:

$$tf - idf(w, d, D) = tf(w, d) \times idf(w, D) \tag{4}$$

8 Conclusion and Perspectives

Using the PRISMA-ScR guidelines, this scoping review has, in the end, given a thorough summary of the state of Arabic essay scoring systems. The investigation has brought to light a variety of methods, from sophisticated machine-learning techniques to rule-based systems. It is clear that there is an increasing interest in automating the assessment of Arabic essays by utilizing computational linguistics and natural language processing methods. The integration of syntactic structures, semantic analysis, and linguistic characteristics shows how sophisticated these scoring systems have become over time.

Despite the progress made, there are still several obstacles to overcome and room for development. The necessity for larger and more varied datasets in Arabic essay-scoring research is one important factor. The creation and assessment of reliable scoring models are hindered by the lack of high-quality, annotated corpora. Addressing the subtleties of Arabic language-specific components, such as morphology and intricate sentence patterns, also poses a special set of difficulties calling for more research.

As a recommendation, developing cross-disciplinary cooperation and a dedication to tackling language-specific issues would help create automated essay grading systems for Arabic that are more precise and sensitive to cultural differences. The authors are hoping this scoping review can be a basis for upcoming studies aiming at improving the efficiency and consistency of Arabic essay scoring in instructional and assessment contexts.

References

1. El kah, A., Zeroual, I.: Sentiment analysis of students' Facebook comments toward university announcements. In: 2022 5th International Conference on Networking, Information Systems and Security: Envisage Intelligent Systems in 5g//6G-based Interconnected Digital Worlds (NISS), pp. 1–5 (2022). https://doi.org/10.1109/NISS55057.2022.10084994
2. Omran, A.M.B., Aziz, M.J.A.: Automatic essay grading system for short answers in English language. JCS. **9**, 1369–1382 (2013). https://doi.org/10.3844/jcssp.2013.1369.1382
3. Ifenthaler, D.: Automated essay scoring systems. In: Handbook of Open, Distance and Digital Education, pp. 1–15. Springer, Singapore (2022). https://doi.org/10.1007/978-981-19-0351-9_59-1
4. Alqahtani, A., Alsaif, A.: Automated Arabic essay evaluation. In: Bhattacharyya, P., Sharma, D.M., Sangal, R. (eds.) Proceedings of the 17th International Conference on Natural Language Processing (ICON), pp. 181–190. NLP Association of India (NLPAI), Indian Institute of Technology Patna, Patna, India (2020)
5. Zeroual, I., Lakhouaja, A.: Arabic corpus linguistics: major progress, but still a long way to go. In: Intelligent Natural Language Processing: Trends and Applications, pp. 613–636. Springer, Cham (2018). https://doi.org/10.1007/978-3-319-67056-0_29
6. Zeroual, I., El Kah, A., Lakhouaja, A.: Integrating corpus-based analyses in language teaching and learning: challenges and guidelines. In: Tabii, Y., Lazaar, M., Al Achhab, M., Enneya, N. (eds.) Big Data, Cloud and Applications, pp. 534–545. Springer International Publishing (2018). https://doi.org/10.1007/978-3-319-96292-4_42
7. Antoun, W., Baly, F., Hajj, H.: AraBERT: transformer-based model for Arabic language understanding. In: Proceedings of the 4th Workshop on Open-Source Arabic Corpora and Processing Tools, with a Shared Task on Offensive Language Detection, pp. 9–15. European Language Resource Association, Marseille, France (2020)
8. Antoun, W., Baly, F., Hajj, H.: AraGPT2: pre-trained transformer for Arabic language generation. In: Habash, N., et al. (eds.) Proceedings of the Sixth Arabic Natural Language Processing Workshop, pp. 196–207. Association for Computational Linguistics, Kyiv, Ukraine (Virtual) (2021)
9. Gunawansyah, Rahayu, R., Nurwathi, Sugiarto, B., Gunawan: Automated essay scoring using natural language processing and text mining method. In: 2020 14th International Conference on Telecommunication Systems, Services, and Applications (TSSA), pp. 1–4 (2020). https://doi.org/10.1109/TSSA51342.2020.9310845
10. Lim, C.T., Bong, C.H., Wong, W.S., Lee, N.K.: A comprehensive review of automated essay scoring (AES) research and development. Pertanika J. Sci. Technol. **29**, 1875–1899 (2021)
11. Tricco, A.C., et al.: PRISMA extension for scoping reviews (PRISMA-ScR): checklist and explanation. Ann. Intern. Med. **169**, 467–473 (2018)
12. Ouahrani, L., Bennouar, D.: AR-ASAG An ARabic Dataset for Automatic Short Answer Grading Evaluation. In: Calzolari, N., et al. (eds.) Proceedings of the Twelfth Language Resources and Evaluation Conference, pp. 2634–2643. European Language Resources Association, Marseille, France (2020)
13. ElNaka, A., Nael, O., Afifi, H., Sharaf, N.: AraScore: investigating response-based Arabic short answer scoring. Proc. Comput. Sci. **189**, 282–291 (2021). https://doi.org/10.1016/j.procs.2021.05.091
14. Attia, M.: Arabic tokenization system. In: Proceedings of the 2007 workshop on computational approaches to Semitic languages: Common Issues Resour., 65–72 (2007)
15. Alajmi, A., Saad, E.M., Darwish, R.R.: Toward an ARABIC stop-words list generation. Int. J. Comput. Appl. **46**, 8–13 (2012)

16. Almazrua, A., Almazrua, M., Alkhalifa, H.: Comparative analysis of nine Arabic stemmers on microblog information retrieval. In: 2020 International Conference on Asian Language Processing (IALP), pp. 60–65 (2020). https://doi.org/10.1109/IALP51396.2020.9310456
17. Darwish, K., Mubarak, H.: Farasa: a new fast and accurate Arabic word Segmenter. In: LREC (2016)
18. Syarief, M.G., Kurahman, O.T., Huda, A.F., Darmalaksana, W.: Improving Arabic stemmer: ISRI stemmer. In: 2019 IEEE 5th International Conference on Wireless and Telematics (ICWT), pp. 1–4. IEEE (2019)
19. Pasha, A., et al.: MADAMIRA: a fast, comprehensive tool for morphological analysis and disambiguation of Arabic. In: LREC, pp. 1094–1101 (2014)
20. Regragui, Y., Abouenour, L., Krieche, F., Bouzoubaa, K., Rosso, P.: Arabic WordNet: new content and new applications. In: Proceedings of the 8th Global WordNet Conference (GWC), pp. 333–341 (2016)
21. Al-Saqqa, S., Awajan, A.: The use of Word2vec model in sentiment analysis: a survey. In: Proceedings of the 2019 International Conference on Artificial Intelligence, Robotics and Control, pp. 39–43. Association for Computing Machinery, New York, NY, USA (2020). https://doi.org/10.1145/3388218.3388229
22. Boudad, N., Ezzahid, S., Faizi, R., Thami, R.O.H.: Exploring the use of word embedding and deep learning in Arabic sentiment analysis. In: Advanced Intelligent Systems for Sustainable Development (AI2SD'2019), pp. 243–253. Springer, Cham (2020). https://doi.org/10.1007/978-3-030-36674-2_26
23. Wang, J., Dong, Y.: Measurement of text similarity: a survey. Information **11**, 421 (2020). https://doi.org/10.3390/info11090421
24. Prasetya, D.D., Prasetya Wibawa, A., Hirashima, T.: The performance of text similarity algorithms (2018)
25. Gomaa, W.H., Fahmy, A.A.: A survey of text similarity approaches. Int. J. Comput. Appl. **68**, 13–18 (2013)

Bridging the Emotional Gap: Google NL-AI Sentiment Analysis in Comparing Moroccan Literary Translations

Khadija Refouh[1(✉)] and Mimoune Daoudi[2]

[1] DISCRESOR Research Lab, Princess Nourah Bint Abdulrahman University, PO Box 84428, Riyadh, Saudi Arabia
Refouh.khadija@usmba.ac.ma

[2] Faculty of Letters and Human Sciences Saïs-Fés, BP 59, Fez, Morocco

Abstract. This preliminary study explores the potential of Google Artificial Intelligence based Natural Language (GNL-AI) sentiment analysis (SA) as a novel and complementary tool for comparing literary translations at the sentiment level. This study investigates how effectively GNL-AI can assess the emotional fidelity of each translation by analyzing the author's emotional sentiment conveyed in the text. It seeks to move beyond traditional methods often driven by subjectivity or literalness and instead explore a different perspective capable of assessing the emotional fidelity of each translation toward the source text (ST). Ahmed Toufiq's Arabic novel, "Abu Musa's Women Neighbors", is the ST that serves as a case study. This research analyzes the sentiment of two translations: English (TT1) by Roger Allen and French (TT2) by Philippe Vigreux. Analyzing the sentiment of 18 ST paragraphs and their corresponding segments in both translations TT1 and TT2 using GNL-AI revealed promising results. Most segments exhibited consistent sentiment patterns, highlighting the potential of this tool for identifying broad emotional trends in literary translations. Three paragraphs showed deviations in sentiment scores, highlighting challenges in achieving perfect alignment between the source text and the translations. Interestingly, the English translation captures well the Arabic author's intended emotional impact, showcasing the potential of GNL-AI SA in evaluating literary translation quality. In contrast, the French translation tends slightly towards neutrality, highlighting both the promise and the limitations of this approach. Future research will involve expanding the dataset and exploring how GNL-AI can be integrated with human expertise for a more comprehensive analysis.

Keywords: literary translation · sentiment analysis (SA) · Google natural language AI (GNL-AI) · emotional fidelity

1 Introduction

Google Cloud technology represents a significant advancement in the field of machine learning and deep learning by offering user-friendly tools that facilitate model building. Traditionally, constructing these models demanded extensive expertise from data scientists, requiring coding and manual input for every step of the process. In contrast, Google

B. Hdioud and S. L. Aouragh (Eds.): ICALP 2024, CCIS 2339, pp. 49–62, 2025.
https://doi.org/10.1007/978-3-031-79164-2_5

Cloud provides tools that automate various aspects of model creation, potentially eliminating the need for such deep specialization. These tools can independently configure and customize machine learning algorithms based on a provided dataset, significantly reducing the user involvement required for successful model development. This innovative approach empowers a wider range of users to leverage the power of machine learning and deep learning, even without extensive data science backgrounds. Building upon this democratization of machine learning, Google Cloud Platform (GCP) offers pre-built sentiment analysis tools within its Natural Language API. These pre-trained models allow users to analyze text data for sentiment with minimal configuration, further reducing the technical expertise required. However, for users with specific domain needs or particularly complex datasets, GCP also offers AutoML Natural Language. In brief, the first provides pre-trained models for immediate use, while the second empowers developers to create custom models for specific domains (White & Rege, 2020). This tool empowers users to train custom sentiment analysis models tailored to their unique requirements. AutoML technology, which emerged in the 1990s, automates various aspects of model development, including sentiment analysis (Mahima et al., 2021). This allows users to leverage the power of custom-built models without the extensive coding expertise traditionally needed (Google, 2024). Overall, GCP's sentiment analysis services cater to a range of user needs, offering both pre-trained models for ease of use and customizable options for more specialized tasks.

This research leverages the user-friendly nature of GCP's Natural Language API by employing its pre-trained sentiment analysis models. Sentiment analysis (SA), a method in natural language processing, originated with the rapid growth of social media and digitalized communication. The increasing demand for sentiment analysis has led researchers to explore various domains, including business and media, where understanding others' emotions is crucial. It is becoming increasingly prominent due to the rise of social media and holds value in capturing public opinion on various topics, informing decision-making. (Mabokela et al., 2022). Sentiment Analysis (SA) is typically used to determine the emotional tone of a text, categorizing it as positive, neutral, or negative. It analyzes not only people's opinions and emotions but also the subjectivity or objectivity of the language itself, classifying text accordingly (Pérez, 2021; Alqurashi, 2023; Mabokela et al., 2022). This study deviates from the typical application of SA by utilizing Google Natural Language API (GNL API) to analyze sentiment in the challenging domain of Moroccan literary works and their translations. This innovative approach offers a new perspective on assessing and comparing literary translations as well as bridging the emotional gap between the ST and its translations.

The emotional core of literary translation remains a challenge to assess. This study explores the potential of sentiment analysis, a technique from Natural Language Processing (NLP), to evaluate emotional fidelity in translations by comparing the sentiment patterns of source texts and their translations. The research focuses on Ahmed Toufiq's Arabic novel, "Abu Musa's Women Neighbors," exploring English and French translations by Roger Allen and Philippe Vigreux, respectively. Ahmed Toufiq's writing, a captivating mix of history and emotional storytelling rooted in Islamic culture, poses a translation challenge. Conveying the full impact of his work requires deep understanding of both the culture and its literary traditions, as emotions and cultural references are intricately intertwined. The aim is to reveal how effectively each translation conveys the hidden emotional currents of the original work. Ahmed Toufiq's writing style is a captivating blend of historical narration, storytelling, and scholarly exploration. This unique approach reflects his understanding of history's role in shaping Islamic culture, where historical narratives have long been interwoven with various fields of knowledge and expressive genres. This unique fusion, however, poses a challenge for translators. Capturing the cultural depth and emotional resonance tied to this heritage requires fluency in both language and Islamic literary traditions. Traditional comparative methods often deal with subjectivity, relying on stylistic preferences or structural analyses. Recognizing these limitations, the investigation suggests that sentiment analysis, a data-driven approach, holds the key to a more comprehensive understanding of emotional integrity in translations.

The original Arabic language has been extensively annotated, reflecting each scene's main emotional mood. This annotated dataset is aligned with its corresponding translations in (TT1) and (TT2) test by the GNL-AI sentiment analysis tool. Comparing sentiment scores in corresponding segments of the original and each translation reveals minor shifts in emotional intensity. Human evaluation, conducted by skilled translators, provides insights into the relevance of the sentiment scores shown by the analysis. A review of existing literature revealed no prior research directly investigating the integration of sentiment analysis for comprehensively evaluating literary translation quality, highlighting a significant gap in this area. While traditional approaches prioritize reliability to the original text and linguistic accuracy, this study underscores the crucial aspect of emotional fidelity.

Using the Google Cloud Natural Language API in this research represents an initial exploration to unlock insights from unstructured text and bridge the gap between the emotional landscape of Arabic literary works and their translations. This research paves the way for scholars to investigate the sentimental aspects of translation that extend beyond surface-level accuracy.

This paper is structured as follows: The methodology section elaborates on data selection, annotation processes, and steps involved in sentiment analysis with GNL-API. Subsequently, the results section presents findings from GNL-AI analysis and human evaluation, highlighting patterns and deviations in sentiment scores. The discussion section delves into the implications of the findings, exploring the potential and limitations of using sentiment analysis for literary translations. Lastly, the conclusion and recommendations section summarize key takeaways, discusses study limitations, and suggests avenues for future research. Through the use of GNL-API, this research aims to pave the way for scholars to investigate the sentimental aspects of translation, moving beyond surface-level accuracy and fostering a deeper understanding of emotional conveyance in translated works.

2 Problem Statement

Evaluating the quality of literary translations often relies on subjective interpretation or literal comparisons, neglecting the crucial aspect of emotional fidelity. Traditional methods can overlook subtle shifts in sentiment between the original text and its translations, potentially misrepresenting the author's intended emotional impact on the reader.

Despite significant advancements in Natural Language Processing (NLP), including validated sentiment analysis techniques and machine learning models, a research gap exists in developing reliable and objective methods for analyzing and comparing the emotional content of Arabic literary translations with their originals. This gap hinders our understanding of how effectively translations convey the original author's emotional nuances, crucial to the aesthetic and artistic value of the work. Addressing this research gap with a focus on the complexities of Arabic literary translations is crucial for ensuring the faithful transmission of not only the literal meaning but also the emotional impact of these works.

3 Research Question

1 How effectively can sentiment analysis tools, like GNL-API, assess emotional faithfulness in Arabic literary translations, considering challenges like cultural nuances and wordplay?
2 Which translated version (TT1 or TT2) maintains closer sentiment coherence to the Arabic original, while acknowledging limitations of sentiment analysis? Anlyse specific deviations for further human evaluation.

This research questions seek to explore the potential of sentiment analysis tools, specifically GNL-API, in the context of assessing emotional fidelity in literary translations as a novel tool for translation comparison, moving beyond subjective assessments and literal comparisons towards a more objective and precise analysis of emotional content. By focusing on the author's emotional resonance, this research aims to contribute to a nuanced understanding of translation quality and fidelity, benefiting translators, scholars, and readers alike.

4 Literature Review

Language and culture significantly influence how emotions are understood and expressed. There are variations in how emotions are conceptualized and expressed in different languages (lexicons and discourses) (Ogarkova et al., 2009). A growing research area focuses on how translators navigate the emotional challenges inherent in translation. This includes managing their own emotions and understanding the emotional tone of the source text, as cultural backgrounds significantly influence how emotions are expressed. These studies emphasize the importance of understanding how a translator's cultural background can impact the accuracy of their work (Fernández Sedano, Itziar, et al. (2000), Hunziker et al., 2021; Cheng, 2022). Consequently, new researchers are moving beyond traditional translation assessment methods and exploring ways to measure a translator's ability to effectively handle these complexities and convey emotions equivalent to those in the source text.

The growing focus on emotion in translation aligns with a broader trend in knowledge discovery: sentiment analysis. With the vast amount of online data generated daily (social media posts, comments, reviews), sentiment analysis has become a focal point for extracting meaning and understanding public opinion. By harnessing these techniques, translation studies can potentially benefit from data-driven approaches to assess emotional fidelity in translations, complementing traditional methods. According to Mabokela et al., (2022), Sentiment analysis employs three main approaches: Machine Learning (ML) trains algorithms on labeled data to classify text as positive, negative, or neutral (e.g., Support Vector Machines). Lexicon-based methods rely on pre-defined sentiment dictionaries (like WordNet) to assign sentiment scores based on individual words. Finally, hybrid methods combine both approaches, potentially using lexicons for initial classification and then training ML models for more nuanced analysis.

Building upon prior research, this work examines the evolving landscape of Sentiment Analysis (SA) for Arabic dialects, highlighting valuable resources and future directions. Sherif et al. (2023) conducted a systematic review of Sentiment Analysis (SA) and data annotations for Arabic dialects from 2015 to 2023. The study offers a refined taxonomy of data annotation methods (manual, automatic, hybrid) and discusses research challenges, motivations, and recommendations. It identifies new gaps, proposes future directions, and emphasizes the growing importance of SA in understanding sentiments and opinions in the context of increasing social media interactions. The review is a valuable resource for scholars in Arabic SA, guiding future research and applications. Bou Nassif et al. (2021) conducted a systematic review spanning from 2000 to June 2020, focusing on the status of deep learning for Arabic Natural Language Processing (ANLP), particularly in Arabic Subjective Sentiment Analysis (ASSA). The study identifies challenges, explores existing research, and proposes future research opportunities. The review highlights the prevalent use of Convolutional Neural Networks (CNN) and Recurrent Neural Networks (RNN), especially Long Short-Term Memory (LSTM) models, in ASSA tasks. The findings stress the need for integrating advanced deep learning techniques into Arabic sentiment analysis systems, emphasizing the significance of ASSA tools in extracting valuable information for various applications, including user feedback, product evaluations, and election predictions.

Concerning the exploration of sentiment analysis as an objective tool for comparing literary translations. Baquero Pérez's study addresses the challenge of comparing translations influenced by reader stylistic taste. It proposes statistical aspects for analysis, including total word count and sentence structure. Additionally, word clouds are suggested to analyze word weight in each context, providing insights into adherence to the original's lexicon. The approach aims to objectively determine the closeness of translations to the original author's feelings, guiding more exhaustive linguistic analyses. The method suggests potential for a broader comparative analysis of multiple translations of Don Quixote (2021).

This study by White & Rege (2020) investigates the effectiveness of Google Cloud Platform (GCP) services for sentiment analysis, comparing pre-built models with custom-trained options. In this project White & Rege (2020) explore sentiment analysis using two Google Cloud Platform (GCP) services: Natural Language API and AutoML Natural Language. The former offers prebuilt models for sentiment analysis, while the latter allows developers to train domain-specific models. The project's experiments indicate the advantages of using AutoML for building custom models, emphasizing ease of use and convenient reporting. The results highlight the subjective nature of sentiment analysis. Despite challenges, the AutoML model demonstrates improvements in correctly identifying positive sentiment compared to Google Cloud Platforms.

More studies agree with this evaluation and underscore the effectiveness of AutoML in specific contexts and showcase its high accuracy for particular cases, especially when considering the efforts required for manually building machine learning or deep learning models. (Mahima et al., 2021) (Soumya & Pramod, 2022). While the literature review explores sentiment analysis (SA) for Arabic dialects and its potential in translation studies, a gap exists regarding the application of user-friendly interfaces like Google Cloud Platform's Natural Language API (GNLP API) for SA in the context of Arabic literary translations.

5 Methodology

The research methodology encompasses several crucial steps to investigate the potential of Google Natural Language AI (NL API) for analyzing the emotional fidelity of literary translations. To achieve this, a sample from a well-regarded Arabic novel and its corresponding English and French translations were selected for a preliminary experiment. This experiment aims to discover the potential of Google NL API in analyzing emotional fidelity and pave the way for deeper investigation concerning translating the emotions within Arabic literature.

The chosen Arabic novel is "Abu Musa's Women Neighbors" by Ahmed Toufiq. The English translation (TT1) by Roger Allen and the French translation (TT2) by Philippe Vigreux are included for comparative analysis. To facilitate a detailed emotional analysis using sentence-level sentiment scores, the text is systematically segmented into paragraphs or even smaller units. Following segmentation, text cleaning is performed on both the Arabic source text and the translated versions (TT1 and TT2) to remove non-textual elements and address formatting issues.

5.1 Data Preparation

The primary stage of this research involved constructing a clean and accurate dataset for sentiment analysis. This process encompassed several steps:

- Digital Transformation: The sample text from the original Arabic novel and its corresponding English and French translations were carefully scanned using high-resolution scanners. This step ensured the digital copies accurately represented the physical books, minimizing potential errors introduced during the scanning process.
- Optical Character Recognition (OCR) with Error Correction: Once scanned, Google's Optical Character Recognition (OCR) technology was employed to extract the textual content from the digital images. OCR technology automatically converts scanned images into editable text formats. However, to guarantee accuracy and consistency, the researchers meticulously reviewed the extracted text and manually corrected any errors introduced by the OCR process. This careful revision ensured the dataset contained the most accurate representation of the original text and its translations.

- Formatting and Cleaning: Following error correction, the researchers standardized the formatting of the extracted text data. This involved addressing inconsistencies in spacing, punctuation, and paragraph breaks across the Arabic source text and its translations. Additionally, any non-textual elements, such as page numbers or headers, were removed during this cleaning process. This meticulous formatting and cleaning ensured the data was consistent and suitable for subsequent sentiment analysis using Google NL API.

5.2 Sentiment Analysis

The prepared text data was broken down into paragraphs or smaller meaningful units. The NL API was adopted for sentiment analysis. Arabic was designated as the primary language for the original novel, while English and French were specified for the translated versions. With each submission, the NL API assessed the emotional undercurrents, generating sentiment scores (ranging from −1 for negative to 1 for positive) and magnitude values (indicating the intensity of emotions).

5.3 Interpreting the Results

The extracted scores and magnitudes were organized into comprehensive tables, offering a clear picture of sentiment trends across the novel and its translations. Graphs further illuminated these trends, allowing for the identification of areas for closer inspection.

5.4 Identifying Deviations

Significant deviations in sentiment scores between the original novel and its translations were identified. Sentences exhibiting such discrepancies were earmarked for deeper investigation, aided by the expertise of human translators. The sentences with notable sentiment score differences were analyzed. The potential causes behind these deviations were explored and explained in the finding paragraph, considering cultural nuances, connotation of expressions and words, sentence structures, and other factors that might influence sentiment analysis. This collaborative approach provided invaluable context and enriched the understanding of the translations' faithfulness to the emotional core of the original work.

6 Finding

The analysis of emotional sentiment within the novel and its translations was conducted using Google Natural Language AI (NL API). Sentence-by-sentence sentiment scores are provided in the Table 1, offering insights into the emotional undercurrents and potential variations across the original text and its English and French translations.

The sentiment analysis conducted on the original Arabic text and its English and French translations is depicted in Fig. 1. The graph illustrates the sentiment analysis at the sentence level of an Arabic novel and its two translations, one into English and the other into French. It displays the sentiment scores assigned by GNL API to sentences from

Table 1. Sentiment Scores for Original Novel, English Translation, and French Translation (Generated by Google NL API)

Sentences	Arabic ST	En TT	Fr TT
1	0.112	0.021	0.025
2	0.14	0.085	0.043
3	−0.144	0.051	0.028
4	−0.043	0.015	0
5	−0.013	−0.005	0.019
6	−0.002	−0.003	0.021
7	0.007	0.047	0.011
8	−0.365	−0.476	0.059
9	−0.262	−0.29	−0.126
10	0.233	0.478	0.035
11	−0.58	0.216	−0.133
12	−0.74	−0.877	−0.348
13	0.22	0.485	0.038
14	0.264	0.147	0.051
15	0.024	0.467	0.066
16	−0.018	0.003	0.004
17	0.598	0.747	0.858
18	−0.002	0.114	0.028

the Arabic novel (Arabic ST) and its translations into English (English TT) and French (French TT). The x-axis represents sentence numbers from 1 to 18, while the y-axis represents sentiment scores ranging from −1.0 (very negative) to 1.0 (very positive).

In general, the translations exhibit a coherent sentiment pattern across sentences, although the French translation tends to hover closer to the neutral line compared to both the original Arabic text (ST) and the English translation. Despite this, specific deviations come to light in certain sentences, as elaborated upon below. To better understand the reasons for these variations, researchers are conducting a comprehensive review. This analysis aims to identify any nuances or challenges in the translation process that may have contributed to the observed discrepancies in sentiment.

Upon analyzing the graph, several points highlight deviations between the Arabic text and its English or French translations:

- Sentence 8: Both the Arabic text and English translation exhibit a negative sentiment, whereas the French translation shows a positive sentiment.
- Sentence 11: Significant deviations in sentiment scores are noted among all three texts, with each displaying different patterns. The French translation has a neutral

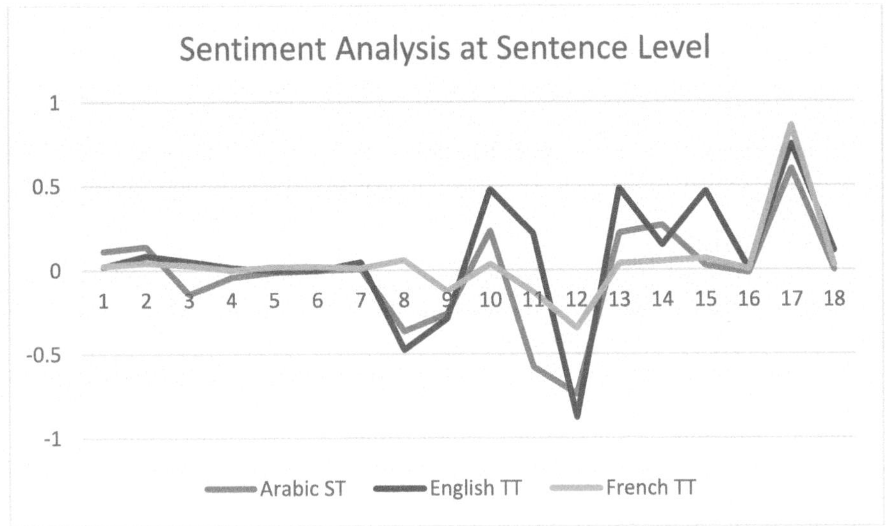

Fig. 1. Sentiment Analysis of the first chapter of the original text in Arabic and the English translations.

sentiment, whereas the Arabic text and English translation sentiments are extremely opposed.

- Sentence 15: The Arabic and French texts have neutral sentiments, while the English translation shows positive sentiment.

6.1 Human Analysis

The subsequent step involves a human review to explain why the translations did not maintain a consistent sentiment pattern across sentences without deviations.

Sentence 8.

Original Arabic Text:

استعظم ابن الحفيد هذا التشريف لمكانة الجورائي من السلطان ولأن هذا الإيثار سيرجح كفة نفوذه في المدينة على حساب العامل الذي لا ينعته القاضي في خاصته إلا باسم «المقيت».

English Translation:

Ibn al-Hafid realized what a great honor was being bestowed on him, not merely because of Al-Jawra'ï's exalted status but also because the obvious preferment involved would enhance his own prestige at the expense of the Governor, someone for whom only one name was ever used in the privacy of the Judge's own home, the odious.

French Translation:

Ibn al-Hafid fit grand cas de l'honneur qu'on lui témoignait, eu égard à la position d'al-Jura i vis-à-vis du sultan et au fait qu'un tel choix assoirait son prestige sur la ville dépens du gouverneur qu'il appelait "L'Abominable" en son for intérieur.

The overall sentiment of all three texts is positive for Ibn al-Hafid. He is honored to be chosen for this task, and he believes it will increase his prestige in the city.

However, there are some subtle differences in the sentiment of the three texts.

Arabic Text:

The Arabic text uses the word استعظم which means "to consider great or important". This suggests that Ibn al-Hafid is very impressed by the honor that has been bestowed on him.

The text also uses the word إيثار which means "preference". This suggests that Ibn al-Hafid believes that he has been chosen for this task because he is more qualified than the Governor.

English Translation:

The English translation uses the word realized, which means "to understand or become aware of something". This suggests that Ibn al-Hafid is aware of the importance of the honor that has been bestowed on him.

The translation also uses the word obvious, which suggests that Ibn al-Hafid believes that he is the clear choice for this task.

French Translation:

The French translation uses the word grand cas, which means "to think highly of something". This suggests that Ibn al-Hafid has a high opinion of the honor that has been bestowed on him.

The translation also uses the word assoirait, which means "to establish or consolidate". This suggests that Ibn al-Hafid believes that this task will solidify his position in the city.

The concluding parts of all three texts express a negative sentiment. In the Arabic text, the use of the term 'المقيت' ('the odious') indicates strong disapproval view. Similarly, in the English and French translations, phrases like 'the odious' and 'L'Abominable' carry derogatory connotations, expressing a negative evaluation of the Governor. The sentiment in all three versions suggests a critical and unfavorable perception of the Governor, emphasizing a sense of displeasure. Even though Ibn al-Hafid may benefit from this situation, an overall negative connotation prevails over any positive sentiments mentioned earlier in the analysis of this sentence and its translations. Therefore, there is no logical explanation for the positive sentiment score assigned by GNL API to the French translation, whereas the sentiment scores of the Arabic sentence and its English translation accurately reflect the real negative sentiment.

Sentence 11.

هي إن كانت حميراء في رقة عود البان كما يصفونها، كانت ذات مزاج حاد ينفعها في زرع الرعب في جميع من في الدار من العيال والخدم حتى ينجز كل شيء بأسرع ما يمكن وعلى أحسن ما يرام.

In the Arabic text, the sentiment is characterized by a mixture of admiration and apprehension towards Tumaymah. She is described as 'حميراء في رقة عود البان'(auburn-haired and as delicate as a reed-stalk) while also emphasizing a 'مزاج حاد'(tough streak in temperament). The expression 'زرع الرعب'(sowing terror) further reinforces the idea of instilling fear to achieve objectives efficiently, giving a more negative connotation to the original text. 'Auburn-haired and as svelte as a reed-stalk (as they described her), she was endowed with a tough streak that served her well when it came to terrorizing everyone, family and servants alike, so that every- thing would be executed as efficiently and as elegantly as possible.'

The English text mirrors this sentiment; Tumaymah is depicted as 'auburn-haired' and possessing a slim physique, yet the mention of a "tough streak" suggests a certain assertiveness or even intimidation in her character. However, the purpose of this toughness is described as ensuring efficiency and elegance in the execution of tasks, implying a level of control or demand.

Generally speaking, the sentiment in both texts appears to convey a similar tone. However, the use of expressions attached to highly positive feelings, such as the adverb 'well' and the noun 'elegancy,' minimizes the negativity of the sentiment and adds a positive connotation to the sentence. The sentiment analysis of the same English sentence without both expressions drops to neutrality. However, the sentiment remains higher than both the Arabic text and the French translation.

Sentence 15.

Original Arabic Text:

التحقت أفواج المرحبين بالقاضي والعامل ووقف أعيان القضاة والمفتين والعلماء وأهل الأدب والتجار والمتمولين وأهل النسبة إلى الشرف والصلاح ومحتسبو البضائع وأمناء الحرف ورؤساء السفن ومن صح لهم الجهاد في عدوة الأندلس أو في البحر وأعوان العامل من مقدمي الأحياء وشيوخها كلٌ في مكانه.

English Translation:

The two men were joined by a huge crowd of officials, there to welcome the distinguished guest: senior Judges, Muftis, religious scholars, littérateurs, merchants, men of wealth, people renowned for their virtue and good deeds, market inspectors, trade representatives, captains of ships, veterans of campaigns in Spain or on the sea, and Governor's aides-quarter-heads and shaykhs, Everyone was stationed in his appointed place.

French Translation:

Les groupes de bienvenue les rejoignirent peu à peu, Se tenaient là hauts magistrats, muftis, oulémas, lettres, commerçants, bourgeois, membres de la lignée du Prophète et des hommes de haute vertu, prévôts des marchés, maîtres des corporations, capitaines de navires, illustres combattants du jihad en terre andalouse ou sur mer, sans oublier les adjoints du gouverneur: juges de police et cheikhs de quartiers, chacun à la place qui lui était assignée.

Overall, the three texts have a similar positive sentiment. The authors all use words and phrases that suggest a sense of excitement, anticipation, order, and harmony. The texts all describe a scene in which a large group of people are gathered to welcome a distinguished guest.

Text 1 (Arabic):

The overall sentiment of this text is positive. The author uses words and phrases like "التحقت أفواج المرحبين"(welcoming crowds), "أعيان القضاة والمفتين والعلماء"(senior judges, muftis, and scholars), and "أهل الأدب والتجار والمتمولين"(literati, merchants, and men of wealth) to create a sense of excitement and anticipation. The author also uses the phrase "كلٌ في مكانه"(everyone in his appointed place) to suggest that there is a sense of order and harmony.

Text 2 (English):

The overall sentiment of this text is also positive. The author uses similar words and phrases to the Arabic text, such as "huge crowd of officials", "distinguished guest", and "men of wealth and virtue". The author also uses the phrase "everyone was stationed in his appointed place" to suggest a sense of order and harmony.

Text 3 (French):

The overall sentiment of this text is also positive. The author uses similar words and phrases to the Arabic and English texts, such as "groupes de bienvenue", "hauts magistrats", and "lettres, commerçants, bourgeois". The author also uses the phrase "chacun à la place qui lui était assignée" to suggest a sense of order and harmony.

However, there are some minor differences in the sentiment of the three texts. The Arabic text tends to be more enthusiastic and positive, perhaps because the Arabic author is from a culture that places a high value on hospitality and welcoming guests. However, the sentiment score generated by GNL API places the Arabic text close to neutrality, even lower than the sentiment score of the French text. In contrast, the sentiment score of the English text accurately mirrors its positive tone.

7 Discussion

In general, the translations exhibit a coherent sentiment pattern across sentences, although the French translation tends to hover closer to the neutral line compared to both the original Arabic text (ST) and the English translation. Despite this, specific deviations come to light in certain sentences, as elaborated upon below. Analyzing the sentiment across the original Arabic text and its translations reveals intriguing patterns. While most sentences maintain a coherent sentiment, as reflected in the consistent patterns for 15 out of 18 sentences, the French translation generally leans closer to neutrality compared to the Arabic and English versions. Notably, three specific sentences (out of 18) exhibit deviations, hinting at nuances that the model might not have fully captured. These deviations could stem from challenges in translating cultural references, wordplay, or subtle emotional shifts. Nonetheless, the overall consistency across most sentences highlights the encouraging performance of GNL API in analyzing sentiment within Arabic literary texts and their translations. For further exploration, the researchers will examine the specific deviations while incorporating contextual information, delving deeper into the three sentences with discrepancies to reveal specific areas for improvement in the model's ability to handle the complexities of literary language. English translation best captures the Arabic author's intended emotional impact compared to French translation.

The researchers used the obtained results the answer research questions:

1. How effectively can sentiment analysis tools, like GNL API, assess emotional fidelity in literary translations, considering challenges like cultural nuances and wordplay?

While capturing all the nuances of literary language remains a challenge, GNL API demonstrated encouraging performance in identifying overall sentiment patterns. Its analysis of 15 out of 18 sentences exhibited consistent coherence across the Arabic text and its translations, highlighting its potential as a valuable starting point for exploring emotional fidelity. While specific deviations require further examination, GNL API 's ability to identify broad trends makes it a promising tool for literary analysis.

2 Which translated version (TT1 or TT2) maintains closer sentiment coherence to the Arabic original, while acknowledging limitations of sentiment analysis? Analyze specific deviations for further human evaluation.

As a sentiment analysis tool, Google NL API (GNL API) cannot definitively determine which translation captures the author's intended emotional impact. However, in this preliminary experiment, it effectively identified a potential trend: the English translation exhibited closer alignment in overall sentiment patterns to the Arabic original compared to the French translation's neutral tendency. It is important to acknowledge that this initial investigation utilizes a limited sample size. Nevertheless, it serves as a valuable exploration within the field of Arabic literature translation. By analyzing a well-regarded Arabic novel, "Abu Musa's Women Neighbors" by Ahmed Toufiq, and its corresponding English and French translations, this experiment paves the way for deeper and more comprehensive research.

8 Conclusion and Recommendation

This research examined GNL API's ability to analyze sentiment in an Arabic literary text and its English and French translations. While acknowledging the inherent challenges of capturing literary nuances, the study provided valuable insights into sentiment patterns and potential areas for improvement.

The majority of sentences (15 out of 18) demonstrated consistent sentiment patterns, demonstrating GNL API's promising potential for literary analysis. Interestingly, the French translation tended towards neutrality compared to its Arabic and English counterparts. Three sentences exhibited sentiment deviations, highlighting potential difficulties with cultural references, wordplay, or emotional nuances. Furthermore, the English translation appeared to better capture the Arabic author's intended emotional impact compared to the French translation. While acknowledging the limitations of using a single Arabic novel and its translations, this initial exploration paves the way for deeper and more comprehensive research in the field of Arabic literature translation using sentiment analysis tools. Examining these deviations and integrating contextual information in future research can contribute to refining the model and gaining a more profound understanding of sentiment patterns in translated literature. In conclusion, this study presents an optimistic perspective on GNL API's capabilities, inviting further exploration and contributing to a nuanced comprehension of the intricacies within translated literary works.

A promising direction for future exploration would be fine-tuning the GNL API sentiment analysis tool with domain-specific data, specifically Arabic literary works. This could potentially enhance the accuracy and effectiveness of the scores obtained in our analysis. Additionally, expanding the dataset to include a larger volume of Arabic literary texts would further refine the model's understanding of the nuances and complexities inherent in this genre, granting deeper insights into sentiment patterns within translations.

References

Alqurashi, T.: Arabic sentiment analysis for twitter data: a systematic literature review. Eng. Technol. Appl. Sci. Res. **13**(2), 10292–10300 (2023)

Araújo, M., Pereira, A., Benevenuto, F.: A comparative study of machine translation for multilingual sentence-level sentiment analysis. Inf. Sci. **512**, 1078–1102 (2020)

Baquero Pérez, P.J.: Comparing translations of literary texts using language technologies: sentiment analysis of translations of Don Quixote. Acad. Lett., 2 (2021)

Cheng, S.: Exploring the role of translators' emotion regulation and critical thinking ability in translation performance. Front. Psychol. **13**, 1037829 (2022)

Fernández Sedano, I., et al.: Differences between cultures in emotional verbal and non-verbal reactions. Psicothema **12**(1), 83–92 (2000)

Google: Cloud AutoML. Google https://cloud.google.com/automl. Accessed 25 Jan 2024

Hunziker Heeb, A., Lehr, C., Ehrensberger-Dow, M.: Situated translators: cognitive load and the role of emotions. Adv. Cogn. Transl. Stud., 47–65. Springer Singapore, Singapore (2021). https://doi.org/10.1007/978-981-16-2070-6_3

Ibrahim, H.S., Abdou, S.M., Gheith, M.: Sentiment analysis for modern standard Arabic and colloquial. arXiv preprint arXiv:1505.03105 (2015)

Mahima, K.T.Y., Ginige, T.N.D.S., De Zoysa, K.: Evaluation of sentiment analysis based on AutoML and traditional approaches. Int. J. Adv. Comput. Sci. Appl., **12**(2) (2021)

Mabokela, K.R., Celik, T., Raborife, M.: Multilingual sentiment analysis for under-resourced languages: a systematic review of the landscape. IEEE Access **11**, 15996–16020 (2023). https://doi.org/10.1109/ACCESS.2022.3224136

Mohammad, S.M., Salameh, M., Kiritchenko, S.: How translation alters sentiment. J. Artif. Intell. Res. **55**, 95–130 (2016)

Monjoor, S.N., et al.: A comparative study for sentiment analysis of raw and translated text. In: The 2nd International Conference on Distributed Sensing and Intelligent Systems ICDSIS 2021, vol. 2021, pp. 220–231. IET (2021)

Nabil, M., Aly, M., Atiya, A.: LABR: a large scale Arabic sentiment analysis benchmark. arXiv preprint arXiv:1411.6718 (2014)

Nassif, A.B., Elnagar, A., Shahin, I., Henno, S.: Deep learning for Arabic subjective sentiment analysis: challenges and research opportunities. Appl. Soft Comput. **98**, 106836 (2021)

Ogarkova, A., Borgeaud, P., Scherer, K.: Language and culture in emotion research: a multidisciplinary perspective. Soc. Sci. Inf. **48**(3), 339–357 (2009)

Sherif, S.M., et al.: Lexicon annotation in sentiment analysis for dialectal Arabic: systematic review of current trends and future directions. Inf. Process. Manage. **60**(5), 103449 (2023)

Soumya, S., Pramod, K.V.: Sentiment analysis of Malayalam tweets—a comparative study of AutoML and conventional ML approaches. In ICT Systems and Sustainability: Proceedings of ICT4SD 2022 (pp. 675–684). Springer Nature Singapore, Singapore (2022). https://doi.org/10.1007/978-981-19-5221-0_64

White, T.E., Rege, M.: Sentiment analysis on google cloud platform. Issues Inf. Syst. **21**(2), 221–228 (2020)

HateTune: Tunisian Dialect Hate Speech Detection Dataset

Ons Kharrat(✉), Fatma Alzahra Mohamed, Ikram Mtimet, Nour Benamor, and Chayma Fourati

Software Engineering, Mediterranean Institute of Technology, Lac 2, Tunis, Tunisia
{ons.kharrat,fatmazahra.mohamed,ikram.mtimet,nour.benamor, chayma.fourati}@medtech.tn

Abstract. In Tunisia, citizens use social media platforms as a space to exercise freedom of speech. However, unchecked and complete freedom of expression can fuel the spread of hateful speech, which is devastating not only for those targeted but also for our society. This alarming situation evokes the need for limiting the spread of hateful content by working on hate speech detection in "Derja", which is the tunisian dialect. Used as a means of communication in daily life and on social media platforms, this dialect is a mixture of many languages, including Arabic, French, and Amazighi, and it can be written using Arabic letters. Due to the complexity of this language, a significant lack of publicly available, large, and annotated datasets for hate speech detection in Tunisian dialect written in Arabic letters is noticeable, making "Tunisian Derja" an underrepresented dialect. In this paper, we introduce the largest publicly available dataset, which consists of more than 12k comments manually annotated as Hate, and Neutral. We also provide an in-depth explanation of the processes of data collection, annotation, and pre-processing. Moreover, we undertake a comprehensive evaluation of the dataset's efficacy through various machine learning models, including Support Vector Machines (SVM), Random Forest, and XGBoost.

Keywords: Tunisian Dialect · Underrepresented · Arabic Letters · Hate Speech

1 Introduction

In recent years, efforts to detect hate speech have intensified, leading to the development of robust mechanisms aimed at mitigating its negative impacts*(https://www.kaggle.com/datasets/ikrammtimet/hate-speech-detection-dataset-in-tunisian-dialect/data). This growing concern has sparked increased interest in using machine learning methodologies to confront this challenge.

Particularly, hate speech detection in Arabic presents challenging tasks because of the lack of available labelled data and the complexity of the Arabic language [1,2]. Furthermore, hate speech is greatly influenced by cultural, political, and religious contexts, as well as factors such as divergent Arabic dialects distinct from Modern Standard Arabic (MSA) [3].

B. Hdioud and S. L. Aouragh (Eds.): ICALP 2024, CCIS 2339, pp. 63–73, 2025.
https://doi.org/10.1007/978-3-031-79164-2_6

Over the last 12 years, Tunisia has struggled with the spread of hateful content. This trend started with the "Freedom and Dignity Revolution" in 2011, when Tunisians overthrew authoritarian rule. This event sparked changes throughout the region. Since then, Tunisia has experienced regime changes, mass protests, and efforts to build democratic institutions. However, as Tunisians have become more connected online, social media platforms like Facebook, Twitter, and Instagram have become key tools for communication. But they have also facilitated the spread of hateful rhetoric, as users exploit the anonymity and reach of these platforms to promote intolerance and division. This issue is best exemplified by the wave of discrimination that started, online, in March of 2023, and targeted a particular racial group, which is sub-Saharan Africans. Written in the Tunisian dialect, "Derja", using Arabic letters, this toxic content exposed those targeted to discrimination, abuse, violence, and racism. Despite this alarming situation, resources for studying and combating hate speech in the Tunisian dialect, especially in Arabic script, are significantly lacking. There is no substantial research or tools for detecting hate speech in this area, highlighting the urgent need for action. To address these challenges, it is crucial to develop a large, clean, annotated, and publicly available dataset that captures instances of hateful content in the Tunisian dialect written in Arabic letters. This dataset would enable deeper analysis and understanding of the issue and support the development of effective strategies to combat online hate speech in this linguistic and cultural context.

As a response to these pressing issues, we introduce HateTune, the largest, publicly available, representative, and balanced dataset that contains more than 12k pre-processed and annotated sentences covering many aspects of Tunisian life, such as sports, politics, daily news, etc. Our motivation is to reduce the underrepresentativeness of the Tunisian dialect by introducing a large publicly available dataset that can help limit the spread of hateful content in Tunisia and allow more researchers to work on Natural Language Processing (NLP) topics covering this dialect.

In this paper, we present the related work, and the process of data composition, including data collection, data annotation, data pre-processing, and data statistics. Then, we introduce the results obtained from evaluating our dataset using machine learning. Finally, we present our conclusion, and future work.

2 Related Work

In the field of hate speech detection for the Tunisian dialect written in Arabic letters, very limited research was previously conducted.

A study "T-HSAB" [2] introduced a publicly available dataset for hate and abusive speech detection in the Tunisian dialect written in Arabic Letters. However, this dataset presents a set of limitations. It only contains 6039 comments labeled as hate, abusive, and normal. Most of these comments are not purely written in the Tunisian dialect as they contain many words and even entire comments which derive from other North African and Middle Eastern Dialects. As a result, this dataset is not representative of the Tunisian dialect. Moreover, this dataset is not balanced as 63.48% of its comments are labeled as normal, while only 17.86% are labeled as Hate and 18.66% are labeled as Abusive. Also, this dataset covers only political and social topics, making it a sociopolitical dataset.

Moreover, in a study [4], authors have presented a dataset of 10000 sentences, labeled as hateful and normal, and used for detecting abusive speech in the Tunisian dialect written in Arabic letters. The data collection process of this dataset followed two steps. The authors have collected 5102 Arabic tweets using the extension for Google Sheets "Twitter Archiver" and have extracted a total of 4898 comments labeled as hateful and normal from the dataset "T-HSAB" [2]. As discussed above, comments presented in the dataset "T-HSAB" [2] contain many words and phrases that do not represent the Tunisian dialect as they derive from other Arabic dialects and cannot be considered as a reference when working on the detection of hateful content for the Tunisian dialect. As a result, this new dataset is also not representative of the Tunisian dialect as approximately 50% of its comments were extracted from "T-HSAB" [2]. Moreover, this dataset is not balanced as 63,36% of its comments are labeled as "normal" and only 36.63% of its comments are labeled as "hateful".

Another study, "TEET" [5] introduces a new annotated dataset containing approximately 10000 comments. Various models and classification tasks have been explored in this project. However, the dataset is unbalanced and is not publicly available for further research work.

More generally, other studies have focused on detecting hateful speech for several Arabic dialects and included the Tunisian dialect as part of their research. However, most Arabic dialects and especially Middle Eastern ones are based on Modern Standard Arabic, while the Tunisian dialect is a complicated mixture of MSA [3], French, Amazighi, and even Turkish. Therefore, it is very challenging to represent the Tunisian dialect, while covering several Arabic dialects under the same study. For instance, in a thesis work [6], data was collected by combining 9 publicly available datasets, with only one dataset focusing entirely on the Tunisian dialect. The Tunisian dataset used in this study is "T-HSAB". Considering the limitations of "T-HSAB", this study is also not representative of the Tunisian context.

Considering the limitations of previous work, our contribution can be summarized as the introduction of the largest, publicly available, balanced, and representative dataset. This dataset contains manually annotated comments specifically targeting hate speech detection in the Tunisian dialect written in Arabic letters.

3 Data

We present HateTune, a dataset that contains **12,012** sentences manually labeled as Hate and Neutral. HateTune covers a large variety of topics such as politics, news, daily life, sports, music, comedy, etc.

3.1 Data Collection

In response to the lack of annotated datasets for hate speech detection in an underrepresented language, such as the Tunisian dialect, we opted to build a dataset for our research. In Tunisia, the internet user count reached 9.80 million users in January 2023, with YouTube having a substantial audience of 7.24 million users, equivalent to 73.88% of the Tunisian population, as per Google's advertising resources[1]. In contrast, other major social media platforms like Facebook and Twitter reached 52.8% and 2.8% of the Tunisian population during the same period.

Given YouTube's extensive user base and the feasibility of performing web scraping from this platform, 85% of our dataset is derived from a Common-Crawl-based dataset that our research team has extracted from tunisian comments on YouTube videos.

To ensure diversity and representation, our research team has manually selected 20 videos from 10 distinct YouTube channels featuring Tunisian content. The criteria for selection were based on popularity metrics, requiring a minimum of 1,000 views and 300 comments per video. The chosen videos covered various topics including sports, economy, education, TV shows, entertainment, politics, health, and Tunisian music videos. Notably, the dataset collected from YouTube comments contained no confidential information, as it solely originated from publicly available videos. However, hate comments included insulting language.

Following the collection of data from YouTube videos, the number of scraped hate comments was fewer than the number of neutral comments. In order to maintain a balanced dataset, we added 1800 comments labeled as hate from a publicly available dataset on Kaggle[2]. The original Kaggle dataset comprised 10,000 comments extracted from comments and posts on Facebook and labeled as positive, negative, and neutral. Although initially focused on "Derja", the dataset contained comments written in both Arabic and Latin letters. To ensure relevance to our study, our research team has manually selected the hate comments written in Arabic letter from the kaggle dataset.

3.2 Annotation Policy

The annotation process was done manually by six engineering students (five females and one male all aged 20) who are all native Tunisian "Derja" speakers. These annotators come from different states in Tunisia, ensuring a diverse team with varied socio-demographic backgrounds capable of identifying the different instances of abusive language used across Tunisia.

To eliminate biases and ensure precise annotation, each comment underwent separate annotation by three distinct annotators. Following individual annotations, the annotators engaged in discussions to review their findings and reach a consensus on the final annotation for each comment.

[1] https://bit.ly/486QtOR.

[2] https://www.kaggle.com/datasets/naim99/ts-naim-mhedhbi/versions/resource=download?selectnegative_tweets.txt.

During the annotation process, hate comments, as shown in Table 1, were carefully identified as the speech containing aggressive language, profanity, bullying, harassment, threats, and aggressive tones. These comments presented attacks against individuals or groups based on various attributes, such as race, religion, gender, minority identification, and ethnicity.

To address conflicts arising from the use of misleading language elements, such as irony, sarcasm, or humor, annotators were allowed to consult the context of the comment. This involved revisiting the corresponding YouTube video or dataset from which the comment was scraped, enabling annotators to better grasp the comment's nature and collectively make an informed decision regarding the nature of the comment.

The annotation result is as follows:

- Neutral label: labeled as '0'.
- Hate label: labeled as '1'.

Table 1. Data Annotation Guideline.

Label	Annotation Definition 2
Hate	A hateful comment is an offensive discourse threatening a group or an individual based on characteristics, such as race, religion, or gender.
Neutral	An unoffensive comment that does not threaten or target any individual or group of people.

Table 2 presents examples of comments of each label in Tunisian Arabic and its translation to English.

Table 2. Examples of comments from the dataset for each label.

Label	Tunisian Arabic Sentence	English Translation
Hate	اكبر منيك هوا العربي المازني فرخ ميبون	he biggest f***ed up person is Arabi Mazni. He is a son of a b*tch.
Neutral	بصراحة ممثلة ممتازة برشا	Honestly, she is an excellent actress.

3.3 Data Pre-processing

Arabic includes various dialects. In many cases, datasets for Tunisian dialect get mixed with other North African and Middle Eastern Arabic dialects. Therefore, in our dataset, we have made sure to only keep the Tunisian dialect comments.

Furthermore, the collected comments were not clean as they included many Latin letters, Emojis, and more. Therefore, the following steps have been followed to properly pre-process every comment in the dataset:

- **Dropping comments containing non-Arabic words:**
It is a very common practice in Tunisian society to include some words written entirely in foreign languages, especially French, while writing in the Tunisian dialect. Our goal is to achieve a dataset that consists purely of Tunisian dialect comments, written in Arabic letters. The solution was to implement an algorithm that dropped all comments containing non-Arabic words from the dataset.
- **Removing Arabic Punctuation:**
The comments in the dataset contained a mix of Arabic and non-Arabic punctuation. Notably, it's worth mentioning that in Arabic writing, including the Tunisian dialect, the use of punctuation in written texts is relatively low compared to other languages. In our initial attempts to train the model with the punctuation, we observed that these punctuation marks often appeared as outliers and did not significantly contribute to the overall understanding of the text. To ensure uniformity, we created a list of possible punctuation marks, and removed them from the dataset.
- **Removing Tunisian Stopwords:** Tunisian dialect contains typical Arabic stopwords. However, it also contains more Tunisian-specific stop words. Words such as 'تي' or 'كي', are stop words used only in the Tunisian dialect. A ready-to-use list of stopwords in the Tunisian dialect is not available. As a result, we proceeded to create our own stop words list. We extracted the list of unique words, then we manually picked and listed Tunisian stop words. This process has greatly aided the learning ability of the models, during the training process.

  Examples of Tunisian stopwords are: ات، تي ، اتف ، كي ، إذ, etc. The stopwords list is also publicly available on the same dataset link.
- **Removing Arabic Diacritical Marks:** In Arabic, diacritical marks (شَكل) are used to specify how a character must be spelled and pronounced. There are at least 8 possible diacritical marks that can be given to each letter of the Arabic alphabet. To simplify the recognition of words, we have proceeded with removing these marks from the words in our dataset.
- **Normalizing Arabic Letters:** In Arabic, some specific letters can take different shapes. Depending on their position in the word, and whether it is a verb or a noun. For example, the letter إ ، أ ، ء ، آ ، ئ spelled as 'Aleef', can also look like [ا]. For learning purposes, we simplified all the forms of 'Aleef' to 'ت'. Another example is 'Tae', spelled as 'Tae', which can also be typed as 'ة'. This normalization process was applied to many letters to simplify and improve the learning of our model.

Table 3. Examples of comment before and after pre-processing.

Comment Before Pre-processing	Comment after Pre-processing
!!! امين عجبني كوستيمك ياااااااسر مزيان	امين عجبني كوستيمك ياسر مزيان

3.4 Data Statistics

In this section, we provide a detailed overview of various characteristics and statistics of our dataset (Table 3).

Table 4 presents a comparative analysis between the Hate and Neutral labels in terms of the number of comments, total word count, and vocabulary size.

Table 4. Data Statistics.

Characteristic	Hate	Neutral
Number of Comments	5,646	6,366
Word Count	19,849	26,513
Vocabulary Size	12,709	13,230

To gain deeper insights into the HateTune dataset, we conducted an analysis of the most frequent words within both the Hate and Neutral labels alongside their frequencies which are reviewed in Table 5. This shows that words such as "ماسط" ("Stupid"), and "طحان" ("Faggot") are widely invoked within Tunisian hateful comments, which proves that many groups and individuals are being directly targeted with hateful language.

Table 5. Top 10 Most Frequent Terms in Hate Comments.

Term	Translation	Frequency
ماسط	Stupid	202
طحان	Faggot	79
ماسيت	Touching Private Areas	62
قحبة	B**ch	57
زبي	My D**k	57
عاهرة	Wh*re	54
القحب	Bullsh*t	53
القحبة	The B**ch	53
امسط	Unlikable	52
زب	D**k	46

Table 6 shows the most common words in the comments labeled as neutral alongside their frequencies. This shows that words such as "شاء" ("Hopefully"), "بالتوفيق" ("Best of luck"), and "تحية" ("Regards") are widely invoked within Tunisian neutral comments, which proves that neutral language is unoffensive and contains mainly some good wishes exchanged between people.

Table 6. Top 10 Most Frequent Terms in Neutral Comments.

Term	Translation	Frequency
شاء	Hopefully	196
جعفور	Jaafar	153
بالتوفيق	Best of Luck	97
تحية	Regards	97
الاحترام	Respect	95
الهي	Divine	84
الطيف	Spectrum	77
احلى	Sweeter	67
التقدير	Appreciation	67
كيما	For example	63

Finally, we divided the dataset into separate training, and test datasets, with a ratio of 8:2 with a balanced split where the number of comments from hate class and neutral class are almost the same. Statistics of the train and test datasets for each label are presented in Table 7.

Table 7. Train & Test Data Statistics.

Characteristic	Train	Test
Hate	4517	1129
Neutral	5093	1273
Total Comments	9610	2402

4 Experiments and Results

In this section, we present the experiments conducted to address the task of hate speech detection in Tunisian dialect using our newly curated dataset. We employed three machine learning models: Random Forest [7], Support Vector Machine (SVM) [8], and XGBoost [9]. The goal of these experiments was to evaluate the performance of each model in handling the intricacies of hate speech detection in the context of Tunisian dialect.

To prepare the data for training, we performed basic pre-processing steps including removing missing values and tokenizing the text. The text data was vectorized using the Term Frequency-Inverse Document Frequency (TF-IDF) technique, which proved effective in capturing word importance while accounting for variations in term frequency.

- **Random Forest Model** [7] The Random Forest model was trained using 100 decision trees. As shown in Table 8 the model achieved an accuracy of **74.49%** on the test set. The classification report revealed a precision of 67% for hate speech class and 90% for neutral speech class. This indicates that the model is effective in identifying hate speech instances, but its performance on the neutral class is relatively lower. The confusion matrix indicated that the model struggles with false positives, misclassifying neutral text as hate speech. This behavior is expected, given the complexities of hate speech detection and the potential linguistic challenges posed by the Tunisia dialect.
- **Support Vector Machine (SVM) Model** [8] The SVM model was employed using a linear kernel with a regularization parameter of 1.0. As shown in Table 8, the model achieved an accuracy of **81.65%**. The SVM model displayed performed better accuracy results compared to the Random Forest model. The precision for both classes was balanced, with 77% for hate speech and 87% for neutral, indicating an improved handling of both classes. The SVM model demonstrated better recall for both classes, achieving 88% recall for hate speech and 76% for neutral. The balanced recall rates suggest that the SVM model is more adept at identifying both hate speech and neutral text, thus providing a more balanced classification approach.
- **XGBoost Model** [9] We also used the XGBoost algorithm for improving hate speech detection models. As shown in Table 8, the XGBoost model achieved competitive results in terms of accuracy, recall, and precision which demonstrates the model's ability to effectively classify hate speech and neutral text.

Table 8 presents results of machine learning models.

Table 8. Machine Learning Models Results.

Model	Accuracy	Precision (1)	Recall (1)	Precision (0)	Recall (0)
Random Forest	0.74	0.67	0.93	0.75	0.60
SVM	**0.81**	**0.77**	**0.88**	**0.80**	**0.83**
XGBoost	0.7	0.67	0.92	0.72	0.58

Comparing the performance of the three machine learning models, the SVM model achieved the best results showcasing balanced performance across classes.

5 Conclusion and Future Work

In this paper, we presented HateTune, a dataset for hate speech detection in Tunisian dialect, 'Derja', written in Arabic letters. Since the Tunisian dialect is an under-represented language, we addressed this gap by introducing this dataset for hate speech detection consisting of 12,012 comments manually annotated by Tunisian native speakers into two labels, hate (1) and neutral (0).

To the best of our knowledge, this dataset presents the largest representative, balanced, and publicly-available dataset for Tunisian dialect hate speech detection. In this paper, we provide insights into the data collection process, and pre-processing methods employed. Moreover, we included an evaluation of the dataset using machine learning models, achieving an accuracy of 0.81 using Support Vector Machine (SVM).

This dataset will be instrumental in advancing research and development of hate speech detection systems for the Tunisian dialect. As a future work, we plan to extend our dataset to include a larger number of comments and build other datasets for other under-represented Arabic dialects dedicated for hate speech detection. In addition, we plan to refine the algorithms used for hate speech detection, test the efficiency of our dataset using deep learning models, explore additional features or linguistic markers for better accuracy, develop user-friendly tools or applications for utilizing the dataset, and collaborate with experts in linguistics to deepen our understanding of hate speech dynamics in online Arabic communities.

By pursuing these future directions, we hope to establish HateTune as a cornerstone for effective hate speech detection in the Tunisian dialect and other under-represented Arabic language variations. This will contribute to creating a safer online environment for Tunisian users and Arabic speakers in general.

Limitations

Despite the contributions and successes of this study, there are certain limitations that should be acknowledged:

- **Imbalance in Topics:** While efforts were made to achieve a balance between hate and neutral classes, the balance within individual topics may vary. Some topics might have more hate speech instances than others, affecting the overall balance within the dataset.
- **Lack of Gold Standard:** The absence of a definitive gold standard for hate speech detection in Arabic dialects poses a significant challenge. Hate speech identification remains a complex and subjective task, influenced by different perspectives and cultural backgrounds. The lack of a universally accepted standard makes it challenging to create an entirely objective dataset.

The limitations discussed underscore the multifaceted nature of the task at hand and emphasize the necessity for continued research and development in hate speech detection, particularly within dialectal contexts like the Tunisian dialect. Confronting these challenges requires a concerted effort from researchers, linguists, data scientists, and policymakers to navigate the complexities inherent in creating datasets and developing algorithms for hate speech detection.

By navigating these challenges effectively, researchers can develop more accurate models that better serve the overarching goal of minimizing harmful content and fostering a safer online environment.

References

1. Mulki, H., Haddad, H., Ali, C.B., Alshabani, H.: L-hsab: A levantine twitter dataset for hate speech and abusive language. In: Proceedings of the Third Workshop on Abusive Language Online, pp. 111–118 (2019). Association for Computational Linguistics
2. Haddad, H., Mulki, H., Oueslati, A.: T-hsab: A tunisian hate speech and abusive dataset. In: Arabic Language Processing: From Theory to Practice: 7th International Conference, ICALP 2019, Nancy, France, October 16–17, 2019, Proceedings, vol. 7, pp. 251–263. Springer (2019)
3. Salomon, P.O., Kechaou, Z., Wali, A.: Arabic hate speech detection system based on arabert. In: 2022 IEEE 21st International Conference on Cognitive Informatics Cognitive Computing (ICCI*CC), pp. 208–213 (2022). https://doi.org/10.1109/ICCICC57084.2022.10101577. Institute of Electrical and Electronics Engineers (IEEE)
4. Schmidt, A., Wiegand, M.: A survey on hate speech detection using natural language processing. In: Proceedings of the Fifth International Workshop on Natural Language Processing for Social Media, pp. 1–10 (2017). Association for Computational Linguistics
5. Gharbi, S., Arfaoui, H., Haddad, H., Kchaou, M.: Teet! tunisian dataset for toxic speech detection. arXiv preprint arXiv:2110.05287 (2021)
6. Harba, S.M.: Detecting hate speech across arabic dialects. PhD thesis, American University of Beirut (2022)
7. Breiman, L.: Random forests. Mach. Learn. **45**(1), 5–32 (2001)
8. Burges, C.J.C.: Support Vector Machines: Theory and Applications. The MIT Press (1998). https://doi.org/10.5555/2627439
9. Bentéjac, C., Csörgő, A., Martínez-Muñoz, G.: A comparative analysis of xgboost. arXiv preprint arXiv:2002.05887 (2020)

DarijaGenie: Learning Moroccan Arabic Through a Multimodal Chatbot

Hamza El Alaoui(✉) and Violetta Cavalli-Sforza

Al Akhawayn University, 53003 Ifrane, Morocco
h.elalaoui@aui.ma

Abstract. The rapid advancement of digital technologies has significantly influenced the landscape of language learning, introducing innovative tools and methodologies to enhance educational experiences. Among these developments, the integration of artificial intelligence and chatbot technology in language education offers a unique approach to teaching less commonly taught languages. This paper introduces "DarijaGenie," an early version of a task-based, multimodal chatbot system designed to facilitate the learning of Moroccan Arabic. Characterized by its spoken nature, non-standard structure, and the scarcity of its resources, Darija presents distinct challenges for learners. DarijaGenie aims to address these challenges by leveraging natural language processing and artificial intelligence to simulate real-life scenarios, providing users with an interactive platform for practical language learning.

Keywords: Chatbots · Task-based Language Learning · Natural Language Processing · Computer Assisted Language Learning · Second Language Learning

1 Introduction and Motivation

The advent of digital technologies has ushered in a transformative era for educational methodologies, particularly in the domain of language learning. The traditional paradigms of language education, largely dependent on textbook and classroom-based instruction, are being supplemented-and in some cases, supplanted-by digital tools that offer interactive, immersive learning experiences [17]. This technological and pedagogical shift heralds a reevaluation of how languages are taught and learned. The potential of artificial intelligence (AI) and chatbot technologies to personalize and enhance the language learning journey presents an especially promising avenue of exploration. However, while significant advancements have been made in developing resources for widely spoken languages, less commonly taught languages such as Moroccan Arabic (Darija) remain notably underserved.

The motivation for this research stems from the scarcity of structured, accessible, and interactive learning materials that incorporate modern pedagogical techniques. We introduce "DarijaGenie," a task-based, multimodal chatbot system designed to leverage AI and natural language processing (NLP) in creating a

B. Hdioud and S. L. Aouragh (Eds.): ICALP 2024, CCIS 2339, pp. 74–89, 2025.
https://doi.org/10.1007/978-3-031-79164-2_7

robust, interactive learning environment. DarijaGenie aims to improve the accessibility and effectiveness of language learning for Darija, a significantly underrepresented language, by embodying the principles of task-based language learning (TBLL) [24] and multimodal learning. Multimodal learning, which involves the use of multiple sensory modalities and representations, has been shown to provide advantages for learners and enhance the learning experience [9]. The system simulates real-life conversational scenarios, facilitating dynamic engagement with the language and its cultural context, thus narrowing the gap between theoretical knowledge and practical application. This paper outlines the development process of an early version of DarijaGenie, including design considerations, technological foundations, and the pedagogical rationale underpinning its functionality. Through this endeavor, the research contributes to the discourse on AI's application in language education, highlighting the potential of such technologies to democratize access to learning resources for low-resource and less commonly taught languages.

2 Related Works

2.1 Pedagogical Uses of Chatbots

Our investigation highlights six primary applications of chatbots: simulation, interaction, recommendation, support, dissemination, and gamification; each application demonstrates unique potential to enhance learning processes and their effects on students' engagement and cognitive development.

- **Simulation:** A critical area where chatbots have shown promise is in creating immersive language learning environments. Chatbots can simulate real-world settings, such as restaurants and supermarkets, to enhance learners' problem-solving skills in a target language [23]. They can provide contextualized conversational practice through speech recognition and virtual worlds, fostering a more authentic experience of language use and a sense of presence within virtual learning environments [6].
- **Interaction:** Chatbots serve as interactive conversational partners, impacting learners' engagement and development of critical thinking and negotiation skills across different proficiency levels [10].
- **Recommendation:** Chatbots have demonstrated the efficacy of learning management systems like Moodle to deliver real-time, personalized educational resource recommendations [22].
- **Support:** In the VILLAGE platform, chatbots assisted students with language grammar practice [23], underscoring their ability to provide immediate assistance and feedback and to create a supportive learning environment.
- **Dissemination:** Chatbots also play an important role in the dissemination of educational content, bridging communication gaps within higher education institutions [4] and streamlining the delivery of educational content, such as essay writing guidelines [15].

- **Gamification:** Lastly, the integration of gamification strategies with chatbots like Quiz-GBot offers a novel approach to learning [18], demonstrating how game-like elements and AI-driven adaptability can enhance engagement and provide personalized learning experiences.

2.2 Examples of Language Learning Tools

Several language learning tools leveraging NLP algorithms have been developed to offer diverse functionalities aimed at enhancing linguistic competencies. One notable example is Alelo [1], established in 2002, which initially concentrated on facilitating language learning for U.S. military personnel with a focus on a variety of languages, including Iraqi Arabic, Pashto, and French [13]. Over time, Alelo has expanded its scope to include English language acquisition, making significant strides in employing AI-driven avatars for immersive conversational practice. This evolution reflects a broader application of its foundational technologies to cater to a wider audience. Alelo combines intelligent tutoring with serious game technologies, utilizing platforms like the Tactical Language and Culture Training System (TLCTS) and Operational Language and Culture Training System (OLCTS) [20], to promote foreign language and cultural proficiency. The initial success in languages such as Iraqi Arabic has highlighted the potential of such technologies in fostering linguistic and cultural competencies across various languages and contexts.

Several popular language learning tools are available online, offering advanced interactive features that surpass traditional learning environments. For instance, Mondly offers an immersive experience in 33 languages, integrating speech recognition and virtual reality (VR) technology to facilitate a comprehensive learning journey through interactive dialogues [14]. Cleverbot, developed by Rollo Carpenter and online since 1996, has accumulated over 10 billion interactions and evolved its language understanding from text-based user interactions [5]. Its vast response repository makes it an engaging conversational partner in various languages and subjects. Rosetta Stone Bot extends Rosetta Stone's language-learning capabilities, providing conversational exercises related to pronunciation, vocabulary, and grammar [7]. Duolingo Max [2] incorporates Generative Pre-trained Transformer (GPT) 4 technology, especially for English, Spanish, and French learners, introducing 'Explain My Answer' and 'Roleplay' features for in-depth grammatical understanding and practical conversational practice. Andy [14] is a language learning application focused on vocabulary and grammar through interactive games and a conversational interface that adapts to user proficiency. Lanny [3], tailored for Korean language learners, combines language instruction with cultural insights and includes audio from native speakers, catering to beginners and advanced students alike. Each of these tools offers unique functionalities, from basic conversation drills to complex grammar exercises, alongside games and activities to reinforce language skills.

Concerning the Arabic language, specifically, KalaamBot and KalimaBot [12] have been developed to assist learners of Arabic as a foreign language. KalaamBot is a speech-based chatbot for conversational practice, while KalimaBot is a text-based vocabulary assistant. However, while these chatbots facilitate basic language learning, they do not incorporate scenario-based training. Additionally, other Arabic language chatbots are often tailored for specific non-educational tasks, such as customer support or medical inquiries. This underscores the need for more comprehensive Arabic language learning chatbots that integrate scenario-based approaches and enhance conversational capabilities and pedagogical effectiveness.

3 System Philosophy

TBLL, a methodology emphasized in modern language education, focuses on the use of authentic tasks as the central unit of learning and the communicative approach to language teaching and learning, which trains learners to develop several practical communication tasks. This approach aligns with the principles of scenario-based learning, where learners engage in structured situations that simulate real-life experiences. Various studies highlight the effectiveness of TBLL and scenario-based learning and its foundations.

Firstly, TBLL facilitates the acquisition of language through activities that mimic real-world usage. Tasks in TBLL should be relevant, appropriate, and engaging, ensuring they are within the learner's competence while gradually increasing in complexity. This approach ensures that learners are actively involved and motivated, essential factors in successful language learning [24]. Moreover, scenario-based learning, as implemented in TBLL, is effective in promoting self-regulated learning strategies. A study based on Oxford's Self-Strategic Regulation (S2R) Model demonstrates that scenario-based instruction significantly increases learners' awareness and use of language learning strategies [21].

The SPELL system [6] integrates virtual worlds and virtual agents with speech recognition technology, providing a practical illustration of TBLL in action and showing how technology can create immersive environments that foster meaningful language practice within contextualized scenarios. The system's design, which includes feedback through reformulations and recasts, effectively aids in language learning within a virtual environment [16].

In summary, TBLL environments provide contexts for language use, opportunities for corrective feedback, and chances for learners to notice gaps in their language production [19]. Such environments can lead to improvements in accuracy, fluency, and the complexity of language production.

We incorporate the above features of TBLL in DarijaGenie. Each task in the system is represented as a scenario, presenting users with learning opportunities that simulate common social interactions in Morocco. Each scenario focuses on specific linguistic skills and cultural competencies necessary for effective communication in Darija. The design ensures relevance and appropriateness by catering to a range of proficiency levels while encouraging active learner involvement. We are in the process of developing a diverse range of scenarios that cover various aspects of daily life in Morocco. The flexibility of the DarijaGenie system means that additional scenarios can be rapidly developed and implemented as needed, ensuring that the learning content remains dynamic, relevant, and effectively aligned with the learners' needs. This approach embodies the principles of TBLL and scenario-based learning, providing an engaging, effective, and culturally immersive language learning experience. Some of these scenarios, including the background, skills to be learned, and roles for both parties, are detailed in Table 1.

Table 1. earning Scenarios

Scenario	Bot Character	User Character	Background	Skills to Learn*
Ordering Food	Server	Customer	Restaurant	Giving/taking advice or suggestions; apologies and excuses; names of food and drinks; tipping; numbers
Buying Clothes	Salesperson	Buyer	Clothing Store	Names of clothing items; sizes; numbers; colors
Shopping & Bargaining Prices	Vendor	Shopper	Market or Shop	Expressing agreement; names of objects; types of currencies (Ryal and Dirham); names of materials; colors; numbers
Exchanging Currency	Bank Teller	Customer	Bank	Dates; large numbers; bank accounts; credit and debit cards; receipts; signatures
Using Public Transportation	Local	Tourist	Town	Buying tickets, making reservations
Asking for Directions	Local	Tourist	Street or Public Place	Names for streets of different sizes, squares, buildings, and shops; numbers; colors
Checking-in	Hotel Receptionist	Guest	Hotel	Making appointments and reservations; obtaining reimbursements; hotel services and amenities (restaurants, bars, meals, WiFi, bathroom, television, room service); dates; numbers
Attending a Family Dinner	Native Speaker	Friend	Native Speaker's Home	Introductions; apologies and excuses; expressing agreement; questions to ask and not ask; dates; numbers
Asking about Moroccan Food	Native Moroccan Speaker	Friend	Moroccan Restaurant or Market	Measurements (volume, weight); containers; numbers; colors

**All scenarios include common communicative skills such as greeting, asking and giving information, expressing requests, and expressing gratitude*

4 System Design

4.1 Architecture

The system architecture of DarijaGenie is designed for optimal efficiency and user engagement across multiple platforms. Central to this architecture is Botpress [8], which acts as the primary chatbot platform, interfacing with Telegram, Messenger, and Slack APIs to extend the chatbot's functionality. Additionally, integration with the Microsoft Bot Framework allows access through Web Chat on the gamified website and Microsoft Teams. This setup operates within a Docker container on an Azure Virtual Machine, ensuring scalability and performance. Complementing the system's front-end, Netlify is used for hosting, providing a responsive and secure user interface, with continuous deployment from the Git repository and SSL certification for enhanced security. The back-end architecture utilizes various Software as a Service (SaaS) solutions, with an Azure VM hosting the Botpress server and a load balancer managing resource allocation to maintain system stability. Figure 1 presents the integrated system architecture, while Fig. 2 illustrates the system's sequence diagram.

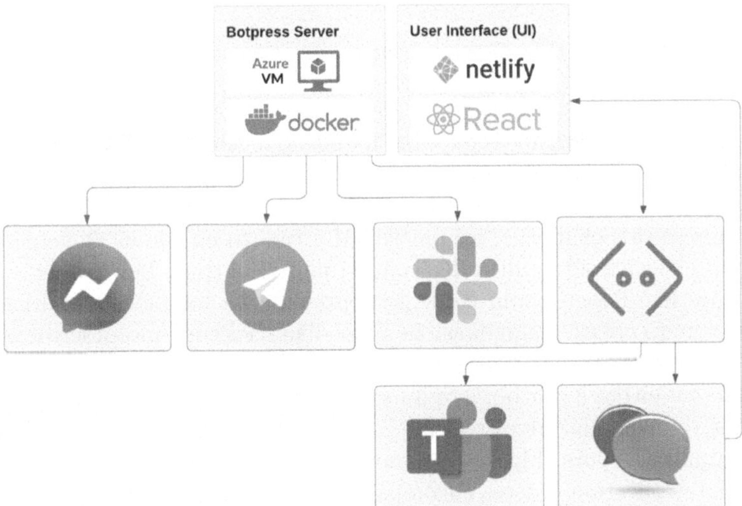

Fig. 1. System Architecture Diagram

4.2 Components

Data Collection Tool: The use of chatbots in language learning requires a corpus of conversations that showcases a variety of language and interactions. There is a conspicuous absence of such a corpus for Moroccan Arabic (Darija). Translating corpora from other languages would not yield the conversation

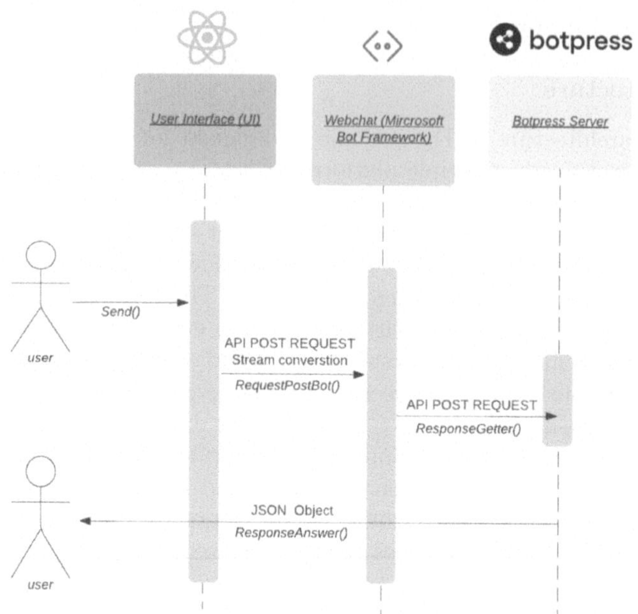

Fig. 2. System Sequence Diagram

structure and cultural richness required for effective learning of Darija and would still require substantial processing to transform conversations into the tree-like structure that is essential for crafting a responsive chatbot.

To address this challenge, we developed a tool to enable us to generate our own comprehensive and culturally contextualized corpus. Leveraging software technologies like React.js and Node.js, it presents an interactive interface that permits users to create dialog flows in a tree-like structure and describe alternative conversational paths around a given topic by dragging and dropping nodes that represent either a chatbot's or a user's response. Thus, the collected dialogs mirror the dynamic nature of real-life conversations, an aspect often overlooked in conventional corpora. Figure 3 presents the data collection tool.

The data collection process encompasses several stages. It begins with a person initiating a dialog using the tool and writing in Arabic script. At this stage, we are not yet enforcing a specific orthography for Darija, relying on the loose coupling option provided by the chatbot technology we use to accept spelling variations. The dialog tree, saved as a JavaScript Object Notation (JSON) file, is then sent back for verification, bias removal, cleaning, and correction by another person. Then, the dialog tree is passed to a third person who adds more conversation pathways, ensuring that the final corpus is diverse and has broad coverage. This process is repeated until the tree is expansive and varied enough to be effectively used for training the chatbot system. To capture the linguistic nuances of Darija, we consulted with native speakers from various parts of Morocco. This helps ensure that the dialogs were not only accurate but also comprehensible to different audiences.

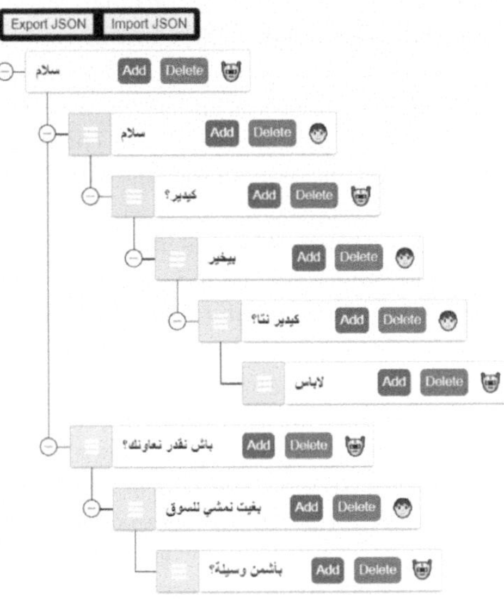

Fig. 3. Data Collection Tool

The outcome of this methodology was a diverse corpus covering various real-life scenarios, such as "Buying Clothes," "Exchanging Currency," and more, which served as the foundation for DarijaGenie.

Chatbot System: The development of DarijaGenie involved experimenting with various chatbot tools and technologies [8], ultimately selecting Botpress, an open-source conversational AI platform, for its comprehensive feature set best suited for our language learning system.

Botpress distinguishes itself with its dual-component structure: Botpress Studio, the visual interface for chatbot design and development, and Botpress Server, which powers the chatbot's backend infrastructure. An important aspect of Botpress is its extensive language support (over 100 languages), including the ability to be trained in new languages. The platform's foundation in JavaScript further contributes to its adaptability and accessibility for developers. In developing DarijaGenie, several key features of Botpress were important:

- **Dialog Flow Creation and Error Control:** Using the flow editor in Botpress Studio, the main conversation flows were constructed and segmented into subflows, as depicted in Fig. 4, 'Main Conversation Flow.' This process is critical for managing complex conversation structures, especially in languages like Darija with dialectical variations. The dialogue tree features fixed

core paths, while variables based on user inputs can dynamically alter the flow, directing users through different paths or trees as required. The system allows for functionalities such as executing functions, waiting for user input, and calling APIs to facilitate interactions. Variables store and reference user input and contextual data throughout the conversation. Figure 5, the 'Buying clothes' subflow, demonstrates how subflows are utilized to separate distinct conversational scenarios and maintain clarity. Error control mechanisms automatically redirect users to previous nodes for corrections when responses deviate from the expected pathway, maintaining the accuracy and continuity of conversations.
- **Integrated Machine Learning:** The machine learning capabilities of Botpress, including Flair and other NLP techniques, were important in utilizing our collected corpus to process user inputs and generate contextually appropriate responses. The platform's NLU module, equipped with algorithms for intent classification and entity extraction, leverages this corpus to adeptly match questions and answers, even in intricate conversational scenarios.
- **Q&A Module:** This module, which was extensively used in DarijaGenie, utilizes the collected corpus to allow the chatbot to respond to queries and facilitate scenario changes or return to previous conversation nodes. The chatbot dynamically adapts to user inputs by leveraging our collected corpus, offering varied responses, and directing users to different sub-trees based on their choices or utterances. This variability ensures that each interaction, even within the same scenario, can lead to a unique conversational path and different learning experiences. By doing so, it enhances the chatbot's ability to maintain dialogue continuity and improves the user experience by providing flexibility and diverse educational possibilities in dialogues.
- **Natural Language Understanding and Context Management:** The NLU module uses intents and entities to improve the recognition of context, which is important for handling the language's diverse spellings and oral variations. Intents organize user inputs into predefined scenarios; for example, the phrase "I want a jacket" triggers the "Buying Clothes" intent, as illustrated in Fig. 6. Entities act as placeholders within these intents, capturing variable user data; in the query "I want to buy *item*," the *item* could be any clothing type like jackets, shirts, or trousers, and other elements such as colors and sizes. This setup allows the chatbot to manage a wide range of inputs without manually programming each variation. To keep the conversation flowing smoothly across different scenarios, the system employs an *append-context* function that stores relevant contextual information from ongoing interactions. This helps the chatbot accurately track the progression of the conversation. Additionally, a *time-to-live (TTL)* variable determines how long this context stays active before being updated, ensuring the chatbot responds appropriately based on both the current interaction and recent exchanges.
- **Misunderstood Module:** This functionality enhances the chatbot's machine learning module by identifying and addressing unrecognized user inputs. It collects all misunderstood inputs and displays them in a dashboard where system administrators can manually decide to ignore or amend them

based on the bot's responses. This continuous learning aspect is important for handling a range of user inputs effectively and improving response accuracy over time. Additionally, this module allows for the review of 'thumbs-down' feedback from system users, providing insights into areas where the system may require adjustments.

- **Analytics:** The analytics module of Botpress provides insights into user interactions, message exchanges, and user feedback. This data is important for understanding user engagement and refining the chatbot's performance.
- **Support For Various Media and Content Types:** Botpress's ability to handle different media types, including interactive elements, was particularly beneficial. This multimodal approach caters to varied learning styles, enhancing user engagement and the educational effectiveness of the chatbot.

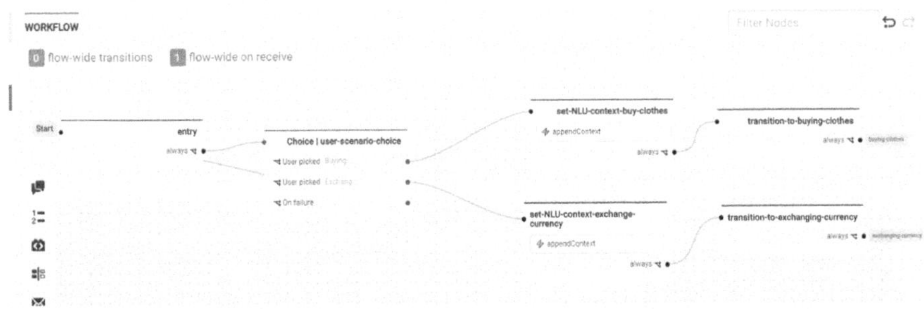

Fig. 4. Main Conversation Flow

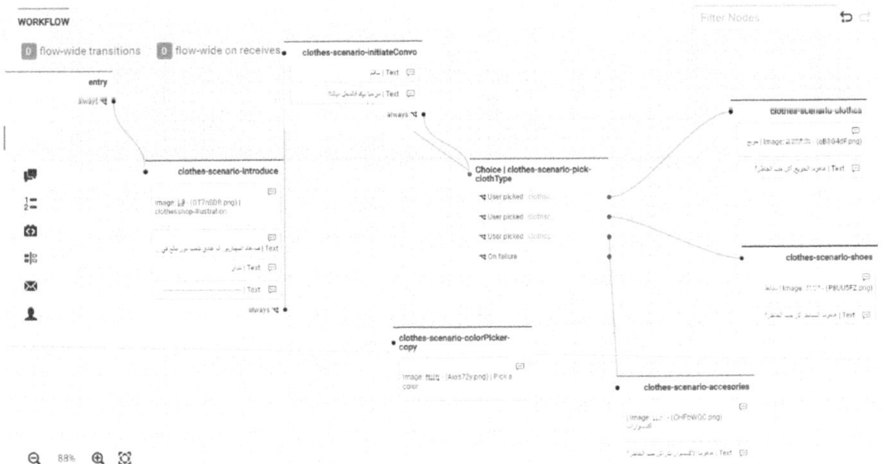

Fig. 5. Subflow for the "Buying Clothes" Scenario

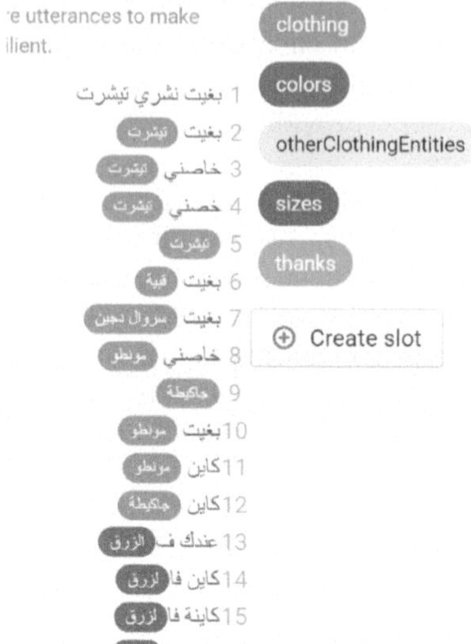

Fig. 6. Intent Panel for the "Buying Clothes" Scenario

Fig. 7. DarijaGenie's Introduction Page

Interactive User Interface: An important part of the DarijaGenie system is the interactive user interface. Inspired by the versatile character of a genie, the interface has been designed to allow for an engaging and interactive user experience. With unique background illustrations and a Moroccan-themed logo, the interface captivates the users and enhances their learning process through gamification. Versions of the introductory pages are available in English, French, Darija (Latin script), and Darija (Roman script), with the language easily selectable via a dropdown menu. Figure 7, Fig. 8, and Fig. 9 present the interactive user interface.

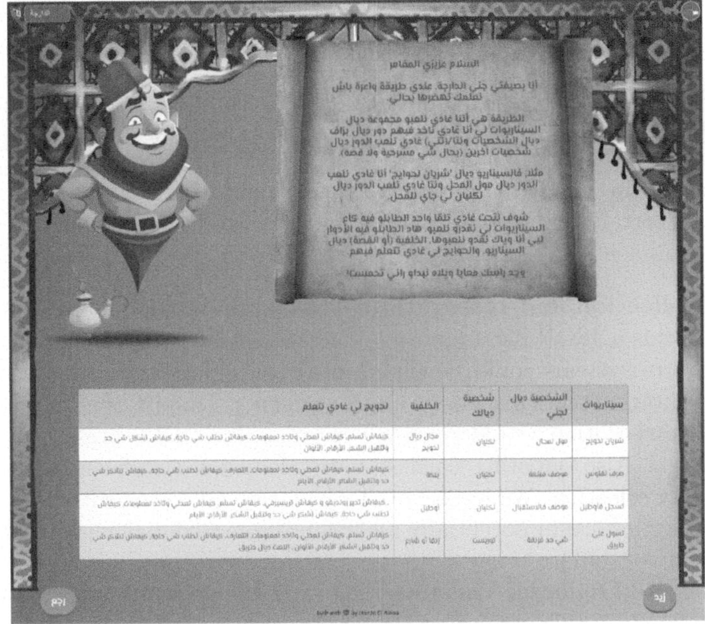

Fig. 8. DarijaGenie's Explanation Page

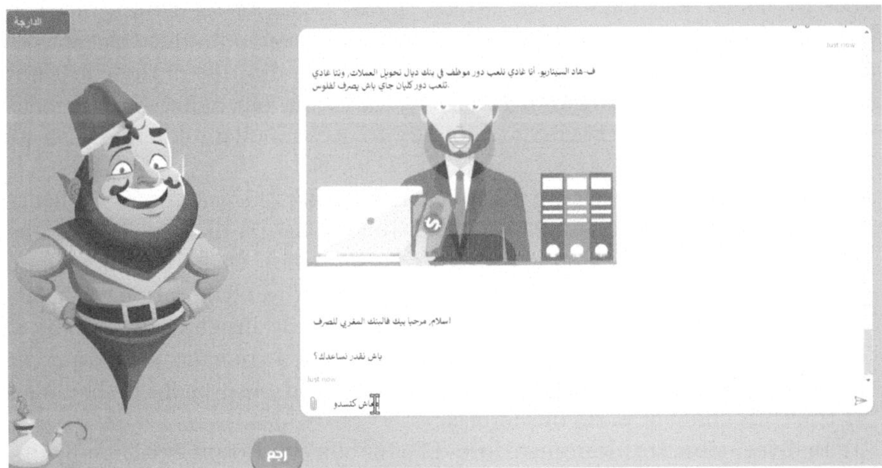

Fig. 9. DarijaGenie's Chat Page

The interface was integrated with the chatbot system using the Microsoft Bot Framework which allows users to interact with the chatbot directly on the platform, circumventing the need for authentication. To ensure a secure user experience, all environment variables, including the authentication key, are stored in the Netlify environment settings.

5 System Limitations

While contributing to the field of language learning tools, the DarijaGenie system exhibits certain limitations. Identifying these areas is important for guiding future developments and enhancing the tool's effectiveness and user experience.

- **Data Collection and Integration:** The current methodology for data collection yields a JSON file, requiring manual adjustment for Botpress integration. Future systems could benefit from an automated transliteration function, facilitating the creation of Q&A segments. Despite this improvement, manual intervention would remain necessary due to Botpress's user interface design. Also, creating each scenario demands significant attention to vocabulary selection. We are currently exploring advancements in generative technology that could potentially allow for automated dialog generation with controlled vocabulary usage.
- **Gender and Dialectal Variance:** The system's current framework has limitations in addressing gender and dialectal variations. To better handle these variations, we are planning to enrich the Natural Language Understanding (NLU) component with corpora that are partially tagged for elements subject to gender and number variations. These tags can then be utilized in conjunction with a morphological analyzer/generator to produce the correct inflections and check user inputs for the accurate realization of these features in their surface form. Regarding dialectal variation, our approach will focus on allowing for a more flexible vocabulary to accommodate different dialects effectively.
- **Dialect Selection:** Selecting an appropriate dialect for learners is challenging. For practical reasons, we are currently focusing on dialects likely to be understood in Central Morocco, as this is the region where our immediate target audience is most likely to use the language. Collaboration with foreign language teaching experts continues to provide insights into the most beneficial dialect choices for learners. Additionally, it remains important for learners to be aware of regional linguistic variations, especially if they plan to travel to different parts of Morocco.
- **Transliteration Implementation:** The inability of Botpress to handle different transliterations within a single flow presents challenges in text inclusion. For learners, we will offer the choice of using an Arabic script or a Latin transliteration. For Arabic, we will adhere to the CODA* conventions [11], which represent the only available standard. For Latin transliteration, the bot will generate a single transliteration style motivated by ease of processing and a one-to-one mapping with Arabic script. For input, we will implement a more flexible approach, likely employing a Minimum Edit Distance algorithm or language models to handle variations and spelling errors, which, when dealing with learners, may often be indistinguishable. A middleware API could

evaluate and adapt user inputs to the selected transliteration style, offering a viable solution for these challenges

- **Speech Integration:** Given the predominantly spoken nature of Darija, the text-based format of the chatbot is admittedly limiting. Introducing a speech feature, either through recorded voices or advanced Text-to-Speech (TTS) models for Darija, will significantly improve user interaction. The implementation of Automatic Speech Recognition (ASR) trained on non-native speech data would be beneficial in understanding user inputs. Additionally, the system could be augmented to assist in pronunciation correction, aligning user speech with native or high-quality TTS standards.
- **Understanding:** The current system's approach, following a decision tree structure, offers clear and structured pathways that are particularly beneficial for beginners by providing a supportive learning environment with clear models to follow. However, it doesn't fully capture the dynamic chain of conversation and events. Integrating an LLM approach alongside the existing dialogue tree structure could significantly enhance the chatbot's understanding of context, allowing for more dynamic and comprehensive conversations while maintaining structured support where needed.
- **Conversational Dynamics:** Improving the conversational aspects of the system could include the addition of visual aids, enhanced error management, and a 'help' feature for language support. Integrating an external API for dictionary or glossary access would be required for this enhancement.
- **Emotional Intelligence:** Incorporating emotional intelligence to understand and respond to users' emotional states could improve the learning experience.
- **Security Risks:** While no personal information is stored, the storage of conversations for fine-tuning the ML module introduces potential security risks. Continuous security enhancements are necessary.

6 Conclusion and Future Work

DarijaGenie aims to create a comprehensive framework for language learning that facilitates the learning of low-resource languages such as Darija. Our work primarily addresses the needs of non-native speakers who come to Morocco and face challenges navigating life in a Darija and French-speaking context. By focusing on Moroccan Arabic, DarijaGenie serves as a model for developing similar systems for other languages that lack extensive digital learning resources.

The system, currently in its prototype phase, uses a functionally oriented, task-based approach. Built on the Botpress platform, it required creating a specialized corpus, for which a bespoke tool to build dialog trees was developed. Despite its innovations, DarijaGenie encounters limitations such as managing dialectal and gender variations and broadening language and cultural content.

Future developments of DarijaGenie will focus on overcoming these challenges and expanding its functionalities. Key objectives include integrating text-to-speech features to emulate real spoken language interactions, implementing automatic speech recognition optimized for non-native speakers, and providing tools for aiding pronunciation correction. The overarching goal is to refine DarijaGenie into a versatile, user-friendly tool for language learning. More broadly, the project aims to establish a replicable chatbot framework that can be adapted to teaching other low-resource languages, thus contributing significantly to the field of computer-assisted language learning.

References

1. Alelo (2023). https://www.alelo.com/
2. Duolingo max (2023). https://blog.duolingo.com/duolingo-max/
3. Lanny (2023). https://web.eggbun.net/
4. Adekunle, I.M., Joy, O.: Development of chatbot system for disseminating information in higher citadel of learning. J. Comput. Sci. Control Syst. **14**(1), 21–26 (2021)
5. Ahmad, N.A., Che, M.H., Zainal, A., Abd Rauf, M.F., Adnan, Z.: Review of chatbots design techniques. Int. J. Comput. Appl. **181**(8), 7–10 (2018)
6. Anderson, J.N., Davidson, N., Morton, H., Jack, M.A.: Language learning with interactive virtual agent scenarios and speech recognition: lessons learned. Comput. Animat. Virtual Worlds **19**(5), 605–619 (2008)
7. Annamalai, N., Ab Rashid, R., Hashmi, U.M., Mohamed, M., Alqaryouti, M.H., Sadeq, A.E.: Using chatbots for english language learning in higher education. Comput. Educ. Artif. Intell. **5**, 100153 (2023)
8. El Alaoui, H., El Aouene, Z., Cavalli-Sforza, V.: Building intelligent chatbots: tools, technologies, and approaches. In: 2023 3rd International Conference on Innovative Research in Applied Science, Engineering and Technology (IRASET), pp. 1–12. IEEE (2023)
9. Gilakjani, A.P., Ismail, H.N., Ahmadi, S.M.: The effect of multimodal learning models on language teaching and learning. Theory Pract. Lang. Stud. **1**(10) (2011)
10. Goda, Y., Yamada, M., Matsukawa, H., Hata, K., Yasunami, S.: Conversation with a chatbot before an online EFL group discussion and the effects on critical thinking. J. Inf. Syst. Educ. **13**(1), 1–7 (2014)
11. Habash, N., Diab, M.T., Rambow, O.: Conventional orthography for dialectal Arabic. In: LREC, pp. 711–718 (2012)
12. Issa, E., Hammond, M.: Kalaambot and kalimabot: applications of chatbots in learning Arabic as a foreign language. In: Trends, Applications, and Challenges of Chatbot Technology, pp. 186–210. IGI Global (2023)
13. Johnson, W.L., Valente, A.: Tactical language and culture training systems: using AI to teach foreign languages and cultures. AI Mag. **30**(2), 72 (2009)
14. Jung, S.K.: Introduction to popular mobile chatbot platforms for english learning: trends and issues. STEM J. **20**(2), 67–90 (2019)
15. Lin, M.P.C., Chang, D.: Enhancing post-secondary writers' writing skills with a chatbot. J. Educ. Technol. Soc. **23**(1), 78–92 (2020)
16. Morton, H., Jack, M.A.: Scenario-based spoken interaction with virtual agents. Comput. Assist. Lang. Learn. **18**(3), 171–191 (2005)
17. Muraviova, O., Arkhypova, V., Krupei, M.: Immersive technologies and the practice of foreign language teaching for students of computer science specialities. Sci. Collect. ≪InterConf+≫ (33 (155)), 136–147 (2023)

18. Neumann, A.T., Conrardy, A.D., Decker, S., Jarke, M.: Motivating learners with gamified chatbot-assisted learning activities. In: International Conference on Web-Based Learning, pp. 189–203. Springer (2023)
19. Robinson, P.: Task-based language learning: a review of issues. Lang. Learn. **61**, 1–36 (2011)
20. Sagae, A., Johnson, W.L., Row, R.: Serious game environments for language and culture education. In: Proceedings of the NAACL HLT 2010 Demonstration Session, pp. 29–32 (2010)
21. Seker, M.: Scenario-based instruction design as a tool to promote self-regulated language learning strategies. SAGE Open **6**(4), 2158244016684175 (2016)
22. Souali, K., Rahmaoui, O., Ouzzif, M., El Haddioui, I.: Recommending moodle resources using chatbots. In: 2019 15th International Conference on Signal-Image Technology & Internet-Based Systems (SITIS), pp. 677–680. IEEE (2019)
23. Wang, Y.F., Petrina, S., Feng, F.: Village—v irtual i mmersive l anguage l earning and g aming e nvironment: immersion and presence. Br. J. Edu. Technol. **48**(2), 431–450 (2017)
24. Wilson, J.: Task-based language learning. ESP for the University, pp. 27–64 (1986)

Morpho-Lexical Based Approach for Arabic WorldNet Extension

Omar Mehdioui[1], Azeddine Rhazi[2](✉), and Khadija Refouh[3](✉)

[1] FLSH, My Ismail University, Meknes, Morocco
[2] FLSH, Cadi Ayyad University, Marrakesh, Morocco
[3] FLSH, USMBA, Fes Sais-Fes, Fes, Morocco
Refouh.khadija@usmba.ac.ma

Abstract. The objective of this research is to present a pilot study for an Arabic WorldNet extension based on morphological and lexical patterns. In this paper, a limited number of Arabic morphological structures (exclusively verbs) have been selected to analyze verb derivational generation. Our goal here is to study the relationship between the verb as a lexical/dictionary entry and the verb as a morphological structure. The specific aim is to demonstrate the role of the morpho-lexical level and its importance for Arabic WorldNet Data, particularly, and for language ontology, in general. Our proposal addresses morphological and lexical problems, focusing on the high degree of pattern derivation, encountered in some structures, as we will demonstrate in this study.

Keywords: morpho-lexical level · Arabic wordNet · extension · Language ontology

1 Introduction to Arabic WordNet (AWN)

Arabic WordNet (AWN) is a lexical database. As mentioned in research, WordNet contains information about nouns, verbs, and adverbs in English. Such WordNet is organized in a synset structure. A synset is a set of words with the same Part-Of-Speech (POS) that can be interchanged in a contextual manner. For example, {, سيارة , سيارة نقل عربة , تاكسي ,... etc} form an Arabic synset because they can be used to convey the same meaning. Consequently, synsets can be related to each other by semantic relations, such as synonymy, antonymy, hyponymy, meronymy, … etc., as illustrated in Fig. 1.

Each of these synsets is related and linked to other synsets, as illustrated for {Car سيارة, {Vehicle}, and {Transport}. Therefore, all word meanings in a language can be interlinked, interconnected, and constitute a relation network (language-internal relations) or WordNet.

With the emergence of Web 2.0, WordNet becomes more and more interesting for the semantic web and crucial for language ontologies. In this paper, we address the problem of Arabic verbal derivation. In Sect. 1, we begin by presenting works related to morphological and lexical approaches for Arabic WordNet focused on the automatic processing

B. Hdioud and S. L. Aouragh (Eds.): ICALP 2024, CCIS 2339, pp. 90–96, 2025.
https://doi.org/10.1007/978-3-031-79164-2_8

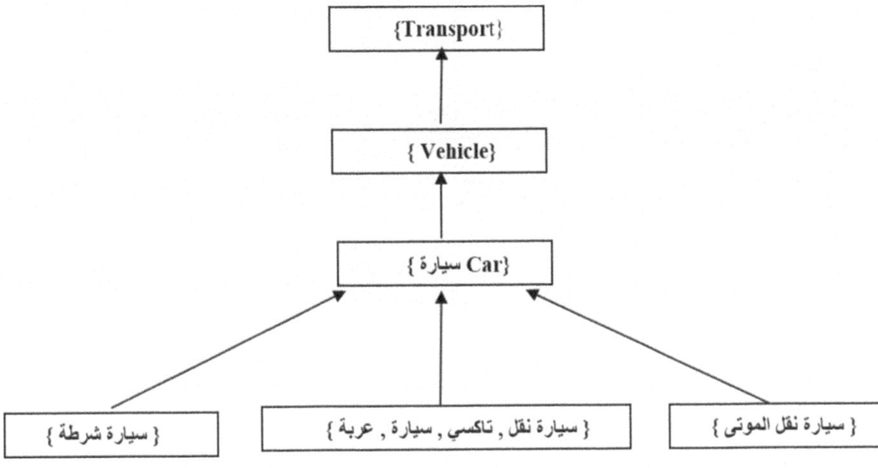

Fig. 1. Synsets related to {Car سيارة}

of verb derivation. In Sect. 2, our proposed approach is described in detail. Section 3 describes the performed experimentation. The evaluation and results are discussed in the following Sect. 4. Conclusion and future works are presented in Sect. 5.

2 The State of Arabic WordNet

Most synsets are connected to other synsets via a number of semantic relations (based on word types), and include [5, 8, 9]:

Nouns:

- hypernyms: Y is a hypernym of X if every X is a (kind of) Y
- hyponyms: Y is a hyponym of X if every Y is a (kind of) X
- coordinate terms: Y is a coordinate term of X if X and Y share a hypernym
- holonym: Y is a holonym of X if X is a part of Y
- meronym: Y is a meronym of X if Y is a part of X

Verbs:

- hypernym: the verb Y is a hypernym of the verb X if the activity X is a (kind of) Y (travel to movement)
- troponym: the verb Y is a troponym of the verb X if the activity Y is doing X in some manner (lisp to talk)
- entailment: the verb Y is entailed by X if by doing X you must be doing Y (sleeping by snoring)
- coordinate terms: those verbs sharing a common hypernym

Adjectives:

- related nouns
- participle of verb

Adverbs:

- Pertain: root adjectives

The morphology functions of the software distributed with the database try to deduce the lemma or root form of a word from the user's input; only the root form is stored in the database unless it has irregular inflected forms (Figs. 2 and 3).

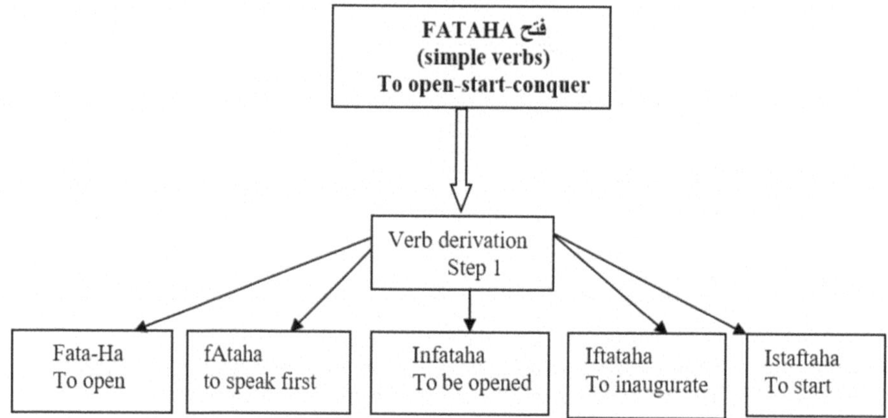

Fig. 2. The architectural morpho-lexical derivation (example of root FA.TA.HA فتح)

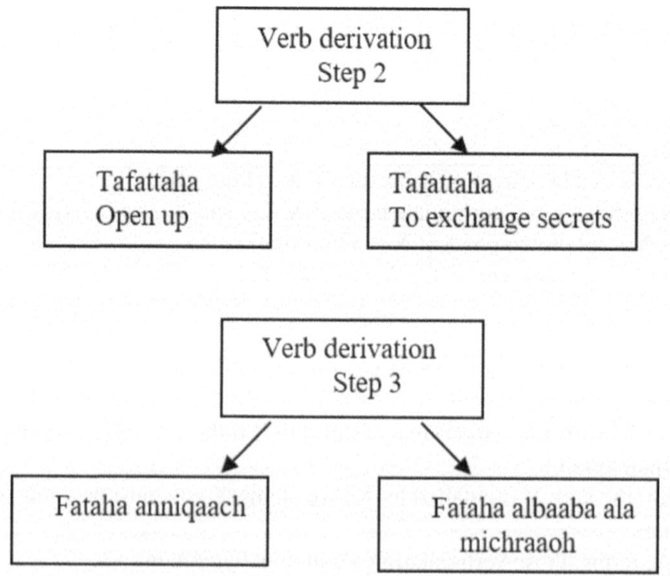

Fig. 3. The architectural morpho-lexical derivation (example of root FA.TA.HA فتح)

3 The Case of Verbal Forms and Derivation Modules

The following figure demonstrate an example of (the root: f,t,h) of the derivation of all Arabic verb lemma (Tables 1, 2 and 3).

Table 1. Forms obtained from darrassa ((درس) to teach) (step 1)

class	Arabic pattern	Arabic root (د.ر.س)
1	فعل	درس
2	فعل	درس
3	فاعل	دارس
4	افعل	ادرس
5	تفعل	تدرس
6	تفاعل	تدارس
7	انفعل	اندرس
8	افتعل	اتدرس
9	افعل	ادرس
10	استفعل	استدرس

Table 2. Table captions should be placed above the tables.

class	English forms	Arabic forms (د.ر.س)
1	(he) learned	درس
2	(i) learned	درست
3	(we) learn	ندرس
4	(he) learns	يدرس
5	(she) learns	تدرس
6	(have to) learn	ادرس
…about 82 forms (references)		

Table 3. Valid derivation forms obtained from darrassa ((درس) to teach) (step3).

class	English forms	Arabic lexicals entries (د.ر.س)
1	To learn, to study ...	درس
2	To teach	درس
3	To study together (someone)	دارس
4	To learn with	ادرس
5	To look for , to discus	تدارس
6	Be informed	مدروس
7	Teaching	تدريس
.......ect		

4 Evaluation of Proposed Methods and Results

Data Collection: It consists of producing a corpus comprising dialectal texts from microblogging (Twitter2), social networks (Facebook3), and political discourse.

Data Preprocessing: It aims to preprocess the produced corpus to preserve only textual contents and filter dialectal texts.

Opinion Classification: It begins by detecting subjective input data, which will be classified according to the opinion polarity.

4.1 Data Collection

In this step, our aim is to create a corpus of MD texts grouped by subjects. For this purpose, we use online data as a source, which is more individual-driven and less formal, and consequently more likely to comprise dialectal contents. We collected texts mainly from Twitter, Facebook, and some political discourse.

We have implemented two modules to automatically collect tweets and Facebook comments. Our Twitter collector module is used to collect a large number of tweets in a reasonable time: an average of 11,000 tweets per hour for 3 computers connected at the same time. The restriction concerning the number of tweets automatically downloaded is imposed by Twitter.

2 https://twitter.com/

3 https://www.facebook.com.

For example, Twitter cuts the connection from the server every quarter of an hour as a security measure. For this, we have created a user account table, in which we created and set 30 accounts. The module 1 alternates between these accounts in the collecting data process.

Another constraint is imposed by Twitter: only 100 tweets per automatic collection. We used a specific source code that overcomes this restriction: starting by a thread connection in a loop and a point to an exception for container collection.

Our component of Tweet Collector consists of a java-client module distributed on several computers and a centralized relational database. The database model is the structure of the Twitter network.

With a Facebook-Developer account, we collect comments for users who agree to participate in our collection. We store these comments in a specific database having the same structure as Facebook databases.

To vary the content of our corpus, we added a dozen political discourse of candidates for local elections.

4.2 Data Preprocessing

In our study, preprocessing aims to clean the collected data first and split it into units later. Cleaning is the removal of non-text data (picture, video) and advertising texts. It aims to keep only scannable text content. For this, we have found a list of HTML-Tags that merely contain non-textual information and a second list with advertising messages. We apply a Python script that eliminates these tags in our corpus.

Once cleaned data, we turn to segmentation. Tokenization is relatively simple, but cutting into a sentence remains a difficult task. Text segmentation into sentences is to determine the boundaries of sentences. Given that punctuation is not enough to detect the end or the beginning of a segment, it is necessary to take into account all typographical markers and specific linguistic markers like "و". Moreover, other linguistic bases are engaged, like the syntactic structure of a sentence and the significance of each typographical marker in a well-defined context. We developed our own segmenter.

5 Conclusion and Perspectives

The approach presented in this paper showed satisfactory results in extracting opinions from social network discourse, with higher performance scores on Facebook and Twitter compared to literary works. Since the evaluation has been conducted over a smaller text corpus size, we assume that using a bigger corpus could yield different results from the ones presented here. Although the analysis presented in this article aims to classify opinions from objective to subjective.

While automatic extraction and classification of opinion from MD and other dialects, such as TD, involving processing might be particularly challenging, we can see that dialect linguistics rules and annotation are indeed powerful sentiment classification tools that can help solve major problems in dialect data processing with more accuracy and coverage. Our system will prove extremely useful not only for the extraction of opinions but also for natural language processing in general. The work in progress will show the ability of the system to expand its applicability to other social media platforms and online communication channels.

References

1. Miller, G.A., Beckwith, R., Fellbaum, C.: Introduction to WordNet: An On-line Lexical Database Derek Gross, and Katherine Miller (Revised August 1993)
2. Diab, Mona, the feasibility of bootsrapping an Arabic wordNet leveraging parallel corpora and an English WordNet. In: Proceeding of the Arabic Language Technologies and Ressources, NEMLAR, Cairo 2004 (2005)

3. Lahcen Abouenour et al,improving Q/Ausing Arabic wordNet
4. Noam, C., Miller, G.A.: L'analyse formelle des langues naturelles (introduction to the formal analysis of natural languages), p. 1968. Traduction de PH. Richard / N.Ruwet. Edition Mouton / Gauthier-VILLARS, Paris (1968)
5. Gardent. Claire, Introduction à la lexicologie explicative et Combinatoire MELC'CUK (OLST) (1995)
6. Ghafry. Mostafa Système d'amélioration de la compétence de l'analyseur. morphologique du LIT2A(EMI) mémoire pour l'obtention du Diplôme d'analyse concepteur en Informatique Institut National de Statistique. Direction de DR Yahya Hlal & Nabil Qasmi Décembre (1995)
7. Igor, M., et al.: Introduction a la lexicologie explicative et combinatoire (1995)
8. Mario, M.: Lexicographie et dictionnaire électroniques, des usages linguistiques aux bases de données lexicales, thèse pour l'obtention du grade du docteur de l'Université de Marne –la-Vallée. Présenté et soutenue le 8 décembre (2003)
9. Alfonseca, E., Manandhar, S.: Extending a lexical ontology by a combination of distributional semantics signatures. In: Gómez-Pérez, A., Benjamins, V.R. (eds.) EKAW 2002. LNCS, vol. 2473, pp. 1–7. Springer, Heidelberg (2002). https://doi.org/10.1007/3-540-45810-7_1
10. Witschel, H.F.: Using decision trees and text mining techniques for extending taxonomies. In: Proceedings of the Learning and Extending Lexical Ontologies by using Machine Learning Methods, Workshop at ICML 2005 (2005)
11. Widdows, D.: Unsupervised methods for developing taxonomies by combining syntactic and statistical information. In: Proceedings of the Human Langauge Technology/North American Chapter of the ACL (2003)
12. Snow, R., Jurafsky, D., Ng., A.Y.: Semantic taxonomy induction from heterogenous evidence. In: COLING 2006 (2006)
13. Piasecki, M., Szpakowicz, S., Broda, B.: Automatic selection of heterogeneous syntactic features in semantic similarity of Polish nouns. In: Matoušek, V., Mautner, P. (eds.) TSD 2007. LNCS (LNAI), vol. 4629, Springer, Heidelberg (2007). https://doi.org/10.1007/978-3-540-74628-7_15
14. Piasecki, M., Szpakowicz, S., Marcinczuk, M., Broda, B.: Classification-based filtering of semantic relatedness in hypernymy extraction. In: Nordström, B., Ranta, A. (eds.) GoTAL 2008. LNCS, vol. 5221, pp. 393–404. Springer, Heidelberg (2008). https://doi.org/10.1007/978-3-540-85287-2_38
15. Hearst, M.A.: Automated discovery of WordNet relations. In: Fellbaum, C. (ed.) WordNet – An Electronic Lexical Database, pp. 131–153. MIT Press, Cambridge (1998)
16. Kurc, R., Piasecki, M.: Automatic acquisition of wordnet relations by the morpho-syntactic patterns extracted from the corpora in Polish. In: 3rd International Symposium Advances in Artificial Intelligence and Applications (2008)

A Hybrid Annotation Model for Arabic Argumentative Debate Corpus

Abdul Gabbar Al-Sharafi[1], Mohammad Majed Khader[2], Mohamed Ahmed[2], Mohamad Hamza Al-Sioufy[3], Wajdi Zaghouani[4], and Ali Al-Zawqari[5(✉)]

[1] Sultan Qaboos University, Muscat, Oman
alsharaf@squ.edu.om
[2] QatarDebate Center, Doha, Qatar
{mkhader,mahmed}@qatardebate.org
[3] Georgetwon University in Qatar, Doha, Qatar
ma2052@georgetown.edu
[4] Northwestern University in Qatar, Doha, Qatar
wajdi.zaghouani@northwestern.edu
[5] Department of Fundamental Electricity and Instrumentation, Vrije Universiteit Brussel, Brussels, Belgium
aalzawqa@vub.be

Abstract. This study introduces the first hybrid annotation model for Arabic argumentation debate corpus. It aims to analyze Arabic argumentation structure in this competitive debate corpus using this hybrid model. The model combines Aristotle's three appeals of logos, ethos and pathos with Toulmin's model of argument structure analysis, in addition to some added labels inspired by the Arabic debate corpus. These added labels are self- repetition, team repetition and reciting, which were added to the hybrid model to reflect the uniqueness of the Arabic argumentation dataset. In addition, the hybrid model further subdivides Toulmin's 'backing' into evidential backing and rational backing reflecting patterns emerging from the dataset annotation. The study presents preliminary findings, and significant patterns of the used labels in Arabic argumentation. The model addresses a gap and an under-representation of Non-English language argument annotation models by enhancing linguistic diversity in argument structure analysis, argument mining and Natural Language Processing (NLP). Thus, the model eliminates Artificial Intelligence (AI) bias by supporting a low-resource language such as Arabic. The multifaceted nature of the corpus on which the model was used, in terms of topics, gender representation, and geographic origins of debaters, serves as a robust resource for validating the model and for analyzing argumentative discourse in the Arabic speaking world. The implications of applying this hybrid model in Arabic argumentation research will be discussed.

Keywords: Argumentation · Annotation · Toulmin's model

B. Hdioud and S. L. Aouragh (Eds.): ICALP 2024, CCIS 2339, pp. 97–113, 2025.
https://doi.org/10.1007/978-3-031-79164-2_9

1 Introduction

Aristotle, in his On Rhetoric, particularly the second chapter of this important treatise argues that persuasion can be achieved in three ways. One is the truthfulness and logicality of the argument, later known as logos. Two is the speaker's ability to get the audience to trust him. Three is the set of emotions the speaker is able to instill in the audience to make it accept his point of view. In modern rhetoric, these three ways have been named logos, ethos and pathos respectively [1]. Stephen Toulmin (1922–2009), who is "one of the founding fathers of modern theory of argumentation" [2], proposed a model that inherited the key features of classical rhetoric [3]. Toulmin's aim was to get argumentation out of the "abstract and formal criteria of mathematical logic" [4,5], and propose a model that takes argumentation as a human endeavor incorporating methods that we "actually use in everyday life" [4]. In this study, we present a hybrid model of argument annotation for Arabic competitive debates mainly based on Aristotle's and Toulmin's models.

Competitive debating, is a rigorous intellectual activity involving oral argumentation. It is highly regulated and is commonly held in debating contests and tournaments. University and school students of both genders from all over the world participate in Arabic debating tournaments on the local and international levels. QatarDebate Center (www.qatardebate.org) is the Arab leading debate institution, promoting debating culture in the Arab world and organizing major debating events. QatarDebate's 3 vs 3 debate format as shown in Fig. 1, which is a customized format of the World Schools Debating Championship (www.wsdcdebating.org), is the adopted format in Arabic competitive debating activities. In this format, two teams debate a motion; each team opposes the other with one representing the 'proposition' and the other the 'opposition'. Each team is composed of three speakers, and each speaker is given a total of 6–7 min to present their arguments. The process begins with the first proposition speaker, and then the first opposition speaker, and so on until the last speaker from the opposition. Then, the Reply Speech which is a 3-min technical speech delivered by each team to conclude the debate. A debate is typically adjudicated by a panel of odd number judges who select the winner based on rigoros rubrics and descriptors that help in designating the right scores for each of the two teams. The quality of the arguments presented and the rebuttal provided are the main focus of the panel to adjudicate the debate.

This study introduces an annotated corpus of Arabic competitive debates. For the implementation and validation of the model, a corpus of Arabic argumentative debate is used. Currently, it stands as the most extensive, diverse and specialized corpus of Arabic argumentative content. The uniqueness of the model originates from the nature of the competitive debate which is rich in structured argumentative content and explicit sentiment inherent in the debating enterprise. The data exploration provides an empirical basis for the hybrid model the authors propose. The expanded model will inform Arabic rhetorical and linguistic studies of spoken Modern Standard Arabic (MSA) argumentation, and will assist in developing Arabic NLP tools for argument mining. This

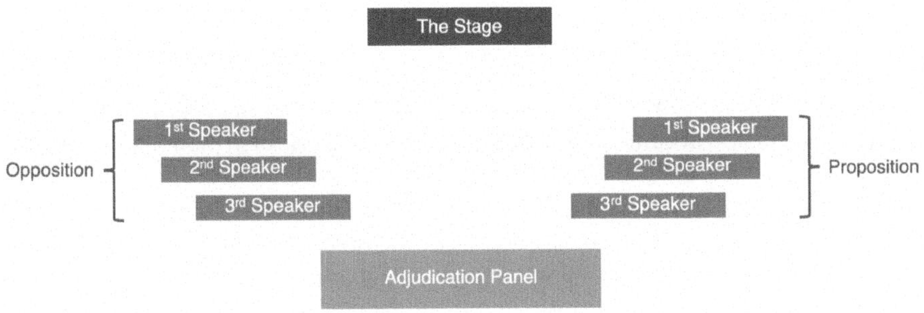

Fig. 1. Illustration of 3 vs 3 Debate Format

unique Arabic annotated corpus of competitive debates can serve as primary training material for Arabic argument mining as well as discourse analysis of Arabic argumentation strategies.

2 Theoretical Framework

2.1 Argument Analysis

Two key models of argumentation analysis are commonly referred to in the literature. The first is Aristotle's model in which he proposed the three key terms logos, ethos and pathos which are used in many argument analyses in different languages. Logos refers to the content of the speech or oration, ethos refers to the credibility of the speaker, and pathos refers to how the audience is emotionally engaged in the speech or oration [1]. The second model is Toulmin's model [6] in which he proposes six main elements of an argument: Claim (C) which is the conclusion we aim to make. This is the statement the arguer makes and needs to justify and support. The support comes in the form of Data (D), later called Grounds. These are the facts we treat as the premise of our claims or arguments. These data might be challenged in the course of an argument, so they need to be supported by a Warrant (W), a proposition showing the logical link between the data and the claim. Toulmin [6] then talks about another element of argument skeleton, which he calls Qualifier (Q), which refers to the scope of certainty or otherwise of the claim. Toulmin then suggests another element in the argument structure and calls it Rebuttal (R) showing the refutation of the claim and the application of a qualifier to produce a more restricted or qualified claim. The last element of Toulmin's model is Backing (B), which is the support that adds authority and legitimacy to the claim, the warrant and the data.

2.2 Related Studies

As research in argumentation analysis and argument mining relies heavily on annotated corpora of argumentative texts, we identify some relevant efforts on corpus creation for argument mining, such as the work of [7]. In this work, the authors describe the creation of the Argument Annotated Essays Corpus containing 302 persuasive student essays annotated for argument components derived from Toulmin's model. The corpus supports the investigation of argument structure in free-text essay writing. Furthermore, [8–10] developed the Qatari Corpus of Argumentative Writing of approximately 200,000 tokens of Arabic and English writing by undergraduate students. The corpus utilized part-of-speech (POS) annotation with TreeTagger for English texts and Farasa for Arabic texts. The students are native Arabic speakers and fluent in English. The team asked the students to write an Arabic and English essay based on specific argumentative prompts and instructed them to include in their essays a clear thesis statement supported by relevant evidence. These studies demonstrate growing efforts to create corpora annotated with argumentation elements to support computational modeling. However, the Qatari Corpus annotation focuses on micro-level categories of argumentative essay writing, hence its purely pedagogical orientation. To the best of our knowledge, the hybrid model proposed in our study is the first model that targets macro-level argument structure in a debate corpus annotating spoken arguments as discourse elements, hence the uniqueness and originality of our hybrid model.

Some studies have proposed various annotation methodologies for languages other than Arabic. For example, [11] conducted an annotation analysis of argument schemes such as expert opinion following the *Argumentum Model of Topics.* [12] annotated claims and evidence in controversial topics for automatic detection in a simple claim/evidence model. There are argument mining efforts in other languages such as Italian [13] and the argument relation annotations from multilingual social media such as X (Twitter, formerly), [14]. [15] presented the UKP Sentential Argument Mining Corpus which annotates 25,492 sentences from online comments according to a simplified model with claims, premises, and major claim tags. The corpus focuses on Components at the sentence level within user-generated web discourse.

Aristotle's rhetorical argumentation model, although has been a source of inspiration for rhetorical studies for centuries, has been critiqued by a number of scholars, including Toulmin. In relation to Aristotle's universal orientation, Toulmin [6] points out that Aristotle was an idealist as he was "much concerned with syllogisms in which both the premises were universal" (p. 100) as opposed to Toulmin's interest in propositions that are used to "justify particular conclusions about individuals" (ibid). The work in [16] describes Aristotle's Rhetoric as "difficult to read, full of discrepancies, gaps and repetitions" (p. 128). Quandahl observes that the model needs to be adapted with caution since it was developed in an entirely different historical context. Kennedy also voices similar concerns in [1]

Similarly, Toulmin's argumentation model has been used in text linguistics, discourse analysis, argument mining, rhetoric, and writing pedagogy [4,7,17–26]. It has not been without drawbacks, however [27,28]. In the numerous applications of Toulmin's model, a number of issues have been raised about the model. For example, some scholars comment on its ambiguity, inconsistency and vagueness [29]. Others describe it as rigid ([19] and needs "to be flexible - not tied to one standard function of argument" (p, 3). [7] highlight "the need for greater efforts in building a framework in which argument mining tasks are carried out, covering all aspects of agreement on the argument theoretical concepts being identified" (p. 806). Toulmin's model is also described as idealistic and gets even frustrating when used to analyze real life data [30]. Scholars have called for a modification or expansion of the model [31].

[25] examine the application of Toulmin's model of argumentation in Chinese EFL argumentative writing. They claim that not all the elements "are explicit, and sometimes warrants may not need to be stated in real life arguments" (p. 445). [32] comments on Toulmin's model referring to the element of warrants. He contends that Toulmin's model is "problematic at points, especially his discussion of warrants, in a way which leads to a confusing misinterpretation of how his model should be understood" (p. xii). He rejects "Toulmin's distinction of data, warrants and backing as appropriate for analyzing arguments as products" (ibid). He devotes a whole chapter to discussing Toulmin's "problematic notion of warrant" (cf. chapter 3). Similarly, Toulmin's notion of data being restricted to 'facts' has been questioned [33]. Toulmin's notion of 'data', according to Herman needs to be expanded to cover other elements such as opinions and interpretations, and Toulmin's notion of 'backing', needs to be expanded to include backing for data and backing for warrant [33].

Despite these comments, Aristotle's and Toulmin's models have been widely used to label argument structure in various linguistic contexts. To accommodate these different contexts, it has been modified and expanded to accommodate various types of data from different genres and language situations. [20] modify Toulmin's model to make the components fit with the purpose of argument analysis of students' writing. Their modified model includes final claim, primary claim, counterclaim, rebuttal, data and other (p. 174). [22] reduce Toulmin's six elements to two "the main components of every argument, and the rest are supporting sub-arguments that may or may not exist in an argument." (p. 5). [24] use a modified model of Toulmin's which is similar to that adapted by [20] referred to above, except in the last category which is 'other' in [20] but 'supporting reason or example' in [24], (p. 160).

Both Aristotle's and Toulmin's models of argument analysis are significant and important in core argumentation theory and analysis because they assist researchers in analyzing and labelling the elements that make an argument in discourse. As shown from the review above, the models seem to have a wide scope of applicability in various areas of inquiry. The current paper contributes with a hybrid argumentation annotation model for Arabic debate used on an original Arabic debate corpus. Both the model and the corpus can serve as a benchmark for argumentation mining methods in the Arabic language. The speeches in the corpus come from competitive debates, which are structured and formal forms of argumentation. The debaters' backgrounds are demographically diverse, resulting in more representation of argumentation among native Arabic speakers. One of the preliminary studies [34] examines using this annotated corpus to classify the modes of persuasion in these debates and considers the evaluation of language models in the classification task with respect to speakers' gender to study the fairness in these language models.

2.3 The Proposed Hybrid Model

The hybrid model proposed in this study is inspired by Aristotle's model of argumentation which sees argumentation as a rhetorical experience involving three main types of argumentative appeals: logos, ethos and pathos [1] and is supported by the various modern applications of these three classical appeals in various types of communication and discourse analysis [35–41]. Another source of support for our hybrid model comes from [42] who argue that the warrant in Toulmin's model that binds both the data and the claim can come in three different ways. These are (1) "relations existing among phenomena in the external world" (p, 48), (2) "an assumption concerning the quality of the source from which the data are derived" (ibid) and (3) "an assumption concerning the inner drives, values or aspirations which impel the behavior of those persons to whom the argument is addressed" (ibid). We use Toulmin's model to bridge the gap of detail in Aristotle's model and we situate Toulmin's model within the Aristotelian logos.

3 Methods

As shown in Table 1, we take (1) in [42] to mean syllogistic argumentation, which is the component directed to the content of the syllogism (rational and dialectical argumentation) and this corresponds to Aristotle's logos and to Toulmin's claim, grounds, warrant, backing, qualifier and rebuttal. We further subdivide Toulmin's 'backing' into two types: rational backing and evidential backing to provide more granulated analysis of the annotated corpus in response to patterns emerging from the data. Moreover, to respond to insights from the data we also added two more elements. The first one is repetition for which we identified two further sub-elements: self-repetition where the speaker repeats himself/herself throughout his/her speech, and team-repetition where the speaker repeats claims, positions, or rebuttals mentioned by his/her team earlier. The second element is 'reciting' where the speaker repeats the argument of the opposing team to refute it. We take (2) in [42] to mean the expressive argumentation, which relates to the speaker's appeal to create their own credibility and trustworthiness, which directly corresponds to Aristotle's ethos. Therefore, we added ethos to the model to account for this kind of expressiveness in argumentation, where the speaker's focus is on expressing, maintaining and preserving his/her

Table 1. The hybrid annotation model based on Aristotle's and Toulmin's models with added labels

No	Argumentation Type
1	**Inferential Argumentation (Logos)**
	Definition: Argumentation based on the logical structure of an argument. This is Aristotle's Logos and is substantiated by the categories proposed by Toulmin with some more labels added in response to the debating corpus of this study
	(1) Position: Team's position in the debate i.e. either proposition or opposition
	(2) Super claim: An assertive statement made by a debating team which outlines the team's overall goal
	(3) Claim: An assertive statement or a conclusion that the proposition team seeks to justify and support and the opposition team seeks to refute and rebut
	(4) Grounds: Usually agreed upon information and facts that support the claim. These include definitions
	(5) Warrant: The logical link that connects Ground to the Claim - often implicit
	(6) Rational backing: Logical and inferential reasoning including justifications, conclusions and mini supported assertions
	(7) Evidential backing: Specific examples or research findings provided to support a claim
	(8) Qualifier: A statement representing a concession on the part of the speaker as to the scope or certainty of the claim, whether in response to a rebuttal or not
	(9) Rebuttal: The refutation of a claim by an opposing team or individual
	(10) Self-repetition: Partial or total repetition of statements made by the same speaker
	(11) Team repetition: Partial or total repetition of statements made by the team of the speaker
	(12) Reciting: Partial or total repetition of statements made by the opposing team
2	**Expressive Argumentation (Ethos)**
	Definition: Argumentation based on the expressive function of discourse whereby a speaker uses statements that help to create their own credibility, morality, trustworthiness, organization, and order. This type of argumentation includes: authority, honesty, trustworthiness, reputation, fairness, transparency, openness, accessibility, etc.
3	**Appellative Argumentation (Pathos)**
	Definition: Argumentation based on the appellative function of discourse whereby a speaker uses statements that appeal to audience emotions and feelings and attempt to engage the receivers in one way or another in the discourse. This type of argumentation includes: empathy, fear, anger, love, compassion, hope, patriotism, uncertainty, etc.

own credibility, moral and ethical standing as a way of persuading the audience to win their trust. Finally, we take (3) in [42] to mean the appellative argumentation, which appeals to audience's feelings and emotions, and attempt to engage the audience in one way or another in the discourse. Thus, we integrated the element of 'pathos' from Aristotle's model to account for this appellative dimension of argumentative discourse. This hybrid model is theoretically grounded in the work of both Aristotle and Toulmin and is empirically grounded in the patterns of data emerging from the annotation process that reflect the nature and uniqueness of Arabic debating argumentation in terms of being spoken and displaying various patterns of repetition in presentation and argumentation. The hybrid model with its new integrated labels would serve as an annotation model for various forms of Arabic debating argumentation. Once, it is finally validated against further data annotation and analysis (the annotation of the entire corpus

120 debates), the model can be tested on Arabic argumentation analysis outside the debating context.

3.1 Corpus Building

In this argument annotation study, we used 40 debate transcripts from Munazarat 1.0 corpus. The corpus has 204,294 word tokens and 21,692 word types. The details of the full corpus are described in [43]. All debates in this corpus comply with the following criteria: (1) follow QatarDebate Center format (3 vs 3) illustrated in Fig. 1 above and explained in more detail in [44], (2) are held in a physical (face-to-face) debate setup, (3) involve university students and native speakers of Arabic. Tables 2, 3, and 4 show some of the important variables of this corpus. We maintain a balanced male-to-female ratio in the corpus as shown in Table 2. The corpus represents debaters from 38 universities that represent 13 Arab countries as shown in Table 3. Also, a variety of debated topics are represented in the corpus (11 topics) as shown in Table 4.

Table 2. Gender Representation

Gender	No of Speeches
Male	126
Female	114
Male/Female Ratio	1.08

Table 3. Country Representation

Country	No of Debating Teams
Qatar	14
Jordan	12
Sudan	11
Oman	10
Tunisia	9
Kuwait	6
Lebanon	5
Libya	5
Palestine	3
Bahrain	2
Iraq	1
Algeria	1
Somalia	1
Total	80

3.2 Corpus Annotation

For the annotation of the corpus, we take every discourse segment in the debate as a piece of argumentation following [45][p. 172] who argues that 'whenever there is persuasion, there is rhetoric. And wherever there is meaning, there is persuasion.' Therefore, we analyze every piece of the debate and treat every text in the corpus as example of argumentation. Some studies classify their corpora into argumentative vs non-argumentative discourse [46]. However, from a critical discourse analysis perspective [47,48], we believe this separating approach is limited and is probably motivated by a reductionist representational view of language. Here we believe that discourse in general is socially constitutive and motivated [48,49]. The annotated corpus so far completed, 40 annotated debates, represents three variables: gender, country and topic as shown in Tables 2, 3 and 4.

Table 4. Topic Representation

Topic	No of Debates
Politics	11
Human rights	8
Ethics/Philosophy	7
Sports	3
Technology	3
Environment	2
Culture	2
Law	1
Lifestyle	1
Education	1
Media	1
Total	40

3.3 Annotation Model

In Table 1, we describe the various elements in our hybrid model (Aristotle, Toulmin + our added labels). The model provides the type of argumentation along with the labels used in each type of argumentation. It also provides a definition for the types and labels used in the annotation process. The labels outlined in Table 1 were used as coding labels for argument structure elements in the corpus. We also provide a set of linguistic triggers that help the annotators to smoothly identify and label the argument segments.

3.4 Annotation Process

In this subsection, we describe the annotation process providing details of the annotation model used, the annotation team and their training, the inter-annotator agreement and briefly outline the challenges encountered.

3.4.1 Annotation Tool

The annotation process is conducted using a paid digital tool called "UBIAI" (https://ubiai.tools/) which is a website that allows for a team of annotators to separately make text labeling on the same text file in a user-friendly environment. Each debate is annotated by analyzing its text using the labels identified in the hybrid model proposed in this study under 14 different labels as shown in Table 1.

3.4.2 Annotation Team

The annotation team was carefully selected to ensure the best quality and high diversity amongst its members. It consisted of four native speakers of Arabic who are also experts in Arabic competitive debates. They have developed considerable expertise within QatarDebate Center as experienced debaters, debate judges, and debate trainers (3 males & 1 female). The annotators come from different academic backgrounds (Engineering, Foreign Affairs, and English Literature) to ensure in-depth knowledge of the annotators in the subject areas covered in the debates. In addition to the annotators' expertise in Arabic competitive debating as debaters, adjudicators, and trainers, they were also provided with intensive training to enhance their annotation and discourse analysis skills.

3.4.3 Annotation Training

The annotator training process entailed the formulation of a structured annotation framework. While this framework is based on Aristotle's and Toulmin's models, custom-made annotation labels were judiciously integrated to reflect the insights emerging from the data as the annotation process evolved. As mentioned earlier, the data exploration in the annotation process provided an empirical foundation for the hybrid model which the authors propose in this study. Subsequent to model development, this hybrid model was thoroughly presented to and discussed with the annotators. Leveraging the annotators' experienced insights as active debaters, the framework underwent meticulous iterative enhancements, ensuring its alignment with the focal argumentation model. This iterative and collaborative refinement process culminated in the ultimate crystallization of a definitive annotation model, which served as the key guide for the annotators' meticulous work.

We used a double annotation process for the first twenty debates where two different annotators separately annotated each debate transcript. Then a reviewer, an academic who was part of the team developing the hybrid annotation model, would look at the IAA rate calculated by the UBIAI tool, read both annotation files, compare the differences and edit the final annotated file. This process was repeated for every debate in the first set of 20 debates. Detailed feedback was given to annotators through a series of 3-hour weekly meetings with the reviewers. Despite the fact that this process was costly in terms of time, effort, and resources, it was necessary to ensure that all debates were being annotated in a consistent manner. The annotation procedure aimed to achieve as precise and descriptive annotation as possible. We did not address the quality, effectiveness, or integrity of the arguments because we did not intend to introduce any further distraction to our descriptive analysis of the corpus by involving evaluative judgments on the quality of the arguments.

3.4.4 Inter-Annotator Agreement (IAA)

When we calculated the IAA for the first 20 debates, we noticed that the IAA ranged mostly between 20 and 50 for the first half of the debates annotated in the early stages. However, after the three weekly meetings between annotators and reviewers (researchers) to fine-tune and closely refine the annotation model, the IAA for the entire corpus increased to be in the range of 50 to 75, corresponding to 0.50–0.75 in Cohen Kappa's test and indicating substantial agreement that is comparable to other studies [7,50].

3.4.5 Challenges Encountered

The argumentation annotation process cannot be as precise as parts-of-speech annotation, for example, due to the subjectivity involved in identifying and analyzing argument segments as discourse segments. For example, two annotators would agree on annotating one segment under the same label, yet they would disagree on the start or end of the segment by one or two words. In addition, one of the annotators might divide the same short paragraph into two or more parts of the same label while the other annotator would keep the whole short paragraph under one label. Thus, most disagreements were insignificant and acceptable as they did not represent contradictions between the annotators. Most disagreements were attributed to the nature of the studied speech corpus which allows for some kind of ambiguity in terms of argument segmentation.

4 Initial Findings and Discussion

In this section, we present some key initial findings from the 40 annotated debates. As shown in Table 5, the highest average word count in the dataset goes to 'rebuttal' 24.24%. Based on the definitions provided in the tool in Table 4, rebuttal is defined as the refutation of a claim by an opposing team or individual. Rebuttal is the second most important element in a debate after 'claim'. It is interesting, however, that 'claim' is less used than rebuttal, only 5.40% of the word count in the dataset. This is justified by the fact that a debate normally includes fewer claims than rebuttals, and a claim can be refuted in different ways by more than one debater. In addition, the label 'rational backing' often includes mini-claims, while in the dataset, it was annotated using a different label which received 15.58% of the word count of the entire corpus, so this also justifies the relatively less frequent mention of 'claim' in the dataset compared to 'rebuttal'. This percentage faithfully reflects the desire of every debating team and every member of the team to support their claims with as much rationalization as possible. In our model, we separated 'rational backing' from 'evidential backing'. If taken together, both types of 'backing' would make 20% of the word count, which puts the label comfortably as the second highest label in terms of word count in the dataset after 'rebuttal'.

The label 'ethos' received 13.72% of the overall word count in the dataset which is a relatively high percentage of use in the corpus. Ethos has two functions: one is expressive, i.e. expressing speaker's credentials to create credibility and believability, and the second is organizational, providing discourse signposting to make it easy for the audience to follow the thread of the argument in the debate, which ultimately feeds into the credibility of the speaker as an organized and confident speaker. This high percentage justifies our hybrid model taking this element from Aristotle's model. In fact, the label of 'ehtos' is so common in our dataset that it cannot just be ignored. In competitive debating as in any other type of debating, the speaker's credibility and image are crucial in making the audience trust and believe the speaker, hence its importance in an argumentation model that seeks to analyze natural language in authentic argumentation settings. This finding echoes the importance of ethos in argumentation and communication in general [35–37, 39–41].

Analyzing the distribution of labels based on the role of the speakers (first, second, third) shows the relevance of the argument labels proposed in the hybrid model to the role of the speaker. As shown in Fig. 2, The labels grounds, position, and super claim appear to be associated mainly with first speakers which is justified given their role in defining the terms of the motion and the stance of the team. Interestingly, the use of rational backing is absent in third speakers' argumentation because of their main role which is refuting the other team. The high use of rational backing compared to evidential backing across the three roles suggests a tendency of debaters to focus more on logical argumentation than using real-life examples which is a distinct feature of competitive debates. The lack of using warrants and qualifiers reflects a long standing problem with Tolmin's model which is the ambiguity of the concept of warrant and qualifier [3, 7, 21, 51–53]. The high use of rebuttal in the three roles suggests that the use of refutation is a very common argumentative component among debaters. Finally, the use of ethos and pathos across the three roles is consistent which suggests a general tendency to use those techniques in argumentation. It is interesting that the use of ethos is particularly higher compared to pathos, which indicates the tendency of debaters to focus more on establishing trust in the audience than relying on emotions.

For male and female, there is a high consistency in the distribution of labels across genders, which suggests that the gender of the speaker is not a factor

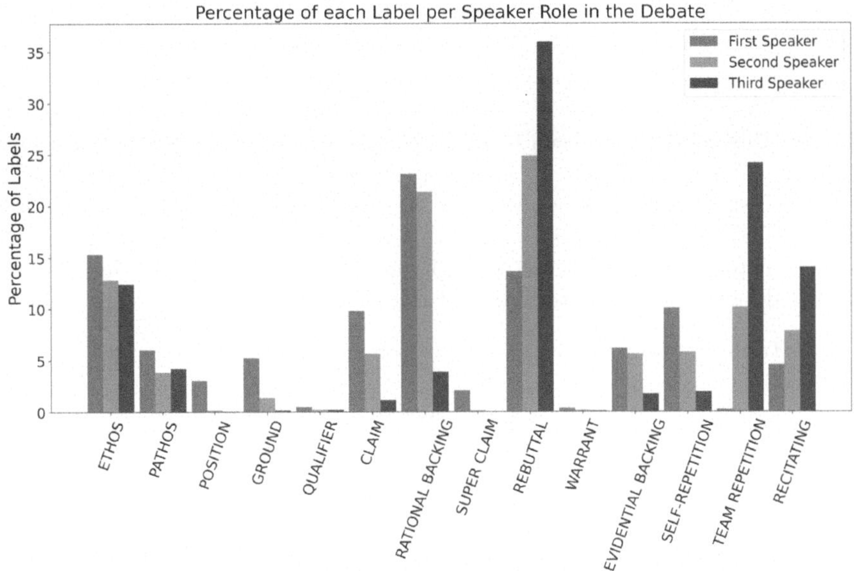

Fig. 2. Label distribution across debaters' roles

that affects the use of argumentation labels by debaters. This consistent pattern between both genders might be attributed to the well-defined structure of competitive debates compared to other forms of argumentation where the structures are relatively less well-defined.

The results also show that the elements added in our hybrid model, i.e. self-repetition, team repetition and reciting, if taken together, make the highest entity in terms of average word count in the entire dataset, 26.27%. This high percentage again explains why this crucial element had to be added to our hybrid model. It reflects the natural language used in spoken argumentative debates where repetition tends to serve an important function, i.e. to state, restate and reaffirm the claims, the backing or the grounds. In competitive debating particularly, debaters are expected to repeat their arguments, the arguments made by their teams and those made by their opponents. Attending to this key feature of debate argumentation in our hybrid model is a move that is supported by these figures which show how significant repetition is in Arabic argumentative debates. This finding echoes arguments by other Arabic argumentation scholars [49,54–59].

Another interesting result is the very low visibility of the argument labels 'warrant' and 'qualifier' in the annotated dataset, only 0.30 and 0.31 of the word count of the entire corpus respectively. This is not surprising because 'warrants' are not easy to identify and annotate. In fact, much of the discussion on Toulmin's model has been on this argument element in particular [3,7,21,51–53]. Similarly, the label 'qualifier' seems to have a very low visibility in the dataset.

However, while the reason behind the low visibility of 'warrants' in the data could be attributed to the difficulty the annotators face in locating it, the reason for the low visibility of 'qualifier' could be due to the reluctance of debaters to use it. Since it is a form of concession, it seems debaters tend to avoid it. However, this conclusion needs to be further examined when the entire corpus is fully annotated. The model we develop for Arabic debate annotation reflects the same issues with the vagueness of 'warrant' as expressed by these scholars [3,7,21,51–53]. The reason behind this vagueness is that it is often implicit and it is expressed as a logical principle or assumption and this implicitness makes it difficult for annotators to spot the warrant.

Table 5. Statistical distribution of argument labels in the dataset

Label	Mean %	Median %	Standard Deviation
Ethos	13.72	13.66	0.0321
Pathos	4.91	4.82	0.0200
Position	1.08	0.83	0.0063
Grounds	2.34	1.93	0.0140
Qualifier	0.31	0.20	0.0069
Claim	5.40	4.88	0.0255
Rational Backing	15.58	14.95	0.0490
Evidential Backing	4.79	4.17	0.0346
Super claim	1.08	0.71	0.0426
Rebuttal	24.24	22.91	0.0853
Warrant	0.30	0.00	0.0087
Self-repetition	5.62	5.57	0.0272
Team-repetition	11.53	11.58	0.0326
Reciting	9.12	9.22	0.0236

5 Conclusion

This study introduces an argument annotation model applied to a corpus of Arabic competitive debates. It uses a hybrid argumentation analysis model combining Aristotle's and Toulmin's models with some extra labels added as a response to insights emerging from the annotation process of the dataset, as shown in Table 5. The study situated Toulmin's model within Aristotle's logos as it is the focus of Toulmin's model to delineate the logical structure of an argument but had to account for the other two appeals of ethos and pathos as these two were quite explicit in the data and could not have been ignored. The authors developed an annotation model and verified and tested it on a sizable and diverse corpus of Arabic debates. The initial findings of the annotation confirm previous research on Arabic argumentation. The model developed in this study will be tested and verified further with more data from the same Arabic debating corpus as the annotation process progresses with the rest of the debates in the corpus.

Acknowledgements. This work was made possible by two QD Fellowship awards [QDRF-2022-01-003] and [QDRF-2022-01-005] from QatarDebate Center.

References

1. Kennedy, G.: Aristotle: On Rhetoric: A Theory of Civic Discourse. Oxford University Press (2006)
2. Eemeren, F., Garssen, B., Krabbe, E., Henkemans, A., Verheij, B., Wagemans, J.: Eemeren Handbook of Argumentation Theory (2014)
3. Van Eemeren, F.H., Grootendorst, R., Kruiger, T.: Handbook of Argumentation Theory: A Critical Survey of Classical Backgrounds and Modern Studies, vol. 7. Walter de Gruyter GmbH & Co KG (2019)
4. Hitchcock, D., Verheij, B.: Arguing on the Toulmin Model, vol. 10. Springer (2006)
5. Van Eemeren, F.H.: Argumentation Theory: A Pragmadialectical Perspective. Springer (2018)
6. Toulmin, S.E.: The Uses of Argument. Cambridge University Press, Cambridge (2003)
7. Lawrence, J., Reed, C.: Argument mining: a survey. Comput. Linguist. **45**(4), 765–818 (2020)
8. Ahmed, A.M., Zhang, X., Rezk, L.M., Zaghouani, W.: Building an annotated L1 Arabic/L2 English bilingual writer corpus: the qatari corpus of argumentative writing (QCAW). Corpus-based Studies across Humanities (2024)
9. Zaghouani, W., Ahmed, A., Zhang, X., Rezk, L.: Qcaw 1.0: building a qatari corpus of student argumentative writing. In: Proceedings of the 2024 Joint International Conference on Computational Linguistics, Language Resources and Evaluation (LREC-COLING) (2024)
10. Ahmed, A., et al.: Qatari Corpus of Argumentative Writing. Linguistic Data Consortium (2022). https://doi.org/10.35111/K307-KG62 . https://catalog.ldc.upenn.edu/LDC2022T04
11. Musi, E., Ghosh, D., Muresan, S.: Towards feasible guidelines for the annotation of argument schemes. In: Proceedings of the First Workshop on Argument Mining, pp. 154–163 (2018)
12. Aharoni, E., et al.: A benchmark dataset for automatic detection of claims and evidence in the context of controversial topics. In: Proceedings of the First Workshop on Argumentation Mining, pp. 64–68 (2014)
13. Durmus, E., Lippi, M., Torroni, P.: Argumentation mining on news editorials and blog posts in Italian. In: Proceedings of the Eighth Italian Conference on Computational Linguistics (CLiC-it 2021), pp. 1–6 (2021)
14. Bosc, T., Cabrio, E., Villata, S.: Dart: a dataset of arguments and their relations on twitter. In: Proceedings of the Tenth International Conference on Language Resources and Evaluation (LREC 2016), pp. 1258–1263 (2016)
15. Stab, C., Gurevych, I.: Parsing argumentation structures in persuasive essays. Comput. Linguist. **43**(3), 619–659 (2017)
16. Quandahl, E.: Aristotle's rhetoric: Reinterpreting invention. Rhetor. Rev. **4**(2), 128–137 (1986)
17. Oswald, S.: Pragmatics for argumentation. J. Pragmat. **203**, 144–156 (2023)

18. Fu, Y., et al.: Hierarchical neural network: integrate divide-and-conquer and unified approach for argument unit recognition and classification. Inf. Sci. **624**, 796–810 (2023)
19. Hinton, M.: Argumentation and identity: a normative evaluation of the arguments of delegates to the cop26 un climate change conference. Argumentation 1–24 (2022)
20. Wan, Q., Crossley, S., Tian, Y.: Automated classification of argumentative components in students' essays. In: International Conference on Intelligent Tutoring Systems, pp. 171–182. Springer (2022)
21. Papadopoulou, T., Theoharakis, V., Jones, M.V., Bhaumik, S.K.: Analysing the macrostructure of spoken strategic communication: an application of argumentation analysis on high-technology newly public firms' earnings conference calls. Br. J. Manag. (2022)
22. Wambsganss, T., Janson, A., Käser, T., Leimeister, J.M.: Improving students argumentation learning with adaptive self-evaluation nudging. Proc. ACM Hum.-Comput. Interact. **6**(CSCW2), 1–31 (2022)
23. Luque, L.B.: Giving Reasons: A Linguistic-pragmatic Approach to Argumentation Theory, vol. 20. Springer (2011)
24. Nussbaum, E.M., Kardash, C.M., Graham, S.E.: The effects of goal instructions and text on the generation of counterarguments during writing. J. Educ. Psychol. **97**(2), 157 (2005)
25. Qin, J., Karabacak, E.: The analysis of Toulmin elements in Chinese EFL university argumentative writing. System **38**(3), 444–456 (2010)
26. Karbach, J.: Using Toulmin's model of argumentation. J. Teach. Writ. **6**(1), 81–92 (1987)
27. Freeman, J.B.: Acceptable Premises: An Epistemic Approach to an Informal Logic Problem. Cambridge University Press, Cambridge (2004)
28. Freeman, J.B.: Dialectics and the Macrostructure of Arguments: A Theory of Argument Structure, vol. 10. Walter de Gruyter (2011)
29. Van Eemeren, F.H., Grootendorst, R., Johnson, R.H., Plantin, C., Willard, C.A.: Fundamentals of Argumentation Theory: A Handbook of Historical Backgrounds and Contemporary Developments. Routledge (2013)
30. Gass, R., Seiter, J.: Arguing, Reasoning, and Thinking Well. Routledge (2019)
31. Verheij, B.: Evaluating arguments based on Toulmin's scheme. Argumentation **19**, 347–371 (2005)
32. Freeman, J.B.: Argument Structure: Representation and Theory, vol. 18. Springer (2011)
33. Herman, T.: A Linguistic Revision of Toulmin's Layout of Arguments. Springer (2018)
34. Al-Zawqari, A., Al-Sharafi, A.G., Ahmed, M., Khader, M.M., Vandersteen, G.: Classifying persuasion modes in Arabic debates: a preliminary language model-based analysis. In: The Eighth International Conference on Arabic Language Processing, ICALP 2023, Rabat, Morocco, 19–20 April 2024. Springer (2024, accepted)
35. Killingsworth, M.J.: Rhetorical appeals: a revision. Rhetor. Rev. **24**(3), 249–263 (2005)
36. Offerdal, T.S., Just, S.N., Ihlen, O.: Public ethos in the pandemic rhetorical situation: strategies for building trust in authorities' risk communication. J. Int. Crisis Risk Commun. Res. **4**(2), 247–270 (2021)
37. Higgins, C., Walker, R.: Ethos, logos, pathos: strategies of persuasion in social/environmental reports. In: Accounting Forum, vol. 36, pp. 194–208. Elsevier (2012)

38. Oeppen Hill, J.H.: Logos, ethos, pathos and the marketing of higher education. J. Mark. High. Educ. **30**(1), 87–104 (2020)
39. Heath, R.L., Millar, D.P.: A rhetorical approach to crisis communication: management, communication processes, and strategic responses. In: Responding to Crisis, pp. 1–17. Routledge (2003)
40. Heath, R.L.: A rhetorical approach to zones of meaning and organizational prerogatives. Public Relat. Rev. **19**(2), 141–155 (1993)
41. Al-Rubai'ey, F., Al-Sharafi, A.G.: Ethos in covid-19 crisis communication: evidence from Oman. J. Risk Res. 1–16 (2023)
42. Brockriede, W., Ehninger, D.: Toulmin on argument: an interpretation and application. Q. J. Speech **46**(1), 44–53 (1960)
43. Khader, M.M., Al-Sharafi, A.G., Sioufy, H., Zaghouani, W., Al-Zawqari, A.: Munazarat 1.0: a corpus of Arabic competitive debates. In: The 6th Workshop on Open-Source Arabic Corpora and Processing Tools with Shared Tasks on Arabic LLMs Hallucination and Dialect to MSA Machine Translation (OSACT 2024)@ LREC 2024. European Language Resources Association (ELRA) (2024, accepted)
44. Khader, M.M.: A digital study on public speaking: NLP & arguments analysis of the first corpus of Arabic debates. Master's thesis, Hamad Bin Khalifa University (Qatar) (2020)
45. Burke, K.: A Rhetoric of Motives. Univresity of California Press, California (1969)
46. Suhartono, D., Gema, A.P., Winton, S., David, T., Fanany, M.I., Arymurthy, A.M.: Argument annotation and analysis using deep learning with attention mechanism in Bahasa Indonesia. J. Big Data **7**, 1–18 (2020)
47. Fairclough, N.: Critical discourse analysis. In: The Routledge Handbook of Discourse Analysis, pp. 11–22. Routledge (2023)
48. Blommaert, J., Bulcaen, C.: Critical discourse analysis. Annu. Rev. Anthropol. **29**(1), 447–466 (2000)
49. Koch, B.J.: Repetition in discourse: cohesion and persuasion in Arabic argumentative prose. Ph.D. thesis (1981)
50. Walker, M.A., Tree, J.E.F., Anand, P., Abbott, R., King, J.: A corpus for research on deliberation and debate. In: LREC, vol. 12, pp. 812–817, Istanbul, Turkey (2012)
51. Walton, D.: Argumentation Methods for Artificial Intelligence in Law. Springer (2005)
52. Walton, D.: Methods of Argumentation. Cambridge University Press, Cambridge (2013)
53. Klumpp, J.F.: Warranting arguments, the virtue of verb. In: Arguing on the Toulmin Model: New Essays in Argument Analysis and Evaluation, pp. 103–113. Springer (2006)
54. Koch, B.J.: Presentation as proof: the language of Arabic rhetoric. Anthropol. Linguist. 47–60 (1983)
55. Koch, B.J.: Arabic lexical couplets and the evolution of synonymy (1983)
56. Johnstone, B.: Repetition in Arabic Discourse: Paradigms, Syntagms, and the Ecology of Language, vol. 18. John Benjamins Publishing (1991)
57. Hatim, B.: A model of argumentation from Arabic rhetoric: Insights for a theory of text types. Br. J. Middle Eastern Stud. **17**(1), 47–54 (1990)
58. Hatim, B.: The pragmatics of argumentation in Arabic: the rise and fall of a text type. Text-Interdisc. J. Study Discourse **11**(2), 189–200 (1991)
59. Hatim, B.: Text politeness: a semiotic regime for a more interactive pragmatics. In: The Pragmatics of Translation, pp. 72–102 (1998)

Alkhalil Platform for Arabic Language Processing

Azzeddine Mazroui[1(✉)], Abdelhak Lakhouaja[1], Safae Berrichi[1], and Naoual Nassiri[2]

[1] LaRI Laboratory, Faculty of Sciences, Mohammed First University, Oujda, Morocco
Azze.mazroui@gmail.com

[2] Engineering and Sustainable Development Team, Ibn Zohr University, Dakhla, Morocco

Abstract. Morphosyntactic analyzers are pivotal in natural language processing, especially during preprocessing. Ensuring open access to these tools is crucial for fostering innovation and research in this field. This necessity is heightened for low-resource languages like Arabic, where available linguistic resources are scarce. In this article, we introduce the Alkhalil platform (http://alkhalil.oujda-nlp-team.net/), designed to provide researchers with a set of open-source morphosyntactic analysis tools for Arabic. Furthermore, researchers can download from this platform some labelled corpora that we have used during the training and testing phases of these tools.

Keywords: Morphosyntactic Analysis · Arabic Language · Labelled corpus

1 Introduction

The morphological complexity of Arabic poses challenges for analysis due to its rich structure [1]. With a system marked by derivation, inflection, and concatenation, it presents hurdles for natural language processing (NLP) tasks. Concatenation, where morphemes are strung together, is prevalent in Arabic and often leads to ambiguity. Single words can express entire sentences, making analysis difficult, as exemplified by the word وسيكتبونه/wsyktbwnh[1]/, which translates as "and they will write it". Moreover, the lack of diacritics in most texts creates even more ambiguity, as an undiacritized Arabic word can typically be segmented in over four different ways on average [2], adding to the ambiguity.

To address these challenges, morphosyntactic analyzers for Arabic were subsequently developed [3]. Their usage has steadily increased over time, as they are frequently utilized in the preprocessing stages of various NLP applications like machine translation, sentiment analysis, and search engines. These analyzers play a crucial role by identifying the word's base form, which can be the stem, lemma, or root. This process helps to disambiguate complex words and improve the overall accuracy of NLP tasks. The stem of a word is obtained by removing any attached clitics. These clitics are grammatical markers that carry additional information, such as tense or person. The lemma

[1] Buckwalter transliteration http://www.qamus.org/transliteration.htm.

B. Hdioud and S. L. Aouragh (Eds.): ICALP 2024, CCIS 2339, pp. 114–123, 2025.
https://doi.org/10.1007/978-3-031-79164-2_10

is the minimal form of the word carrying its main meaning and representing dictionary entries. For a verb, the lemma is the active form, conjugated in the past tense, third person singular, without clitics. For an adjective, the lemma is its masculine singular form without clitics, and for a noun, it's the masculine singular form (if possible) without clitics. Lastly, for a function word, the lemma is obtained by removing clitics. The root is an abstract entity composed of three or four letters, occasionally five.

Morphological analysis delves into the structure of words, breaking them down into their meaningful units. There are two primary approaches to this analysis, each with its own strengths [1]:

- Context-Free Analysis: This method examines words in isolation, without considering their surrounding context. While this straightforward approach allows the system to generate all potential morphological breakdowns, it may introduce ambiguity. For instance, when analyzing the word "play," which could function as both a noun and a verb, context-free analysis would present both possibilities.
- Context-Sensitive Analysis: In contrast, this approach considers the context in which words appear, aiming to provide a single, most likely morphological interpretation. By analyzing the surrounding words and sentence structure, the system can make more precise determinations. Consider the word "كتب"/ktb/, a contextual analysis would be crucial to determine its role in a sentence. Depending on its surrounding words and grammatical markers, "كتب"could function as a noun (like in the word كُتُبٌ/kutubN/ meaning "books") or a verb (like in the word كَتَبَ/kataba/ meaning "to write").

The choice between these analysis types often depends on the specific NLP task at hand.

In this paper, we present the Alkhalil platform for automatic processing of the Arabic language. Within this platform, we have incorporated an out-of-context morphosyntactic analyzer alongside several open-source in-context analysis tools, including a stemmer, lemmatizer, root extractor, POS tagger, and parser. The source codes for these tools are available for download directly from the platform. Additionally, the platform provides downloadable corpora, which are large collections of Arabic text used to train and test these tools. By providing both source code for these tools and access to the corpora, the Alkhalil platform empowers users to incorporate them into their applications.

2 Presentation of the Alkhalil Platform for Arabic Language Processing

Within the platform, we've incorporated numerous morphosyntactic analyzers developed through various projects by our NLP team at the computer science research laboratory of Mohammed First University. Users can download both the source code and the corresponding JARs or APIs of these analyzers directly from the platform. Additionally, the platform offers downloadable corpora used within its framework. In the following sections, we'll offer a summary of the platform's analyzers and available corpora.

2.1 Analyzers on the Platform

With the exception of the Alkhalil Morpho Sys out-of-context analyzer, all other analyzers installed on the platform conduct in-context analysis.

Context-Free Analysis

Alkhalil Morpho Sys: Alkhalil Morpho Sys is a powerful tool for analyzing Arabic words without considering their context [4]. Developed using Java, the analyzer offers all potential vowelized forms of a given word, considering both partial and complete diacritic presence. It offers for each vowelized form a wealth of information, including:

- The stem of the word;
- The clitics attached to the stem;
- The lemma;
- The root;
- The POS tag;
- The syntactic state (the case for nouns and the mode for verbs);
- The stem and lemma schemes.

Table 1 details the linguistic resources used to develop the Alkhalil Morpho Sys analyzer.

Table 1. Statistics of Linguistic Resources for Alkhalil Morpho Sys.

Linguistic resources	Size
Proclitics	67
Enclitics	68
Roots	7 716
Lemmas	155 238
Stems	3 126 354
Proper nouns	24955
Tool words	418

Context-Sensitive Analysis. Contextual analysis plays a critical role in Arabic language processing. It leverages the surrounding words in a sentence to pinpoint the most likely canonical form (the root, lemma or stem) for each individual word. This approach helps to resolve ambiguities that can arise due to the rich morphology of Arabic. The proposed system, as illustrated in Fig. 1, operates in two distinct stages. To identify each canonical form, we employed the same two-stage approach.

In the initial stage of the system, the goal is to identify the potential labels for each word within the sentence. To achieve this, we employed the Alkhalil Morpho Sys analyzer, which suggests potential labels for each word. Recall that this analyzer tackles words in isolation, considering all possible vowelized forms. The second stage

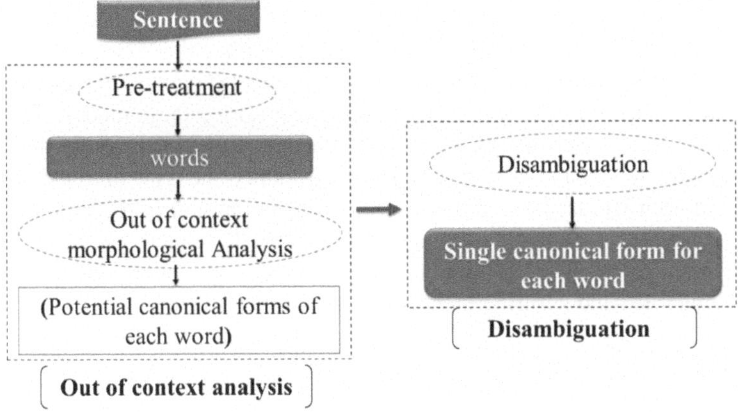

Fig. 1. Contextual analysis architecture.

addresses the challenge of ambiguity. With a list of potential labels for each word, the system needs to pinpoint the single most accurate one. We employed two methods for this disambiguation process. The initial one relies on a statistical method employing hidden Markov models, while the second method utilizes spline functions.

- Statistical Technique with Hidden Markov Models (HMMs): This approach leverages statistical analysis to identify the most likely label based on the surrounding words and their historical probabilities [5]. Given a sentence *Ph* composed of words $w_1, w_2, \ldots, w_k$, then the task of disambiguation involves finding the most probable labels $(e_1^*, e_2^*, \ldots, e_k^*)$ by searching through a list of solutions for the following problem:

$$\left(e_1^*, \ldots, e_k^*\right) = \underset{\substack{e_i^{j_i} \in L_i \\ 1 \leq i \leq k}}{\text{argmax}} \; Pr\left(e_1^{j_1}, \ldots, e_k^{j_k} | w_1, \ldots, w_k\right) \tag{1}$$

where $E_i = \{e_i^1, \ldots, e_i^{n_i}\}$ represents the list of potential labels for the word w_i as provided by the Alkhalil Morpho Sys analyzer during the initial analysis phase.

- Spline Function Approach: This method utilizes mathematical functions to analyze the relationships between words in the sentence [6]. For a potential list of labels $\left(e_1^{j_1}, \ldots, e_k^{j_k}\right)$ of the sentence words ($e_i^{j_i}$ is a potential label of the word w_i), we associate a quadratic spline $\Psi_{e_1^{j_1},\ldots,e_k^{j_k}}$ defined on the interval [1,k]. The list of labels $(e_1^*, e_2^*, \ldots, e_k^*)$ we ultimately choose will be the one that corresponds to the spline with the largest area under the curve. In mathematical terms, we can say this list solves the following problem:

$$\left(e_1^*, \ldots, e_k^*\right) = \underset{\substack{e_i^{j_i} \in L_i \\ 1 \leq i \leq k}}{argmax} \int_1^k \Psi_{e_1^{j_1},\ldots,e_k^{j_k}}(x)dx \tag{2}$$

For speedy resolution of Eqs. (1) and (2), we implemented a modified version of the Viterbi algorithm [7]. This powerful algorithm streamlines these calculations, ensuring faster processing times. The Nemlar labelled corpus [8], containing approximately 500,000 words, served as the dataset for training and testing these models. During the training and testing phases, we randomly partitioned 90% of the corpus for the learning phase, reserving the remaining 10% for testing. To address the issue of transitions (relationships between words) present in the test corpus but absent in the training corpus, we implemented the Absolute Discounting method [9]. This technique helps the models assign small probabilities to these unseen transitions, preventing them from being entirely disregarded and ensuring more robust performance.

Alkhalil Stemmer. We have explored the two distinct approaches to disambiguation: Hidden Markov Models (HMMs) and spline functions [6]. Both techniques aim to pinpoint the most likely stem label for each word within a sentence. To evaluate their effectiveness, we conducted a series of tests on the 10% Nemlar test corpus. The results, presented in Table 2, compare the two approaches in terms of accuracy (how well they identify the correct stem labels) and calculation speed (how many words they can analyze per second). This comparison allows us to assess the trade-off between precision and processing speed for each approach.

Table 2. A comparative analysis of the two approaches to stemmer development.

Model based on	Accuracy	Speed
Quadratic Splines	94.15%	290
HMM	92.35%	254

The spline-based model offers an efficiency advantage, achieving higher accuracy while maintaining fast processing times.

Alkhalil Lemmatizer. In developing the Alkhalil Lemmatizer analyzer, we followed a similar approach to that used in creating the Stemmer analyzer [6, 10]. The test results obtained from the test corpus are summarized in Table 3.

Table 3. A comparative analysis of the two approaches to lemmatizer development.

Model based on	Accuracy	Speed
Quadratic Splines	94,98%	296
HMM	94.45%	210

Just like with stemming, the lemmatizer based on splines outperforms the HMM-based approach in overall performance.

Alkhalil Root Extractor. We have extended the methodology used for the lemmatizer and stemmer analyzers to the Alkhalil Root Extractor analyzer [6, 11]. This powerful tool identifies the root tags of each word in a sentence. To evaluate its effectiveness, we carried out tests on a sample of 10% of the test corpus. Detailed results are presented in Table 4.

Table 4. A comparative analysis of the two approaches to root extractor development.

Model based on	Accuracy	Speed
Quadratic Splines	95.87%	301
HMM	94.12%	240

Comparing the performance of the two models, we conclude that the spline-based model achieves the best performance.

Alkhalil POS tagger. The Alkhalil POS tagger is equipped with a comprehensive tagset, specially designed to handle the agglutination phenomenon prevalent in Arabic text [12]. Agglutination refers to the formation of words by combining multiple morphemes. To address this complexity, the tagset boasts 82 labels, categorized into two groups:

- Simple Labels (22): These labels represent basic parts of speech like nouns, verbs, adjectives, etc.
- Compound Labels (60): These labels account for words formed by attaching clitics to stems.

This rich tagset empowers the Alkhalil POS tagger to provide a more nuanced and accurate analysis of Arabic text by considering the intricate ways words are built and modified. This analysis is very useful for further development of a parser.

The Alkhalil POS tagger employs a slightly adapted version of the approach depicted in Fig. 1. In the initial out-of-context analysis phase, the system augments the tags assigned to a word by the Alkhalil Morpho Sys analyzer with those found in the Nemlar corpus for the same word. For the disambiguation phase, we utilize a statistical approach based on Hidden Markov Models. We conducted the training phase on 90% of the randomly extracted Nemlar corpus, and the remaining 10% were used in the testing phase. We conducted a comparison on the same test corpus between our POS Tagger and those developed by Stanford [13] and Qatar Computing Research Institute (QCRI) [14]. The comparison outcomes are outlined in Table 5.

It's worth noting that the performance achieved by the Alkhalil POS Tagger significantly surpasses that of the other two POS taggers in terms of both accuracy and F-measure.

Syntactic Analysis: Alkhalil Parser. To address this complexity, the tagset boasts 82 labels, categorized into two groups: Drawing on prior comparisons between traditional Arabic grammar and modern linguistic theories, we've been able to pinpoint the unique features of the Arabic language. This rich grammatical tradition, along with its detailed annotations, has provided valuable insights in resolving syntactic ambiguities. We've learned how to leverage these linguistic characteristics to build a robust

Table 5. A Comparison between the three POS taggers.

Model based on	Stanford_POS	QCRI_POS	Alkhalil_POS
Accuracy	72.68	84.54	94.02
Precision	75.65	73.11	87.30
Recall	54.66	64.62	88.98
F-measure	63.46	68.60	88.13

lexico-semantic database. This database forms a cornerstone for our syntactic parser development approach.

The Alkhalil Parser offers a method for representing sentences, enabling the specification of their constituents and the syntactic relationships among them [15]. It begins by identifying core phrases such as noun phrases (including annexations), adjectival phrases, and prepositional phrases. Subsequently, it establishes syntactic dependencies that link the heads of these constituents.

The good performance achieved by this parser is largely due to the exploitation of the following characteristics of the Arabic language:

- The integration of the main phrase concept, derived from the widely studied theory of العمدة(AlEmdp) in Arabic linguistics, has been pivotal in syntactic sentence analysis. This concept has enabled the parser to effectively manage the diverse compositions of phrases resulting from the prevalent phenomenon of annexation in Arabic. Consequently, it has significantly reduced the number of potential segmentations, leading to more accurate syntactic analysis.
- The use of conventional rules of the Arabic language to detect and correct analysis errors.
- Extracting lexico-semantic relationships from untagged resources to resolve specific ambiguities.

The different stages of the parser are presented in Fig. 2.

While the lack of a labeled corpus prevented a formal evaluation of the Alkhalil parser, its performance on a sample sentence set suggests promise. This set specifically targeted common ambiguity scenarios in Arabic, and Alkhalil's analyses emerged as superior when compared to other parsers tested on the same data.

2.2 Corpora on the Platform

We integrated three corpora into the platform. These corpora played a crucial role in the development process, serving as valuable training and testing data for several of our analyzers.

Nemlar Corpus. The Nemlar corpus is a valuable collection of Arabic texts initially annotated by the Egyptian company RDI on behalf of the NEMLAR consortium which holds the rights. It consists of approximately 500,000 Arabic words distributed across

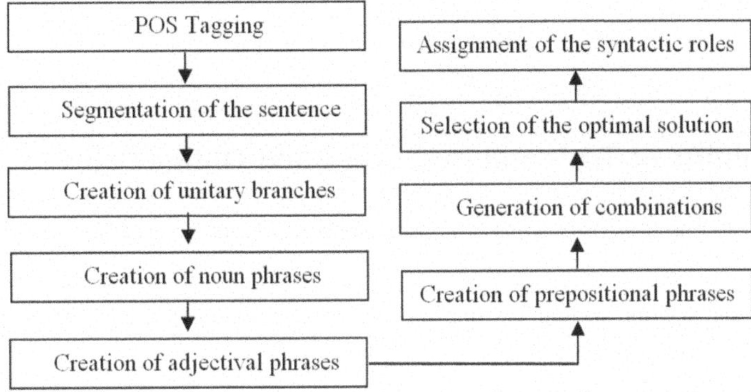

Fig. 2. Architecture of the Alkhalil Parser architecture.

489 files, spanning 13 different domains. Our team meticulously cleaned and enhanced the corpus by adding lemma label. Additionally, we have converted the corpus into the widely-used XML format, and securing approval from the NEMLAR consortium to make this valuable resource publicly available [8]. Each word in the Nemlar corpus is accompanied by the following labels:

- The vowelled form of the word;
- Its lemma;
- Its stem;
- The clitics attached to the stem;
- Its POS tag;
- Its grammatical category;
- Its pattern.

AL Mus'haf Corpus. The AL Mus'haf corpus is the Quranic corpus annotated using a semi-automatic method [16]. We utilized the morphosyntactic analyzer AlKhalil Morpho Sys on the corpus's words, followed by manual verification to ensure accurate annotation. As a result, every word within the AL Mus'haf corpus is enriched with various morphosyntactic details, including:

- The vowelled form of the word;
- Its root;
- Its lemma;
- Its stem;
- The clitics attached to the stem;
- The vowelled patterns of the stem and lemma.

OSIAN Corpus. OSIAN is an impressive collection of international Arabic news articles, meticulously compiled from 32 leading Arab newspapers worldwide [17]. This corpus comprises approximately 3.5 million articles containing roughly 1 billion words across more than 37 million sentences. To ensure clarity and organization, each article is enriched with detailed metadata, including the source publication and the date it was extracted.

3 Availability of Tools and Resources, and Online Demo

Each tool on the platform (http://alkhalil.oujda-nlp-team.net/) offers downloadable resources:

- Source code: This allows examining the tool's inner workings and potentially modifying it for your needs.
- JAR file: This file is specifically for Java projects and provides all the necessary components to run the tool.
- Language-agnostic API: This integration layer lets incorporate the tool's functionalities into other projects regardless of the programming language you're using.

The platform also provides a demo to try these tools with short texts.

4 Conclusion and Perspectives

This article introduces the Alkhalil platform, designed for Arabic language processing. Within this platform, we've incorporated the context-free morphosyntactic analyzer Alkhalil Morpho Sys, alongside various open-source morphosyntactic analyzers. These analyzers leverage word context in the analysis process, and include a stemmer, lemmatizer, root extractor, POS tagger, and parser. Additionally, the platform includes labelled corpora utilized during the training and testing phases of these analyzers. Both the source codes of these tools and the various corpora are freely available for download on the platform.

In the future, we plan to add more tools to the platform. More precisely, we plan to integrate a diacritization system, as well as new, more efficient versions of the tools already present, developed using deep learning approaches. Additionally, we intend to enhance the collection of labelled corpora by incorporating additional datasets.

Acknowledgment. The development of this platform and some of its integrated tools is a product of collaborative projects between the NLP team at Mohammed First University's Computer Science Research Laboratory and the Arab League Educational, Cultural and Scientific Organization (ALECSO). We are grateful for their support.

References

1. Habash, N.Y.: Introduction to Arabic natural language processing. Morgan & Claypool Publishers (2010)
2. Boudchiche, M., Mazroui, A.: Evaluation of the ambiguity caused by the absence of diacritical marks in Arabic texts: statistical study. In: Proceedings of the 5th International Conference on Information & Communication Technology and Accessibility (ICTA) (pp. 1–6). IEEE (2015)

3. Pasha, A., Al-badrashiny, M., Diab, M., El Kholy, A., Eskander, R., Habash, N., et al.: MADAMIRA: a fast, comprehensive tool for morphological analysis and disambiguation of Arabic. In: Proceedings of the 9th Language Resources and Evaluation Conference (LREC'14), pp. 1094–1101 (2014)
4. Boudchiche, M., Mazroui, A., Bebah, M.O.A.O., Lakhouaja, A., Boudlal, A.: AlKhalil Morpho Sys 2: a robust Arabic morpho-syntactic analyzer. J. King Saud Univ.-Comput. Inf. Sci. **29**(2), 141–146 (2017)
5. Chennoufi, A., Mazroui, A.: Morphological, syntactic and diacritics rules for automatic diacritization of Arabic sentences. J. King Saud Univ. – Comput. Inf. Sci. **29**(2), 156–163 (2017)
6. Boudchiche, M., Mazroui, A.: Spline functions for Arabic morphological disambiguation. Appl. Comput. Inform. (2020). https://doi.org/10.1016/j.aci.2020.02.002
7. Neuhoff, D.L.: The Viterbi algorithm as an aid in text recognition. In: Proceedings of the IEEE Transaction on Information Theory, pp. 222–226 (1975)
8. Boudchiche, M., Mazroui, A.: Enrichment of the Nemlar corpus by the lexical label lemma. In: Proceedings on Arabic Language Resources for NLP: Construction, Standardization, Management and Exploitation, Rabat, Morocco (2015)
9. Ney, H., Essen, U.: On smoothing techniques for bigram-based natural language modelling. [Proceedings] ICASSP 91: 1991 International Conference on Acoustics, Speech, and Signal Processing, vol. 2. IEEE, pp. 825–828 (1991). https://doi.org/10.1109/ICASSP.1991.150464
10. Boudchiche, M., Mazroui, A.: A hybrid approach for Arabic lemmatization. Int. J. Speech Technol. **22**(3), 563–573 (2019)
11. Boudchiche, M., Mazroui, A.: Improving the Arabic root extraction by using the quadratic splines. In: Proceeding of the International Conference on Intelligent Systems and Computer Vision, Fez, Morocco (2018)
12. Ababou, N., Mazroui, A.: A hybrid Arabic POS tagging for simple and compound morphosyntactic tags. Int. J. Speech Technol. **19**, 289–302 (2016)
13. Toutanova, K., Klein, D., Manning, C.D., Singer, Y.: Feature-rich part-of-speech tagging with a cyclic dependency network. In: Proceedings of the 2003 conference of the North American chapter of the Association for Computational Linguistics on Human Language Technology, vol. 1, pp. 173–180. Association for Computational Linguistics (2003)
14. Abdelali, A., Darwish, K., Durrani, N., Mubarak, H.: Farasa: a fast and furious segmenter for Arabic. In: Proceedings of the 2016 Conference of the North American Chapter of the Association for Computational Linguistics: Demonstrations, pp. 11–16 (2016)
15. Ababou, N., Mazroui, A., Belehbib, R.: From extended chunking to dependency parsing using traditional Arabic grammar. Lang. Resour. Eval. **57**(3), 1011–1043 (2023)
16. Zeroual, I., Lakhouaja, A.: A new Quranic Corpus rich in morphosyntactical information. Int. J. Speech Technol. **19**, 339–346 (2016)
17. Zeroual, I., Goldhahn, D., Eckart, T., Lakhouaja, A.: OSIAN: open source international Arabic news corpus-preparation and integration into the CLARIN-infrastructure. In: Proceedings of the Fourth Arabic Natural Language Processing Workshop, pp. 175–182 (2019)

Advancements in Deep Learning for Arabic Language Processing: Generation, Translation, and QA

Exploring Semantic Hadith Overlap Across Topics

Devi G. Kurup[1(✉)], Amina Daoud[1], Jens Schneider[1], Wajdi Zaghouani[2(✉)], Saeed Mohd H. M. Al Marri[3], Hamada R. H. Al-Absi[1], and Younss Ait Mou[1]

[1] College of Science and Engineering, Hamad Bin Khalifa University, Doha, Qatar
{dkurup,aminadaoud,jeschneider,haalabsi,ymou}@hbku.edu.qa

[2] Northwestern University in Qatar, Doha, Qatar
wajdi.zaghouani@northwestern.edu

[3] College of Shariah and Islamic Studies, Qatar University, Doha, Qatar
saealmarri@qu.edu.qa

Abstract. Semantic sentence similarity measures the degree of resemblance between multiple sentences. This similarity is a foundational element in information retrieval, machine translation, etc. This paper focuses on natural language processing techniques to analyze the semantic similarity in Hadiths, which are significant religious texts in Islam. Our objective is to investigate the extent of semantiv overlap between Hadiths across various topics, with the aim to provide insights into the cohesion and interconnectedness of Hadiths. We use AraVec and GPT embeddings to represent Hadiths numerically, followed by UMAP (Uniform Manifold Approximation & Projection) to project these embeddings to 2D. The projection serves to visually interpret the relationships between Hadiths, facilitating a deeper understanding of content and semantic interrelations. Our results unveil semantic clusters and connections within Hadiths, contributing to the exploration of Islamic textual heritage through modern computational methodologies. This study suggests that GPT outperforms AraVec, providing a more advanced representation that discerns intricate semantic relationships and subtle nuances within the Hadiths.

Keywords: Hadith · Hadith Corpus · Semantic relatedness · Arabic Natural Language Processing · AraVec & GPT · UMAP

1 Introduction

According to Islamic tradition, a Hadith refers to the recorded sayings and actions of Prophet Muhammad, peace be upon him (pbuh). This literature is considered as the second major source of religious law and moral guidance after the Qur'an [1]. Hadith are composed of two key components: Sanad (سند), the chain

D. G. Kurup and A. Daoud—Joint first authors.

B. Hdioud and S. L. Aouragh (Eds.): ICALP 2024, CCIS 2339, pp. 127–138, 2025.
https://doi.org/10.1007/978-3-031-79164-2_11

of narrators who report, and a matn (متن), the actions of Prophet Mohammed (pbuh) [2]. Hadith studies have been a popular subject for Islamic scholars and researchers, who seek to analyze their contents and uncover profound wisdom! [3]. We aim at discerning shared principles and values, unearthing underlying connections and dependencies. These discoveries could greatly aid scholars and individuals seeking a comprehensive understanding of Hadiths. Our approach measures similarity even across takhreej (clusters of Hadith with the same matn but different sanads) and topics to enable intelligent queries and searches in the setting of a knowledge base system. As data, e.g., commentaries and explanations, expand rapidly, it is increasingly vital to provide intelligent tools to extract knowledge from Islamic resources to discern between authentic and counterfeit information. Traditional methods such as manual analysis and interpretation is often time-consuming, labor-intensive, and susceptible to errors [4]. Thus, natural language processing (NLP) stands out as an excellent candidate to process texts at scale, in particular for Hadith research. NLP has the potential to automate the workflow of scholars. Tasks such as disambiguating the names of narrators, visualizing the propagation of a Hadith through narration trees, and even offering initial assessments of a Hadith's authenticity can benefit from NLP techniques [3]. By leveraging computational linguistics and machine learning, NLP techniques can aid Hadith scientists in more efficient and effective processing, analysis, and understanding of Hadith texts. This union of NLP and Hadith studies unveils numerous possibilities, revolutionizing how researchers interact with these sacred texts and expanding the knowledge obtainable from them.

Contributions. We present a study of semantic overlaps between Hadiths that goes beyond clustering into takhreej. Our method is fully automated and unsupervised, offering ease of use and a reduced need for manual labeling of data. We also demonstrate that similarities based on GPT embeddings, for which Arabic is a relatively low-resource language, can outperform LLMs that have been designed specifically for Arabic such as AraVec or AraBERT. We attribute that to GPT's large number of model parameters and extensive training time. We therefore believe this work to be an important step for information retrieval systems with a potential to suggest further readings to users.

Organization. The rest of the paper is organized as follows. In the next section, we provide a background of linguistics (cf. Sect. 2). We then review related work, with a focus on Arabic NLP. We then describe the Hadith data that has been used, the preprocessing applied to it and the methodology (cf. Sect. 4) followed by a discussion of our results (cf. Sect. 5) before concluding and providing potential directions for future research (cf. Sect. 6).

2 Linguistic Background

Linguistic Characteristics of Hadith Texts. Hadith literature, composed in classical Arabic, exhibits unique linguistic features like a specialized lexicon, formulaic expressions (e.g., قال رسول الله - "The Prophet said"), and syntactic structures distinct from modern Arabic. Grasping these traits is crucial for effective semantic analysis [5].

Embedding Models and Linguistic Nuances. The AraVec model captures semantic relationships based on word co-occurrence within a window, but its static representation might not fully grasp contextual nuances of Hadith texts. In contrast, GPT's transformer architecture excels in contextual understanding, capturing subtleties like different usages of صلاة (prayer) in varied contexts [6].

Semantic Similarity and Linguistic Contexts. Analyzing semantic similarity through embeddings involves understanding polysemy (e.g., نية (intention) having multiple meanings) and synonymy, which is critical for determining semantic similarity. GPT's dynamic embeddings offer a nuanced understanding of such terms in varied contexts compared to AraVec's static embeddings [7].

Semantic Overlap Across Topics. Despite addressing diverse topics, Hadiths exhibit semantic overlap reflecting unified Islamic principles and values. For example, لا تحقرن من المعروف شيئا (Do not belittle any good deed) and الحسنات والسيئات إن الله كتب (Verily, Allah has recorded the good and the bad deeds) converge on the significance of actions, demonstrating semantic linkage captured by embeddings [8].

Common Lexical and Conceptual Foundations. Certain recurring words (إِيمَان - faith), phrases, and concepts permeate through various Hadith topics, creating an interconnected web of meanings and associations. For example, الْمُؤْمِنُ بِالطَّعَّانِ...لَيْسَ and ...لَا يَزْنِي الزَّانِي share the concept of "faith" despite addressing different themes [5].

Contextual and Pragmatic Considerations. While lexical and conceptual overlaps contribute to interconnectedness, contextual and pragmatic factors also determine meaning nuances. GPT's contextual embeddings account for linguistic context, capturing subtle differences like من غش فليس منا referring to deception towards the Muslim community versus من غشنا فليس منا having a more general scope [7].

Linguistic Interpretation of UMAP Projections. The UMAP projections visually represent semantic relationships, revealing how different topics or themes cluster together based on linguistic and thematic overlap, offering insights into the interconnections within Hadith literature [6].

3 Arabic Natural Language Processing

NLP has been applied to different languages, including Arabic [9]. ANLP (Arabic Natural Language Processing) is a major research challenge. This is both due to the complex and rich grammar of Arabic, as well as the fact that Arabic is the most-spoken semitic language. Arabic is a complex language, with many dialects. Working with Arabic text in NLP projects, there are at least four unique challenges [9].

1. Orthographic Ambiguity: The form of characters and spelling of words can vary depending on their context.
2. Morphological Richness: The same verb can have thousands of different forms.
3. Dialectal Variation: There are many dialects of Arabic and there are big differences between them.
4. Orthographic Inconsistency: Since Arabic is a phonetic language, there can be different ways to write the same word when writing in dialectal Arabic, for which there is no agreed-upon standard.

These four different characteristics of Arabic all contribute to data sparsity, with estimates that a full NLP vocbulary would contain millions of words [9]. For example, a single verb in Arabic can have up to 5,400 forms [10]. Before dealing with Arabic words or sentences, texts are usually pre-processed using stemming or lemmatization to mitigate such challenges [11]. To this end, full Arabic text processing tool kits have been developed over the decade, e.g., FARASA by Qatar Computing Research Institute (QCRI) [12], Stanford's Arabic Parser and Word Segmenter [13], etc. In this work, we are concerned only with classical Arabic and a very specific vocabulary and grammar subset. We therefore chose to specialize pre-existing and more general language processing tools to this task to achieve better accuracy, robustness, and reliability.

4 Materials and Methods

4.1 Hadith Dataset

We have chosen the LK-Hadith-Corpus [14] because it provides enough data for our NLP tasks until our work in progress, the completion of a research-specific and clean data set, is completed. In this paper, we consider only the Arabic Hadiths from Sahih al-Bukhari [15], a collection of Hadith compiled by Imam Muhammad al-Bukhari (died 256 AH/870 AD) (pbuh). This collection is considered the most authentic by the majority of the Muslim world and contains over 7,500 hadiths (with repetitions), organized into 97 books, mostly by topic.

4.2 Hadith Data Preprocessing

We first extracted the Arabic matns from the LK-Hadith Corpus [14], specifically from the Sahih Al-Bukhari collection [15]. A new subset was created, focusing on two significant topics: كتاب الصلاة (Prayers, "Salat") and كتاب الوضوء (Ablutions "Wudu'"). The goal was to analyze potential overlaps within these topics, with plans to expand the scope to other relevant topics over time. The subset consisted of 282 Hadiths, 168 from كتاب الصلاة and 114 from كتاب الوضوء . We then follow pre-processing with data cleaning to reduce noise and gain reliable insights. General Arabic stopwords defined in the NLTK Arabic library,

Non-Arabic characters, digits, whitespaces, and tashkeel (diacritics indicating Arabic pronunciation) were removed. Post-cleaning, the araby.tokenize() tokenizer from the Python PyArabic package split the corpus into words, with only words longer than three characters retained. Figure 1 shows preprocessing steps that were applied to the LK Hadith dataset.

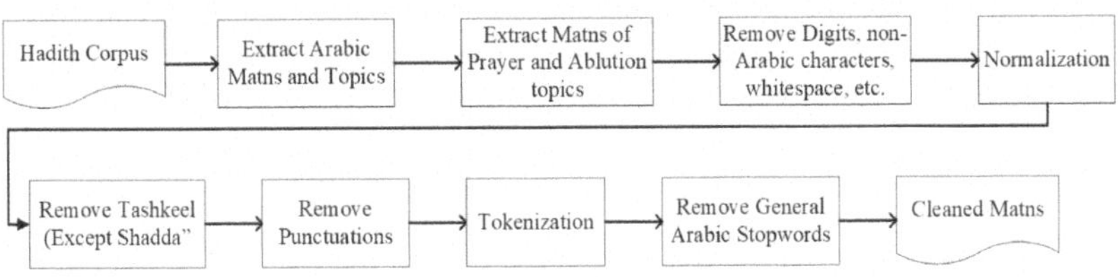

Fig. 1. Hadith Data Preprocessing.

4.3 Methods

Our approach combines text embeddings generated using AraVec [16] and Generative Pre-trained Transformers (GPT) [17] and dimensionality reduction using Uniform Manifold Approximation and Projection (UMAP) [18]. The rationale is to provide a unsupervised analytics pipeline that allows for visual inspection of the semantic overlap of Hadiths across different topics. At the beginning of our pipeline stands a well-structured corpus of Hadith literature which encompasses the Hadith texts sourced from the six canonical collections. Although there are several studies in the Hadith literature, the vast and diverse nature of the texts combined with their inconsistent structure presents challenges in preparing such a well-structured corpus [14].

We use a two-step methodology for this task. Initially, we transformed the matn in the Hadiths into to a vector space using either AraVec [16] or OpenAI's GPT embedding [17] methods. Subsequently, we projected the embedded Hadiths onto a two-dimensional UMAP visualization [18]. We also carried out a comparative analysis of the results from both embedding methods, aiming to identify the more effective approach. We will then use this analysis to guide our choice of the best embedding model for future work for developing a knowledge base system. AraVec, an Arabic adaptation of word2vec, is an open-source initiative offering pre-trained distributed word representations, or word embeddings. Its primary purpose is to equip the Arabic NLP research community with freely accessible and potent word embedding models. These models prove invaluable for several NLP tasks involving Arabic text analysis, allowing researchers and practitioners to harness the advantages of word embeddings in their Arabic language applications. The generative pre-trained transformer (GPT) is a cutting-edge language model created and maintained by OpenAI. As part of the neural network models' family, it utilizes a transformer architecture based on a self-attention mechanism [19]. This feature enables the model to capture relationships between words or tokens within a text. GPT represents a significant breakthrough in artificial intelligence, underpinning generative AI applications such as

ChatGPT. GPT was trained on vast online text data, learned word semantics, grammar, and patterns, enriching its language understanding and generation abilities. OpenAI also provides text embedding models, converting text strings into embedding vectors, or vectorized data preserving content meaning—similar input is expected to produce similar embeddings. These models, which input text strings and output embedding vectors, assess text relatedness effectively. Closer distances indicate higher relatedness, and vice versa. These embeddings benefit search, clustering, recommendations, anomaly detection, diversity measurement, and classification. To generate an embedding, input the text to the embeddings API endpoint with the chosen model ID, such as "text-embedding-ada-002". The resulting API [20] provides the necessary embedding for subsequent processes. Overall, GPT's language modeling advances and OpenAI's text embedding models have significantly transformed AI applications, offering superior text generation, understanding, and analysis capabilities. UMAP [18] is a powerful, scalable dimensionality reduction algorithm and data analysis tool. It competes well with advanced methods like t-distributed stochastic neighbor embedding (t-SNE) [21] and is popular for unsupervised clustering. UMAP addresses the "curse of dimensionality" by identifying clusters in high-dimensional space and retaining both intra- and inter-cluster distances (unlike t-SNE which can struggle with inter-cluster distances) in lower-dimensional embeddings. In addition, it matches the speed of Principal Component Analysis (PCA) [22], making it significantly faster than t-SNE. Figure 2 shows the workflow that has been followed in this study for semantic overlap of Hadith across topics.

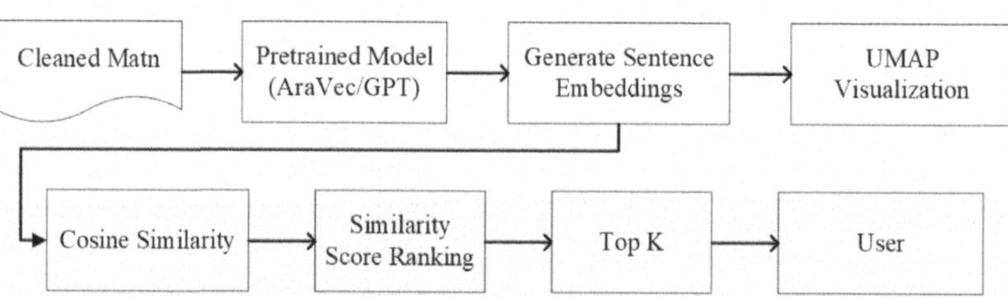

Fig. 2. Workflow adopted in this study.

5 Results and Discussion

The cleaned corpus totaled 60,311 words from the subset covering the chosen topics from the Sahih Al-Bukhari collection, with a vocabulary of 35 unique words. The longest single matn in the subset had 236 words. Figure 3 shows a word cloud of matns for the topics كتاب الصلاة and كتاب الوضوء . As can be seen, several terms are closely linked to ablution and prayer, such as الصلاة (prayer), المسجد (mosque), الكعبة (Kaaba), البيت (house), الجنة (paradise), القبلة (qibla), فتوضأ (perform ablution), فغسل وجهه (washing the face), ركعتين ركعتين (two units of prayer), الوضوء (ablution),

Fig. 3. Word cloud for topics كتاب الصلاة and كتاب الوضوء .

وجهه ثلاثا (wiping the face three times), فمسح (wiping), والعصر (Asr prayer), and المغرب (maghrib prayer). These terms are essential within the context of ablution and prayer, representing crucial elements, actions, and locations related to these practices. In Fig. 3, some words are repeated with different weights. This is due to the collocations, combination of words that frequently occur together and convey specific meanings or cultural connotations. These combinations often consist of multi-word expressions or phrase that are deeply rooted in Arabic culture, religion, literature and everyday communication. For example صلى الله عليه و سلم ("peace be up on him") is a phrase or a multi word expressions and the word cloud generator will attempt to identify and include these collocations in the word cloud. In the future, we plan to detect these collocations and remedy this effect. After preprocessing the matn in the data set, the subsequent step involved embedding the matn using the AraVec and GPT models, ensuring that similar documents clustered closely. These embeddings could be utilized for other tasks such as corpus visualization or running clustering algorithms like KMeans or DBSCAN [23]. To check sentence overlap and compare the mentioned embedding models, we initially embedded the matn using the AraVec model. We loaded the AraVec model with the Python "gensim" module to generate high-dimensional vector word embeddings, placing semantically similar words close to each other in the vector space. We computed sentence embeddings by averaging word embeddings in each sentence. We embedded the matn using the GPT model by submitting each matn to the embeddings API endpoint with the embedding model ID. Specifically, we used the second-generation ada model (text-embedding-ada-002) from OpenAI GPT's four base embedding models (davinci, curie, ada, and babbage). This model, simpler, cheaper, and faster, produces 1,024 dimensions and outperforms older models on text search, code search, and sentence similarity tasks. After obtaining the data set's matn embeddings, we saved the data set and embeddings in a CSV file for future use. The next step involved

Table 1. High similarity between matns using GPT and AraVec.

№	Matn	Topic	GPT	AraVec
1	خَرَجَ رَسُولُ اللَّهِ صلى الله عليه وسلم بِالْهَاجِرَةِ فَصَلَّى بِالْبَطْحَاءِ الظُّهْرَ وَالْعَصْرَ رَكْعَتَيْنِ، وَنَصَبَ بَيْنَ يَدَيْهِ عَنَزَةً، وَتَوَضَّأَ، فَجَعَلَ النَّاسُ يَتَمَسَّحُونَ بِوَضُوئِهِ.	كتاب الصلاة	0.95	0.91
2	خَرَجَ عَلَيْنَا رَسُولُ اللَّهِ صلى الله عليه وسلم بِالْهَاجِرَةِ، فَأُتِيَ بِوَضُوءٍ فَتَوَضَّأَ، فَجَعَلَ النَّاسُ يَأْخُذُونَ مِنْ فَضْلِ وَضُوئِهِ فَيَتَمَسَّحُونَ بِهِ، فَصَلَّى النَّبِيُّ صلى الله عليه وسلم الظُّهْرَ رَكْعَتَيْنِ وَالْعَصْرَ رَكْعَتَيْنِ، وَبَيْنَ يَدَيْهِ عَنَزَةٌ.	كتاب الوضوء	0.91	0.91

Table 2. Low similarity between matns using GPT and AraVec.

№	Matn	Topic	GPT	AraVec
1	أَنَّ زَيْدَ بْنَ خَالِدٍ، أَرْسَلَهُ إِلَى أَبِي جُهَيْمٍ يَسْأَلُهُ مَاذَا سَمِعَ مِنْ، رَسُولِ اللَّهِ صلى الله عليه وسلم فِي الْمَارِّ بَيْنَ يَدَىِ الْمُصَلِّي فَقَالَ أَبُو جُهَيْمٍ قَالَ رَسُولُ اللَّهِ صلى الله عليه وسلم لَوْ يَعْلَمُ الْمَارُّ بَيْنَ يَدَىِ الْمُصَلِّي مَاذَا عَلَيْهِ لَكَانَ أَنْ يَقِفَ أَرْبَعِينَ خَيْرًا لَهُ مِنْ أَنْ يَمُرَّ بَيْنَ يَدَيْهِ . قَالَ أَبُو النَّضْرِ لاَ أَدْرِي أَقَالَ أَرْبَعِينَ يَوْمًا أَوْ شَهْرًا أَوْ سَنَةً.	كتاب الصلاة	0.76	0.76
2	سَمِعْتُ النَّبِيَّ صلى الله عليه وسلم يَقُولُ `` لاَ يَتَوَضَّأُ رَجُلٌ فَيُحْسِنُ وُضُوءَهُ، وَيُصَلِّي الصَّلاَةَ إِلاَّ غُفِرَ لَهُ مَا بَيْنَهُ وَبَيْنَ الصَّلاَةِ حَتَّى يُصَلِّيَهَا ". قَالَ عُرْوَةُ الآيَةُ إِنَّ الَّذِينَ يَكْتُمُونَ مَا أَنْزَلْنَا مِنَ الْبَيِّنَاتِ.	كتاب الوضوء	0.75	0.79

fitting the UMAP embedding to the matn embeddings from both models and examining the resulting two-dimensional embedding. We used default values for UMAP's parameters (min_dist=0.1, n_neighbors=15, and metric="cosine"). UMAP's min_dist parameter defines the minimum distance between points in the low-dimensional embedding space, controlling the visualization's granularity. Generally, these values balance global structure preservation and local relationship capture. Adjusting the min_dist value can fine-tune visualization based on data characteristics. In UMAP, we selected the cosine metric, which measures vector similarity or dissimilarity by computing the angle between them, especially beneficial for high-dimensional or vector-represented text data. For two points $\mathbf{x}, \mathbf{y}$ embedded onto a unit hyper-sphere, maximizing the cosine norm is equivalent to minimizing the Euclidean distance, but is faster to compute:

$$(\mathbf{x}-\mathbf{y})^2 = \underbrace{\mathbf{x}^T\mathbf{x}}_{=1} + \underbrace{\mathbf{y}^T\mathbf{y}}_{=1} - 2\langle \mathbf{x}, \mathbf{y} \rangle = 2\left(1 - \underbrace{\langle \mathbf{x}, \mathbf{y} \rangle}_{\cos \angle \mathbf{x}, \mathbf{y}}\right), \tag{1}$$

Common alternatives include Manhattan, and correlation distances. The chosen metric depends on data nature and analysis requirements. In our case, to identify the most similar matns from given topics, the cosine metric best computed the distance. We perform ranking followed by a selection of the top-k (e.g., k = 10) most similar matns. This allows users to select further readings from suggested Hadith. Tables 1 and 2 show top two high and low similar matns (respectively) using cosine similarity for the given matn ``خَرَجَ عَلَيْنَا رَسُولُ اللَّهِ صلى الله عليه وسلم بِالْهَاجِرَةِ، فَأُتِيَ بِوَضُوءٍ فَتَوَضَّأَ فَصَلَّى بِنَا الظُّهْرَ وَالْعَصْرَ وَبَيْنَ يَدَيْهِ عَنَزَةٌ، وَالْمَرْأَةُ وَالْحِمَارُ يَمُرُّونَ مِنْ وَرَائِهَا."

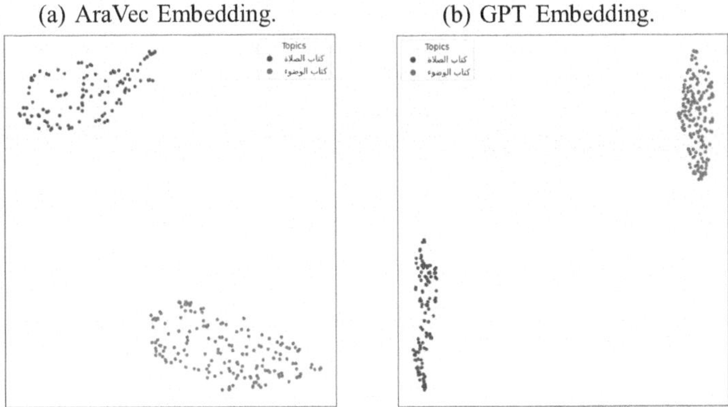

Fig. 4. Supervised UMAP reduction to 2D AraVec vs. GPT embeddings.

UMAP's n_neighbors controls the number of neighboring points used to construct the neighborhood graph of the manifold in the high-dimensional space (perplexity) and affects local structure preservation and the low-dimensional embedding's overall fidelity. Higher values provide a more global data view, capturing broader relationships between high-dimensional space points. Conversely, lower values focus on more local relationships and finer data details. The appropriate value depends on data set characteristics and the desired embedding granularity. Generally, smaller data sets may require a lower n_neighbors value (5–50), while larger data sets may benefit from a higher values (50–200). Different values are often tested to identify the setting that best represents the data's underlying structure in the low-dimensional embedding. Figure 4 shows the resulting UMAP embeddings for AraVec and GPT embeddings.

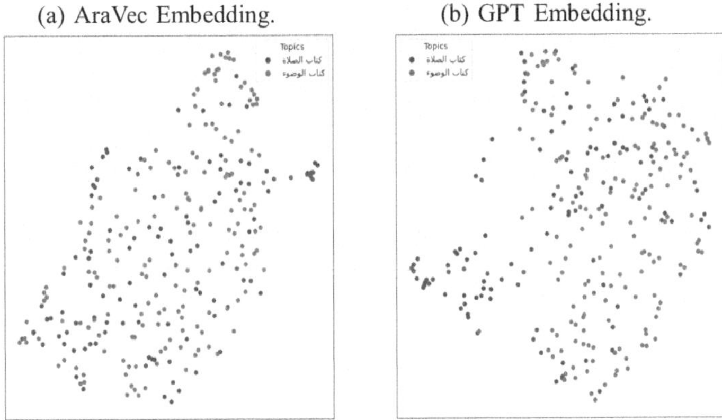

Fig. 5. Unsupervised UMAP reduction to 2D of AraVec vs. GPT embeddings.

Figure 5 shows the UMAP visualization of *unsupervised* clustering, that means clustering based only on the similarity of the matns in the data set. Figure 4 presents a *supervised* UMAP, exploiting both the matns' embeddings as well as their class labels. Since supervised UMAP uses class labels directly in the dimension reduction process, the result is a low-dimensional projection that not only retains the intrinsic data structure but also the class information [24]. In contrast, Fig. 5 depicts an unsupervised UMAP projection without class labels. The fitting and transformation occur solely due to the data's intrinsic structure, enabling the algorithm to reveal patterns and relationships without prior class data [24]. From this result, it is evident that there is significant overlap in the matns, as suggested by the similarity scores. This figure allows identification of Hadith clusters with substantial semantic overlap, signifying a specific interrelation between prayer and ablution topics. Furthermore, it is apparent from these figures that GPT embeddings surpass AraVec embeddings. GPT embeddings deliver a superior data representation, yielding more insightful clusters and enhanced visualization. This can be seen in Fig. 4 by the more localized clusters, and implies that the GPT embedding model more effectively discerns semantic relationships and subtleties within the Hadiths than the AraVec model.

6 Conclusion and Future Work

The comparison drawn from these visual representations indicates the superiority of GPT embeddings over AraVec embeddings. The evidence suggests that GPT embeddings capture a more better and refined representation of the data, resulting in the creation of clusters that offer deeper insights and a more enriched visual interpretation. In particular, GPT clusters in Fig. 4 show better localization and even the unsupervised case (cf. Fig. 5) shows better topic separation to the left of the figure. These outcome suggests that the GPT embedding model outperforms the AraVec model in its ability to accurately discern intricate semantic relationships and subtle nuances present within the Hadiths. In the future, we will continue our ongoing efforts together with Islamic scholars to proof-read and cleanse the data, and to obtain an authoritative ground truth of similarities between Hadith. This goes beyond the clustering of takhreej, which offers variations in the chains of narrators of the same Hadith. At the same time, we are exploring how textual similarity measures, such as presented in this work, can be used for presenting recommended Hadiths to readers, primarily laypersons, who seek topic-based guidance from the Hadith. We will make the resulting data set containing the embeddings available to the public for further academic dissemination in the future.

Acknowledgment. This work has been supported by Qatar National Research Fund (QNRF), now known as the Qatar Research Development and Innovation (QRDI) Council, under grant number (NPRP13S-0129-200194).

References

1. Sulisto, B., Ramadhan, A., Abdurachmal, E., Zarlis, M., Trisetyarso, A.: The utilization of machine learning on studying hadith in Islam: a systematic literature review. Educ. Inf. Technol. (2023). https://doi.org/10.1007/s10639-023-12008-9
2. Mughal, M.A.: Ibtidā' Al-sanad/اِبْتِدَاء اَلسَّنَد [Beginning of the chain of narrators of Ḥadīth] [a term of science of Ḥadīth]. SSRN (2016). https://ssrn.com/abstract=2717633
3. Azmi, A., Al-Qabbany, A., Hussain, A.: Computational and natural language processing based studies of hadith literature: a survey. Artif. Intell. Rev. **52**, 1369–1414 (2019). https://doi.org/10.1007/s10462-019-09692-w
4. Najeeb, M.: Towards innovative system for hadith isnad processing. Int. J. Comput. Trends Technol. **18**, 257–259 (2014). https://doi.org/10.14445/22312803/IJCTT-V18P154
5. Al-Azawei, R.: Linguistic features of hadith texts for authenticity: a machine learning approach. Int. J. Islamic Arabic Stud. **9**(3), 1–10 (2019). ISSN 2520-2218. https://doi.org/10.1186/s40092-019-00204-6
6. Al-Azawei, R.: A comprehensive study on the use of hadith in learning Arabic as a second language. Int. J. Islamic Arabic Stud. **10**(1), 1–13 (2020). ISSN 2520-2218. https://doi.org/10.1186/s40092-020-00219-3
7. Al-Azawei, R.: A survey of computational and natural language processing-based studies of hadith literature. Int. J. Islamic Arabic Stud. **9**(2), 1–12 (2019). ISSN 2520-2218. https://doi.org/10.1186/s40092-019-00203-7
8. Al-Azawei, R.: Translation of hadiths into english: challenges and opportunities. Int. J. Islamic Arabic Stud. **9**(4), 1–8 (2019). ISSN 2520-2218. https://doi.org/10.1186/s40092-019-00205-5
9. Bourahouat, G., Abourezq, M., Daoudi, N.: Systematic review of the Arabic natural language processing: challenges, techniques and new trends. J. Theor. Appl. Inf. Technol. **101**(3), 1333–1343 (2023). http://www.jatit.org/volumes/hundredone3.php
10. Alsayed, A., Qadah, T.M., Arif, M.: A performance analysis of transformer-based deep learning models for Arabic image captioning. J. King Saud Univ.-Comput. Inf. Sci. **35**(9), 101750 (2023)
11. Oueslati, O., Cambria, E., HajHmida, M.B., Ounelli, H.: A review of sentiment analysis research in Arabic language. Future Gener. Comput. Syst. **112**, 408–430 (2020)
12. Abdelali, A., Darwish, K., Durrani, N., Mubarak, H.: Farasa: a fast and furious segmenter for Arabic. In: Proceedings of the 2016 Conference of the North American Chapter of the Association for Computational Linguistics: Demonstrations, pp. 11–16 (2016). https://doi.org/10.18653/v1/N16-3003
13. Green, S., Manning, C.D.: Better Arabic parsing: baselines, evaluations, and analysis. In: Proceedings of the 23rd International Conference on Computational Linguistics, pp. 394–402 (2010). https://aclanthology.org/C10-1045
14. Altammami, S., Atwell, E., Alsalka, A.: The Arabic-English parallel corpus of authentic hadith. Int. J. Islamic Appl. Comput. Sci. Technol. (IJASAT) 1–10 (2019). http://www.sign-ific-ance.co.uk/index.php/IJASAT/article/view/2199/1908

15. Muḥammad ibn Ismāʻīl Al-Bukhārī. الجامع المسند الصحيح المختصر من أمور رسول الله الجامع المسند الصحيح المختصر من أمور رسول الله (The shortened authentic collection with isnads from the affairs of the messenger, peace be upon him, and his traditions and his days). ISBN: 978-1-56744-519-0. 846
16. Soliman, A.B., Eissa, K., El-Beltagy, S.R.: Aravec: a set of Arabic word embedding models for use in Arabic NLP. Procedia Comput. Sci. **117**, 256–265 (2017). https://doi.org/10.1016/j.procs.2017.10.117
17. OpenAI. GPT-4 technical report (2023). arXiv:2303.08774v3
18. McInnes, L., Healy, J., Melville, J.: UMAP: uniform manifold approximation and projection for dimension reduction. arXiv:1802.03426v3 (2023)
19. Vaswani, A., et al.: Attention is all you need. In: Advances in Neural Information Processing Systems, vol. 30 (2017)
20. Keita, Z.: Introduction to text and code embeddings in the openai API (2023). https://www.datacamp.com/tutorial/introduction-to-text-embeddings-with-the-open-ai-api. Accessed 8 Oct 2023
21. van der Maaten, L.J.P., Hinton, G.E.: Visualizing data using t-SNE. J. Mach. Learn. Res. **9**(86), 2579–2605 (2008). http://jmlr.org/papers/v9/vandermaaten08a.html
22. Pearson, K.: On lines and planes of closest fit to systems of points in space. Phil. Mag. **2**(11), 559–572 (1901). https://doi.org/10.1080/14786440109462720
23. Reades, J., Williams, J.: Clustering and visualising documents using word embeddings (2023). https://programminghistorian.org/en/lessons/clustering-visualizing-word-embeddings. Accessed 8 Oct 2023
24. Ghosh, T., Kirby, M.: Supervised dimensionality reduction and visualization using centroid-encoder. J. Mach. Learn. Res. **23**(1), 901–934 (2022). https://jmlr.csail.mit.edu/papers/v23/20-188.html

Stance Detection in Arabic Dialects: Preliminary Experiments

Imene Bensalem[1,2(✉)], Ivan Grubišić[3,4], Abdelmoumen El Goual[5], Paolo Rosso[3], Anis Charfi[6], and Wajdi Zaghouani[7]

[1] ESCF de Constantine, Constantine, Algeria
ibensalem@escf-constantine.dz
[2] MISC Laboratory, Constantine 2 University, Constantine, Algeria
[3] Universitat Politècnica de València, Valencia, Spain
grubisic@irb.hr, prosso@dsic.upv.es
[4] Ruđer Bošković Institute, Zagreb, Croatia
[5] Polytech Marseille, Aix-Marseille Université, Marseille, France
abdelmoumen.EL-GOUAL@etu.univ-amu.fr
[6] Carnegie Mellon University, Doha, Qatar
acharfi@andrew.cmu.edu
[7] Northwestern University in Qatar, Doha, Qatar
wajdi.zaghouani@northwestern.edu

Abstract. Stance detection is a classification task that determines whether a text is in favour, against or neutral towards a particular target. Arabic stance detection remains under-explored. This paper describes our work, which consists in evaluating a new dataset composed of user-generated texts in dialectal and formal Arabic on three targets: general labour union, illegal immigration, and administrative capital. We carried out experiments employing AraBERT-Twitter and Qarib transformers in addition to several machine learning classification models trained using different settings including target-specific and dialect-specific. The results show that training a model for each target, using Qarib, yields the best performance.

Keywords: Stance detection · Arabic dialects · Cross-target stance detection

1 Introduction

Stance detection is a textual analysis process that aims to discern, whether the standpoint of the text's writer regarding a target entity is supportive, opposing, or neutral. The target could encompass individuals, governmental measures, social movements, products, and more [1]. In the era of social media, detecting the stance from user-generated texts has become an essential task for social and political studies [2].

There are only a limited number of works on stance detection in the Arabic language. Some earlier works, such as [2–6] concentrated on the application

B. Hdioud and S. L. Aouragh (Eds.): ICALP 2024, CCIS 2339, pp. 139–150, 2025.
https://doi.org/10.1007/978-3-031-79164-2_12

aspect. Their goal was primarily to analyse the stance on one controversial topic, for example, analysing the political polarization in Egypt during the military intervention in 2013 [2] and studying the opinions on women's driving in Saudi Arabia [6], among others. Other works, such as [7,8] introduced multi-target datasets to foster the development of stance detection solutions, independently of the application domain. To the best of our knowledge, in all the existing Arabic stance detection works, the experiments were carried out using only one experimental setting, which is training one classification model to distinguish between in favour, against and neutral classes regardless of the number of targets (one or multiple) and the present Arabic dialects in the dataset.

Our work is the first that evaluates the performance of Arabic stance detection by comparing different settings:

- a specific model for each target vs. one model for multiple targets;
- a specific model for each dialect vs. one model for multiple dialects;
- mono-target vs. cross-target settings.

Our objective is to pave the way for further studies on this underexplored research topic. Concretely, we aim to address three research questions:

RQ1. What performance can we achieve in Arabic stance detection by training the models on a multi-targets and multi-dialects dataset?

RQ2. What are the settings that allow achieving the best results: target-specific, dialect-specific or one general model stance detection?

RQ3. To what extent a model trained on one target can generalize to data of a different target?

The rest of this paper is organized as follows. Section 2 summarizes some previous works on Arabic datasets used for text analysis and Arabic stance detection. Section 3 describes the dataset we used in our experiments. Section 4 describes the experimental setup and discusses the results. Finally, Sect. 5 concludes the paper and outlines directions for future work.

2 Related Work

The study and analysis of Arabic corpora has been a subject of considerable interest in the field of Natural Language Processing (NLP). Several researchers have dedicated their efforts to the development and study of Arabic corpora for various NLP tasks. In this context, [9] and [10] presented comprehensive surveys of freely available Arabic corpora, providing valuable insights into the existing resources and their potential applications. Furthermore, [11] and [12] conducted extensive surveys on author profiling, deception, and irony detection as well as toxic language detection, respectively, in the context of the Arabic language, highlighting the challenges and opportunities in these specific domains.

In the domain of natural language processing, stance detection is a pivotal task that involves determining the attitude or position of the author towards a specific target, such as an entity, issue, or claim. This task is multifaceted and can be bifurcated into two primary categories: intrinsic and extrinsic stance detection. Intrinsic stance detection focuses on analysing the text itself to identify the author's stance, often relying on linguistic cues and textual content. On the other hand, extrinsic stance detection goes beyond the text, incorporating external knowledge or context to ascertain the stance. This distinction is crucial as it underscores the varying approaches and methodologies employed in the field, each with its unique challenges and applications. The importance of stance detection is underscored by its wide array of applications, ranging from opinion mining and sentiment analysis to media bias detection and fake news identification, highlighting its significance in the broader landscape of computational linguistics and information retrieval. Based on its wide range of applications, the term stance detection may refer to two distinct tasks:

- **Target-based stance detection**, which is defined above.
- **Claim-based stance detection**, which consists in checking whether a given claim agrees, disagrees or is unrelated to an article. The applications of claim-based stance detection comprise fact-checking [13] as well as rumours and fake news detection [14,15].

In this work, we are specifically interested in target-based stance detection. In the following, we report on some Arabic target-based stance detection works.

Magdy et al. [5] presented an SVM-based approach to classifying Arabic tweets referring to ISIS into pro-ISIS and anti-ISIS. The trained classifier can predict future support or opposition to ISIS with an accuracy of 87%.

Kaati et al. [3] proposed a method that detects the tweets and the accounts that support jihadists on Twitter based on linguistic, stylistic, and temporal features. The experiments have been carried out for both Arabic and English and showed that detecting jihadists is much more challenging in Arabic than in English, especially in terms of precision.

Darwish et al. [4] proposed a method for the automatic detection of what they called "seminar users", meaning users who actively and consistently support a political entity and promote its agenda. As a case study, the authors trained a classifier to identify and study pro- and anti-Sisi seminar users. The authors affirm that seminar users are quite different from bots. The developed method can identify seminar users with an F1 measure of 80%.

Mubarak et al. [16] proposed a method of detecting the stance toward COVID-19 vaccination. The tweets are annotated with labels specifying their stance towards vaccination: positive (pro-vaccination), negative (against vaccination) or neutral. The study shows that the transformer models obtain better results than SVM, with a difference of about 10% in the performance score.

Jaziriyan et al. [7] proposed a multi-target dataset collected from Twitter, which comprises more than 200 targets. In their experiments, the authors fine-tuned the BERT model with different inputs, resulting in 70.69% as the best F1.

Recently, significant contributions have been made by recent studies to create stance datasets such as Laabar and Zaghouani's analysis of multi-dimensional insights in 5000 Facebook comments [17] and Shestakov and Zaghouani's dataset on the digital framing of the Sheikh Jarrah evictions [18] and finally Alturayeif et al. [8] who created a stance dataset of more than 4000 tweets focusing on three targets: women empowerment, COVID-19 vaccine and digital transformation. The authors fine-tuned several BERT-like models on this dataset and reported the overall and per-target performance.

3 Dataset

In this section, we introduce the Arabic stance dataset used in our experiments and explain how the data was collected and annotated by our project partner team at Carnegie Mellon University in Qatar. We worked with an early version of the MARASTA corpus [19].

3.1 Data Collection

The dataset for the Arabic stance detection was collected between the 27th of September 2022 and the 31st of August 2023 by our project partner team at CMU Qatar. The dataset comprised 1827 sentences from two Arab countries: Tunisia and Egypt. The dataset includes three targets: two controversial topics from Tunisia and one topic from Egypt as shown in Table 1. Sentences in this dataset were then collected based on these topics. Below are the criteria used for topic selection:

- A topic could apply to a single country or multiple ones;
- A topic could be a previously relevant topic (less than 15 years) or a recent one;
- A topic should be one that was trending or is recent enough to have a lot of discussion so that we can find posts with varying viewpoints: in favour, against and neutral.

Initially, sentences in dialectal and formal Arabic were manually collected from social media (Facebook, Twitter, and YouTube) and news Websites. Then, the team reverted to using Python scripts that call Twitter and YouTube APIs to collect tweets and video comments, respectively, using a set of keywords.

3.2 Annotation Guidelines

The collection and annotation of the stance corpus were done by a team of 4 individuals at CMU Qatar who were all native Arabic speakers. The annotators were familiar with several Arabic dialects and we had at least one expert in each of the dialects included in the dataset. After a sentence is collected, the annotator would decide which class of stance annotation the sentence falls under by reading it and based on words that express the tone of the sentence. Below are the three possible stance classes:

- pro: the sentence mentions/discusses the topic and supports it

- neutral: the sentence mentions/discusses the topic and does not have a stance
- against: the sentence mentions/discusses the topic and disapproves of it

After the first round of annotation, the initial stance annotations were hidden and given to another annotator who was also familiar with the dialect for a second round of stance annotation. After the second annotations were completed, a script was run to detect sentences with annotation conflicts. In such a case, a third annotator was involved, and another script was run to decide on the final stance annotation based on the majority. Detailed statistics on the stance dataset we used are displayed in Table 1.

We split the dataset into a training set (80%) and a test set (20%) while keeping the same distribution of the three targets (Tunisian General labour union, Illegal immigration, Administrative capital), the classes (pro, against and neutral), and the dialects (Tunisian, Egyptian, Modern Standard Arabic (MSA))[1].

Table 1. Our dataset statistics

Target	Dialect	Pro	Against	Neutral	Total size
Illegal immigration	Tunisian: 522, MSA: 795	178	240	174	592
Tunisian General Labour Union		251	308	166	725
Administrative capital	Egyptian: 260, MSA: 250	178	198	134	510
Total	Tunisian: 522, Egyptian: 260, MSA: 1045	607	746	474	1827

4 Experiments

We conducted three experiments that aim to:

- Evaluate the performance of several machine learning models to detect the stance on the whole Arabic dataset (Experiment 1);
- Gain insights into the best training settings in a multi-target and multi-dialect context (Experiment 2);
- Assess the performance of cross-target stance detection (Experiment 3).

For performance evaluation, we used the Accuracy and the Macro-averaged F1, which are computed as shown in Eqs. 1 and 2.

$$Accuracy = \frac{The\ number\ of\ the\ correctly\ classified\ examples}{Total\ number\ of\ examples} \quad (1)$$

$$MacroF1 = \frac{F1_{pro} + F1_{against} + F1_{neutral}}{3} \quad (2)$$

$F1_{class}$ ($class \in \{pro, against, neutral\}$) is the harmonic average of $precision_{class}$ and $recall_{class}$, computed in each of the 3 classes: pro, against

[1] Note that Modern Standard Arabic is not a dialect but the formal Arabic, which is used in news, media, official communication and education.

Table 2. Hyper-parameters used for fine-tuning AraBERT-Twitter and Qarib models.

Epochs	10
Loss	Cross Entropy Loss
Optimizer	Adam
Adam_epsilon	1E-08
Learning_rate	2E-05
Per_device_train_batch_size	16
Gradient_accumulation_steps	2

and neutral as displayed in Eqs. 3, 4 and 5, respectively. Note that TP, FP, FN stand for true positive, false positive and false negative examples, respectively. The subscripts used with them indicate the classes in which they are counted.

$$F1_{class} = \frac{2 \times Precision_{class} \times Recall_{class}}{Precision_{class} + Recall_{class}} \quad (3)$$

$$Precision_{class} = \frac{TP_{class}}{TP_{class} + FP_{class}} \quad (4)$$

$$Recall_{class} = \frac{TP_{class}}{TP_{class} + TN_{class}} \quad (5)$$

4.1 Experiment 1: General Stance Detection

Our objective is to address **RQ1**, which is to identify the most effective stance detection model without making distinctions based on either targets or dialects.

We have used 2 transformers that have been pre-trained on dialectal Arabic: AraBERTv0.2-Twitter [20][2] and Qarib [21][3]. AraBERTv0.2-Twitter has been pre-trained using about 60 Million tweets in dialectal Arabic. Qarib is a BERT-like model that was pre-trained on a collection of over 420 Million tweets and 180 Million sentences of formal Arabic text (i.e., MSA). The hyper-parameters used for fine-tuning both models are presented in Table 2. The remaining parameters are set as the default values within the 'TrainingArguments' class from the 'transformer' library, with the exception of the seed parameter, which was set to 25. Regarding the dropout rates, we maintained the default settings, which are the same in both models.

In addition to the transformers, as baselines, we implemented 4 traditional machine learning classification methods, namely Support Vector Machines (SVM), Logistic Regression (LR), Decision Trees (DT), and Multilayer Perceptron (MLP). To extract features for the 4 traditional classifiers, we implemented two commonly used verctorizers with each classification method, which are:

[2] https://huggingface.co/aubmindlab/bert-base-arabertv02-twitter.

[3] https://huggingface.co/qarib/bert-base-qarib.

Table 3. Comparison of different machine learning models trained using the whole training data and tested on the whole test data.

Model	Accuracy	F1
AraBERT-Twitter v.2	**80.6%**	**80.6%**
Qarib	**76.5%**	**76.7%**
MLP (TF-IDF)	68.0%	70.1%
SVM (TF-IDF)	64.2%	63.1%
MLP (BOW)	61.7%	63.8%
LR (TF-IDF)	61.7%	64.3%
LR (BOW)	59.8%	62.8%
SVM (BOW)	58.2%	58.1%
DT (BOW)	49.2%	49.0%
DT (TF-IDF)	43.0%	45.5%

- Bag of Words (BoW)
- Term Frequency-Inverse Document Frequency (TF-IDF)

As shown in Table 3, AraBERT-Twitter and Qarib significantly outperformed all the models. Among the traditional machine learning models, MLP stands out as the top performer, especially when utilizing TF-IDF features.

Based on these results, we carried out the following experiments using the models that yielded the best results, namely AraBERT-Twitter and Qarib models.

4.2 Experiment 2: Target-Specific and Dialect-Specific Stance Detection

Since the stance dataset we used is composed of 3 targets and 2 dialects in addition to MSA, the goal of this experiment is to answer the question **RQ2**, which focuses on finding the best training settings among the following ones:

- **One general model**: Training one model using the whole training dataset (the same setting used in Experiment 1)
- **Target-specific**: Training a model for each target, meaning both training and test sets are divided into 3 parts corresponding to the 3 targets. Then, each part is used to train and test a model specific to one target. For example, a model is trained on a subset of the training set whose target is illegal immigration and tested on the subset of the test set that has the same target (i.e., illegal immigration). The same process is carried out using the data of the two other targets, resulting in 3 models.
- **Dialect-specific**: Training a model for each dialect, meaning both training and test sets are divided into 3 parts corresponding to Tunisian, Egyptian and MSA. Then, each part is used to train and test a stance detection model

Table 4. Table The training data used in the different experimental settings

Training setting	Models: Training data
Target-specific	Model 1: General labour union Model 2: Illegal immigration Model 3: Administrative capital
Dialect-specific	Model 4 Tunisian texts from General labour union + Illegal immigration Model 5: Egyptian texts from Administrative capital Model 6: MSA texts from the three targets
One general model	Model 7: General labour union + Illegal immigration + Administrative capital

specific to one of these variants of Arabic. The predictions obtained by each model in each part of the test set are then combined to compute the performance measures.

These settings are summarised in Table 4 and the results of these experiments are shown in Table 5. In all the experiments, we computed the results, on the test set, per target and on the whole dataset (displayed in the column Overall). Note that for the target-specific and dialect-specific experiments, the results are computed by combining the predictions produced by the models (1, 2, 3) and (4, 5, 6) on the corresponding part of the test set, respectively. For example, the results computed on the Illegal immigration target of the dialect-specific experiments are obtained by combining the predictions of models 4 (on the Tunisian data) and 6 (on the MSA data).

Table 5. Comparison of three training settings using AraBERT-Twitter and Qarib models. The results are in terms of Accuracy (Acc.) and macro-averaged F1 (F1). The best results for each model are in bold.

Training settings ↓	Test set →	Tunisian General Labour Union		Illegal immigration		Administrative capital		Overall	
	Models	F1	Acc.	F1	Acc.	F1	Acc.	F1	Acc.
Dialect-specific models	AraBERT Twitter	87.6%	87.6%	65.5%	66.4%	74.4%	74.5%	77.0%	77.0%
	Qarib	89.3%	89.7%	71.1%	71.4%	72.4%	71.6%	79.0%	78.7%
Target-specific models	AraBERT Twitter	89.8%	90.3%	69.2%	68.9%	**78.3%**	**78.4%**	80.2%	80.1%
	Qarib	**89.7%**	**90.3%**	**71.7%**	**71.4%**	**78.6%**	**78.4%**	**80.9%**	**80.9%**
One general model	AraBERT Twitter	**91.5%**	**91.7%**	**69.4%**	**69.7%**	77.1%	77.5%	**80.6%**	**80.6%**
	Qarib	84.5%	84.8%	69.2%	68.9%	73.6%	73.5%	76.7%	76.5%

In the following, we present observations that could be extracted from Table 5.

4.2.1 Qarib Results

The target-specific training yields the best results. This could be noticed in the target-specific results computed on the data of each target and the overall test data. In the latter, for example, we can notice a difference of +4.2% in terms of F1 score (80.9% vs. 76.7%) in comparison with the results obtained by training with the whole training data. On the other hand, training a model for each dialect improves the results in comparison with training one model on the whole data.

4.2.2 AraBERT-Twitter Results

Unlike when using Qarib, the best results in each target are achieved by employing diverse settings, with the best overall performance (more than 80% in terms of accuracy and F1) coming from training a single model on the entire training dataset. Nonetheless, the overall results obtained by employing the target-specific settings are not so different from the best ones.

4.3 Experiment 3: Cross-Target Stance Detection

The experiments described in this section aim to address the research question **RQ3**.

To answer this question, we tested each target-specific model on the test data from the two other targets.

As depicted in Table 6, the stance detection accuracy on a given target's data decreases significantly when the classification model (either AraBERT-Twitter or Qarib) is not originally trained on data from that same target. For instance, if AraBERT-Twitter is trained on the Tunisian general labour union data, it correctly classifies 90.3% of the examples with the same target. However, if the model is trained on the Illegal Immigration data, the accuracy score drops to 53.1%. The same pattern holds true in the rest of the results. Intriguingly, even when the training and test data share the same dialect (such as in the case of the targets Tunisian General Labour Union and Illegal Immigration), this dialect similarity does not improve the model's ability to generalize across different targets.

Table 6. Cross-target results using AraBERT-Twitter and Qarib models. Note that the target-specific results are results already presented in the target-specific row in Table 5.

Training set ↓	Test set→	Tunisian general labour union		Illegal immigration		Administrative capital	
	Model	F1	Acc.	F1	Acc.	F1	Acc.
Tunisian general labour union	AraBERT Twitter	**89.8%**	**90.3%**	48.6%	52.9%	62.4%	63.7%
	Qarib	**89.7%**	**90.3%**	49.7%	52.9%	69.8%	70.6%
Illegal immigration	AraBERT Twitter	52.8%	53.1%	**69.2%**	**68.9%**	38.9%	49.0%
	Qarib	62.6%	62.1%	**71.7%**	**71.4%**	50.5%	54.9%
Adminstrative capital	AraBERT Twitter	55.7%	62.1%	33.9%	44.5%	**78.3%**	**78.4%**
	Qarib	65.2%	68.3%	51.3%	55.5%	**78.6%**	**78.4%**

5 Conclusions and Future Work

In this paper, we used a stance dataset that includes user-generated comments in MSA as well as the Tunisian and Egyptian dialects. The dataset focuses on three targets: general labour union, illegal immigration, and administrative capital.

We conducted a series of experiments using different settings for the first time on Arabic data. The results obtained when using the Qarib model are in line with stance detection results in other languages, showing that the best setting is to train a model for each specific target. This observation was less evident when we used the AraBERT-Twitter model as this model generated almost similar overall performance using target-specific models and one general model. However, the comparison of dialect-specific models with one general model is inconclusive, as the performance improves with the dialect-specific models of Qarib, but it is not the case with AraBERT-Twitter.

Since training a model for each target is not realistic, regarding the countless targets in a real scenario [22], we conducted preliminary cross-target experiments to assess the generalizability of models. Those experiments resulted in a significant deterioration of the model's performance, even if the dialect is the same across data of different targets. This highlights the need to develop generalizable language models, which is still an unexplored research area for Arabic.

A limitation of our work is the small size of the dataset we used, comprising only 3 targets. A more extensive version of the dataset called MARASTA [19] was recently completed, which covers eight targets and additional dialects such as Gulf and Levantine. In our future work, we plan to redo the experiments described in this paper with the extended version of the dataset, which may lead to improving the generalizability of the models.

Acknowledgement. This publication was made possible by NPRP13S-0206-200281 from the Qatar National Research Fund/Qatar Research Development and Innovation Council (QRDI). The contents herein reflect the work and are solely the authors' responsibility.

References

1. Mohammad, S.M., Sobhani, P., Kiritchenko, S.: Stance and sentiment in tweets. ACM Trans. Internet Technol. (TOIT) **17**(3), 1–23 (2017)
2. Borge-Holthoefer, J., Magdy, W., Darwish, K., Weber, I.: Content and network dynamics behind Egyptian political polarization on twitter. In: Proceedings of the 18th ACM Conference on Computer Supported Cooperative Work & Social Computing, pp. 700–711 (2015)
3. Kaati, L., Omer, E., Prucha, N., Shrestha, A.: Detecting multipliers of jihadism on twitter. In: Proceedings of ICDMW 2015, pp. 954–960 (2015)
4. Darwish, K., Alexandrov, D., Nakov, P., Mejova, Y.: Seminar users in the Arabic twitter sphere. In: Ciampaglia, G.L., Mashhadi, A., Yasseri, T. (eds.) SocInfo 2017. LNCS, vol. 10539, pp. 91–108. Springer, Cham (2017). https://doi.org/10.1007/978-3-319-67217-5_7

5. Magdy, W., Darwish, K., Weber, I.: #FailedRevolutions: using Twitter to study the antecedents of ISIS support. First Monday **21**(2) (2016)
6. Addawood, A., Alshamrani, A., Alqahtani, A., Diesner, J., Broniatowski, D.: Women's driving in Saudi Arabia-analyzing the discussion of a controversial topic on twitter. In: BRiMS 2018, pp. 1–8 (2018)
7. Jaziriyan, M.M., Akbari, A., Karbasi, H.: ExaASC: a general target-based stance detection corpus in Arabic language. In: ICCKE 2021 - 11th International Conference on Computer Engineering and Knowledge (ICCKE), pp. 424–429 (2021)
8. Alturayeif, N.S., Luqman, H.A., Ahmed, M.A.K.: Mawqif: a multi-label Arabic dataset for target-specific stance detection. In: Proceedings of the The Seventh Arabic Natural Language Processing Workshop (WANLP), pp. 174–184 (2022)
9. Ahmed, A., Ali, N., Alzubaidi, M., Zaghouani, W., Abd-alrazaq, A.A., Househ, M.: Freely available Arabic corpora: a scoping review. Comput. Methods Programs Biomed. Update **2**, 100049 (2022)
10. Zaghouani, W.: Critical survey of the freely available Arabic corpora. In: International Conference on Language Resources and Evaluation (LREC 2014), OSACT Workshop, Reykjavik, Iceland, 26–31 May 2014 (2014)
11. Rosso, P., Rangel, F., Farías, I.H., Cagnina, L., Zaghouani, W., Charfi, A.: A survey on author profiling, deception, and irony detection for the Arabic language. Lang. Linguist. Compass **12**(4), 12275 (2018)
12. Bensalem, I., Rosso, P., Zitouni, H.: Toxic language detection: a systematic review of Arabic datasets. Expert Syst. 13551 (2024). https://doi.org/10.1111/exsy.13551
13. Baly, R., Mohtarami, M., Glass, J., Màrquez, L., Moschitti, A., Nakov, P.: Integrating stance detection and fact checking in a unified corpus. In: NAACL HLT 2018 - 2018 Conference of the North American Chapter of the Association for Computational Linguistics: Human Language Technologies - Proceedings of the Conference, vol. 2, pp. 21–27 (2018). https://doi.org/10.18653/v1/n18-2004
14. Haouari, F., Elsayed, T.: Detecting stance of authorities towards rumors in Arabic tweets: a preliminary study. In: European Conference on Information Retrieval, pp. 430–438. Springer (2023)
15. Khouja, J.: Stance prediction and claim verification: an Arabic perspective. In: Proceedings of the Annual Meeting of the Association for Computational Linguistics, pp. 8–17 (2020). https://doi.org/10.18653/v1/2020.fever-1.2
16. Mubarak, H., Hassan, S., Chowdhury, S.A., Alam, F.: ArCovidVac: Analyzing Arabic Tweets About COVID-19 Vaccination (i) (2022). arXiv:2201.06496
17. Laabar, S., Zaghouani, W.: Multi-dimensional insights: annotated dataset of stance, sentiment, and emotion in Facebook comments on Tunisia's July 25 measures. In: Proceedings of 2nd Workshop on Natural Language Processing for Political Sciences Co-located with LREC 2024 (2024)
18. Shestakov, D., Zaghouani, W.: A dataset on the digital framing of the sheikh jarrah evictions. In: Proceedings of the Second Workshop on Natural Language Processing for Political Sciences Co-located with LREC 2024 (2024)
19. Charfi, A., Bessghaier, M., Atalla, A., Akasheh, R., Al-Emadi, S., Zaghouan, W.: Marasta: a multi-dialectal Arabic cross-domain stance corpus. In: Proceedings of the 2024 Joint International Conference on Computational Linguistics, Language Resources and Evaluation, LREC-COLING 2024 (2024)
20. Antoun, W., Baly, F., Hajj, H.: AraBERT: transformer-based model for Arabic language understanding. In: Proceedings of the 4th Workshop on Open-Source Arabic Corpora and Processing Tools, with a Shared Task on Offensive Language Detection, pp. 9–15. ELRA, Marseille, France (2020)

21. Abdelali, A., Hassan, S., Mubarak, H., Darwish, K., Samih, Y.: Pre-training bert on Arabic tweets: practical considerations (2021). arXiv:2102.10684
22. Allaway, E., McKeown, K.: Zero-shot stance detection: a dataset and model using generalized topic representations. In: EMNLP 2020 - 2020 Conference on Empirical Methods in Natural Language Processing, Proceedings of the Conference, pp. 8913–8931 (2020). https://doi.org/10.18653/v1/2020.emnlp-main.717

MAGENTA: Generating and Detecting Arabic Machine-Generated Text in Multiple Domains

Saad Yaquine[1], Amine Hmimou[1], and Paolo Rosso[2](✉)

[1] Polytech Marseille, Aix-Marseille Université, Marseille, France
{saad.yaqine,amine.hmimou}@etu.univ-amu.fr
[2] Universitat Politècnica de València, Valencia, Spain
prosso@dsic.upv.es

Abstract. This paper studies the detection of Machine-Generated Text (MGT) in Arabic. In this context, we aim to study Arabic MGT detection by constructing (**M**ulti-domain **A**utomatically **Gen**erated **T**exts in **A**rabic), a comprehensive dataset of diverse human and machine-generated Arabic texts from multiple domains: news, reviews and wiki-how articles. Our approach ensures comparability between human and generated texts, emphasizing their contextual alignment. We additionally train and evaluate various Arabic MGT detectors encompassing both traditional machine learning techniques and state-of-the-art deep models. Our findings further underscore the suitability of Transformers for MGT detection, outperforming other models by considerable margins of over 12 points of Macro-F_1.

Keywords: Machine-Generated Text · Large Language Models · Arabic

1 Introduction

While the increasing popularity of strongly capable Large Language Models (LLMs) has created new applications,[1] efforts in democratizing LLMs [1–3] have also lowered the barrier of entry for users to generate high-quality malicious texts.

Defense against high-scale generated spam and propaganda attacks, together with efforts in increasing AI regulation[2] motivate the detection of Machine-Generated Text (MGT). The task consists in identifying whether a particular text has been written by humans or generated automatically via machines. MGT

[1] https://tinyurl.com/reuters-chatgpt.
[2] European Commission, Proposal for a Regulation of the European Parliament https://eur-lex.europa.eu/legal-content/EN/TXT/?uri=celex%3A52021PC0206.

S. Yaquine, A. Hmimou and P. Rosso—Contributing authors.

B. Hdioud and S. L. Aouragh (Eds.): ICALP 2024, CCIS 2339, pp. 151–159, 2025.
https://doi.org/10.1007/978-3-031-79164-2_13

detection is most often studied in Indo-European languages [4,5], but the defense against large scale automatically generated text attacks extend to other languages as well. The case of Arabic is especially important due to an observed rise in violence-driven propaganda [6,7] and hateful speech [8] in social media.

Generally, MGT detection is studied in specific scenarios where detectors obtain high scores in single-model settings [9,10], with few works studying the task in realistic scenarios for practical use [4,5,11]. Few works have explored detecting MGT in Arabic [12], potentially due to a lack of high-quality text generators in the past. However, the multilingual capabilities of current LLMs [13,14] make it paramount to explore Arabic MGT detection in realistic scenarios. In this short paper, we take the first step towards this prospect by: (i) compiling a multi-domain and multi-generator dataset of diverse human and generated Arabic texts and (ii) studying the behaviour of various supervised MGT detectors on the task.

2 Related Work

Current LLMs exhibit remarkable text generation capabilities, achieved through self-supervised pre-training on large datasets and via instruction tuning to match human preferences [13,15]. However, Arabic-only text generation models are scarce and not as capable as English or multilingual models. Some works [16] study Arabic generations with existing monolingual models such as `AraGPT-2` [17] or `AraT5` [18], while others [11] leverage multilingual LLMs such as `GPT-3.5` [15].

Most work on MGT detection is in English, with some works providing generations and studying the behaviour of detectors in other languages such as Russian [19] and Spanish [4]. There are few works which study MGT detection in Arabic, namely [12] and [13]. Authors of [12] generate text via POS tags and k-nearest-neighbor similarities of word embeddings, where the studied detectors obtain great results in a single-domain scenario. However, these generation methodologies are less relevant today, with LLMs leading in the text generation landscape. In more recent work, [11] generate Arabic texts with `GPT-3.5-turbo` [15], and they consider a multilingual scenario where they experiment with training and testing on different languages. The authors find that, when not trained with Arabic texts, multilingual detectors achieve high performance with specific configurations, showing promise in cross-language MGT detection capability transference. However, they also only consider a single domain for Arabic generations.

In addition to language, there are many more dimension where MGT detectors are studied. Specifically, some works frame the task in a white-box zero-shot manner, where one has access to the token logits of the generator and is able to detect MGT based on the model's generation process [9]. While this is an impressive feat, it offers little in terms of generalization to new text generation models, making it impractical in nature. This is why most works, in addition to this one, focus on supervised MGT detectors, where detectors, usually using statistical features or embeddings from pre-traind Transformers [20], are trained with MGT and human-authored texts [5,10]. This way, Transformer-based MGT detectors have been shown to effectively generalize to new domains [4], and new models [5].

3 MAGENTA

In this section we describe the generation of the MAGENTA (Multi-domain Automatically GENerated Texts in Arabic) dataset and the way that the detection of Machine-Generated Texts (MGTs) was addressed.

3.1 Data Gathering Process

In order to compile a dataset for Arabic MGT detection, we follow the data gathering process in [4], obtaining a set of human-authored and machine-generated continuations to the same prefix. Given a sentence written by a human ليوم الجو حار في مدينة فالنسيا (Today it's hot in Valencia), we can split it into a prefix, اليوم (today), and continuation, الجو حار في مدينة فالنسيا, labeling the latter as human text. Next, we provide the prefix as input to an LLM and label its generated continuation, e.g. الطقس طيب (the weather is fine) as a generated text. This way, both machine-generated and human texts are plausible continuations of the same prefix, reducing domain bias and making them fairly comparable. We carry out this process with datasets containing various human-written texts in different domains, removing empty generations and unwanted artefacts in the process.

3.2 Dataset

In order to obtain the MAGENTA dataset, we consider three domains: (i) `news` articles, where we leverage human news from XLSUM [21]; (ii) `reviews`, where human texts were obtained mainly from Arabic 100k reviews [22], a collection of reviews extracted and cleaned from HARD [23], and BRAD [24]; and (iii) `wikihow` articles, employing human written articles in Wikihow Arabic Summarization.[3]

We generate texts using monolingual Arabic text generation models, `aragpt-2-base`[4] and `aragpt-2-medium`[5] [17], as well as multilingual models, `bloom-1b1`[6] and `bloom-1b7`[7] [14], making use of the HuggingFace ecosystem [2]. We employ nucleus sampling [25] with $p = 0.8$ so the generations are diverse,

[3] huggingface.co/datasets/Abdelkareem/wikihow-arabic-summarization.
[4] huggingface.co/aubmindlab/aragpt2-base.
[5] huggingface.co/aubmindlab/aragpt2-medium.
[6] huggingface.co/bigscience/bloom-1b1.
[7] huggingface.co/bigscience/bloom-1b7.

Table 1. MAGENTA dataset statistics.

Domain	Hum	Gen
`news`	5,468	4,881
`reviews`	2,320	2,385
`wikihow`	5,361	4,747
Total	13,149	12,013

Table 2. Repetition and diversity mean scores. Subscripts denote n-gram size.

Subset	Label	rep_2	rep_3	rep_4	diversity
`news`	Gen	2.72	1.28	0.98	96.06
`news`	Hum	0.14	0.42	1.30	98.60
`reviews`	Gen	6.33	4.65	4.46	91.28
`reviews`	Hum	5.74	12.57	21.72	78.08
`wikihow`	Gen	4.97	3.52	3.22	93.11
`wikihow`	Hum	3.18	4.68	8.09	91.50
All	Gen	4.33	2.83	2.55	93.95
All	Hum	2.37	4.30	7.67	92.09
All	Both	3.30	3.60	5.23	92.97

limiting them to 300 tokens to ensure that they are also concise and not veering off-topic. Table 1 presents the statistics of our dataset (human and machine-generated texts).

3.3 Evaluation

We further evaluate the generations with two standard measures for text generation: rep_n and diversity [26] of n-grams with $n \in \{2, 3, 4\}$.

Given a text y, rep_n measures the repeated n-grams as $\text{rep}_n(y) = 1.0 - \frac{|\text{unique } n\text{-grams}(y)|}{|\text{total } n\text{-grams}(y)|}$. It can be used to obtain diversity scores, which measure text degeneration, meaning that lower scores suggest more severe degenerations $\text{diversity}(y) = \prod_{n=2}^{4}(1.0 - \text{rep}_n(y))$. These measures are local to each text, and that reported scores are usually percentages of means in the whole dataset, which is also the case in this work. Note that lower values of rep_n are better, while a higher diversity is better.

Table 2 shows per-domain, per-label and aggregated mean repetition and diversity scores.[8] We observe that most subsets exhibit low values of repetition and high values of diversity, with the exception of the `reviews` domain in human texts. We hypothesize this to be due to the nature of review texts with respect to the other domains, where content is mostly short form and often including

[8] We used the implementation released by SimCTG [27].

Table 3. Per-domain and global Macro-F_1 scores of 5-split cross-validation. Best results in bold, second best underlined.

Domain	TRF	LR	MLP	DT	SVM
news	**92.4**	79.4	76.8	78.2	<u>79.8</u>
reviews	**98.2**	84.2	78.6	<u>84.6</u>	83.4
wikihow	**98.6**	86.8	83.4	<u>90.6</u>	87.8
Mean$_{std.dev.}$	**96.4**$_{2.8}$	83.4$_{3.1}$	79.6$_{2.8}$	<u>84.5</u>$_{5.1}$	83.6$_{3.3}$

similar forms when expressing opinions about different topics. We see this further evidenced by the lower repetition and higher diversity scores of `news` with respect to `wikihow`, where the former has a more formal but less strict style, when compared to the latter which most often is comprised of instructions.

We also find that both human and generated texts have similar repetition and diversity scores, which is expected and desirable, reinforcing that the generations are of high quality, contain few artefacts, and will more closely mimic outputs of massive-scale generations produced by malicious users. Overall, human texts appear more repetitive and slightly less diverse than generated texts, which may hint at either: (i) a better capability for LLMs to express ideas using various alternative wordings, or (ii) a stronger capacity for degeneration in LLMs where longer generations do not reference expressions in the start of the texts.

4 Experiments

We carry out a set of experiments for MGT detection using the aforementioned dataset. For this, we employ a 5-fold cross validation scheme to split the dataset, reporting per-detector and per-domain Macro-F_1 scores as well as means and std. deviations across domains to ensure the performance differences are statistically significant. These experiments leveraged the infrastructure provided by Kaggle[9] and Google Colab.[10]

We apply conventional fine-tuning to `AraBERT-base`[11] [28] for 3 epochs with a batch size of 8 using AdamW [29] with a learning rate of 1e-5 and default parameters (TRF), as well as four classical classifiers trained on TF-IDF features of the text: Logistic Regression (LR), Multi-Layer Perceptron (MLP), Decision Trees (DT) and Support Vector Machines (SVM), using default parameters for all cases. Table 3 presents these results. When observing the differences with respect to each domain, we find that it is easier to detect MGT in the `wikihow` domain, with every detector reaching Macro-F_1 scores higher than 80%. This is in contrast to the other two domains, where models obtain lower Macro-F_1 scores in every case with respect to their performance on `wikihow`. This is especially relevant in the `news` domain, where detectors obtain their worst scores

[9] kaggle.com.

[10] colab.research.google.com.

[11] huggingface.co/aubmindlab/bert-base-arabert.

and exhibit special difficulty in discriminating between human and generated news. Specifically, having observed the repetition and diversity scores, we find that higher repetition or lower diversity scores do not necessarily translate to easier detection of MGT. Detector performance in `reviews` and `wikihow` is similar, but their repetition and diversity scores were vastly different both when comparing between domains in the same label and between labels in the same domain. However, we observe that very low repetition and high diversity scores do have an effect, given that models obtain the worst scores in `news`.

Overall, we clearly observe how fine-tuned transformers perform much better than other approaches, always obtaining Macro-F_1 scores higher than 90%. Decision Trees follow as the second best performers, with the remaining ones being slightly below these. However, none of the traditional machine learning approaches compare to the results of the Transformer, with their differences being statistically significant.

5 Conclusions

This work contributes to the Arabic MGT detection research by: (i) compiling a dataset of human and generated Arabic texts with monolingual and multilingual LLMs in three domains: news, reviews, and wiki-how articles; and (ii) training a set of machine and deep learning models to act as MGT detectors in these different domains. The generation process is carried out such that there is comparability between human and generated texts, ensuring both are plausible continuations of the same prefix. The MGT quality is evaluated with common repetition and diversity, two common text generation evaluation metrics that measure the degeneration of generated text. In most cases we observe desirable values of repetition (low) and diversity (high) with scores being highly similar for human and generated texts. Regarding the detectors, we find further evidence that Transformers are more adequate models for MGT detection, surpassing most other detectors by over 12 points of Macro-F_1.

5.1 Future Work

Several avenues of research offer promising directions in improving the community's understanding of Arabic MGT detectors' behaviour. One such avenue is the exploration and expansion of this study to a wider range of domains, e.g. social media, legal documents, medical reports, considering in the learning phase the entire corpus composed of texts from all the domains, and aiding in understanding whether Arabic MGT is more difficult to identify in particular domains. Similarly, one can study the generalization capabilities of Arabic MGT detectors into new domains and new models. Moreover, we consider incorporating zero-shot MGT detection techniques, and exploring the impact of larger text generation models on detection performance. Another important research question involves delving into fine-grained analyses of Arabic generators and detectors in comparison to those for Indo-European languages. The impact of writing direction in MGT detection, particularly for multilingual detectors where both left-to-right and right-to-left texts are observed by these models, could uncover challenges and nuances unique to Arabic and its interactions to other languages. Exploring these research directions could promote the progress of Arabic machine-generated text detection and its practical real-world applications.

6 Limitations

While in this work we provide various important findings, there still remain many limitations. Specifically, we primarily use small models for text generation, which may impact the quality of the generated text when compared to human text. While in this work we obtain very high scores for our best detectors, the usage of larger text generation models could strongly reduce these scores. Additionally, this work has only included supervised detectors, whereas it would be valuable to also study zero-shot white-box techniques proven effective for detecting MGT in English [9]. Furthermore, the limited computational resources for experimentation may have restricted the extent and scope of this work. These limitations collectively highlight the need for further research to advance the field of Arabic machine-generated text detection.

Acknowledgements. This publication was made possible by NPRP13S-0206-200281 from the Qatar National Research Fund/Qatar Research Development and Innovation Council (QRDI). The contents herein reflect the work and are solely the authors' responsibility.

References

1. Touvron, H., et al.: Llama: open and efficient foundation language models. arXiv preprint arXiv:2302.13971 (2023)
2. Wolf, T., et al.: Transformers: state-of-the-art natural language processing. In: Proceedings of the 2020 Conference on Empirical Methods in Natural Language Processing: System Demonstrations, pp. 38–45. Association for Computational Linguistics (2020). https://doi.org/10.18653/v1/2020.emnlp-demos.6. https://aclanthology.org/2020.emnlp-demos.6
3. Seger, E., Ovadya, A., Garfinkel, B., Siddarth, D., Dafoe, A.: Democratising AI: multiple meanings, goals, and methods. arXiv preprint arXiv:2303.12642 (2023)
4. Sarvazyan, A.M., González, J.Á., Franco-Salvador, M., Rangel, F., Chulvi, B., Rosso, P.: Overview of autextification at iberlef 2023: Detection and attribution of machine-generated text in multiple domains. Procesamiento del Lenguaje Natural **71**, 275–288 (2023)
5. Sarvazyan, A.M., González, J., Franco-Salvador, M., Rosso, P.: Supervised machine-generated text detectors: Family and scale matters. In: Information Access Evaluation Meets Multilinguality, Multimodality, and Visualization, vol. 71. Springer (2023)
6. Badawy, A., Ferrara, E.: The rise of jihadist propaganda on social networks. J. Comput. Soc. Sci. **1**, 453–470 (2018)

7. Alam, F., Mubarak, H., Zaghouani, W., Da San Martino, G., Nakov, P.: Overview of the WANLP 2022 shared task on propaganda detection in Arabic. In: Proceedings of the The Seventh Arabic Natural Language Processing Workshop (WANLP), pp. 108–118. Association for Computational Linguistics, Abu Dhabi, United Arab Emirates (Hybrid) (2022). https://doi.org/10.18653/v1/2022.wanlp-1.11. https://aclanthology.org/2022.wanlp-1.11
8. Alshehri, A., Nagoudi, E.M.B., Abdul-Mageed, M.: Understanding and detecting dangerous speech in social media. In: Proceedings of the 4th Workshop on Open-Source Arabic Corpora and Processing Tools, with a Shared Task on Offensive Language Detection, pp. 40–47. European Language Resource Association, Marseille, France (2020). https://aclanthology.org/2020.osact-1.6
9. Mitchell, E., Lee, Y., Khazatsky, A., Manning, C.D., Finn, C.: DetectGPT: zero-shot machine-generated text detection using probability curvature. arXiv preprint arXiv:2301.11305 (2023)
10. Fröhling, L., Zubiaga, A.: Feature-based detection of automated language models: tackling GPT-2, GPT-3 and grover. PeerJ Comput. Sci. **7** (2021)
11. Wang, Y., et al.: M4: multi-generator, multi-domain, and multi-lingual black-box machine-generated text detection. arXiv preprint arXiv:2305.14902 (2023)
12. Nagoudi, E.M.B., Elmadany, A., Abdul-Mageed, M., Alhindi, T.: Machine generation and detection of Arabic manipulated and fake news. In: Proceedings of the Fifth Arabic Natural Language Processing Workshop, Barcelona, Spain, pp. 69–84. Association for Computational Linguistics (2020). https://aclanthology.org/2020.wanlp-1.7
13. Brown, T., et al.: Language models are few-shot learners. Adv. Neural. Inf. Process. Syst. **33**, 1877–1901 (2020)
14. Scao, T.L., et al.: Bloom: A 176b-parameter open-access multilingual language model. arXiv preprint arXiv:2211.05100 (2022)
15. Ouyang, L., et al.: Training language models to follow instructions with human feedback. In: Advances in Neural Information Processing Systems (2022)
16. Harrag, F., Dabbah, M., Darwish, K., Abdelali, A.: Bert transformer model for detecting Arabic GPT2 auto-generated tweets. In: Proceedings of the Fifth Arabic Natural Language Processing Workshop, Barcelona, Spain, pp. 207–214. Association for Computational Linguistics (2020). https://aclanthology.org/2020.wanlp-1.19
17. Antoun, W., Baly, F., Hajj, H.: AraGPT2: pre-trained transformer for Arabic language generation. In: Proceedings of the Sixth Arabic Natural Language Processing Workshop, Kyiv, Ukraine (Virtual), pp. 196–207. Association for Computational Linguistics (2021). https://aclanthology.org/2021.wanlp-1.21
18. Nagoudi, E.M.B., Elmadany, A., Abdul-Mageed, M.: AraT5: text-to-text transformers for Arabic language generation. In: Proceedings of the 60th Annual Meeting of the Association for Computational Linguistics (Volume 1: Long Papers), Dublin, Ireland, pp. 628–647. Association for Computational Linguistics (2022). https://doi.org/10.18653/v1/2022.acl-long.47. https://aclanthology.org/2022.acl-long.47
19. Shamardina, T., et al.: Findings of the the RUATD shared task 2022 on artificial text detection in Russian. arXiv preprint arXiv:2206.01583 (2022)
20. Vaswani, A., et al.: Attention is all you need. In: Advances in Neural Information Processing Systems, vol. 30 (2017)

21. Hasan, T., et al.: XL-sum: large-scale multilingual abstractive summarization for 44 languages. In: Findings of the Association for Computational Linguistics: ACL-IJCNLP 2021, pp. 4693–4703. Association for Computational Linguistics (2021). https://doi.org/10.18653/v1/2021.findings-acl.413. https://aclanthology.org/2021.findings-acl.413
22. Khooli, A.: Arabic 100k reviews. Kaggle (2023)
23. Elnagar, A., Khalifa, Y.S., Einea, A.: Hotel Arabic-Reviews Dataset Construction for Sentiment Analysis Applications, pp. 35–52. Springer, Cham (2018). https://doi.org/10.1007/978-3-319-67056-0_3
24. Elnagar, A., Einea, O.: Brad 1.0: book reviews in Arabic dataset. In: 2016 IEEE/ACS 13th International Conference of Computer Systems and Applications (AICCSA), pp. 1–8 (2016)
25. Holtzman, A., Buys, J., Du, L., Forbes, M., Choi, Y.: The curious case of neural text degeneration. In: International Conference on Learning Representations (2020). https://openreview.net/forum?id=rygGQyrFvH
26. Welleck, S., Kulikov, I., Roller, S., Dinan, E., Cho, K., Weston, J.: Neural text generation with unlikelihood training. In: International Conference on Learning Representations (2020). https://openreview.net/forum?id=SJeYe0NtvH
27. Su, Y., Lan, T., Wang, Y., Yogatama, D., Kong, L., Collier, N.: A contrastive framework for neural text generation. Adv. Neural. Inf. Process. Syst. **35**, 21548–21561 (2022)
28. Antoun, W., Baly, F., Hajj, H.: AraBERT: transformer-based model for Arabic language understanding. In: Proceedings of the 4th Workshop on Open-Source Arabic Corpora and Processing Tools, with a Shared Task on Offensive Language Detection, Marseille, France, pp. 9–15. ELRA (2020)
29. Loshchilov, I., Hutter, F.: Decoupled weight decay regularization. In: International Conference on Learning Representations (2019). https://openreview.net/forum?id=Bkg6RiCqY7

Transformers and Spark for Automated CV Classification in Arabophone Regions

Soumia Chafi(✉), Mustapha Kabil, and Abdessamad Kamouss

FSTM, Hassan II University Mohamedia, Mohammedia, Morocco
Soumia.Chafi@gmail.com, Mustapha.kabil@fstm.ac.ma

Abstract. The growing demand for skilled labor in Arabophone regions has led to increased interest in automating the Curriculum Vitae (CV) classifying process. In this study, we present an innovative methodology that exploits the power of Transformers models and the flexibility of the Spark platform for the automatic classification of CVs written in Arabic. We start by preprocessing CVs using Arabic-specific text processing techniques, including tokenization and normalization. Then, we use a pre-trained Transformer model, adapted to the Arabic linguistic context, to extract relevant features from the CVs. These features are then fed into a Spark pipeline for classification. Thanks to the scaling of Spark, we were able to process large quantities of CVs in record time, making it a practical solution for recruitment companies. This research paves the way for more efficient and accurate automation of Arabic CV classifying, helping to facilitate the recruitment process in Arabic-speaking regions.

Keywords: Text Classification · Transformers · Deep Learning · BERT · ArabicBERT · NLP · Apache Spark

1 Introduction

Word processing is a fundamental field of computer science and artificial intelligence, it plays a vital role in the analysis, generation and understanding of human language [1]. Among the world's languages, Arabic occupies a particularly important place due to its historical, cultural and linguistic richness [13]. Word processing in Arabic represents a fascinating and complex challenge, as this language has unique characteristics that require a specific and tailored approach. One such crucial application is Curriculum Vitae (CV) classifying, which is a fundamental part of the recruitment process in Arabic-speaking regions.

The process of classifying and analyzing Curriculum Vitae (CV) is an essential element in the field of recruitment, allowing companies and organizations to select the most qualified candidates for vacant positions. In the context of Arabic-speaking regions, where the demand for qualified labor is constantly increasing, word processing of CVs in Arabic has become a crucial issue. Faced with this requirement, a convergence of advanced technologies has emerged to address this complex challenge, including the

B. Hdioud and S. L. Aouragh (Eds.): ICALP 2024, CCIS 2339, pp. 160–169, 2025.
https://doi.org/10.1007/978-3-031-79164-2_14

use of natural language processing (NLP) models such as ArabicBERT [2] and the power of the Spark platform.

BERT (Bidirectional Encoder Representations) from Transformers) is a revolutionary NLP model that excels at contextual understanding of human language [3]. By adapting BERT to the Arabic language context, researchers and engineers have opened the door to significant advances in CV text processing. BERT is able to automatically extract relevant information from resumes, identifying skills, work experience, education, and other key elements needed to evaluate candidates. To further improve the efficiency of this approach, we leverage the Spark platform, a distributed data processing solution. Spark offers exceptional scaling, enabling it to process vast volumes of CVs in record time, making it a practical solution for recruitment companies looking to manage large amounts of data efficiently.

In this article, we will explore in detail the application of BERT on the Spark platform for text processing of Arabic CVs. We will discuss specific challenges related to Arabic, including tokenization, normalization, and named entity recognition, and how BERT can overcome them through its ability to understand the context and semantics of Arabic sentences.

Ultimately, this innovative combination of BERT and Spark paves the way for more efficient and accurate automation of Arabic CV classifing, thereby improving the recruitment process in Arabic-speaking regions. In the sections ahead, we'll dive deeper into the methodology, highlighting the benefits it offers for recruiters and companies looking for talent.

2 Related Works

Many studies have been carried out in the field of text classification using BERT in Arabic, also known as Arabert, in the context of Big Data with Spark. In addition, several research studies have explored the use of this model to classify CVs in the field of e-recruitment. This work strongly confirmed the effectiveness of this model for extracting relevant information from CVs.

In this context [2] explores the use of the Arabic BERT model to create universal contextualized sentence representations with the aim of categorizing Arabic texts using two approaches: knowledge transfer and feature extraction. The results show that the refined AraBERT model achieves exceptional performance, with F1 score and accuracy reaching up to 99%.

Also [4] looks at misinformation related to COVID-19 vaccination in Arabic. It proposes the use of supervised machine learning and natural language processing techniques to classify information into real and fake news. And it demonstrates the use of Python's NLTK package for data preprocessing and classification using the RF model.

On the other hand, Much scientific work has been carried out to develop methods [5] and [6] and approaches to align CVs with job offers such as [7, 8] and others. This research focuses on extracting essential information from CVs and job advertisements, as well as comparing and evaluating their match.

Other research has also focused on the use of Spark [9], for distributed processing of large amounts of textual data. Spark helps leverage parallel computing power to perform natural language processing-intensive tasks [10] [11], improving the efficiency and scalability of text classification [12].

3 Methodology

As part of our Arabic language CV classification project using the Arabert model, including the integration of our model into a Spark pipeline, we followed a life cycle structured in five essential steps:

1- Data collection
2- Data preparation
3- Design of the classification model
4- Model deployment
5- Monitoring or supervision of the model

The first step was **data collection**, where we gathered a diverse corpus of Arabic-language CVs from online sources. Next, we undertook **data preparation**, a crucial process for cleaning, normalizing and pre-processing the raw CVs. This step includes tokenization and transformation of the data into a format suitable for training the model (Fig. 1).

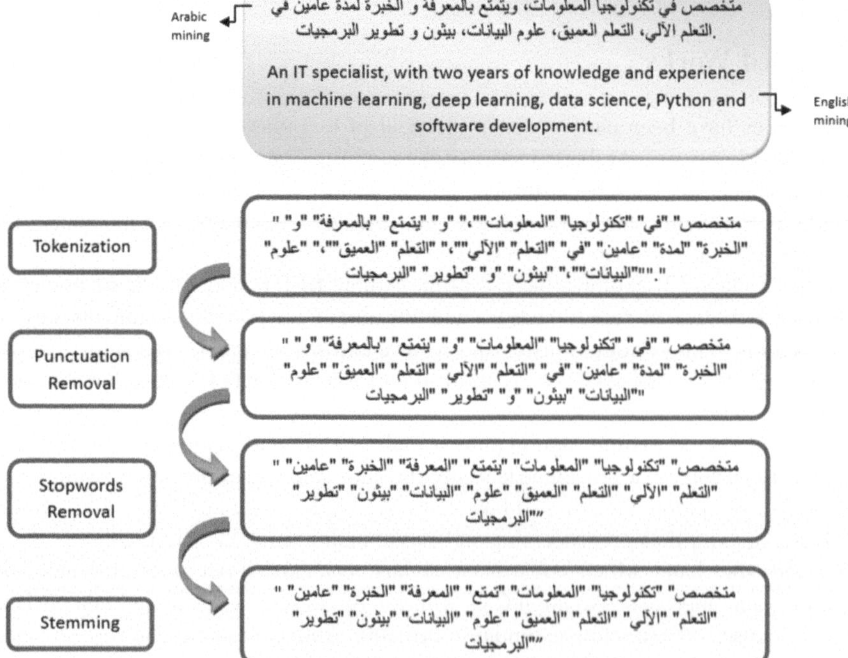

Fig. 1. The implementation of the different stages of NLP

Our dataset is subdivided into two distinct parts: the first, reserved for the training phase, includes 80% of all the data in our dataset, while the second portion contains the remaining 20% intended for testing. Figure 3 illustrates the distribution of labels between the training and testing data (Fig. 2).

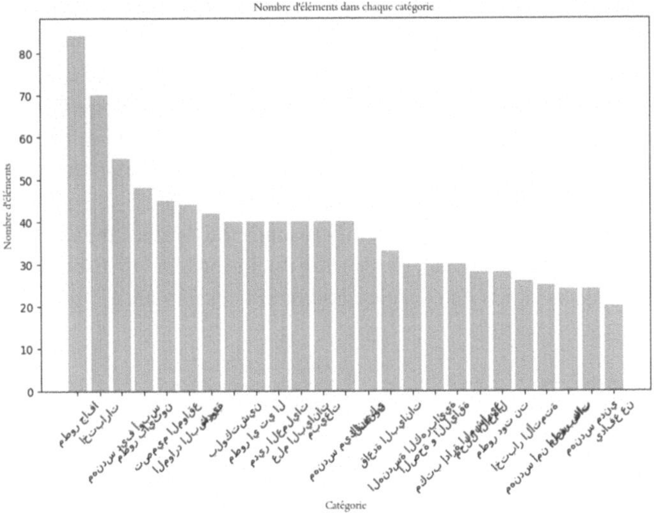

Fig. 2. CVs by category

Our prototype system was subjected to experiments in a distributed environment, deployed on a virtual machine running on a personal computer with an 11th generation 64-bit Intel Core processor clocked at 2.8 GHz (i7-1165G7) and equipped 16 GB of RAM memory. The operating system used was Ubuntu 20.04 LTS, while the version of Spark used was 3.2.1.

This data is preloaded into the Hadoop HDFS file system and then undergoes a preprocessing process using natural language processing (NLP) techniques.

The results relating to the calculation of the weight of each functionality are obtained using the Term technique Frequency -Inverse Document Frequency (TF-IDF). This method involves counting the occurrences of tokens present in the corpus for each CV, followed by normalization by the total number of occurrences of these same tokens in the entire corpus.

$$\mathrm{tf}(\mathrm{t},\ \mathrm{d}) = \frac{f_{\mathrm{d}}(\mathrm{t})}{\max\limits_{w \in d} f_{\mathrm{d}}(\mathrm{w})}$$

$$\mathrm{idf}(\mathrm{t},\ \mathrm{D}) = \ln \frac{|\mathrm{D}|}{|\{d \in D : t \in d\}|}$$

$$tfidf(t, d, D) = tf(t, d).idf(t, D)$$

$$f_{\mathrm{d}}(\mathrm{t}) := \text{frequency of term t in document d}$$

$$D: = corpus\ of\ documents$$

The third step was **the design of the classification model**, where we chose Arabert as the natural language processing model for its compatibility with the Arabic language, the results found by Rabert will be compared with other models, such as SVM and RNN. We then trained the model on our prepared dataset, making sure to tailor it specifically to the CV classification task.

After training, we proceeded to the fourth step, **model deployment**, to make it accessible through an online interface with Spark, allowing users to perform CV classifications in a distributed and scalable manner. Finally, to ensure **monitoring or supervision of the model** and guarantee its continued performance, we have implemented monitoring, error management, and user feedback mechanisms.

A Spark pipeline allows you to efficiently manage the Arabic language resume classification process by automating data processing operations and distributing computation across a Spark cluster, which can accelerate data processing and classification at scale.

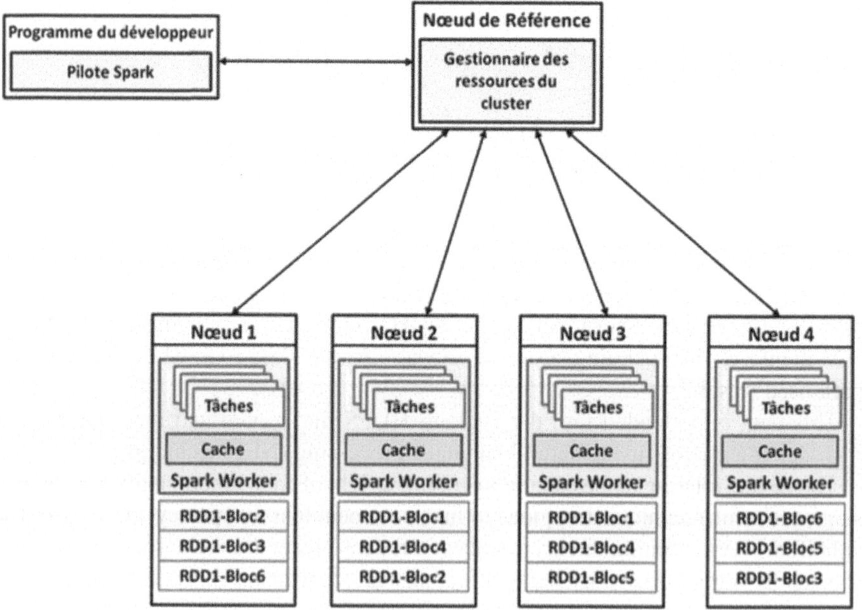

Fig. 3. Distributed system architecture with Spark

This well-structured life cycle allowed us to arrive at an effective Arabic language CV classification model, meeting the specific needs of our project, while guaranteeing the quality of the results and the security of the data (Fig. 4).

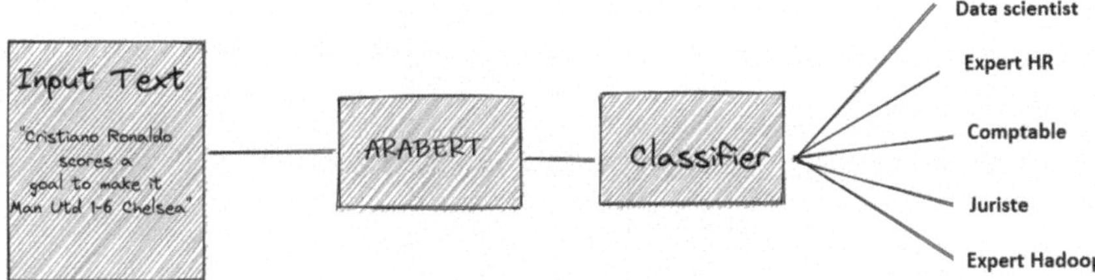

Fig. 4. Proposed system

4 Positional Encoding Avec ARABERT

The integration of Positional Encoding into transformer-based natural language processing models is a crucial step in enabling them to effectively capture sequence information. In the context of the Arabic language, a complex linguistic domain with distinct sentence structures, the adoption of this technique holds particular significance. ARABERT, a pre-trained model specifically tailored for the Arabic language based on the Transformer architecture, also incorporates Positional Encoding to account for the relative position of words in a sequence. Following a similar approach to standard Transformer models, ARABERT associates each token in the sequence with a position vector that encodes its location in the sentence. This enriched representation enables ARABERT to better understand the structure and context of the Arabic language, thereby contributing to improved performance across various natural language processing tasks such as text classification, machine translation, and text generation (Figs. 5 and 6).

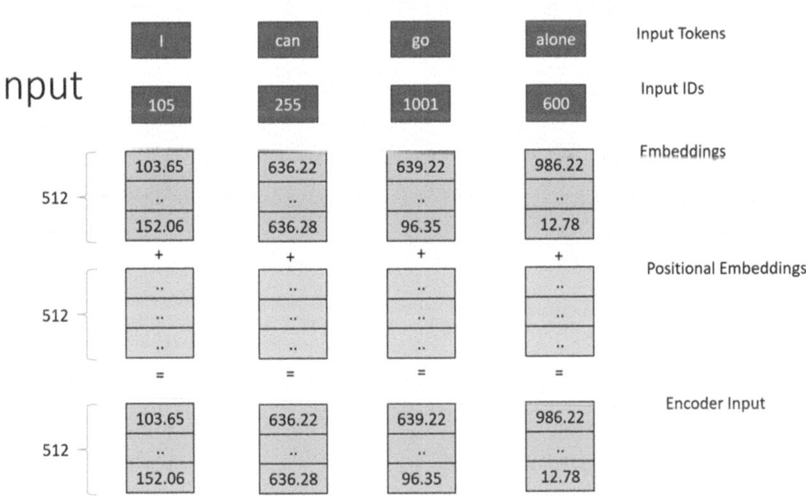

Fig. 5. Positional Encoding

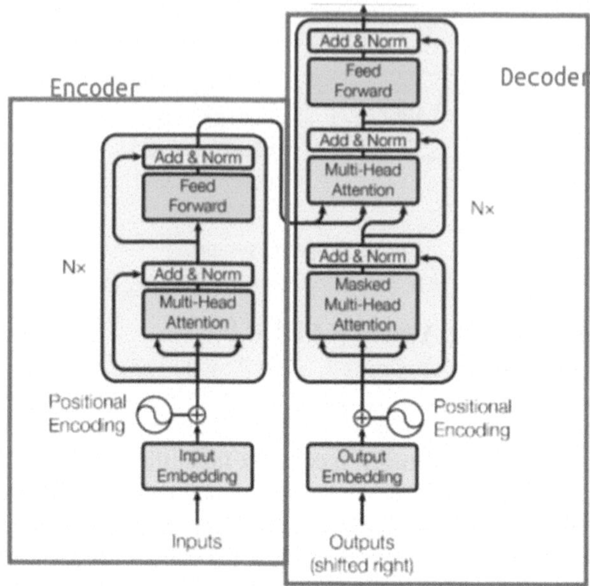

Fig. 6. Transformer encoder-decoder model diagram

5 The Results

Evaluating the machine learning algorithms used is of crucial importance because a model may produce satisfactory results when evaluated according to certain metrics, such as accuracy score, while showing poor performance when evaluated according to other metrics, including log loss or other similar criteria. Often, we rely on classification

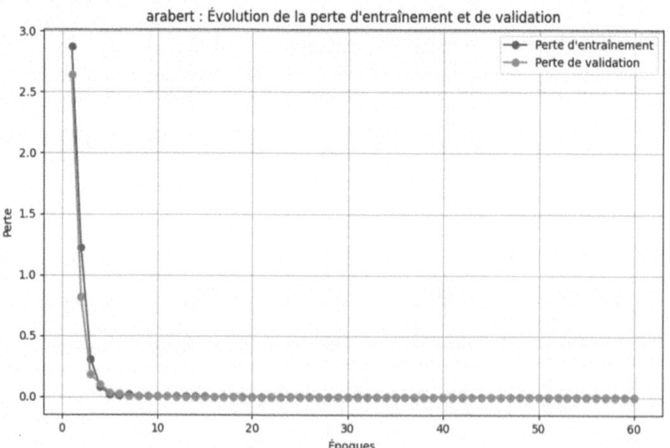

Fig. 7. Arabert Model

accuracy to evaluate the performance of our model. However, this measurement may be insufficient for a complete analysis of model performance.

With this in mind, it is essential to explore various types of evaluation metrics available. Classification accuracy is commonly used and measures the proportion of correct predictions out of the total set of samples.

Another effective evaluation metric that is particularly suitable for multiclass classification is logarithmic loss, also known as Log Loss. When Log Loss is used as shown in the figures below, the classifier must assign a probability to each class for each sample, which allows incorrect classifications to be penalized (Figs. 7, 8 and 9).

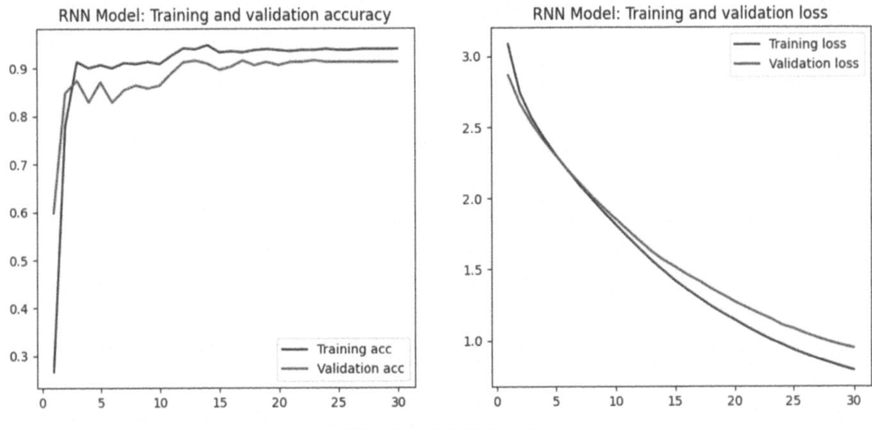

Fig. 8. RNN Model

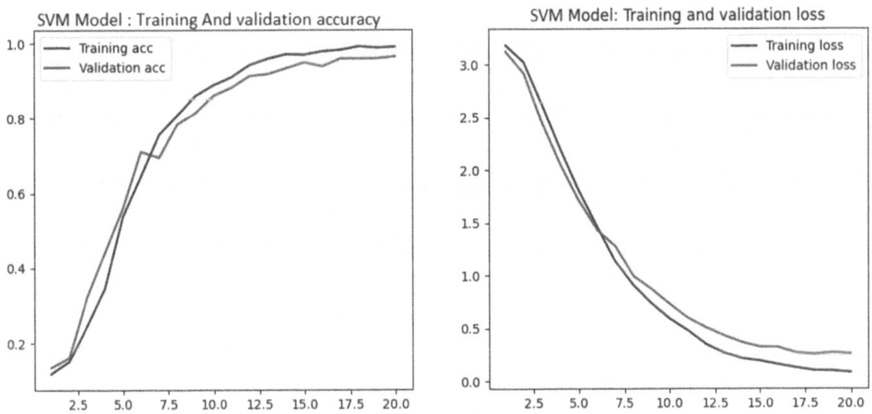

Fig. 9. SVM Model

6 Comparative Discussion

The results of the automatic CV classification experiment using the Arabert, RNN and SVM models are summarized in the table below (Table 1):

Table 1. Performance results of the proposed methods.

Model	Accuracy	Precision	Reminder	F1 score
Arabert	0.9889	0.9901	0.9882	0.9892
RNN	0.9275	0.9279	0.9275	0.9234
SVM	0.9377	0.9324	0.9377	0.9252

The Arabert model clearly stands out with a remarkable Accuracy score of 98.89%, meaning it correctly classified almost 99% of resumes. This demonstrates the power of this pre-trained model for text processing in Arabic.

Regarding Accuracy, which measures the proportion of correct predictions compared to the total number of positive samples predicted, the Arabert model displays an exceptional accuracy of 99.01%. This indicates an extremely high ability to minimize false positives. The SVM model tracks with an accuracy of 93.24%, which is respectable, although significantly lower than Arabert. The RNN model has a similar accuracy of 92.79%.

Recall, which measures the proportion of positive samples actually predicted correctly, is also impressive for Arabert with a score of 98.82%. The SVM model shows a recall of 93.77%, which is solid, but less efficient compared to Arabert. The RNN model has a similar recall of 92.75%.

The F1 Score, which is a harmonic average between Precision and Recall, highlights the overall capability of each model. The Arabert model achieves a remarkable F1 Score of 98.92%, while the SVM model achieves 92.52%, and the RNN model obtains 92.34%.

In summary, the results highlight the overwhelming superiority of the Arabert model, with exceptional performance in terms of Precision, Recall and Accuracy. The SVM and RNN models, although having reasonable performance scores, fail to compete with Arabert in this experiment. The choice of model will therefore depend on the specific needs of the classification task, but Arabert clearly stands out as the optimal choice in this context.

7 Conclusion

This article introduced a new active strategy for the automatic classification of CVs in the field of e-recruitment, highlighting the performance of the Arabert algorithm. Furthermore, we managed to integrate our system into a Big Data environment based on Spark, taking advantage of its speed thanks to data processing carried out via in-memory RDDs.

The next steps of our work will focus on improving our CV classification results by exploring other more appropriate techniques, including other types of transformers.

References

1. Korde, V.: Text classification and classifiers a survey. Int. J. Artif. Intell. Appl. **3**(2), 85–99 (2012). https://doi.org/10.5121/ijaia.2012.3208
2. FZ. El-Alami, S. O. El Alaoui, N. En Nahnahi , Contextual semantic embeddings based on fine-tuned AraBERT model for Arabic text multi-class categorization, February 2021, Journal of King Saud University - Computer and Information Sciences 34(2), https://doi.org/10.1016/j.jksuci.2021.02.005
3. Cui, H., Wang, C., Yu, Y.: News short text classification based on BERT model and fusion model. Highlights Sci. Eng. Technol. **34**, 262–2680 (2023). https://doi.org/10.54097/hset.v34i.5482
4. Mahmoudi, O., Filali Bouami, M., Badri, M.: Arabic language modeling based on supervised machine learning (2023). https://doi.org/10.18280/ria.360315
5. Shawal Chowdhury, S.M., Chowdhury, M., Sultana, A.: Matching job circular with resume using different natural language processing based algorithms. In: Machine Intelligence and Emerging Technologies, pp. 428–442 (2023). https://doi.org/10.1007/978-3-031-34619-4_34
6. Dong, Z.: Resume recommendation based on text similarity. Appl. Comput. Eng. **6**(1), 848–853 (2023). https://doi.org/10.54254/2755-2721/6/20230937
7. Bouhoun, Z., Guerrois, T., Li, X., Baker, M.: Information retrieval using domain adapted language models: application to resume documents for HR recruitment assistance. In: Computational Science and Its Applications – ICCSA 2023 Workshops, pp. 440–457 (2023). https://doi.org/10.1007/978-3-031-37105-9_30
8. Rojas-Galeano, S., Posada, J., Ordoñez, E.: A bibliometric perspective on AI research for job-résumé matching. Sci. World J. **2022**(3), 1–15 (2022). https://doi.org/10.1155/2022/8002363
9. Semberecki, P., Maciejewski, H.: Distributed classification of text documents on apache spark platform. In: International Conference on Artificial Intelligence and Soft Computing (2016). https://doi.org/10.1007/978-3-319-39378-0_53
10. Oğul, İ.Ü., Ozcan, C., Hakdağlı, Ö.: Text Classification with Spark Support Vector Machine, Conference: 1. Ulusal Bulut Bilişim Ve Büyük Veri Sempozyumu B3S'17, At: Antalya (2017)
11. The Deep Learning and Apache Spark Enabled Architecture for Improving the Performance of Big Data Classification. Int. J. Innovat. Technol. Exploring Eng. **8**(11), 2908–2914 (2019), https://doi.org/10.35940/ijitee.K2445.0981119
12. Gonzalez-Lopez, J., Cano, A., Ventura, S.: Large-scale multi-label ensemble learning on spark (2017). https://doi.org/10.1109/Trustcom/BigDataSE/ICESS.2017.328,Conference: IEEETrustcom/BigDataSE/ICESS
13. Bourahouat, G., Abourezq, M., Najima, D.: Word embedding as a semantic feature extraction technique in Arabic natural language processing: an overview. Int. Arab J. Inf. Technol. **21**(2) (2024). https://doi.org/10.34028/iajit/21/2/13

Fine-Tuning AraBART on AHS Dataset for Arabic Abstractive Summarization

Mustapha Benbarka(✉) and Moulay Abdellah Kassimi

ESTIDMA, ENSA Agadir, Ibn Zohr University, Agadir, Morocco
{mustapha.benbarka,moulayabdellah.kassimi}@edu.uiz.ac.ma

Abstract. Recent studies dealing with Abstractive Summarization are dominated by the use of Pre-trained Language Models based on Transformers. While the main contributions are applied to English, a review of the literature highlights the existence of a trend towards applying this framework on Arabic. This paper describes the full pipeline of Fine-tuning a Pre-trained Language Model based on Transformers for Arabic Abstractive Summarization. The model used is AraBART. The experiments are conducted on AHS dataset. Our work also challenges the quality of this dataset regarding the effects of repetitive summaries on the performances of the model. We found that their effect is substantial pointing out the need of a thorough study to be conducted on this dataset. A score of 54.69 $ROUGE_1$ is obtained on the test dataset. This score drops to 46.32 when the repetitive summaries are removed. A detailed analysis is provided discussing this issue.

Keywords: Arabic Abstractive Summarization · Pre-trained Language Models · Transformers · AraBART · AHS Dataset

1 Introduction

Automatic Text Summarization (ATS) is a Natural Language Processing (NLP) task that aims to produce a reduced text from an original document. This reduced version captures, ideally, the most relevant elements (Fig. 1).

There are, mainly, two approaches that tackle this problem : Abstractive Methods and Extractive Methods [1]. Extractive Models focus on extracting the most important sentences in the input text. Those sentences should belong to the original text. On the contrary, Abstractive Models try to mimic the behavior of a human by generating a summary that captures the meaning of the original text without any need to use passages from the original text.

Recent papers dealing with Abstractive Summarization are dominated by the use of Deep Neural Networks in which the task is designed as a *Sequence-to-Sequence (Seq2Seq)* problem [2] (e.g. as *Encoder/Decoder* architecture) and the models are Pre-trained models [3–6]. These models are based on the Transformer [7] architecture and become the "*De Facto*" for multiple downstream NLP tasks including Summarization.

B. Hdioud and S. L. Aouragh (Eds.): ICALP 2024, CCIS 2339, pp. 170–182, 2025.
https://doi.org/10.1007/978-3-031-79164-2_15

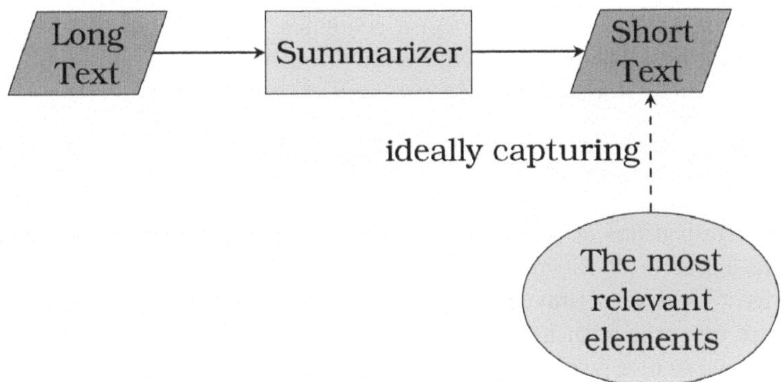

Fig. 1. ATS System Overview

Those models are mainly applied to English. There promising results encouraged researchers interested in Arabic to adopt them to solve the same tasks in the context of Arabic [8–13].

Our work focuses on this class of models regarding their performances in Arabic Abstractive Summarization. Our main contribution is providing a detailed pipeline of fine-tuning a specific pre-trained model which is AraBART [8] on Arabic Headline Summary (AHS) dataset [14]. This includes a comparison between our findings and the original results produced by Al Maleh and Desouki. Our study also provides some analyses regarding the quality of AHS dataset and its impact on our results.

To the best of our knowledge, there are only two works dealing with this dataset with in-depth analyses : the original works of Al Maleh and Desouki and a recent study [9] bench-marking some Transformer Language Models.

2 Background

2.1 Encoder-Decoder Sequence-to-Sequence Models

Encoder-Decoder Sequence-to-Sequence (Seq2Seq) Models were originally introduced by Sutskever *et al.* [2] in 2014 and applied to Machine Translation.

The framework is very straightforward, which consists of two main blocks : the encoder component, *A Recurrent Neural Network (RNN)* [15], which deals with the input sequence (source) and produces an intermediary representation, which in turn taken by the decoder component in order to produce another sequence as output (target). In other words, given an input text, which can be considered as a sequence of tokens $(x_1, x_2, ..., x_n)$; the encoder transforms this sequence into a latent representation with fixed length, which in turn transformed by the decoder in order to produce an output $(y_1, y_2, ..., y_m)$, hence the name *Sequence-to-Sequence (Seq2Seq)*.

Despite the fact that the experiments of the original paper were applied to Machine Translation, the model itself is agnostic which means that it can be used whenever we want to transform a sequence into another. Therefore, this framework can also be applied to Summarization by considering the problem as a transformation of a long sequence into a short one.

2.2 Attention Mechanism

Among the limitations of the Encoder-Decoder Architecture is that the encoder can fail to capture all the relevant information of the source sentence. This is mainly due to the fact that the encoding part is done by mapping the source sequence to a vector with fixed length, which can lead to lose contextual information, in particular when it comes to dealing with long sequences [16]. To overcome this issue, *Attention* was introduced.

As the name might suggest, *Attention* means that on every step of the decoding process, the decoder directly interacts with the encoder in order to put its focus (i.e. *pay attention*) on a specific subset of the source sequence [17].

2.3 Transformers

The vanilla Transformer was introduced by Vaswani *et al.* in 2017 [7]. This work presented a new neural architecture based solely on attention without any use of recurrence or convolution. This work also led researchers to take the main components of the Transformer model and create other variants and augmentations such as Pre-trained Language Models based on Transformers (e.g. BERT [18] and BART [5]).

2.4 Pre-trained Language Models Based on Transformers

Pre-training models on large corpora and fine-tune them on downstream tasks, becomes the "*De Facto*" especially when dealing with Summarization [4–6]. This is mainly because the pre-training phase can teach the model some generalizations [19] and some statistical properties of the language, then the model can be used as initialization step for some downstream NLP tasks (Fig. 2).

2.5 BART Model

BART stands for *Bidirectional and Auto-Regressive Transformers*, a Denoising Autoencoder for pre-training sequence-to-sequence models [5]. Autoencoders are special case of the Encoder-Decoder models in which the input and the output belong to the same domain [20]. This particularity can lead the model to learn the identity function. To prevent this, a strategy (i.e. denoising) is used which consists of corrupting the inputs, by adding noise or a mask, then the network tries to reconstruct the original input [21].

BART architecture is based on the vanilla Transformer except for some modifications. The encoder is Bidirectional like BERT [18] and the decoder is Left-to-Right like GPT [22] (Fig. 3).

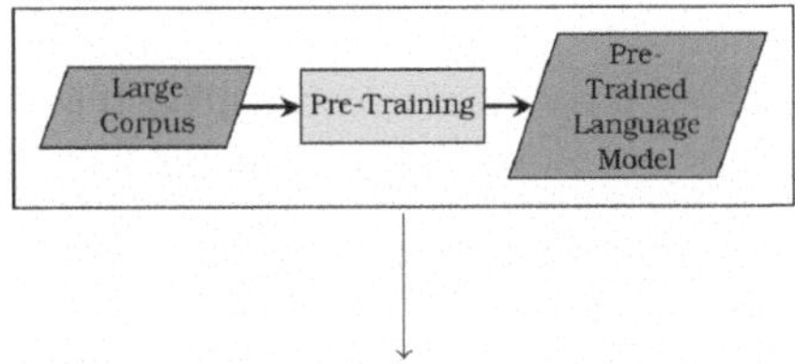

- Teaching the model some generalizations
- Learning statistical properties of the language
- Using the model as initialization step

Fig. 2. Importance of Pre-Training

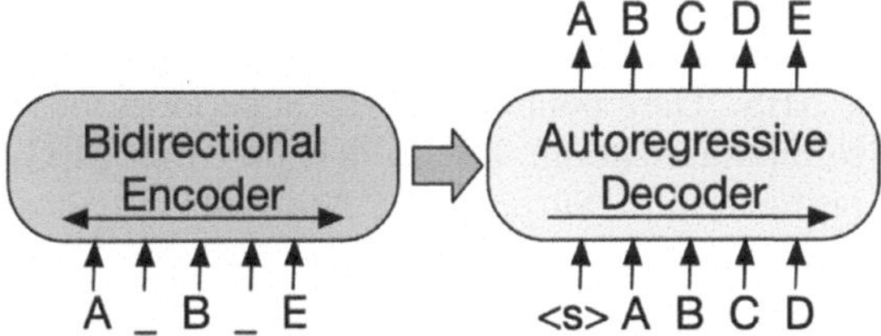

Fig. 3. A representation of BART [5]

3 Related Works

Recent advances in Abstractive Summarization applied to English become a source of inspiration to other researchers interested in Arabic. Many studies are now taking the main blocks of state-of-the-art models, originally designed for English, and apply them to Arabic.

3.1 Models

We can mention :

mBART. [23] a pre-trained language model based on BART architecture and trained on large-scale monolingual corpora in many languages including Arabic.

AraBART. [8] the first Arabic model in which the encoder and the decoder are pre-trained end-to-end based on BART architecture. The model was pre-trained on the same dataset used by AraBERT [24]. Eddine *et al.* [8] fine-tuned this model on multiple Abstractive Summarization datasets ; AHS was not included. Their results outperform many models including mBART.

AraGPT. [12] a pre-trained language model based on GPT-2 [25] architecture. The model was trained on a large Arabic corpus constructed from web text and news articles. The model has 1.46 billion parameters.

AraT5. [13] another pre-trained model based on T5 architecture [26] which uses a particular framework. This particularity resides in converting all downstream NLP tasks into a unified text-to-text format. The pre-training was done on huge corpora including non Modern Standard Arabic (MSA) materials (e.g. tweets).

3.2 Bench-Marking Studies

Some bench-marking studies were also conducted by fine-tuning some of the previous models on different Arabic datasets :

Chouikhi and Alsuhaibani [9] performed a comparison between multiple Transformers based Language Models (TLMs) fine-tuned on three different datasets including AHS. They pointed out the superiority of those models for Arabic Abstractive Summarization. The models based on PEGASUS [6] architecture achieved better results. Surprisingly, AraBART scores a very low value on AHS dataset.

Bani-Almarjeh and Kurdy [10] conducted a study by comparing some RNN based models with some TLMs. They first constructed a new dataset named *SumArabic* following the same steps of creating AHS dataset by Al Maleh and Desouki [14]. Then they fine-tuned some TLMs models (e.g. AraGPT and AraT5) on this new dataset and performed a comparison between them and some RNN based models considered as baselines. They reported a gain, in terms of performance, in the favor of the former models.

Kahla *et al.* [11] also fine-tuned mBERT [18], AraBERT [24] and mBART [23] on their own corpus. They reported that cross-lingual strategies can lead to better results.

3.3 Datasets

Following recent studies, one can distinguish between two main classes of datasets used in Abstractive Summarization :

Datasets Constructed as Pairs of Article/Title. Those datasets are compiled by crawling the web and extracting the entire article or a chunk of it to be used as the original text. The title of this article is considered as a summary of the extracted text (e.g. AHS [14] and SumArabic [10]). The Summarization methods applied to this class of datasets are also referred to, in the literature, as

Headlines Generation. The main advantages of compiling those datasets is that they are less tedious to create and more suitable, heuristically, to be evaluated by ROUGE metrics [27] because the tokens of the references tend to belong to the original text[1].

Datasets Crafted by Experts Manually or Using a Well Designed Protocol. These datasets can be considered as gold-standard (e.g. XL-Sum dataset [28]). They have multiple level of abstractivness and penalize extractive approaches. Despite their high quality, they are expensive to produce and less suitable to be evaluated automatically using ROUGE as a metric.

4 Experiments

4.1 Method

Our study highlights the potential gains to be made by adopting a strategy based on Transformers Pre-trained Language Models in the context of Arabic Abstractive Summarization.

Our approach is to take a pre-trained model, AraBART in our case, and fine-tune it on AHS dataset [14] following the pipeline described in (Fig. 4).

We choose AraBART because it is the first Arabic pre-trained model based on BART architecture and available to public.

The choice of this dataset is justified by the fact that it covers a wide range of topics which may make our model more robust in terms of generalizations. In addition, and as we mentioned before, this dataset is more suitable, heuristically, with ROUGE metrics [27] during the evaluation.
Despite the relevance of these intuitions regarding our choices, the experiments challenge the quality of this dataset and the degree of bias induced into our results. More details are provided in the next sections.

4.2 Dataset Description

Arabic Headline Summary (AHS) is a dataset of arabic articles combined with their corresponding summaries (i.e. references). This dataset is compiled by Al Maleh and Desouki [14] by crawling the website mawdoo3. The authors gathered and processed 294 839 entries by taking the introduction paragraph of an article as the original text and the title of this article as a summary.

The dataset is made available to public at https://osf.io/btcnd/ which contains two *txt* files : *articles introductions* and *articles titles*.

[1] They are more extractive datasets than abstractive.

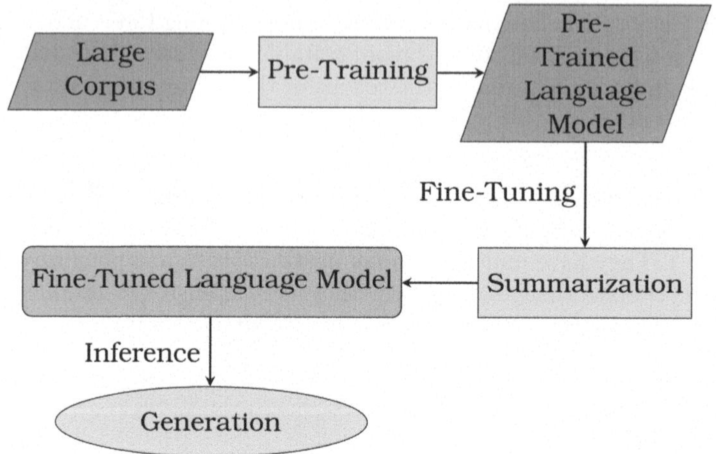

Fig. 4. Workflow of fine-tuning a Pre-Trained Language Model for Summarization

4.3 Dataset Preparation

In order to use this dataset, we added some extra preprocessing by creating a *csv* file with two columns *Article* and *Title*. Each row is a combination of an introduction paragraph and the title of the original article.

We split the dataset into three subsets : *train*, *dev* and *test*. We took the same proportions (i.e. 235871, 38968, 20000) used by the authors to compare their findings with ours.

We should also mention that the dataset has a substantial level of repetitive summaries. This is justified because the summaries are mainly just headlines and it is natural to find the same headline describing different articles. However, we should take this into consideration to avoid biasing our results.

4.4 Evaluation

The metrics used to quantify automatically "*the quality*" of a summary are usually ROUGE-1, ROUGE-2 and ROUGE-L. ROUGE stands for *Recall-Oriented Understudy for Gisting Evaluation* and was originally introduced by Lin [27] in 2004 in order to overcome a manual evaluation, which is a tedious and expensive task even for small corpora.

1, 2 and L associated with ROUGE respectively means that we are scoring based on Unigrams, on Bigrams and on the Longest common Subsequence (LCS) [29].

In order to compute this metric, we need a candidate summary and a set of reference summaries. Then, we calculate a recall between them. As defined by Lin [27], ROUGE-N can be computed using the following formula :

$$ROUGE_N = \frac{\sum_{S \in \{ReferemceSummaries\}} \sum_{gram_n \in S} Count_{match}(gram_n)}{\sum_{S \in \{ReferemceSummaries\}} \sum_{gram_n \in S} Count(gram_n)} \quad (1)$$

where :

- n is the size of n-gram
- $gram_n$ is the n-gram
- $Count_{match}(gram_n)$ is the maximum number of n-grams co-occurring in a candidate summary and a set of reference summaries

By default, $ROUGE_N$ is a Recall measure which means that it favors the long summaries. So in practice, a Precision measure is added in order to compute F-1 score as a trade-off :

$$Precision = \frac{| grams_{reference} \cap grams_{infered} |}{grams_{infered}} \tag{2}$$

$$Recall = \frac{| grams_{reference} \cap grams_{infered} |}{grams_{reference}} \tag{3}$$

$$F_1 - score = 2 \times \frac{Precision \times Recall}{Precision + Recall} \tag{4}$$

Despite the usefulness of this measure, it suffers from a number of limitations, in particular its lack of ability to identify synonyms [30] because it relies on the overlapping of tokens. This penalizes Abstractive Methods during the evaluation.

4.5 Training

We fetched the pre-trained model *AraBART* and fine-tune it on AHS dataset following the adapted version (Fig. 5) of the previous general workflow (Fig. 4).

The training configuration is described in Table 1.

Table 1. Training Configuration

Model Architecture	BART
Optimizer	Adam
Learning Rate	0.00002
Evaluation Strategy	Epoch
Epochs	4
Weight Decay	0.01
Metrics	R_1, R_2 and R_L
Training Time	Approximately 10 h including the evaluation time per epoch
Hardware	GPU : RTX 3070, RAM : 34G

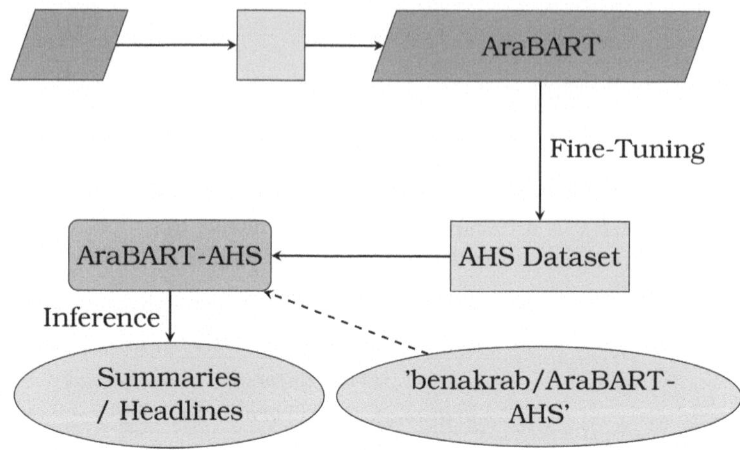

Fig. 5. Adapted Workflow

5 Results and Discussion

5.1 Evaluation on the *Dev* Dataset

On each training epoch, we evaluated our model on a subset of the *dev* (i.e. validation) dataset. The results are described in Table 2.

Table 2. Evaluation results during the fine-tuning

Epoch	Training Loss	Validation Loss	R_1	R_2	R_L
1	1.334300	1.213489	53.63	38.78	53.14
2	1.128200	1.198254	53.93	39.05	53.44
3	1.012300	1.197924	54.65	39.71	54.18
4	0.943200	1.191044	54.86	39.91	54.38

As one can see, the training was stable and the performances were improving on each epoch.

5.2 Evaluation on the *Test* Dataset

As a final step, once the training was completed, we evaluated our model on the *test* dataset which contains 20000 instances (Table 3).

Our fine-tuned model is available on *Huggingface* platform via this link using the name benakrab/AraBART-AHS.

An instance of a generated summary is described in (Fig. 6). The English translation was added manually to assist no Arabic speakers.

Table 3. Evaluation results on the *test* dataset

Model	R_1	R_2	R_L
AraBART-AHS	54.69	39.76	54.24

index	text	reference	topic	summary
5023	ينصح بممارسة الكتابة بشكل يومي ، وجعلها روتينا يوميا ؛ و ذلك لتطوير المهارات اللغوية و الكتابية و تحسينها ، إذ إنه كلما كتب الشخص أكثر كلما شعر بتطور أكبر ، و لذلك يجب تخصيص وقت لكتابة فقرة على الأقل ، أو صفحة كاملة يوميا ، و يمكن الاستيقاظ باكرا للكتابة ، أو النوم متأخرا بعد كتابة فقرة ما ، و لو لفترة قصيرة لا تتعدى خمس عشرة دقيقة عند عدم وجود وقت كاف أثناء النهار .	الكتابة بشكل يومي	تعليم	ممارسة الكتابة يوميا
	It is recommended to practice writing on a daily basis, and make it a daily routine; This is to develop and improve linguistic and writing skills, as the more a person writes, the more developed he feels. Therefore, time must be allocated to write at least a paragraph, or a full page daily, and one can wake up early to write, or sleep late after writing a paragraph. Even for a short period not exceeding fifteen minutes when there is not enough time during the day.	Writing on a daily basis	Education	Practicing writing daily

Fig. 6. Instance of the original text, its reference and the generated summary

5.3 Results Comparison

The scores achieved by our model are larger by 10 points R_1 compared to the findings of Al Maleh and Desouki and using their best model [14]. This comparison is presented in Table 4.

Table 4. Comparison of fine-tuned AraBART with the best results of Al Maleh and Desouki [14] and Chouikhi and Alsuhaibani [9] on AHS dataset

Study	Model	R_1	R_2	R_L
Al Maleh and Desouki [14]	Pointer-generator + length penalty	**44.23**	-	-
Chouikhi and Alsuhaibani [9]	Fine-tuned AraBART	**34.74**	17.50	34.08
Ours	AraBART-AHS	**54.69**	39.76	54.24

5.4 Repetitive Summaries (i.e. References)

The dataset has a substantial level of repetitive summaries ($\simeq$ 30%). This is consistent with the way in which the AHS dataset was built. Figure 7 illustrates an instance of these repetitive summaries.

In order to isolate the effect of the repetitive summaries on our results, we eliminated all the rows of the test dataset that share the same summary with the training dataset.

The evaluation shows a significant effect of those repetitive summaries on the training. We witnessed a drop of 9 R_1 compared to what we achieved when those summaries were included in our test dataset and an increase of 14 R_1 if we test our model only on those repetitive summaries.

	subset	text	reference	summary
0	train	عرفت القصيدة العربية في العصر العباسي شكلا و بناء جديدا اختلفت فيه عن باقي العصور ؛ فقد ابتعدوا فيه عن كتابة القصائد المطولة و لجأوا إلى كتابة القطع القصيرة ، و قد جددوا في مقدمات القصائد فقاموا مثلا بكتابة مقدمات جديدة تلائم طبيعة العصر العباسي كمقدمات وصف الطبيعة و الحكمة و غيرها ، و قد برز الشاعر أبو نواس الحكمي الدمشقي في هذا المجال حيث ابتكر مقدمات فريدة من نوعها و التي تسمى الخمريات ، ويشار أخيرا إلى أنه غلب على الشعر في هذا العصر الحماسة و الوصف و الغزل بقسميه الحسي و الصريح بالإضافة إلى الزهد و الحكمة أيضا .	الشعر العباسي	الشعر في العصر العباسي
1	train	طورت الأساليب الشعرية في العصر العباسي بسبب اطلاع الشعراء على الثقافات الأجنبية التي وسعت مداركهم ، و زادت من معلوماتهم ، إلى جانب تطور الحياة الحضارية . فنجد أن الشعراء قد مالوا إلى الأساليب السهلة و المفهومة المنسوجة من واقع الحياة ، و ابتعدوا عن الألفاظ الصعبة التي قل استعمالها أو هجرت ، واعتمدوا على المحسنات البديعية ، و التجديد في الألفاظ تبعا لتطور الأمور ، حتى وصلت الحال عند مجموعة من الشعراء إلى استخدام ألفاظ غير عربية في الشعر . و عليه ، يمكننا أن نقول أن مفهوم الأسلوب يعني الطريقة السلوكية التي يعتمدها الشاعر في شعره ، بحيث كان لكل شاعر أو مجموعة من الشعراء تلك الطريقة التي عرفوا بها . لقد نظم شعراء الدولة العباسية الأساليب الشعرية في ضوء حضارة الدولة وثقافتها ، وطريقة تذوقها للفنون ، لذا جاء الأسلوب الشعري أقرب من يكون إلى الرقة في النسج ، والدقة في التصوير ، و شاعت في الحواشي ألوان من الزخرفة اللفظية ، و الصنعة اللغوية ، إضافة إلى النغمة الموسيقية التي تحرك المشاعر و الوجدان . و عليه ، نجد أن الشعراء كلما كانوا أكثر تحضرا مالوا إلى الزينة و الاطافة في كل شيء ، فالطابع الحضري تغشاه الأناقة في كل جوانبه ، و هو ما يدل على التطور في الأذواق ، الرقي في الأفكار ، ورقيها ، و هو السبب الذي دفع بالشعر إلى إيجاد أسلوب جديد تركن فيه النفس لتستريح عند جماله و تناسقه ورقته . من أشهر شعراء العصر العباسي نذكر المتنبي ، و الأصمعي ، و أبا فراس الحمداني ، و أبا العلاء المعري ، و أبا نواس ، و ابن الرومي ، و ابن الفارض ، و أبا العتاهية ، و غيرهم من الشعراء . (4)	الشعر العباسي	الأساليب الشعرية في العصر العباسي
2	test	يعرف الشعر العباسي على أنه إبداع فني ظهر في فترة العصر العباسي ، و الذي كان يتأرجح منذ بدايته بين الطابع الأموي و الطابع العباسي ، و يجدر بالذكر أن العصر العباسي هو ذلك العصر الذي يمتد من عام 750م إلى عام 1258م ، حيث بدأ حكم خلفاء بني العباس الذين بلغ عددهم 37 خليفة ، بدءا بالخليفة عبد الله بن محمد بن علي بن عبد الله بن عباس بن عبد المطلب المعروف بالسفاح ، و انتهاء بالخليفة العباسي أبي أحمد عبد الله المستعصم بالله .	الشعر العباسي	الشعر العباسي
3	test	تميز الشعر العباسي بخصائص وميزات مختلفة كل الاختلاف عن الشعر في العصور الأخرى ، و يعتبر أبو تمام واحدا من أشهر شعراء ذلك العصر ، حيث كان له دور مميز في وضع التجديد في بنية القصيدة ، و في موضوعاتها ، و أحدث أبو تمام نتاج فني بمذهب فني جديد و مختلف ، و كان شعره لا يشبه أشعار القدماء ، و يجدر القول هنا أن أبا تمام استطاع أن يثير قضايا متعددة في الشعر العباسي ، و أفاد البناء الأدبي من نواحي عديدة ، و خرج الشعر العباسي من إطار التقليد إلى إطار التجديد .	الشعر العباسي	شعر أبي تمام

Fig. 7. Case of a repetitive summary

The results still slightly high compared to Al Maleh and Desouki (Table 5) but the drop amount is so significant that it calls for a very thorough examination of the dataset.

Al Maleh and Desouki did not mention any pre-processing regarding the repetitive summaries. This suggests that their results might also be biased.

Chouikhi and Alsuhaibani [9] conducted the same experiment but they did not also provide more details about the pre-processing done in order to deal with this issue. They mentioned that they eliminated repetitions which may indicate that the repetitive summaries are removed from the whole dataset. This may explain the very low R_1(34.74) score obtained by their study.

Table 5. Isolating the effect of repetitive summaries on our fine-tuned AraBART

Study	Model	Test Dataset	R_1	R_2	R_L
Ours	AraBART-AHS	All the instances of the test dataset	**54.69**	39.76	54.24
Ours	AraBART-AHS	Removing repetitive summaries	**46.32**	29.32	45.91
Ours	AraBART-AHS	Only repetitive summaries	**68.48**	56.96	67.98

6 Conclusion

The results achieved during our experiments show potential gains in terms of performances despite the fact that our results may have some degree of bias due to the repetitive summaries. A score of 54.69 $ROUGE_1$ is obtained on the test dataset. This score drops to 46.32 when the repetitive summaries are removed.

The observed effects of repetitive summaries on our results should be followed up by further studies in order to isolate their origins.

This work can be followed by investigating more in depth the AHS dataset in order to eliminate any known source of bias and to enhance its quality. Furthermore, more datasets can be used in addition to AHS, like SumArabic [10], in order to analyze the effects of the repetitive summaries. Then, a training phase can be conducted to assess our models in an appropriate context.

References

1. Hou, S.L., et al.: A survey of text summarization approaches based on deep learning. J. Comput. Sci. Technol. **36**(JCST-1912-10207.R2), 633 (2021). https://doi.org/10.1007/s11390-020-0207-x, https://jcst.ict.ac.cn/en/article/doi/10.1007/s11390-020-0207-x
2. Sutskever, I., Vinyals, O., Le, Q.V.: Sequence to sequence learning with neural networks. CoRR abs/1409.3215 (2014). arxiv:1409.3215
3. Narayan, S., Cohen, S.B., Lapata, M.: Don't give me the details, just the summary! Topic-aware convolutional neural networks for extreme summarization. In: Proceedings of the 2018 Conference on Empirical Methods in Natural Language Processing. Brussels, Belgium (2018)
4. Liu, Y., Lapata, M.: Text summarization with pretrained encoders. CoRR abs/1908.08345 (2019). arxiv:1908.08345
5. Lewis, M., et al.: BART: denoising sequence-to-sequence pre-training for natural language generation, translation, and comprehension. CoRR abs/1910.13461 (2019). arxiv:1910.13461
6. Zhang, J., Zhao, Y., Saleh, M., Liu, P.J.: PEGASUS: pre-training with extracted gap-sentences for abstractive summarization. CoRR abs/1912.08777 (2019). arxiv:1912.08777
7. Vaswani, A., et al.: Attention is all you need. CoRR abs/1706.03762 (2017). arxiv:1706.03762
8. Eddine, M.K., Tomeh, N., Habash, N., Roux, J.L., Vazirgiannis, M.: AraBART: a pretrained Arabic sequence-to-sequence model for abstractive summarization (2022)
9. Chouikhi, H., Alsuhaibani, M.: Deep transformer language models for Arabic text summarization: a comparison study. Appl. Sci. **12**(23) (2022). https://doi.org/10.3390/app122311944, https://www.mdpi.com/2076-3417/12/23/11944
10. Bani-Almarjeh, M., Kurdy, M.B.: Arabic abstractive text summarization using RNN-based and transformer-based architectures. Inf. Process. Manag. **60**(2), 103227 (2023)
11. Kahla, M., Yang, Z.G., Novák, A.: Cross-lingual fine-tuning for abstractive Arabic text summarization. In: Proceedings of the International Conference on Recent Advances in Natural Language Processing (RANLP 2021), pp. 655–663. INCOMA Ltd., Held Online (2021). https://aclanthology.org/2021.ranlp-1.74
12. Antoun, W., Baly, F., Hajj, H.M.: AraGPT2: pre-trained transformer for Arabic language generation. CoRR abs/2012.15520 (2020). https://arxiv.org/abs/2012.15520
13. Nagoudi, E.M.B., Elmadany, A.A., Abdul-Mageed, M.: Arat5: text-to-text transformers for arabic language understanding and generation. CoRR **abs/2109.12068** (2021). https://arxiv.org/abs/2109.12068
14. Al-Maleh, M., Desouki, S.: Arabic text summarization using deep learning approach. J. Big Data **7**(1), 1–17 (2020). https://doi.org/10.1186/s40537-020-00386-7

15. Rumelhart, D.E., Hinton, G.E., Williams, R.J.: Learning representations by back-propagating errors. Nature **323**, 533–536 (1986)
16. Bahdanau, D., Cho, K., Bengio, Y.: Neural machine translation by jointly learning to align and translate (2014)
17. Olah, C., Carter, S.: Attention and augmented recurrent neural networks. Distill (2016). https://doi.org/10.23915/distill.00001, http://distill.pub/2016/augmented-rnns
18. Devlin, J., Chang, M., Lee, K., Toutanova, K.: BERT: pre-training of deep bidirectional transformers for language understanding. CoRR abs/1810.04805 (2018). arxiv:1810.04805
19. Jurafsky, D., Martin, J.H.: Speech and Language Processing An Introduction to Natural Language Processing, Computational Linguistics, and Speech Recognition Understanding, vol. Third Edition draft (2023). http://web.stanford.edu/~jurafsky/slp3/ed3book_jan72023.pdf
20. Minaee, S., Boykov, Y., Porikli, F., Plaza, A., Kehtarnavaz, N., Terzopoulos, D.: Image segmentation using deep learning: a survey. IEEE Trans. Pattern Anal. Mach. Intell. **44**(7), 3523–3542 (2022). https://doi.org/10.1109/TPAMI.2021.3059968
21. Vincent, P., Larochelle, H., Lajoie, I., Bengio, Y., Manzagol, P.A.: Stacked denoising autoencoders: learning useful representations in a deep network with a local denoising criterion. J. Mach. Learn. Res. **11**, 3371–3408 (2010)
22. Radford, A., Narasimhan, K.: Improving language understanding by generative pre-training (2018)
23. Liu, Y., et al.: Multilingual denoising pre-training for neural machine translation. CoRR abs/2001.08210 (2020). https://arxiv.org/abs/2001.08210
24. Antoun, W., Baly, F., Hajj, H.: AraBERT: transformer-based model for Arabic language understanding. In: Proceedings of the 4th Workshop on Open-Source Arabic Corpora and Processing Tools, with a Shared Task on Offensive Language Detection, pp. 9–15. European Language Resource Association, Marseille, France (2020). https://aclanthology.org/2020.osact-1.2
25. Radford, A., Wu, J., Child, R., Luan, D., Amodei, D., Sutskever, I.: Language models are unsupervised multitask learners (2019)
26. Raffel, C., et al.: Exploring the limits of transfer learning with a unified text-to-text transformer. CoRR abs/1910.10683 (2019). arxiv:1910.10683
27. Lin, C.Y.: ROUGE: a package for automatic evaluation of summaries. In: Text Summarization Branches Out, pp. 74–81. Association for Computational Linguistics, Barcelona, Spain (2004). https://aclanthology.org/W04-1013
28. Hasan, T., et al.: XL-Sum: Large-scale multilingual abstractive summarization for 44 languages. In: Findings of the Association for Computational Linguistics: ACL-IJCNLP 2021, pp. 4693–4703. Association for Computational Linguistics, Online (2021). https://doi.org/10.18653/v1/2021.findings-acl.413, https://aclanthology.org/2021.findings-acl.413
29. Bergroth, L., Hakonen, H., Raita, T.: A survey of longest common subsequence algorithms. In: Proceedings Seventh International Symposium on String Processing and Information Retrieval. SPIRE 2000, pp. 39–48 (2000). https://doi.org/10.1109/SPIRE.2000.878178
30. Ganesan, K.: ROUGE 2.0: updated and improved measures for evaluation of summarization tasks. CoRR abs/1803.01937 (2018). arXiv:1803.01937

Qur'an Passage Ranking Using Transformer Models

Sarah Alnefaie[1,2(✉)], Eric Atwell[1], and Mohammed Ammar Alsalka[1]

[1] School of Computing, University of Leeds, Leeds, UK
salnefaie@kau.edu.sa, {e.s.atwell,m.a.alsalka}@leeds.ac.uk
[2] Faculty of Computing and Information Technology, King Abdulaziz University, Jeddah, Saudi Arabia

Abstract. Passage ranking is arguably one of the most important natural text-processing tasks. It is based on retrieving a passage from a larger corpus that contains an answer to a specific question. This task has not been fully explored in the Classical Arabic (CA) language. Because the size of the only available CA corpus was small, we created a new, larger CA dataset. This dataset was used to train eight Arabic pre-trained transformer-based models, which had been used in different approaches to passage ranking. The highest result we achieved was in using AraBERT Base (Arabic bidirectional encoder representations from transformers) as a bi-encoder model in the dense passage retrieval approach. This model outperformed BM25 (best match 25), which is considered a traditional approach. It obtained a 0.244 mean average precision (MAP) and 0.413 mean reciprocal rank (MRR), compared to the 0.170 MAP and 0.313 MRR obtained by BM25.

Keywords: Arabic Passage Retrieval · Arabic Transformer Models · Quran Retrieval Model

1 Introduction

The concept of passage ranking (PR) is based on retrieving an ordered list of passages that answer a question from a larger corpus. This list of passages is sorted based on a score assigned to each that is computed based on a chosen approach. There are three general categories of approaches: an exact match, semantic match and hybrid approach [1].

Exact match is a traditional approach that is based on statistical information about the query terms and corpus or set of passages; an example is BM25 (best match 25) [2]. This approach suffers from a vocabulary mismatch problem, which means that it is unable to retrieve passages or documents that contain different words that are semantically similar to those in the question.

To tackle this challenge, researchers use several techniques, including query expansion, passage expansion, and semantic match. The idea of expanding the query or passage is based on adding synonyms of terms found in a query or passage. Recently, the semantic

B. Hdioud and S. L. Aouragh (Eds.): ICALP 2024, CCIS 2339, pp. 183–194, 2025.
https://doi.org/10.1007/978-3-031-79164-2_16

match approach has shown promising results from its use with pre-trained transformer-based models to capture meaning [1]. The semantic match approach is based on dense representations and relevance classification [1].

The abundance of research on the dense representation approach has been in a small number of languages, such as English [3] and Modern Standard Arabic (MSA) [4] and research on the relevance classification approach has been in English [5]. Thus, there are still a number of unanswered questions in applying these approaches in Classical Arabic (CA). The first addressed in this study was the following: **RQ1**: Is using the dense representation or relevance classification approach better than the traditional statistical approach BM25 in CA for the PR task?

A hybrid approach ranks the relevant passages in two steps. First, the passages are ranked using an initial approach, such as the exact match approach BM25. The top passages are then selected and re-ranked using another approach, such as a semantic match. Results have shown that the hybrid approach outperformed the use of BM25 with the English language [1]. Thus, our second research question was as follows: **RQ2**: Does the hybrid approach outperform BM25 in CA for the PR task?

The transfer learning technique and the ensemble technique improve the pre-trained transformer-based model's performance in many natural language processing tasks (NLP) [6]. Thus, our third research question was as follows: **RQ3**: Does the transfer learning technique or the ensemble technique improve the performance of using the pre-trained transformer-based models for the PR task?

There are three main Arabic variants: dialect Arabic, Modern Standard Arabic (MSA) and Classical Arabic (CA). The importance of CA lies in the fact that it is considered the official version of the Arabic language. Most history, science and religious books have been written using it, including the Qur'an. In our study, we chose to use the Qur'an dataset because the Qur'an is the primary book for Muslims, the language of the Qur'an is complex, requires more exploration through academic research, including empirical studies (such as this one), and provides many unique challenges. First, the orthography (spelling conventions), for example, is different from other Arabic variants. Second, the meanings of the terms in the Qur'an are often different from their general meanings in the Arabic language [7]. Currently, there is only one dataset available in CA, the Text Retrieval Conference (TREC) AyaTEC, which is specific to the Qur'an. It is very small, containing only 199 questions [8, 9]. Therefore, the CA language was considered a low-resource language [10].

In this paper, we built a QuranTrec dataset to use in the training phase and then verified the performance of the dense representation approach compared to the BM25 and the relevance classification approach compared to the BM25. In addition, we explored the performance of the hybrid approach. Finally, we studied the effect of the optimisation methods (the transfer learning or ensemble technique) on the dense representation, relevance classification and hybrid approaches.

2 Related Work

2.1 Semantic Match Approach

The PR semantic match method is an approach based on dense representations and relevance classification [1]. These two concepts are described in the following paragraphs.

First, dense representations are utilised in dense passage retrieval (DPR) techniques. The concept behind DPR is to generate a representation vector for the query and all passages in the corpus using the transformer model. To compute the similarity score for each passage with a query, the dot product of the passage and query vectors are then calculated. Finally, the passages are sorted based on these scores. The pre-trained model in this approach is called a bi-encoder model [3]. Karpukhin et al. [3] studied the performance of the DPR technique using BERT [11] as a bi-encoder model with the following English datasets: SQuAD (Stanford Question Answering Dataset), CuratedTREC, WebQuestions, TriviaQA and Natural Questions. The results showed that the DPR approach outperformed the BM25 in terms of accuracy of the top-20 passage retrieval by 9%-19%. In addition, Alsubhi et al. [4] proposed applying the DPR approach to MSA. They used the dpr-ctx encoder-bert-base-multilingual BERT model and the ARCD (Arabic Reading Comprehension Dataset) and TyDiQA-GoldP (Typologically Diverse Question Answering – Gold Passage) dataset. They conducted many experiments using different datasets for fine-tuning and testing. In fine-tuning, they used the ARCD alone, the TyDiQA-GoldP dataset alone and ARCD and the TyDiQA-GoldP dataset together. In the testing, they used the ARCD test set, the ARCD development set, the TyDiQA-GoldP test set and the TyDiQA-GoldP development set. They used the top-20 and top-100 PR accuracy as evaluation metrics. The results of all these experiments showed that the DPR approach outperformed the traditional approach of TF-IDF (term frequency-inverse document frequency).

Second, the approach was based on relevance classification. The pre-trained transformer-based model in this approach is used as a classifier and is called a cross-encoder model. The input to the model is two sentences and the output from the model is a score from zero to one, which indicates the semantic similarity between them. In the PR, each passage in the dataset will be entered with the question into the model. The passages will be sorted based on the scores obtained when they were retrieved as relevant passages to each question [1]. Grundmann et al. [12] investigated the performance of the BioBERT transformer-based model when used as a cross-encoder model and bi-encoder model for the clinical domain. In general, the recall of the top-ranked passage (R@1) of the cross-encoder model outperformed the bi-encoder model and the classical approach TF-IDF and BM25 in the WikiSection, MedQuAD (Medical Question Answering Dataset), HealthQA and MIMIC-III datasets. The highest score achieved by the cross-encoder model was 77.90 R@1 with the MedQuAD dataset. While the bi-encoder model achieved 46.74 R@1, BM25 achieved 31.98 R@1 and TF-IDF achieved 24.87 R@1.

2.2 Hybrid Approach

The hybrid approach is based on the retrieve-and-re-rank architecture, which consists of two stages. First, the top passages that answer the question are retrieved from the corpus using a first approach, such as the traditional BM25 or DPR. These top candidate passages are then re-ranked using a second approach, such as the relevance classification or DPR approach [1]. Nogueira and Cho [5] and Xie et al. [13] proposed a PR model that retrieved the top passages using BM25. Then re-ranked them with a BERT model in cross-encoder mode. The first study was in the English language, while the second was in Chinese. The model proposed by Nogueira and Cho [5] outperformed BM25 in terms of mean average precision (MAP) and mean reciprocal rank (MRR@10) on the TREC-CAR (Complex Answer Retrieval) dataset and MSMARCO (Microsoft Machine Reading Comprehension) dataset. The performance of the proposed model could potentially double that of BM25. For example, with the TREC-CAR dataset, the proposed model produced a MAP score of 33.5, while the BM25 generated a MAP score of 15.3. Furthermore, the Chinese hybrid approach outperformed the BM25 by 0.15 MRR@10 on the T2Ranking dataset.

3 Datasets

In this research, four Arabic datasets were used in the experiments. The first dataset was used for training and evaluation, and the remaining three datasets were used only for training. The questions in the first two datasets were written in MSA, while the passages were written in CA. The language in the last two datasets was MSA.

TREC AyaTEC: This dataset consists of three files: Qur'anic passage collection (QPC), AyaTEC questions and query relevance judgements (QRels). The QPC consists of 1,266 passages that represent the entire Holy Qur'an. The Qur'an was divided into these passages using the Thematic Holy Qur'an[1] that divides the Qur'an verses into groups according to the topics of the verses. Each passage has an ID number. The question file includes 199 questions. Each question has its own ID. The questions were divided into 70% for training, 10% for development and 20% for the test sets. The QRels file is composed of 1,132 gold records. Each record is a pairing of a question ID and the ID of the passage that answers it [8, 9]. This dataset is the only one available for PR tasks in CA, but it has a limitation in the number of questions. There are only 199 questions. There is a relationship between the size of the training data and the pre-trained transformer-based model's performance; the larger the dataset, the better the model's performance. Therefore, we decided to build a larger CA dataset to use for training [6].

QuranTrec: The creation process of this dataset included two steps: using the available dataset by working on it (cleaning the data and putting them in the required format) and then using available information from books to enlarge it. We found only one question-answer dataset for CA related to the Qur'an called the Arabic Al-Qur'an Question and Answer Annotated Corpus (AQQAC) [14] After extracting answers that included only Qur'anic verses, we obtained 611 records. We added these records to our dataset as a basic step. We then extracted questions and answers from five books: The Doctrine of Every Muslim in a Question-and-Answer Book [15, 16], Inference on Children's Treasure [17], 100 Qur'anic Questions and Answers [18], 900 Questions and Answers

[1] http://archive.org/details/Quran_Tafseel-Mawdo.

in Managing the Verses of the Book [19], and Prayer (1770) Questions and Answers [20]. After adding the book questions and answers to our dataset, the total number of records reached 3,382. The number of questions was 2,189, as some questions had more than one answer. Each record in our dataset consists of a question, answer, the sura number of the answer, the start verse number of the answer and the end verse number. The answers in this dataset are very short, consisting of only a part of a verse from the Holy Qur'an. To use this dataset in training for the PR task, we needed a passage for each record. Using the sura number and the start and end verse number for each record, we extracted the passage from the QPC file of the TREC AyaTEC dataset. Sometimes, the first part of the answer was located in a passage, and the second part was located in the next passage. In this case, our passage containing the answer consisted of the first passage and part of the second passage. This dataset is available in the GitHub repository[2].

ARCD: This dataset consists of 1,395 question–passage–answer triplets from Wikipedia website [21].

Arabic SQuAD: This dataset contains 48.3k triplets of (question–passage–answer) for machine translation of the SQuAD dataset [21].

4 Model Overview

In our proposed model, we used eight Arabic pre-trained transformer-based models in the DPR approach as bi-encoder models and in the relevance classification approach as cross-encoder models. The models were AraBERT Base [22], ArabicBERT [23], AraELECTRA [24], QARiB [25], CAMeL-BERT [26], ARBERT, MARBERT [27], and CL-AraBERT [28]. In addition, in the relevance classification approach, we used six multi-language transformer-based models: mmarco-mMiniLMv2-L12-H384-v1[3], stsb-roberta-base[4], ms-marco-MiniLM-L-12-v2[5], sts-bdistilroberta-base[6], qnli-distilroberta-base[7], ms-marco-TinyBERT-L-2-v2[8]. In the experiment, the parameters were set as follows: the batch size was 16, the learning rate was 1e-4 and the number of epochs was 4.

DPR Approach: The process of building a training dataset consisted of two steps. First, we extracted all the question–passage pairs from the training set of the TREC AyaTEC dataset and the QuranTrec dataset. Second, we put each record in the following format: [question, positive passage, negative passage]. The question and positive passage (relevant to the question) were extracted from question–passage pairs from the dataset. The negative passage (not relevant to the question) was chosen using the in batch negatives method [3]. We then used this dataset to fine-tune the transformer-based model. Next,

[2] https://github.com/scsaln.

[3] https://huggingface.co/corrius/cross-encoder-mmarco-mMiniLMv2-L12-H384-v1.

[4] https://huggingface.co/cross-encoder/stsb-distilroberta-base.

[5] https://huggingface.co/cross-encoder/ms-marco-MiniLM-L-12-v2.

[6] https://huggingface.co/cross-encoder/stsb-distilroberta-base.

[7] https://huggingface.co/cross-encoder/qnli-distilroberta-base.

[8] https://huggingface.co/cross-encoder/ms-marco-TinyBERT-L-2-v2.

we used this model to map each passage to a d-dimensional, real-valued vector and constructed an index for these vectors. In the run time, a d-dimensional vector was generated for each question. To determine the closest passage vectors to the question vector, we calculated the dot product on their vectors. The passages were then sorted based on the calculated scores. Finally, we retrieved the passage with the highest value.

Relevance Classification Approach: First, each record in the training dataset was represented as follows [question, passage, 1]. The question and passage pairs were extracted from the training set of the TREC AyaTEC and the QuranTrec datasets. A value of 1 indicated that they were semantically similar. To build the negative samples of non-relevant pairs, we paired each question with a passage that answered another question in the datasets with the following format [question, passage, 0]. We then fine-tuned the transformer-based model using this dataset. After that, we built an index for all passages in the evaluated dataset (the TREC AyaTEC dataset). At run time, the model computes the semantic similarity scores for the questions with each passage. These scores are then used to sort the passages. Finally, the top passages are extracted.

Hybrid Approach: First, we used BM25 to retrieve the passages relevant to the question. The top relevant passages were then selected. Finally, we implemented the previously described DPR approach or relevance classification approach to re-rank the passages. In fact, the number of top relevant passages selected is a factor that affects performance. Therefore, we ran experiments to determine how adjusting the number of documents selected improved the results with this dataset.

Improvement Techniques: Most of the studies that used the pre-trained transformer-based models in NLP tasks used the transfer learning technique or ensemble technique to enhance the results.

Transfer Learning Technique: The idea of the transfer learning technique is that if the dataset available for training is small, the model can be trained on another large dataset, the weights of the model are saved, and it can then be trained on the small basic dataset. This technique showed good results when used in a machine reading comprehension (MRC) transformer-based model with the Arabic Qur'an dataset [28]. They further fine-tuned the CL-AraBERTv0.1-base model with the MSA dataset. In this study, we applied this technique by building four models. The only difference between these models was the training dataset. In the first model, we trained the AraBERT base model to be used as a bi-encoder in the hybrid approach using only the primary dataset (TREC AyaTEC), which is considered a CA dataset. In the second model, we trained the same model with TREC AyaTEC and QuranTrec, which is considered a CA dataset. The third model was fine-tuned, using only the MSA ARCD and Arabic SQuAD. The two CA datasets and two MSA datasets were used together to fine-tune the fourth model.

Ensemble Technique: ElKomy and Sarhan in [29] applied the ensemble technique to the results of five Arabic different models that run individually for the MRC task. They obtained results that exceeded the results of the individual models. In this study, we applied this ensemble technique to all the PR models (using the different approaches) we built to answer our questions. To implement this technique, we followed the following steps: First, for each question, we selected the top 20 candidate passages from each individual model. Next, for each of those passages, we computed the summation of its score from all the models. We then calculated the average score for each passage. Finally, the top-10 candidate passages were considered as the retrieved passages for the question.

5 Results

5.1 A Subsection Sample

We used MAP and the MRR as the evaluation metrics for these experiments. We considered MAP as the main metric.

To answer **RQ1**, which compared the performance of the dense representation and relevance classification approaches with BM25, we conducted three experiments. First, we built a PR model using BM25. BM25 obtained a 0.170 MAP and 0.313 MRR. Second, we built a PR model using the DPR approach; those results appear in the "Bi-Encoder" column in Table 1. Third, we used the relevance classification approach to build a PR model, and the results of using Arabic models appear in the column "Cross-Encoder" in Table 1 while the results of using multi-language models appear in Table 2. The BM25 obtained 0.170 MAP and 0.313 MRR. From the results, we note that five models out of eight achieved higher results than the BM25 in terms of MAP when used in the DPR approach. The models were AraBERT Base, ArabicBERT, CAMeL-BERT, AraELECTRA and CL-AraBERT. The highest-performing model among them was AraBERT, which achieved a 0.244 MAP and 0.413 MRR. From Table 1, we note that all the Arabic models achieved worse results than the BM25 when used with the relevance classification approach. The best of them was CAMeL-BERT, with a 0.125 MAP and 0.219 MRR. The only model that outperformed the BM25 with the multi-language models was qnli-distilroberta-base with a 0.198 MRR, as shown in Table 2.

To address **RQ2**, which related to the performance of the hybrid approach compared to the BM25 in CA, we followed the following steps. First, we needed to determine the number of passages retrieved by the BM25. We conducted three experiments for the hybrid approach, which involved using the BM25 to retrieve the top passages and then re-ranked them using the AraBERT Base model as a DPR approach. In these three experiments, we fixed all the parameters except the number of passages selected from the BM25 list. In the first experiment, it was 100; in the second, it was 50; and in the third, it was 20. Based on the results shown in Table 3, 50 was the value that achieved the best result. Therefore, we used it in the upcoming experiments. Second, we conducted experiments for the following hybrid approach: ranking using BM25 and then re-ranking using the DPR approach (bi-encoder model). The results in Table 4 show that the Arabic pre-trained models, when used as a bi-encoder model in the hybrid approach, achieved better results than the BM25 on at least one metric—except for MARBERT, which achieved a 0.165 MAP and 0.294 MRR. The best model among them was AraBERT Base, which achieved a 0.227 MAP and 0.365 MRR. Third, we conducted experiments for the hybrid approach that ranked the passages using the BM25 and then re-ranked them using the relevance classification (cross-encoder model). From the results shown in Table 4 and Table 5, we noticed that BM25 was better than the hybrid approach, which

Table 1. Results of the DPR and relevance classification approaches using the Arabic transformer-based model.

	Bi-Encoder		Cross-Encoder	
Model	MAP	MRR	MAP	MRR
AraBERT Base	0.244	0.413	0.077	0.131
ArabicBERT	0.172	0.281	0.119	0.199
QARiB	0.164	0.305	0.096	0.183
ARBERT	0.161	0.300	0.114	0.195
MARBERT	0.154	0.277	0.057	0.122
CAMeL-BERT	0.182	0.315	0.125	0.219
AraELECTRA	0.172	0.307	0.090	0.184
CL-AraBERT	0.179	0.302	0.093	0.168
Ensemble All	0.219	0.360	0.098	0.173
Ensemble Best	0.171	0.288	**0.139**	**0.220**

Table 2. Results of the relevance classification approach using the multilingual transformer-based model.

Model	MAP	MRR
mmarco-mMiniLMv2-L12-H384-v1	0.169	**0.298**
stsb-roberta-base	0.084	0.159
ms-marco-MiniLM-L-12-v2	0.107	0.192
stsb-distilroberta-base	0.080	0.145
qnli-distilroberta-base	**0.198**	0.198
ms-marco-TinyBERT-L-2-v2	0.088	0.174
Ensemble All	0.130	0.261
Ensemble Best	0.170	**0.298**

used relevance classification (cross-encoder model) as a re-ranker in all the Arabic pre-trained models and the multi-language model.

The final question in this study, **RQ3**, was related to whether the transfer learning or ensemble technique enhanced the performance of utilising the pre-trained transformer models for the PR task. The question was divided into two parts. The first part concerns training the pre-trained PR model using different datasets. Table 6 shows the results.

The results show that training the AraBERT Base model on the two CA datasets when it is used as a bi-encoder in the hybrid approach performed best with a 0.168 MAP and 0.276 MRR. The second highest result was achieved by the model when trained using the two CA datasets and two MSA datasets with a 0.152 MAP and 0.29 MRR.

Table 3. Comparison of the different numbers of passages retrieved from the BM25 in a hybrid approach.

Model	Number of the document	MAP	MRR
AraBERT Base	100	0.168	0.276
	50	**0.227**	**0.365**
	20	0.118	0.223

Table 4. Results of the hybrid approach that retrieved the passage using BM25 and then re-ranked them using the DPR and relevance classification approaches.

	Bi-Encoder		Cross-Encoder	
Model	MAP	MRR	MAP	MRR
AraBERT Base	0.227	0.365	**0.167**	0.273
ArabicBERT	0.198	0.328	0.155	**0.290**
QARiB	0.204	0.347	0.140	0.234
ARBERT	0.222	0.405	0.105	0.227
MARBERT	0.165	0.294	0.098	0.157
CAMeL-BERT	0.180	0.294	0.093	0.205
AraELECTRA	0.219	0.373	0.093	0.164
CL-AraBERT	0.139	0.315	0.119	0.233
Ensemble All	**0.240**	**0.41**	0.159	0.273
Ensemble Best	–	–	0.083	0.180

Table 5. Results of the hybrid approach that retrieved passages using BM25 then re-ranks with the relevance classification approach (a multi-language transformer-based model).

Model	MAP	MRR
qnli-distilroberta-base	0.116	0.207

Training the model on only the two MSA datasets achieved the lowest result, with a 0.039 MAP and 0.149 MRR. The second part is related to applying the ensemble technique to the results of the individual models. The results of applying the ensemble technique to the PR models that implemented the DPR approach are shown in Table 1. Tables 1 and 2 show the results of applying the ensemble technique to the Arabic and multi-language PR pre-trained models that implement the relevance classification. In addition, the results of ensembling the PR Transformer models that used the hybrid approach are shown in Table 4. The results of applying the ensemble technique to all the models are shown in the row **Ensemble All** of these tables. From Table 1, Table 2 and Table 4, we note that using the ensemble technique did not improve the results, as the results of some individual models were better. For example, the model ensemble technique in Table 1 achieved a score of 0.219 MAP and 0.360 MRR, while the AraBERT Base model alone received a score of 0.244 MAP and 0.413 MRR. The only example in which the ensemble technique improved performance was when it was implemented on the result of bi-encoder models used in the hybrid approach, where it achieved a score of 0.240 MAP and 0.41 MRR. Based on these results, we conclude that the ensemble technique provides good results if the performances of the individual models are close to each other. Very poor performance of the models affects the ensemble technique. Therefore, we decided to study the application of the ensemble technique on the results of only the two best models, as shown in the **Ensemble Best** row in Table 1, Table 2 and Table 4. **Ensemble Best** and **Ensemble All** did not improve the performance except when the pre-trained model was used as a cross-encoder achieved scores of 0.139 MAP and 0.220 MRR, as shown in Table 1.

Table 6. Comparison of the different datasets used to train the hybrid approach that retrieved the top-100 passages using BM25 then re-ranked using the DPR approach.

Model	Dataset	MAP	MRR
AraBERT Base	TREC AyaTEC	0.056	0.170
	TREC AyaTEC + QuranTrec	0.168	0.276
	ARCD + Arabic SQuAD	0.039	0.149
	TREC AyaTEC + QuranTrec + ARCD + Arabic SQuAD	0.152	0.29

6 Conclusion

This paper investigated the performance of pre-trained transformer-based models with a CA dataset for a passage retrieval task. The CA language is considered a low-resource language. Therefore, we built a dataset called Qur'anQA, which was used as a training dataset in this research. We explored the performance of these models when used in the dense passage retrieval approach as a bi-encoder, in the relevance classification approach as a cross-encoder and in the hybrid approach. Many Arabic pre-trained models outperformed the BM25 in terms of MAP and the MMR when used as a bi- encoder. The best model was AraBERT Base, with a 0.244 MAP and 0.413 MRR, while the BM25 score was a 0.170 MAP and 0.313 MRR. This result was the best in all experiments. The BM25 outperformed all the Arabic and multi-language models except the qnli-distilroberta-base model with a 0.198 MAP and 0.198 MMR. The best result in the hybrid approach was a 0.227 MAP when using AraBERT Base as a bi-encoder. We tried to improve the performance of these models by further fine-tuning the models using an additional dataset (including our dataset) or using the ensemble technique. The results of the ensemble technique showed improvement in some cases. Using our dataset in training improved the results, opening the door to creating a larger classical Arabic dataset and studying its impact.

References

1. Yates, A., Nogueira, R., Lin, J.: Pretrained transformers for text ranking: BERT and beyond. In: Proceedings of the 14th ACM International Conference on Web Search and Data Mining, pp. 1154–1156 (2021)
2. Robertson, S., Zaragoza, H., et al.: The probabilistic relevance framework: Bm25 and beyond. Found. Trends® Inf. Retrieval **3**(4), 333–389 (2009)
3. Karpukhin, V., et al.: Dense passage retrieval for open-domain question answering. arXiv preprint arXiv:2004.04906 (2020)
4. Alsubhi, K., Jamal, A., Alhothali, A.: Deep learning-based approach for Arabic open domain question answering. PeerJ. Comput. Sci. **8**, 952 (2022)
5. Nogueira, R., Cho, K.: Passage re-ranking with BERT. arXiv preprint arXiv:1901.04085 (2019)
6. Malhas, R., Mansour, W., Elsayed, T.: Qur'an qa 2022: Overview of the first shared task on question answering over the holy qur'an. In: Proceedings of the 5th Workshop on Open-Source Arabic Corpora and Processing Tools with Shared Tasks on Qur'an QA and Fine-Grained Hate Speech Detection, pp. 79–87 (2022)
7. Altammami, S.: Artificialintelligencefor understandingthehadith. PhD thesis, UniversityofLeeds (2023)
8. Malhas, R.R.: Arabic question answering on the holy qur'an. PhD thesis, QATARUNIVERSITY (2023)
9. Malhas, R., Elsayed, T.: AyaTEC: building a reusable verse-based test collection for Arabic question answering on the holy Qur'an. ACM Trans. Asian Low-Resour. Lang. Inf. Process. (TALLIP) **19**(6), 1–21 (2020)
10. Kazi, S., Khoja, S., Daud, A.: A survey of deep learning techniques for machine reading comprehension. Artif. Intell. Rev. 1–61 (2023)
11. Devlin, J., Chang, M.-W., Lee, K., Toutanova, K.: BERT: Pre-training of deep bidirectional transformers for language understanding. arXiv preprint arXiv:1810.04805 (2018)
12. Grundmann, P., Arnold, S., L¨oser, A.: Self-supervised answer retrieval on clinical notes. arXiv preprint arXiv:2108.00775 (2021)
13. Xie, X., et al.: T2Ranking: A large-scale Chinese benchmark for passage ranking. arXiv preprint arXiv:2304.03679 (2023)
14. Alqahtani, M.M.A.: Quranic Arabic semantic search model based on ontology of concepts. PhD thesis, University of Leeds (2019)
15. Zeno, M.b.J.: The Abbreviation of the Islamic Belief from the Qur'an and Sunnah (2004)
16. Zeno, M.b.J.: The Doctrine of Every Muslim in a Question and Answer (2007)
17. Al-Wadi, F.b.M.b.M.: Inference on Children's Treasure (2016)
18. Alakeel, F.: Quranic Questions and Answer (2018)
19. ALmuselli, D.: 900 Questions and Answers in Managing the Verses of the Book. Altafseer, Erbil (2020)
20. Al -Alami, F.b.M.b.M.: Prayer (1770) Question and Answer (2022)
21. Mozannar, H., Hajal, K.E., Maamary, E., Hajj, H.: Neural Arabic question answering. arXiv preprint arXiv:1906.05394 (2019)
22. Antoun, W., Baly, F., Hajj, H.: AraBERT: Transformer-based model for Arabic language understanding. arxiv 2020. arXiv preprint arXiv:2003.00104 (2020)
23. Safaya, A., Abdullatif, M., Yuret, D.: KUISAIL at semeval-2020 task 12: BERT-CNN for offensive speech identification in social media. arXiv preprint arXiv:2007.13184 (2020)
24. Antoun, W., Baly, F., Hajj, H.: AraELECTRA: Pre-training text discriminators for Arabic language understanding. arXiv preprint arXiv:2012.15516 (2020)

25. Abdelali, A., Hassan, S., Mubarak, H., Darwish, K., Samih, Y.: Pre-training BERT on Arabic tweets: Practical considerations (2021)
26. Inoue, G., Alhafni, B., Baimukan, N., Bouamor, H., Habash, N.: The interplay of variant, size, and task type in Arabic pre-trained language models. In: Proceedings of the Sixth Arabic Natural Language Processing Workshop. Association for Computational Linguistics, Kyiv, Ukraine (Online) (2021)
27. Abdul-Mageed, M., Elmadany, A., Nagoudi, E.M.B.: ARBERT & MARBERT: Deep bidirectional transformers for Arabic. arXiv preprint arXiv:2101.01785 (2020)
28. Malhas, R., Elsayed, T.: Arabic machine reading comprehension on the holy Qur'an using Cl-AraBERT. Inf. Process. Manage. **59**(6), 103068 (2022)
29. ElKomy, M., Sarhan, A.M.: TCE at Qur'an QA 2022: Arabic language question answering over holy Qur'an using a post-processed ensemble of BERT-based models. arXiv preprint arXiv:2206.01550 (2022)

Question Answering over the Arabic Hadith Sharif Using Transformer Models

Sarah Alnefaie[1,2(✉)], Eric Atwell[1], and Mohammed Ammar Alsalka[1]

[1] School of Computing, University of Leeds, Leeds, UK
salnefaie@kau.edu.sa, {e.s.atwell,m.a.alsalka}@leeds.ac.uk
[2] Faculty of Computing and Information Technology, King Abdulaziz University, Jeddah, Saudi Arabia

Abstract. Studies have shown the promising performance of transformer-based models in machine reading comprehension task. However, the performance of these models has not been explored extensively and deeply with Classical Arabic texts. To fill this gap, we first created two datasets: one for the Qur'anic text and the other for the Hadith Sharif, which are considered the main sources of Islam. We chose these two sources because they are more challenging. Their text requires a deep understanding of the content, and their terminology can have an interpretation that is different from that of other books. We then made them available to the research community. Second, we explored the performance of all the pre-trained transformer-based models available for the Arabic language when used as an answering model for the Hadith Sharif questions. Third, we studied the impact of further training the models on a Classical Arabic dataset, such as the Qur'an dataset and/or Modern Standard Arabic datasets. Finally, we selected the best-performing models and applied the ensemble method to their results. The model that achieved the best result was the ensemble of the CAMeL-BERT and CL-AraBERT, with a 0.187 EM, 0.711 F1 score, and 0.631 pRR.

Keywords: Arabic NLP · Question Answering · Machine Reading Comprehension

1 Introduction

In natural language processing (NLP), One of the most challenging tasks is machine reading comprehension (MRC). In the MRC task, a text passage and question are the two inputs to the MRC model. The model then needs to create a thorough understanding of the passage to extract the correct answer [1].

Recently, most MRC task studies in the Arabic language that have achieved state-of-the-art performance have tended to use pre-trained transformer-based models [2, 3]. The Arabic language mainly consists of three variants: Modern Standard Arabic (MSA), Classical Arabic (CA), and dialect Arabic [4]. Mozannar et al. in [5] and Alsubhi et al. in [2] studied different Arabic BERT (bidirectional encoder representations from transformers) models using four available MSA datasets.

B. Hdioud and S. L. Aouragh (Eds.): ICALP 2024, CCIS 2339, pp. 195–206, 2025.
https://doi.org/10.1007/978-3-031-79164-2_17

QRCD is the only MRC dataset available in CA [6]. It consists of 169 questions about the Quran text. Some questions have more than one answer. Thus, it consists of 1,093 question–passage pairs. This dataset has been used for the Qur'an 2022 QA Shared Task competition and has encouraged research in this area [3]. Participants in this competition used transformer models. Some improved the performance by further training the model utilising a MSA and/or CA corpus [7–9], and others enhanced performance using an ensemble of five Arabic BERT models [10].

CA is an important language because it is the language of a large number of basic historical and Islamic books. The most important books are the Holy Qur'an and the Hadith Sharif, which are the two foundational books for a huge number of Muslim people around the universe. These are two sources from which Muslims derive rulings and legislation in all matters of their lives. Therefore, they are considered fertile sources for finding answers to their queries. The language of these two Islamic books is very challenging because they contain terms that have meanings that are different from other Arabic variants [4]. In addition, CA is classified as a low-resource language due to the availability of only one small dataset (the QRCD) specific to the Qur'an [11]. This limitation hinders the development of MRC models for CA, keeping them largely unexplored.

Therefore, in this paper, we built two MRC datasets: the Qur'an machine reading comprehension (QMRC) dataset and the Hadith machine reading comprehension (HMRC) dataset. Both were made publicly available. We then investigated the performance of all available Arabic pre-trained transformer-based models on the HMRC corpus. After that, we applied two improvement approaches. First, we fine-tuned the models using large CA such as QMRC and/or MSA datasets such as ARCD. We then ensembled the models result.

The research questions in this study:

RQ1: Do the pre-trained models perform well when used in the MRC task to answer questions of the Hadith Sharif?
RQ2: Does further fine-tuning of the models with large MSA and/or CA datasets enhance their performance?
RQ3: Does applying the ensemble approach for the pre-trained models improve the results for the Hadith Sharif MRC?

2 Related Work

2.1 Machine Reading Comprehension Models

Recently, some papers have concentrated on the performance of pre-trained models for MRC with CA text. They used the QRCD for training and testing. This dataset contain of questions for and answers from the text of the Qur'an. The main differences between these studies were the model used and the method of improvement. This research has been used Different Arabic BERT models, such as QARiB, MARBERT, ARBERT, and AraBERT. The optimisation methods they used can be divided into two types: using transfer learning and applying an ensemble approach to the different models.

Transfer Learning Approach
MSA datasets were used in some studies to further fine-tune the model, in addition to the QRCD. Mostafa and Mohamed in [7] proposed using three MSA datasets to train the ARAELECTRA model. They were the Arabic Reading Comprehension Dataset (ARCD), Ar-TyDi and Arabic-SQuAD. Their system achieved a 0.23, 0.54, and 0.52 in exact match (EM), partial reciprocal ranking (pRR), and F1@1, respectively. Additionally, Malhas and Elsayed in [6] conducted three experiments. First, only the ArabicSQuAD and ARCD datasets, which are MSA datasets, were used to fine-tune the AraBERT and CL-AraBERT models. Second, only QRCD was utilised to train the two models. Third, the ARCD and ArabicSQuAD datasets were utilised to train the two models, and then the two models were fine-tuned further on the QRCD. The highest results were achieved by AraBERT and CL-AraBERT when the models were further fine-tuned utilising all three datasets: 49.53 and 53.28 partial average precision (paP)@10, respectively.

Other papers try to use a CA dataset to fine-tune the model. There is no currently available MRC dataset for CA other than the QRCD, so they used this questions and answers dataset and put it into the appropriate MRC format. Sleem et al. in [8] suggested using the AQQAC dataset for a fine-tuned AraBERTv02Base model. The results showed a 0.5 F1@1, 0.25 EM, and 0.52 pRR. Aftab and Malik in [9] proposed fine-tuning the baseline BERT using the AQQAC and QRCD. The model results reach a 0.30 pRR, 0.08 EM, and 0.26 F1@1.

Ensemble Approach
ElKomy and Sarhan in [10] developed an MRC system for the Arabic Qur'an by training five BERT models using the QRCD. The models were AraBERT Large, AraBERT Base, ARBERT, MARBERT, and QARiB. They obtained the answers for the test set of the QRCD using each model individually. They then applied an ensemble approach to these models to obtain better results. This system achieved a 0.50 F1@1, 56.6 pRR, and 26.8 EM.

To the best of our knowledge, no one built an MRC model for the Hadith Sharif. In addition, no study could be found that has explored the classical Arabic language in depth. All previous studies found in the literature have used the QRCD dataset, which consists of only 169 questions.

2.2 Machine Reading Comprehension Datasets

There are many MSA datasets, such as Arabic SQuAD, ARCD, and Ar-TyDi. Mozannar et al. [5] developed two datasets: ARCD and Arabic SQuAD. They built the Arabic SQuAD by translating the English version of SQuAD. It comprised 48.3k records. For ARCD, they ask crowdsourced workers to create questions from Wikipedia passages. It consists of 1,395 triplets. Clark et al. in [12] proposed Ar-TyDi, which consists of 16,305 samples. The questions were written by people who wanted to know these particular answers. After they were written, the data were collected.

For the CA dataset, only one was available: QRCD [6]. The creation process for this dataset consisted of a number of stages. First, a number of questions were gathered from the internet. Freelancers were then asked to answer the questions using the Qur'an.

Specialist religious scholars reviewed all the questions and answers in the dataset. Finally, specific passages were associated with each of the answers. Some studies used the question-and-answer dataset and added a passage to each record so that it would be an appropriate format for the MRC task, but the customised dataset was not available [8, 9].

The size of the Qur'an collection is very small, and there is no collection specifically for the Hadith Sharif.

3 Datasets

In this section, we explain the methodology for building the two MRC datasets for CA: the Qur'an MRC (QMRC) dataset and the Hadith MRC (HMRC) dataset. These two datasets are publicly available in our repository[1].We hope that researchers in the NLP field will benefit from them.

Quran MRC (QMRC) Dataset: The language of the questions was available in MSA. The passages were a group of verses from the Qur'an. Each answer was an extracted span from a passage. This dataset was built in two stages. First, the existing dataset was integrated. Second, we enlarged it using available books. These stages are described in more detail in the following paragraphs.

For the first stage, there were two available Qur'an datasets: the QRCD Malhas and Elsayed in [6] and AQQAC [13]. The QRCD is an MRC dataset. It is available in the required format; therefore, we added it directly to our dataset. In contrast, the AQQAC is a question–answer dataset, consisting of 1,224 records. This means that each record contains only a question and answer. In addition, the answer consists of two parts. The first part is the entire Qur'anic verse written in the CA language.

The second part is a scholar's answer to the question in modern language, which is similar to the meaning of part of the verse but in MSA terminology. Therefore, we manually extracted the part of the verse that answers the question and considered it to be the answer. Moreover, a large number of questions were answered using the interpretations of scholars and not from verses of the Holy Qur'an. The scope of our study limited the questions and answers to those that could be associated specifically with the text from the Qur'an. Therefore, we filter out and remove all answers from books of interpretation (i.e. those that did not have a corresponding passage). The number of records after filtering was 611. For AQQAC to be in the required format, we needed to add passages for the remaining records. We followed the same procedure to add the passages as proposed by [6]. We collected the verses of the Qur'an into groups using the Thematic Holy Qur'an[2]. This book divides the Holy Quran into groups based on topic. The process of finding the passage for each answer was as follows: (1) we determined the beginning and end numbers of the verses in the answer; (2) we identified the passage that contained these verses and considered it to be the passage for this record (sometimes a passage may include part of the answer verses; in those cases, we expanded the passage until it included the answer completely); (3) finally, we added the appropriate passage

[1] https://github.com/scsaln

[2] http://archive.org/details/quran Tafseel-Mawdo

for each record in the dataset. Once this was done for all records, they were added to our MRC dataset.

For the second stage, we initially identified five available books that met our two requirements. These contained questions and answers relevant to verses from the Qur'an. The owners of the books allowed us to publish our dataset with that content. The books were 100 Qur'anic Questions and Answers [14], 900 Questions and Answers in Managing the Verses of the Book [15], Inference on Children's Treasure [16], Prayer (1770) Questions and Answers [17], and The Doctrine of Every Muslim in a Question-and-Answer Book [18, 19]. Next, we extracted the questions and answers from the books. We then cleaned the text using both automated and manual procedures. Removing non-Arabic characters and extra spaces using regular expressions is an example of one of the automated procedures. Detecting duplicate and missing information is an example of one of the manual procedures. We applied the aforementioned procedure to find the passage for each question based on the answer provided. Thus, each record became a question–passage–answer. We added these records to enlarge our dataset. The number of records in this dataset was then 3,382.

Hadith MRC (HMRC) Dataset: This dataset consists of triplets: question, passage, and answer. The language of the questions is in MSA, while the language of the passage is in CA because it is a collection of the Hadith Sharif. We followed the same procedures used in building the QMRC dataset. First, it was built using the three books that were available and that we were authorised to use. They had to meet our requirements, which included focusing on answers from the Hadith Sharif. The books were The Doctrine of Every Muslim in a Question-and-Answer Book [18, 19], Prayer (1770) Questions and Answers [17], and Inference on Children's Treasure [16]. The questions and answers were extracted, and the text was cleaned. Finally, a passage was assigned for each record in the dataset. Hadith books are divided into sections, and each section deals with a specific topic. Therefore, we collected the four consecutive hadiths in each book into one longer text and numbered each passage. Thus, every record included a question, a passage, and an answer. Each passage can appear with more than one question. The resulting corpus consisted of 1,359 questions and 1,598 records. We explored the hadiths in the dataset.

4 The Proposed Models

Implementing pre-trained models for the Arabic Qur'an MRC task has shown promising results in many experiments [3, 6]. Therefore, our methodology was based on these models. Our methodology consisted of two steps. First, the HMRC dataset was used to fine-tune the Arabic transformer-based models. The available Arabic models were ArabicBERT [20], AraBERT large, AraBERT base [21], ARBERT, MARBERT [22], QARiB [23], AraELECTRA [24], CAMeL-BERT [25], and CL-AraBERT [6]. After the initial fine-tuning, we used the following improvement methods to attempt to enhance the results.

4.1 Transfer Learning

Transfer learning is one of the techniques used to enhance the performance of an MRC transformer-based model when the initial training dataset is small in size, as in our case; the HMRC training dataset had only 1,038 question–passage–answer triplets. The concept behind this technique is to use a large dataset to fine-tune the model. The model weights are then saved. Finally, these saved weights are used at the beginning of the training process of the model with a small dataset. This approach showed good results with an Arabic Qur'an MRC model [6]. In their experiment, they trained the CL-AraBERTv0.1-base with the MSA dataset and saved the weights of the model to use when they trained the model with the QRCD.

The language of the questions in the HMRC dataset is MSA, while the language of the passages and answers is CA. Therefore, we decided to study the effect of fine-tuning the model using MSA or/and CA corpus and then fine-tuning it using the HMRC. Three experiments were conducted. In the first, we used the ARCD, which was considered an MSA corpus, to train all models. Second, we utilized the QMRC, which was considered a CA corpus, to train all models. Third, we identified the model that showed improvement in both previous experiments. We then fine-tuned these models using the ARCD and QMRC datasets.

4.2 Ensemble Approach

The idea of an ensemble approach is based on identifying the scored candidate answers for each question of all models and then applying majority voting to them to calculate the final score for each candidate. This approach usually achieves better results than the results of each individual model because it avoids the noise of any particular single model [10].

In our experiment, for each question, we chose the 20 highest-scoring candidate answers from each model. For each candidate answer, we then calculated the summation of its score obtained from all models. The new score for the candidate answer was the summation score divided by the number of models. Next, the candidate answers were sorted using the new score. Finally, we considered the 10 highest-scoring candidates to be the final answers to the question.

The code of the proposed models are publicly available[3].

5 Results

In this study, we used three evaluation metrics: F1, exact match (EM), and score partial reciprocal rank (pRR). EM is a binary score (0 or 1). If one of the gold answers fully matches the top candidate answer. Then the EM equals 1. The value of the pRR is based on the position of the first candidate answer that is relevant to the gold answers in a ranked list. The F1 score is computed based on the recall and precision scores [6, 26]. Each of these three metrics was computed for each question. We then computed the overall score for each metric by averaging it across all questions. The EM focuses on the top answer,

[3] https://github.com/scsaln.

the pRR focuses on the first relevant answer, and the F1 focuses on the system's overall performance. Therefore, we chose F1 as the key metric in our experiments.

Table 1 shows the results of the experiments when using the transformer-based models in the MRC task with CA text.

Table 1. Results of using different Arabic MRC datasets to train different Arabic pre-trained transformer-based models.

Training Datasets	HMRC			HMRC + ARCD			HMRC + QMRC		
Model	EM	F1	pRR	EM	F1	pRR	EM	F1	pRR
AraBERT Large	0	0.158	0.099	0.239	0.663	0.588	0.209	0.642	0.56
AraBERT Base	0.118	0.67	0.604	0.215	0.676	0.612	0.178	0.662	0.584
MARBERT	0.015	0.509	0.329	0.054	0.595	0.454	0.012	0.52	0.325
ARBERT	0.072	0.645	0.556	0.16	0.661	0.579	0.1	0.613	0.516
QARiB	0.009	0.381	0.224	0.009	0.412	0.235	0.009	0.368	0.207
CAMeL-BERT	0.106	0.68	0.604	0.181	0.684	0.606	0.166	0.662	0.589
ArabicBERT	0.093	0.598	0.504	0.121	0.596	0.507	0.106	0.579	0.49
AraELECTRA	0	0.408	0.301	0.006	0.342	0.228	0	0.613	0.551
CL-AraBERT	0.13	0.68	0.597	0.154	0.673	0.599	0.145	0.668	0.587

First, we began by addressing **RQ1**, which was related to the pre-trained model's performance in the MRC task of answering the questions of the Hadith Sharif. The results are shown in the "HMRC" columns in Table 1. The results showed that the models performed well in general when they were trained using only the HMRC dataset. Most models had F1 and pRR scores between 0.5 and 0.6. The best models were CAMeL-BERT and CL-AraBERT with an F1 score of 0.68. The CAMeL-BERT had the best pRR score (0.604) and the third-best EM score (0.106).

To address **RQ2**, which was related to studying the effects of fine-tuning the models using larger CA datasets (such as QMRC) or/and MSA datasets (such as ARCD) on their performance. The columns under "HMRC + ARCD" and "HMRC + QMRC" in Table 1 and the columns under "HMRC + ARCD + QMRC" in Table 2 show the result. The answer to this research question is split into three sections. First, fine-tuning the models with the ARCD led to improvement in all three evaluation metrics in six models: AraBERT Large, AraBERT Base, MARBERT, ARBERT, QARiB, and CAMeL-BERT. The EM and pRR were the most improved evaluation metrics, with eight models out of nine showing improvement in these two. The CAMeL-BERT model achieved a 0.684 F1, which is considered the highest result. After that, using the QMRC dataset in the training phase enhanced three models: AraBERT Large, MARBERT, and AraELECTRA. Six of the nine models improved their EM scores when the QMRC was used. When we used this training dataset, the highest F1 score was 0.668, which was obtained by the CL-AraBERT model. Third, only the EM improved when fine-tuning the AraBERT Large model using the ARCD and QMRC dataset. The EM was 0.242, compared with 0.209 when fine-tuning with QMRC and 0.239 when fine-tuning with ARCD, as shown in Table 2. The other two metrics, F1 and pRR, were 0.647 and 0.578, respectively, which were worse than when training the model using only ARCD and better than when training the model using only QMRC. The F1 and pRR of training the model with only ARCD were 0.663 and 0.588, respectively, while the F1 and pRR of training the model with only QMRC were 0.642 and 0.56, respectively. We chose the AraBERT Large model because it obtained improved results when trained individually using the ARCD and QMRC.

Table 2. Results of using a combination of HMRCD, ARCD, and QMRC to fine-tune the AraBERT Large model.

Training Datasets	HMRC + ARCD			HMRC + QMRC			HMRC + ARCD + QMRC		
Model	**EM**	**F1**	**pRR**	**EM**	**F1**	**pRR**	**EM**	**F1**	**pRR**
AraBERT Large	0.239	0.663	0.588	0.209	0.642	0.56	0.242	0.647	0.578

RQ3 was related to whether the ensemble approach enhanced the performance of Hadith Sharif MRC models. This question was answered by choosing the best performing version of each model and then applying the ensemble approach to them and comparing the results. Table 3 shows these results. Unfortunately, the result of the ensemble approach performed worse than eight of the nine individual models, as shown in Table 3. The result of the ensemble approach achieved a 0.586 F1, 0.5 pRR, and 0.221 EM, while the best model alone (CAMeL-BERT) achieved a 0.684 F1, 0.606 pRR, and 0.181 EM. We noticed that the poor performance of some models negatively affected the performance of the ensemble approach. Therefore, we decided to choose only the best models and then apply the ensemble approach to them: CAMeL-BERT Base and CL-AraBERT. The results of this ensemble showed improvement in all three metrics: (0.711 F1, 0.631 pRR, 0.187 EM) compared to (0.684 F1, 0.606 pRR, 0.181 EM) and (0.68 F1, 0.597 pRR, 0.13 EM), respectively. In summary, the ensemble approach improved the results when the included models' individual results were close. However, if there was a severe contrast in the models' individual results, then the poorer-performing models negatively affected the ensemble approach results.

Table 3. Results of the ensemble approach. The best results for all model are presented first. "Ensemble All" means the result of implementing the ensemble to the results of all models. "Ensemble Best" refers to implementing the ensemble to the best models that achieved the highest results: CAMeL-BERT and CL-AraBERT.

	Best Results		
Model	EM	F1	pRR
AraBERT Large	0.239	0.663	0.588
AraBERT Base	0.215	0.676	0.612
MARBERT	0.054	0.595	0.454
ARBERT	0.16	0.661	0.579
QARiB	0.009	0.412	0.235
CAMeL-BERT	0.181	0.684	0.606
ArabicBERT	0.093	0.598	0.504
AraELECTRA	0	0.613	0.551
CL-AraBERT	0.13	0.68	0.597
Ensemble All	0.221	0.586	0.5
Ensemble Best	0.187	0.711	0.631

6 Analysis and Discussion

We analysed the expected Arabic answers to determine why the models failed to predict the correct answer in some cases. We noted the following points: The model does not deeply "understand" the question to predict the answer correctly but rather applies a direct and simple matching method, leading to an incorrect answer, such as Example 1 in Table 4. Example 2 in Table 4 is an example of the model having difficulty answering a question. The reason may be that the terms in the passage are synonymous with the terms in the question.

Table 4. Examples of wrong model predictions.

Question	Passage	Gold	Predict
1- What is the meaning of **more** in saying of Allah Most High: And **for those who have done good is the best and even more**?	…from the Prophet peace be upon him, regarding the saying of Allah Most High: And **for those who have done good is the best and even more (10:26)** - He Peace be upon him said: "When the inhabitants of Paradise have entered Paradise a caller will call out: 'Indeed there remains for you a promise with Allah, and He wants to reward you with it.' They will say: 'Have your faces not been made bright, have we not been saved from the Fire, and have we not been admitted into Paradise?'" He said: "So the Veil will be lifted." He said: "By Allah! Nothing given to them [by Allah] will be more beloved to them than looking at Him….."	looking at Him	for those who have done good is the best and even more
2-What is the thing that **evil runs away** from and cannot bear to hear?	…God's Messenger says, "When a summons to prayer is made **the evil turns his back**"…	When a summons to prayer is made	2-What is the thing that **evil runs away** from and cannot bear to hear?

7 Conclusion

This research investigated transformer-based models with Classical Arabic, which is classify as a low-resource language. Making the research more challenging was the choice of religious texts because they require a deep and extensive understanding, and the terms in these texts are interpreted with meanings specific to religion. We focused on a machine reading comprehension task for the Hadith Sharif. To achieve this, we first expanded the Holy Qur'an dataset with a machine reading comprehension dataset to fine-tune the model, and we also created a Hadith Sharif dataset for use in fine-tuning and testing. We then conducted different experiments to explore all Arabic transformer-based models efficiency. First, we trained the models on only the Hadith Sharif dataset. After that, we trained them on a different dataset, a Classic Arabic dataset (such as the Holy Qur'an dataset) and a Modern Standard Arabic dataset (such as the ARCD), and finally applied the ensemble method to the results of the best-performing models. The models that achieved the highest score when trained on only the Hadith Sharif were CL-AraBERT and CAMeL-BERT, with a 0.68 F1. The highest-scoring model trained on additional data was CAMeL-BERT trained on the ARCD, with a 0.181 EM, 0.684 F1, and 0.606 pRR. Finally, when we applied the ensemble method to our top models (CL-AraBERT and CAMeL-BERT), we obtained a 0.187 EM, 0.711 F1, and 0.631 PRR.

References

1. Baradaran, R., Ghiasi, R., Amirkhani, H.: A survey on machine reading comprehension systems. Nat. Lang. Eng. **28**(6), 683–732 (2022)
2. Alsubhi, K., Jamal, A., Alhothali, A.: Pre-trained transformer-based approach for Arabic question answering: A comparative study. arXiv preprint arXiv:2111.05671 (2021)
3. Malhas, R., Mansour, W., Elsayed, T.: Qur'an QA 2022: overview of the first shared task on question answering over the holy Qur'an. In: Proceedings of the 5th Workshop on Open-Source Arabic Corpora and Processing Tools with Shared Tasks on Qur'an QA and Fine-Grained Hate Speech Detection, pp. 79–87. European Language Resources Association, Marseille, France (2022)
4. Altammami, S., Atwell, E.: Challenging the transformer-based models with a classical Arabic dataset: Quran and hadith. In: Proceedings of the 13th Language Resources and Evaluation Conference (2022)
5. Mozannar, H., Hajal, K.E., Maamary, E., Hajj, H.: Neural Arabic question answering. arXiv preprint arXiv:1906.05394 (2019)
6. Malhas, R., Elsayed, T.: Arabic machine reading comprehension on the holy Qur'an using Cl-AraBERT. Inf. Process. Manage. **59**(6), 103068 (2022)
7. Mostafa, A., Mohamed, O.: GOF at Qur'an QA 2022: towards an efficient question answering for the holy Qu'ran in the Arabic language using deep learning-based approach. In: Proceedings of the 5th Workshop on Open-Source Arabic Corpora and Processing Tools with Shared Tasks on Qur'an QA and Fine-Grained Hate Speech Detection, pp. 104–111(2022)
8. Sleem, A., Elrefai, E.M., Matar, M.M., Nawaz, H.: Stars at Qur'an QA 2022: building automatic extractive question answering systems for the holy Qur'an with transformer models and releasing a new dataset. In: Proceedings of the 5th Workshop on Open-Source Arabic Corpora and Processing Tools with Shared Tasks on Qur'an QA and Fine-Grained Hate Speech Detection, pp. 146–153 (2022)
9. Aftab, E., Malik, M.K.: eRock at Qur'an QA 2022: Contemporary deep neural networks for Qur'an based reading comprehension question answers. In: Proceedings of the 5th Workshop on Open-Source Arabic Corpora and Processing Tools with Shared Tasks on Qur'an QA and Fine-Grained Hate Speech Detection, pp. 96–103 (2022)
10. ElKomy, M., Sarhan, A.M.: TCE at Qur'an QA 2022: Arabic language question answering over holy Qur'an using a post-processed ensemble of BERT-based models. arXiv preprint arXiv:2206.01550 (2022)

11. Kazi, S., Khoja, S., Daud, A.: A survey of deep learning techniques for machine reading comprehension. Artif. Intell. Rev. **56**(Suppl 2), 2509–2569 (2023)
12. Clark, J.H., et al.: TyDI QA: a benchmark for information-seeking question answering in ty pologically di verse languages. Trans. Assoc. Comput. Linguist. **8**, 454–470 (2020)
13. Alqahtani, M.M.A.: Quranic Arabic semantic search model based on ontology of concepts. PhD thesis, University of Leeds (2019)
14. Alakeel, F.: Quranic Questions and Answer (2018)
15. ALmuselli, D.: 900 Questions and Answers in Managing the Verses of the Book. Altafseer, Erbil (2020)
16. Al-Wadi, F.b.M.b.M.: Inference on Children's Treasure (2016)
17. Al -Alami, F.b.M.b.M.: Prayer (1770) Question and Answer (2022)
18. Zeno, M.b.J.: The Abbreviation of the Islamic Belief from the Qur'an and Sunnah (2004)
19. Zeno, M.b.J.: The Doctrine of Every Muslim in a Question and Answer (2007)
20. Safaya, A., Abdullatif, M., Yuret, D.: KUISAIL at SemEval-2020 task 12: BERT- CNN for offensive speech identification in social media. In: Proceedings of the Fourteenth Workshop on Semantic Evaluation, pp. 2054–2059. International Committee for Computational Linguistics, Barcelona (online) (2020)
21. Antoun, W., Baly, F., Hajj, H.: AraBERT: Transformer-based model for Arabic language understanding. arXiv preprint arXiv:2003.00104 (2020)
22. Abdul-Mageed, M., Elmadany, A., Nagoudi, E.M.B.: ARBERT & MARBERT: Deep bidirectional transformers for Arabic. In: Proceedings of the 59th Annual Meeting of the Association for Computational Linguistics and the 11th International Joint Conference on Natural Language Processing (Volume 1: Long Papers), pp. 7088–7105. Association for Computational Linguistics, Online (2021)
23. Abdelali, A., Hassan, S., Mubarak, H., Darwish, K., Samih, Y.: Pre-training BERT on Arabic tweets: Practical considerations. arXiv preprint arXiv:2102.10684 (2021)
24. Antoun, W., Baly, F., Hajj, H.: AraELECTRA: pre-training text discriminators for Arabic language understanding. In: Proceedings of the Sixth Arabic Natural Language Processing Workshop, pp. 191–195. Association for Computational Linguistics, Kyiv, Ukraine (Virtual) (2021)
25. Inoue, G., Alhafni, B., Baimukan, N., Bouamor, H., Habash, N.: The interplay of variant, size, and task type in Arabic pre-trained language models. In: Proceedings of the Sixth Arabic Natural Language Processing Workshop, pp. 92–104. Association for Computational Linguistics, Kyiv, Ukraine (Virtual) (2021)
26. Malhas, R., Elsayed, T.: Ayatec: Building a reusable verse-based test collection for Arabic question answering on the holy Qur'an. ACM Trans. Asian Low-Resour. Lang. Inf. Process. **19**(6) (2020)

Deep Reinforcement Learning for Arabic Machine Translation: A Study on Reward Signals

Mohamed Zouidine[1(✉)], Mohammed Khalil[1], and Abdelhamid Ibn El Farouk[2]

[1] FSTM, LMCSA, Hassan II University of Casablanca, Casablanca, Morocco
mohamed.zouidine-etu@etu.univh2c.ma, mohammed.khalil@univh2c.ma
[2] FLSH, LLEC, Hassan II University of Casablanca, Casablanca, Morocco
abdelhamid.farouk@univh2c.ma

Abstract. Machine translation training with reinforcement learning has shown improvement in the translation quality. In previous works, the BLEU score was used as a reward function for reinforcement learning being the metric the most widely employed for evaluating machine translation models. Nevertheless, BLEU is not the only metric available to evaluate machine translation models. In this work, we use four different measures as reward functions, and we study their impact on the translation quality. We use these rewards to train a transformer model with reinforcement learning to perform translation between Arabic and English. Experimental results with the IWSLT dataset reveal that the GLEU score enhances the Arabic-to-English translation quality and the BLEU score improves the English-to-Arabic one.

Keywords: Machine translation · Transformer · Reinforcement Learning · BLEU · GLEU · METEOR · TER

1 Introduction

Machine translation (MT) is a crucial tool that helps to bridge language barriers, expand international communication, and promote cross-cultural interactions. As a result of advances in artificial intelligence (AI) and deep learning (DL), MT has made significant advancements in the last decade. Sequence to Sequence [13], attention-based LSTM [3], and transformer [14] are examples of DL models that have been employed successfully in MT.

The Arabic language has benefited from the success of DL in machine translation. Several improvements based on DL models have been observed in the literature related to translation to and from Arabic. Almahairi *et al.* [2] used an attention-based neural machine translation model in both directions, Arabic to English and English to Arabic translation. Oudah *et al.* [10] employed an encoder-decoder model with global attention [9] to examine the effects of

B. Hdioud and S. L. Aouragh (Eds.): ICALP 2024, CCIS 2339, pp. 207–217, 2025.
https://doi.org/10.1007/978-3-031-79164-2_18

pre-processing approaches on Arabic-to-English translation. Bensalah *et al.* [5] introduced a model for machine translation from Arabic to English by combining the convolutional neural network (CNN) and the transformer [14].

Most of these models were trained employing the maximum likelihood estimation approach. The key idea of this approach is to minimize the cross-entropy loss between the model-generated translation and a reference translation. However, machine translation models are generally evaluated using sequence-level metrics like the BLEU score [11]. This contradiction between training and evaluation leads to a mismatch problem (cross-entropy loss vs. BLEU). This problem was addressed through reinforcement learning [16,18]. Reinforcement learning allows direct optimization of the evaluation metric (BLEU score as an example) during training by considering it as a reward signal and trying to maximize it.

Most work on machine translation training with reinforcement learning has used the BLEU score [11] as the reward signal, but BLEU is not the only evaluation metric that exists for machine translation. Several evaluation metrics have been proposed for machine translation; we cite, for example, GLEU [17], METEOR [4], etc. Therefore, using other evaluation metrics as reward signals besides the BLEU score can further improve reinforcement learning-based machine translation.

This paper analyses the use of four different machine translation evaluation metrics as reward signals for training with reinforcement learning. In addition to the BLEU score [11], we use the GLEU score [17], METEOR [4], and the translation edit rate (TER) [12]. We train a transformer-based model using REINFORCE [15], a reinforcement learning algorithm, and we examine the former four metrics for reward calculation and translation quality evaluation. To the best of our knowledge, this is the first study on the use of different metrics in Arabic machine translation training with reinforcement learning. Experimental results on the IWSLT Arabic-English dataset [6] showed that using the BLEU score as a reward function improved all the other metrics (except TER) for the translation from English to Arabic. Whereas for the Arabic-to-English translation, when used as reward signals, all metrics improve the performance.

This paper is structured as follows: Sect. 2 illustrates our followed methodology. Section 3 describes the details of the experimental protocols. Section 4 delves into the discussion of the results. Section 5 summarises the findings of this analysis.

2 Methodology

This section presents the methodology of this work. First, we describe the transformer used as the machine translation model. Second, we introduce reinforcement learning training for machine translation. Finally, we outline the machine translation metrics that will be used as a reward signal for reinforcement learning.

2.1 Transformer Model

A transformer [14] is a sequence-to-sequence model that is composed of an encoder and a decoder. Both are a stack of N layers, where each encoder layer is made up of two sub-layers: a self-attention mechanism and a feed-forward network. Given an input sentence $(x_1, x_2, \ldots, x_n)$ in a source language (Arabic, for example), the encoder extracts a representation $z = (z_1, z_2, \ldots, z_n)$ of this input sequence. On the other hand, in addition to the sub-layers employed by the encoder, the decoder employs another sub-layer called the cross-attention layer, which calculates the attention over the encoder output. Starting from the representation z extracted by the encoder, the decoder generates the translation $y = (y_1, y_2, \ldots, y_m)$ in a target language (English, for example).

The overall form of the transformer attention function is a mapping of a query (Q), a key (K), and a value (V) to an output. This output is calculated as [14]:

$$\text{Attention}(Q, K, V) = \text{softmax}\left(\frac{QK^T}{\sqrt{d_k}}\right) V \tag{1}$$

where d_k is the output dimension.

During training, the model tries to maximize the probability of generating a word y_t conditioned on the input sentence x and the words generated so far $y_{1:t-1} = (y_1, y_2, \ldots, y_{t-1})$. Given a training set of N sentence pairs $\{x^i, y^i\}_{i=1}^N$, the maximum likelihood estimation approach is used to train such a model, and the objective function is given by:

$$\begin{aligned} L_{mle} &= -\sum_{i=1}^{N} \log p\left(y^i | x^i\right) \\ &= -\sum_{i=1}^{N}\sum_{t=1}^{m} \log p\left(y_t^i | y_1^i, \ldots, y_{t-1}^i, x^i\right) \end{aligned} \tag{2}$$

2.2 Reinforcement Learning Training

Reinforcement learning is used to overcome the mismatch problem between training and evaluation of machine translation models, since it may directly optimize the evaluation metrics throughout the training process. Specifically, machine translation can be formulated as a reinforcement learning task, wherein the model undergoes training to maximize a reward function which is defined as the evaluation metric.

Examining the machine translation model, specifically the transformer in our context, can be viewed as a reinforcement learning agent in interaction with an environment (the input sentence x and the words generated so far $y_{1:t-1}$) at a training time step t. The agent acts following a policy defined as the conditional probability of generating the next token $p\left(y_t | y_1, \ldots, y_{t-1}, x\right)$. Following this policy, the agent chooses an action, generating the next word y_t, and receives a reward R_t defined as follows:

$$R_t = R\left(y_{1:t}, \hat{y}\right) - R\left(y_{1:t-1}, \hat{y}\right) \tag{3}$$

where $\hat{y}$ is the reference translation . In machine translation, the reward can be any metric used for evaluation. Reinforcement learning training is designed to maximize the expected reward. Following the policy gradient algorithm REINFORCE [15], this maximization can be reached by minimizing the following objective function:

$$L_{rl} = -\frac{1}{N}\sum_{i=1}^{N}\sum_{t=1}^{m} R_t \log p\left(y_t|y_1, \ldots, y_{t-1}, x\right) \tag{4}$$

Training a machine translation model directly with reinforcement learning is challenging as the action space (the vocabulary size) is tens of thousands of words. As a result, we initially pre-train the model employing the maximum likelihood estimation approach (Eq. 2), and then we continue the training with a linear combination between the maximum likelihood estimation (Eq. 2) and reinforcement learning (Eq. 4), with a trade-off controlled by a hyperparameter λ as follows:

$$L = \lambda L_{mle} + (1 - \lambda) L_{rl} \tag{5}$$

It has been proved that this combination leads to better training stabilization [16].

2.3 Reward Signals

Several machine translation evaluation metrics are available and can be used as reward signals for reinforcement learning training. In this work, we use the following metrics:

BLEU. BiLingual Evaluation Understudy (BLEU) metric [11] is commonly employed in machine translation. It is an automatic evaluation metric that compares the similarity of a candidate translation (C) to a set of reference translations (R).

BLEU starts by counting the highest frequency of n-gram matches. To prevent the count of the same n-gram in the candidate several times, BLEU restricts the count to the maximum count of n-grams that occur in any reference. The formula of this clipped count is given by:

$$\text{Count}_{\text{clip}} = \min\left(\#\text{n-gram}, \max_{r\in R}\left(\#\text{n-gram in r}\right)\right)$$

Then a precision is calculated by taking the division of the clipped count of the matching n-grams by the total count of n-grams:

$$p_n = \frac{\sum_{\text{n-gram}\in C} \text{Count}_{\text{clip}}\left(\text{n-gram}\right)}{\sum_{\text{n-gram}\in C} \text{Count}\left(\text{n-gram}\right)}$$

Next, BLEU calculates a Brevity Penalty (BP). This BP is applied to minimize the impact of sentence length on the score. It is calculated by the given formula:

$$\mathrm{BP} = \begin{cases} 1 & \text{if } |c| > |r| \\ \exp^{(1-|r|/|c|)} & \text{if } |c| \leq |r| \end{cases}$$

where $|c|$ is the candidate length and $|r|$ is the length of the reference. Then, the BLEU score is calculated as:

$$\mathrm{BLEU} = \mathrm{BP}.\exp\left(\sum_{n=1}^{4} w_n \log p_n\right) \tag{6}$$

where w_n is the weight of each n-gram.

METEOR. Metric for Evaluation of Translation with Explicit ORdering (METEOR) [4] is another machine translation evaluation metric. METEOR starts by searching for the longest matching uni-gram (chunk) between the candidate and the reference translation. During this search, words with the same meaning (synonyms) are considered the same. Then, it calculates the precision p, the recall r, and the F-score as follows:

$$p = \frac{\#\text{ matched uni-grams}}{\#\text{ uni-gram in candidate}}$$

$$r = \frac{\#\text{ matched uni-grams}}{\#\text{ uni-gram in reference}}$$

$$F\text{-score} = \frac{10pr}{r + 9p}$$

Next, METEOR calculates a penalty function that penalizes short matches and rewards long matches. This penalty is given by:

$$\text{Penalty} = 0.5 \times \left(\frac{\#\text{ chunks in candidate}}{\#\text{ matched uni-grams}}\right)^3$$

Finally, METEOR is calculated using the following formula:

$$\text{METEOR} = F\text{-score} \times (1 - \text{Penalty}) \tag{7}$$

GLEU. GLEU [17] starts by recording all sub-sequences of 1-gram, 2-gram, 3-gram, and 4-gram in the candidate and the reference translation. It calculates then a recall and a precision. The recall (r) and the precision (p) are calculated as the ratio of matched n-grams to the total number of n-grams in the reference and the candidate, respectively. Finally, the GLEU score is calculated by taking the minimum between the recall and the precision:

$$\text{GLEU} = \min(r, p) \tag{8}$$

TER. Translation Edit Rate (TER) [12] calculates machine translation accuracy by comparing the model-generated translation to a reference. TER measures the minimum count of editing operations (insertion, deletion, substitution, and shift) needed to align a candidate with a reference translation. It is calculated by dividing the number of edits by the total of words in a reference:

$$\text{TER} = \frac{\#\text{edits}}{\#\text{reference words}} \tag{9}$$

All of the above metrics always range between 0 and 1. While for the TER metric, a value close to 0 is the best, for the first three metrics, the best value is the one close to 1. Therefore, for our reward calculation, we directly use the score calculated by the first three metrics, and for the last one, we use one minus the score.

3 Implementation Details

This section provides the implementation details. We start with the dataset used for training and evaluation. We then describe the pre-processing pipeline applied to the input and output sentences. Finally, we present the experimental settings.

3.1 Dataset

IWSLT [6] dataset, which includes translated TED talks, was employed to train and evaluate our machine translation models. It contains a total of 224k of Arabic/English translation training pairs. We created a validation set of 3255 samples by combining the 'dev2010', 'tst2011', and 'tst2013' sub-sets. We also made a test set of 4378 samples by combining the 'tst2010', 'tst2012', and 'tst2014' sub-sets. During the experiments, we only used sentences of length less than 30 words. This reduces the size of the training, validation, and test sets to 122394, 1675, and 2474 samples, respectively.

3.2 Pre-processing

A good pre-processing pipeline has been proven to enhance the Arabic machine translation performances [19]. Therefore, we apply the same pre-processing as in [19].

We start with a cleaning process to eliminate any special characters that are not alphabets, digits, or punctuation signs in both languages, Arabic and English. Then, for English, we apply an additional lower-casing step to convert uppercase characters to lowercase. For Arabic, two additional steps were applied, a normalization and a segmentation step. The normalization was used to convert 'إأآٱ' to 'ا', 'ى' to 'ي', and 'ة' to 'ه'. The segmentation was used to break an Arabic word into stems, prefixes, and suffixes using the FARASA segmenter [1]. Table 1 illustrates an example of these pre-processing steps application. This pre-processing results in a vocabulary size of 18121 tokens for Arabic and 21011 for English.

Table 1. Pre-processing application example.

Language	Pre-processing	Text
Arabic	Original	معظم مياة كواكب الأرض محيطات.
	Cleaning	معظم مياة كواكب الأرض محيطات.
	Normalization	معظم مياه كواكب الارض محيطات.
	Segmentation	معظم مياه كواكب ال+ ارض محيط+ ات .
English	Original	Most of the planet is ocean water.
	Cleaning	Most of the planet is ocean water.
	Lower-casing	most of the planet is ocean water.

3.3 Experimental Settings

We employed the transformer [14] as the base model machine translation. The model parameters were set to 4 layers, 8 heads, 256 dimensions, and a dropout rate of 0.3. The model was firstly pre-trained for 5 epochs employing the MLE method (Eq. 2) and the Adam optimizer [7] with a learning rate of 0.001. We then continue the training for another 5 epochs with reinforcement learning (Eq. 2.2) using the Adam optimizer with a learning rate of 0.0001 and $\lambda = 0.5$. The batch size was set to 128. We used greedy generation during the inference, where the highest probability token is generated at each decoding step t. The implementation was done using the deep learning library Pytorch[1].

We used the machine translation evaluation metrics of Sect. 2.3 to calculate the reward and to evaluate the performance. We used the nltk implementation of BLEU[2], GLEU[3], and METEOR[4]. For TER, we used the pyter[5] python library.

4 Results

Tables 2 and 3 reveal the evaluation results for both directions of Arabic/English translation. The first line of both tables is the baseline model, where the training was done without reinforcement learning. Each other line represents the result when reinforcement learning is applied with the mentioned reward as well as the improvement over the baseline.

For the Arabic into English translation (Table 2), whatever the metric we use as a reward, we achieve improvement when we train with reinforcement learning overall evaluation metrics. The best gain was obtained for the TER metric (−1.75) when it was used as a reward function. With the GLEU score as the reward signal, we achieve the best improvement for both BLEU and GLEU

[1] https://pytorch.org/.
[2] https://www.nltk.org/_modules/nltk/translate/bleu_score.html.
[3] https://www.nltk.org/api/nltk.translate.gleu_score.html.
[4] https://www.nltk.org/api/nltk.translate.meteor_score.html.
[5] https://pypi.org/project/pyter/.

Table 2. Machine translation performance on Arabic-to-English translation (bold indicates the best improvement)

Reward	BLEU (%)	METEOR (%)	GLEU (%)	TER (%)
–	30.20	63.15	34.50	45.46
BLEU	31.19 (+0.99)	**63.96 (+0.81)**	35.52 (+1.02)	44.17 (−0.29)
METEOR	30.70 (+0.50)	63.78 (+0.63)	35.26 (+0.76)	44.00 (−1.46)
GLEU	**31.23 (+1.03)**	63.94 (+0.79)	**35.59 (+1.09)**	43.92 (−1.54)
TER	30.68 (+0.48)	63.50 (+0.35)	35.29 (+0.79)	**43.71 (−1.75)**

Table 3. Machine translation performance on English-to-Arabic translation (bold indicates the best improvement)

Reward	BLEU (%)	METEOR (%)	GLEU (%)	TER (%)
–	34.34	57.3	36.73	48.76
BLEU	**34.63 (+0.29)**	**57.85 (+0.55)**	**36.82 (+0.09)**	48.9 (+0.14)
METEOR	33.90 (−0.44)	56.97 (−0.33)	36.21 (−0.52)	49.71 (+0.95)
GLEU	34.53 (+0.19)	57.59 (+0.29)	36.57 (−0.16)	49.68 (+0.92)
TER	33.1 (−1.24)	56.54 (−0.76)	35.32 (−1.41)	50.94 (+2.18)

evaluation metrics. For the METEOR evaluation metric, the best improvement was obtained with the BLEU as a reward function. On average, we consider the GLEU score as the most suitable reward function when translating from Arabic to English.

On the other hand, for the inverse direction (English-to-Arabic, Table 3), with the BLEU as a reward, we get improvement in the BLEU, METEOR, and GLEU evaluation metrics with a gain of +0.29, +0.55, and +0.09, respectively. When using the GLEU score as a reward signal, only the BLEU and the METEOR metrics are improved while the GLEU and TER metrics have deteriorated. On the other hand, using the METEOR or the TER scores as rewards leads to deterioration in all evaluation metrics. These poor performances can be explained by the fact that all of these metrics are proposed for the English language, which makes it difficult for them to deal with the complex morphological structure of the Arabic language. Overall, we can consider the BLEU score as the most suitable reward function for the translation from English to Arabic.

All of the above metrics are lexical-based metrics. They calculate a translation score by comparing a lexical item, such as a word, between a candidate and a reference translation. While they are simple to calculate, fast to compute, and able to provide quick translation quality assessment. However, they suffer from limitations in capturing the translation's fluency and general meaning. These limitations make them less correlated with human evaluation [8]. Recently, new deep learning-based automated metrics have been proposed. These new metrics measure the similarity with a better understanding of the context by using the embedding representations of the sentence. Using such metrics can further improve machine translation training with reinforcement learning.

5 Conclusion

In this work, we investigated four different evaluation metrics as reward signals to train machine translation models with reinforcement learning. BLEU, METEOR, GLEU, and TER scores were employed as reward functions to train a transformer model to translate between Arabic and English languages. Experimental results illustrated that the GLEU score is the most suitable reward function for the Arabic into English translation, whereas the BLEU score is the best reward for the English into Arabic one. As a perspective, we scheme employing some deep learning-based metrics instead of the lexical-based ones used in this work.

Acknowledgements. This work received support from the Ministry of Higher Education, Scientific Research and Innovation, the Digital Development Agency, and the National Center for Scientific and Technical Research (Alkhawarizmi/2020/01).

References

1. Abdelali, A., Darwish, K., Durrani, N., Mubarak, H.: Farasa: a fast and furious segmenter for Arabic. In: Proceedings of the Demonstrations Session, NAACL HLT 2016, The 2016 Conference of the North American Chapter of the Association for Computational Linguistics: Human Language Technologies, San Diego California, USA, June 12-17, 2016, pp. 11–16. The Association for Computational Linguistics (2016). https://doi.org/10.18653/V1/N16-3003
2. Almahairi, A., Cho, K., Habash, N., Courville, A.C.: First result on Arabic neural machine translation. CoRR abs/1606.02680 (2016). arxiv:1606.02680
3. Bahdanau, D., Cho, K., Bengio, Y.: Neural machine translation by jointly learning to align and translate. In: Bengio, Y., LeCun, Y. (eds.) 3rd International Conference on Learning Representations, ICLR 2015, San Diego, CA, USA, May 7-9, 2015, Conference Track Proceedings (2015). arxiv:1409.0473
4. Banerjee, S., Lavie, A.: METEOR: an automatic metric for MT evaluation with improved correlation with human judgments. In: Goldstein, J., Lavie, A., Lin, C., Voss, C.R. (eds.) Proceedings of the Workshop on Intrinsic and Extrinsic Evaluation Measures for Machine Translation and/or Summarization@ACL 2005, Ann Arbor, Michigan, USA, June 29, 2005, pp. 65–72. Association for Computational Linguistics (2005). https://aclanthology.org/W05-0909/
5. Bensalah, N., Ayad, H., Adib, A., Farouk, A.I.E.: Transformer model and convolutional neural networks (CNNs) for Arabic to English machine translation. In: Lazaar, M., Duvallet, C., Touhafi, A., Achhab, M.A. (eds.) BDIoT'21: Proceedings of the 5th International Conference on Big Data and Internet of Things, Rabat, Morocco, March 17-18, 2021. Lecture Notes in Networks and Systems, vol. 489, pp. 399–410. Springer (2021). https://doi.org/10.1007/978-3-031-07969-6_30

6. Cettolo, M., Girardi, C., Federico, M.: WIT3: web inventory of transcribed and translated talks. In: Cettolo, M., Federico, M., Specia, L., Way, A. (eds.) Proceedings of the 16th Annual Conference of the European Association for Machine Translation, EAMT 2012, Trento, Italy, May 28-30, 2012, pp. 261–268. European Association for Machine Translation (2012). https://aclanthology.org/2012.eamt-1.60/
7. Kingma, D.P., Ba, J.: Adam: a method for stochastic optimization. In: Bengio, Y., LeCun, Y. (eds.) 3rd International Conference on Learning Representations, ICLR 2015, San Diego, CA, USA, May 7-9, 2015, Conference Track Proceedings (2015). arXiv:1412.6980
8. Lee, S., et al.: A survey on evaluation metrics for machine translation. Mathematics **11**(4), 1006 (2023). https://doi.org/10.3390/math11041006
9. Luong, T., Pham, H., Manning, C.D.: Effective approaches to attention-based neural machine translation. In: Màrquez, L., Callison-Burch, C., Su, J., Pighin, D., Marton, Y. (eds.) Proceedings of the 2015 Conference on Empirical Methods in Natural Language Processing, EMNLP 2015, Lisbon, Portugal, September 17-21, 2015, pp. 1412–1421. The Association for Computational Linguistics (2015). https://doi.org/10.18653/V1/D15-1166
10. Oudah, M., Almahairi, A., Habash, N.: The impact of preprocessing on Arabic-English statistical and neural machine translation. In: Forcada, M.L., Way, A., Haddow, B., Sennrich, R. (eds.) Proceedings of Machine Translation Summit XVII Volume 1: Research Track, MTSummit 2019, Dublin, Ireland, August 19-23, 2019, pp. 214–221. European Association for Machine Translation (2019). https://aclanthology.org/W19-6621/
11. Papineni, K., Roukos, S., Ward, T., Zhu, W.: BLEU: a method for automatic evaluation of machine translation. In: Proceedings of the 40th Annual Meeting of the Association for Computational Linguistics, July 6-12, 2002, Philadelphia, PA, USA, pp. 311–318. ACL (2002). https://doi.org/10.3115/1073083.1073135
12. Snover, M.G., Dorr, B.J., Schwartz, R.M., Micciulla, L., Makhoul, J.: A study of translation edit rate with targeted human annotation. In: Proceedings of the 7th Conference of the Association for Machine Translation in the Americas: Technical Papers, AMTA 2006, Cambridge, Massachusetts, USA, August 8-12, 2006, pp. 223–231. Association for Machine Translation in the Americas (2006). https://aclanthology.org/2006.amta-papers.25/
13. Sutskever, I., Vinyals, O., Le, Q.V.: Sequence to sequence learning with neural networks. In: Ghahramani, Z., Welling, M., Cortes, C., Lawrence, N.D., Weinberger, K.Q. (eds.) Advances in Neural Information Processing Systems 27: Annual Conference on Neural Information Processing Systems 2014, December 8-13 2014, Montreal, Quebec, Canada, pp. 3104–3112 (2014). https://proceedings.neurips.cc/paper/2014/hash/a14ac55a4f27472c5d894ec1c3c743d2-Abstract.html
14. Vaswani, A., et al.: Attention is all you need. In: Guyon, I., von Luxburg, U., Bengio, S., Wallach, H.M., Fergus, R., Vishwanathan, S.V.N., Garnett, R. (eds.) Advances in Neural Information Processing Systems 30: Annual Conference on Neural Information Processing Systems 2017, December 4-9, 2017, Long Beach, CA, USA, pp. 5998–6008 (2017). https://proceedings.neurips.cc/paper/2017/hash/3f5ee243547dee91fbd053c1c4a845aa-Abstract.html
15. Williams, R.J.: Simple statistical gradient-following algorithms for connectionist reinforcement learning. Mach. Learn. **8**, 229–256 (1992). https://doi.org/10.1007/BF00992696

16. Wu, L., Tian, F., Qin, T., Lai, J., Liu, T.: A study of reinforcement learning for neural machine translation. In: Riloff, E., Chiang, D., Hockenmaier, J., Tsujii, J. (eds.) Proceedings of the 2018 Conference on Empirical Methods in Natural Language Processing, Brussels, Belgium, October 31 - November 4, 2018, pp. 3612–3621. Association for Computational Linguistics (2018). https://doi.org/10.18653/V1/D18-1397
17. Wu, Y., et al.: Google's neural machine translation system: Bridging the gap between human and machine translation. CoRR abs/1609.08144 (2016). arxiv:1609.08144
18. Zouidine, M., Khalil, M., Farouk, A.I.E.: Policy gradient for Arabic to English neural machine translation. In: Lazaar, M., Duvallet, C., Touhafi, A., Achhab, M.A. (eds.) BDIoT'21: Proceedings of the 5th International Conference on Big Data and Internet of Things, Rabat, Morocco, March 17-18, 2021. Lecture Notes in Networks and Systems, vol. 489, pp. 469–480. Springer (2021). https://doi.org/10.1007/978-3-031-07969-6_35
19. Zouidine, M., Khalil, M., Farouk, A.I.E.: Pre-processing and pre-trained word embedding techniques for Arabic machine translation. In: Abraham, A., Pllana, S., Casalino, G., Ma, K., Bajaj, A. (eds.) Intelligent Systems Design and Applications - 22nd International Conference on Intelligent Systems Design and Applications (ISDA 2022) Held December 12-14, 2022 - Volume 2. Lecture Notes in Networks and Systems, vol. 715, pp. 115–125. Springer (2022). https://doi.org/10.1007/978-3-031-35507-3_12

ARAP-IRONY: A Multi-dialectal Arabic Irony Corpus for Irony Detection

Anis Charfi(✉), Syed Hassan Mehdi, Esraa Mohamed, and Mabrouka Bessghaier

Carnegie Mellon University in Qatar, Education City, Doha, Qatar
{acharfi,smehdi,emohamad,mbessgha}@andrew.cmu.edu

Abstract. In this paper, we present ARAP-IRONY, a multi-dialectal Arabic irony corpus including 21,120 tweets covering 11 Arabic dialects, which we developed to enable the detection of irony in dialectal Arabic using machine learning. In fact, Arabic dialects exhibit important differences in pronunciation, grammar, and vocabulary so that it is quite hard from someone from the Gulf region for instance to understand someone from the Maghreb region. Our irony corpus is balanced in terms of gender and age groups. It includes 20 ironic and 20 non-ironic tweets from each of the 48 users per dialect region that are manually annotated. We conducted various machine learning experiments using this corpus to identify irony in Dialectal Arabic. The highest accuracy and F1-score of 70% was achieved using a Logistic Regression classifier with character n-gram feature extraction.

Keywords: Irony · Dialectal Arabic · Corpus · Irony Detection · Natural Language Processing

1 Introduction

According to Merriam-Webster dictionary, Irony is defined as "the use of words to express something other than and especially the opposite of the literal meaning". The fact that the intended meaning is the opposite of the literal meaning poses several challenges both for humans and computer systems. Research on child development [1] reported that children under the age of five years are not able to understand irony.

With the increasing popularity of social media platforms, it has become very important to have tools for the identification of figurative language such as irony and sarcasm. This is relevant in several applications such as opinion mining, sentiment analysis [2] and human-computer interactive systems such as customer service chat-bots. For example, when online product or service reviews are processed automatically for opinion mining, ironic texts have to be identified as such. Otherwise, the opinion mining results will be wrong.

A. Charfi, S. H. Mehdi, E. Mohamed, M. Bessghaier—Equal contribution.

B. Hdioud and S. L. Aouragh (Eds.): ICALP 2024, CCIS 2339, pp. 218–229, 2025.
https://doi.org/10.1007/978-3-031-79164-2_19

Several approaches have been proposed for the automatic detection of irony, especially in the context of social media platforms. Most research in this field focused on Twitter [3–6]. Furthermore, many works targeted English and other European languages such as Portuguese, Spanish and Italian. These works address irony detection as a classification problem and they use machine learning classification algorithms such as support vector machine and decision trees [7]. Often, explicit hashtags such as #irony and #ironic were used to retrieve the ironic tweets.

More recently, we witnessed an increasing interest in irony detection for Arabic especially on Twitter, such as the proposed work in [8,9]. In addition, the first shared task on irony detection in Arabic was organized in the context of FIRE 2019, in which 10 teams from seven different countries participated and the best team achieved an F-measure result of 84%.

While there was some progress in the last few years on irony detection for Arabic, a key challenge that remains is the lack of annotated language resources, i.e., irony corpora. To the best of our knowledge, there are no publicly available corpora that can be used for irony detection in Arabic except the corpus of [8], which was made available to the research community at the IDAT 2019 shared task [10]. The authors of that corpus relied on some keywords such as the name of Arab politicians and the presence of explicit hashtags as markers for ironic tweets (such as the Arabic translation of #irony and #sarcasm). Another challenge is that for Arabic there are multiple dialects in different regions of the Arab world. In addition, Arab users often use their dialects on social media rather than using Modern Standard Arabic (MSA). This adds an additional complexity dimension to the language resources, which should support the variety of Arabic dialects.

In this paper, we present ARAP-IRONY, a manually-annotated multi-dialectal corpus including 21,120 tweets of 528 anonymized Twitter users. A distinctive feature of our corpus is its meticulous balance across various dimensions, including dialect, gender, and age groups. Furthermore, we have ensured a harmonious distribution of both ironic and non-ironic tweets. We believe that this balance contributes to a comprehensive exploration of the dynamics of irony across diverse linguistic and demographic factors. Through ARAP-IRONY, we aim to provide a valuable and versatile resource that caters to the nuanced intricacies of irony detection in the context of Arabic, including its various dialects and demographic considerations.

2 Related Work

Computational irony detection is a relatively recent research field that witnessed strong interest in the last decade. Research has been done on irony detection in several languages such as English, Portuguese, Italian, Spanish and Dutch.

In [6], Reyes et al. proposed a set of textual features to detect irony in English Tweets. They experimented with four freely available Twitter datasets that were retrieved using keywords such as Toyota and which also had some user-generated tags such as #irony. The reported accuracy in terms of F-measure was 73% using naive bayes and 76% when using decision trees.

In [3], the authors presented a system for automatic irony detection in Italian tweets. The used corpus included ironic tweets from the Twitter account Spinoza and the non-ironic tweets were retrieved from seven popular Italian newspapers. The authors used semantic and lexical features and reported an F-measure precision of 76%, which was obtained using decision trees.

Regarding the Arabic language, there are fewer works on irony detection than for European languages. A survey on irony and deception detection in Arabic is presented in [11].

In [9], the authors presented a classifier model for sarcasm detection in Arabic. They defined specific features to identify sarcasm, including, the presence of exclamation marks, question marks, ellipses, brackets, quotation marks, laughter, and positive words. The absence of positive marks was considered an indicative factor of sarcasm. Also, presence of both positive and negative words in a tweet was recognized as a potential indicator of sarcasm. The data was manually collected from 11 different trending hashtags on Twitter in Saudi Arabia. This process resulted in a dataset comprising 344 tweets, with 238 classified as sarcastic and 106 as non-sarcastic. The authors used Weka for data mining and achieved an accuracy of 66% and F-measure of 68%.

In [8], the authors presented a binary classification system for detecting ironic tweets in Arabic. That work is based on several features such as surface, sentiment, context and shifter features. The underlying corpus included 5479 tweets: 1/3 of them were ironic tweets that used explicit markers such as the Arabic translation of #irony and #sarcasm: 2/3 of the tweets were non-ironic. The tweets were retrieved based on keywords such as the names of politicians from the Arab world. The corpus included tweets in MSA and other Arabic dialects and it was made available to the research community at the shared task [10]. The best performing system at that shared task achieved and F-measure of 84%.

In [12], the authors introduced a multilingual irony detection system for French, English, and Arabic. Their approach integrates feature-based models and neural architectures with monolingual word representation. This study incorporated datasets in Arabic, French, and English. Specifically, the Arabic corpus, consisting of 11,225 tweets, expanded upon the corpus constructed by [8]. This expansion addressed political issues in the Middle East and the Maghreb from 2011 to 2018. For tweet collection, the authors used a set of predefined keywords targeting specific political figures or events. Besides, the collection included tweets with or without Arabic ironic hashtags, which all mean irony in Arabic. Tweets containing these hashtags were categorized as ironic. The reliability of initial tweet labels was assessed by two native Arabic speakers, resulting in 2,636 instances of ironic tweets and 2,876 instances of non-ironic tweets, with an agreement score of 0.6. In experimental results, the Neural Model with Monolingual Embeddings for Arabic achieved 80.5% accuracy and 80.4% F-score. For cross-lingual irony detection, the authors used a CNN architecture with bilingual embedding and a Random Forest model with surface features, conducting experiments by training on one language and testing on another. The CNN provided the best performance, particularly when training on Arabic and French and testing on each other.

The work proposed by [13] focused on building a new open domain Arabic corpus annotated for irony detection. Data was gathered from Twitter by querying the platform using hashtags related to irony without using any specific keywords. The resulting corpus comprises 5,358 tweets written in MSA, dialectal Arabic, and a combination of both, with more than 70% of the tweets written in Gulf and Egyptian dialects. Subsequently, two linguists manually annotated the collected tweets, and 4,809 were categorized as "Ironic" (89.75%), 435 (8.12%) as "Not Ironic," and 114 (2.13%) as "Ambiguous."

The authors in [14] investigated the application of deep learning methods for detecting irony in the Arabic language. They used Convolutional Neural Network (CNN) and Bidirectional Long Short-Term Memory (BiLSTM) models, employing word2vec term representation. The authors used a new dataset collected via Tweet Scraper by searching for tweets containing the Arabic translation of #irony and #Sarcasm hashtags. For the non-ironic dataset, they employed a random sample from an existing Arabic sentiment corpus. Both datasets were manually labeled by two Arabic speakers. The final corpus comprised 11,240 annotated tweets in Arabic, with 5,620 labelled as ironic and 5,620 as non-ironic. For the experimental results, the CNN model achieved the highest performance, with an F1 score of 87%.

While there have been efforts to detect irony in Arabic text, a notable gap exists in the specific exploration of Arabic dialects. MSA significantly differs from various Arabic dialects, and Arabic dialects vary from one another. Despite these linguistic distinctions, existing studies often categorize all Arabic dialects under one group, which neglects the nuanced features inherent in Arabic dialects, preventing the development of accurate and context-aware irony detection models. Recognizing the diversity and unique linguistic characteristics of different Arabic dialects is crucial for advancing irony detection in Arabic language processing.

2.1 Corpus Overview

ARAP-IRONY is a multi-dialectal Arabic irony corpus, which covers 11 Arabic dialects from 7 different regions as shown in Table 1. In fact, Arabic is spoken by over 370 million people worldwide, and its dialects are surprisingly unique. There are dozens of Arabic dialects, and they are all geographically and culturally different. There are also some notable pronunciation differences in these dialects. For example, many speakers of these dialects pronounce the same Arabic letters differently. There are also particular nuances to the grammar of these dialects. Table 1 shows an illustration of how diverse Arabic dialects can be. It includes basic greetings in each dialect, as well as how to ask someone how she is doing.

Our proposed irony corpus includes 48 users for each dialect and 40 tweets per user: 20 ironic and 20 non-ironic. Overall, ARAP-IRONY includes 21,120 tweets with around 200,000 words and each tweet has on average 12.85 words. Some examples of ironic tweets from our corpus along with their respective dialects are shown in Table 2.

Table 1. Dialects and regions of our irony corpus

Region	Dialects	How are you?
South Levant	Palestine-Jordan	(kefak?)
Egypt	Egyptian	(ezzayak?)
Gulf	Qatari	(shlonak?)
Gulf	Saudi Arabian	(kif halsh?)
Maghreb	Tunisian	(shono hwailk?)
Maghreb	Moroccan	(ki dayer?)
Gulf	Omani	(ieshhaleeg?)
North Levant	Lebanon-Syrian	(kefak sava?)
Iraq	Iraqi	(Kif halaj?)
Yemen	Yemeni	(keef halik?)
Sudan	Sudani	(akhbarak?)

ARAP-IRONY is perfectly balanced with respect to gender and three age groups (under 25, 25 to 34, 35 and above), i.e., for every dialect we have 24 male authors and 24 female authors. Moreover, we have 16 authors from each of the three age groups.

For the annotation, we hired three experienced native Arabic annotators and asked them to independently annotate 30 ironic and 30 non-ironic tweets for each user. Then, we took a majority vote as described later in this paper and we included in the corpus for each user only 40 tweets that have a majority vote of 2/3 at least (20 ironic tweets and 20 non-ironic tweets).

2.2 Data Collection

In order to create our corpus, we used a subset of the user accounts from ARAP-Tweet 2.0 [15], which is a large scale multi-dialectal manually annotated Arabic corpus covering 15 regions in the Arab world. ARAP-Tweet 2.0 user accounts were already annotated with respect to gender, dialect and three age groups (under 25, 25 to 34 and 35 and up) and that corpus covers 17 Arabic speaking countries and includes 5 million tweets of about 3000 Twitter users. All user information was anonymized in ARAP-Tweet and also in our irony corpus.

From each Dialect in ARAP-Tweet, we randomly selected eight male and eight female users for each of the three age groups, leading to a total of 48 users for each dialect. Hence the corpus data is perfectly balanced with respect to age

Table 2. Examples of dialectal Arabic ironic tweets

Dialect	Example of Ironic Tweet
Egypt	اخبارك؟ يخرب بيت الغياب اللي يخلينا نحضر محاضرات مش فاهمين منها حرف
Saudi Arabia	انا لازم ارتبط حياتي الساده ذي م عجبتني
Qatar	لو مضيع لي ياهل جان لقيته اسرع
Palestine Jordan	والله ما حدا داري عنك
Oman	خفي سخافتش وسماجتش وينحل الموضوع ترا بسيطة
Lebanon Syria	عم فكر غير عيلتي وحط بدل الأطرش حيدر

group, gender and dialect. The average number of words per tweet in our corpus is 12.85.

2.3 Data Annotation

The main annotation task for this corpus was to read the tweet and indicate if it is ironic or non-ironic. To that end, we hired three experienced annotators as part time employees. These annotators were native Arabic speakers and were also familiar with the dialects included in our corpus, which was very important because irony is subjective and often requires an understanding of the social, cultural and geopolitical norms of the respective regions.

For each region, we assigned a lead annotator who was responsible to identify 30 ironic and 30 non-ironic tweets for each of the 48 selected users. All the lead annotators were given clear instructions and examples of ironic tweets, which allowed us to have an initial set of ironic and non-ironic tweets for all users of a given region.

To ensure a high quality of our data set, we decided to have each tweet annotated independently by all three annotators. The lead annotator was asked to select and annotate an initial set of 60 tweets (30 ironic and 30 non-ironic) for each of the 48 users from each dialect. Then, we asked the other two annotators to read blindly annotate each of the 60 tweets for each user.

Once three annotations for each of the tweets were made blindly, we selected 20 ironic and 20 non-ironic where at least two of the three annotators agreed.

Preference was given to the tweets that were given a vote of 3/3. Once we had the finalized set of the annotations we calculated instances with a vote of 3/3 and 2/3. We found that 87% of the tweets in our corpus were labeled as ironic or non-ironic with a 3/3 vote, while 13% of the tweets received a 2/3 vote.

We used Fleiss' Kappa [16] to quantify the extent of annotator agreement, as shown for each region in Table 3. Overall, the Kappa score for our irony corpus is 0.83.

Table 3. Kappa scores for each dialect

Dialect	Kappa	Majority 3 (%)
Palestine-Jordan	0.75	81
Lebanon-Syria	0.86	89
Egyptian	0.73	80
Qatari	0.77	82
Saudi Arabian	0.83	88
Omani	0.88	91
Tunisian	0.86	89
Moroccan	0.82	87
Iraqi	0.76	82
Yemeni	0.87	95
Sudani	0.89	91
Overall	0.83	87

3 Experiments

This section describes the setup and results of some machine learning experiments, which we carried out to evaluate our irony corpus for the task of irony detection.

3.1 Setup

In these experiments, our models were provided with Arabic text data from our corpus, along with the associated dialect information. The output of the models is a binary classification result: either 'Ironic' or 'Non-ironic'. The inclusion of dialect information is crucial because the interpretation of expressions can vary significantly based on the specific dialect associated with the text.

We split our dataset into training and testing sets using a 75:25 ratio. For data pre-processing, we eliminated URLs, emails, stop words, punctuation, and non-Arabic characters. Then, we applied various techniques for extracting features,

Table 4. Performance Comparison of different Models on our Irony Detection Corpus

Classifier	Features		Accuracy	Precision	Recall	F1-Score
SVM	n-grams	Char	0.69	0.70	0.69	0.69
		Word	0.64	0.65	0.64	0.64
	TF-IDF		0.67	0.67	0.67	0.67
LR	**n-grams**	**Char**	**0.70**	**0.70**	**0.70**	**0.70**
		Word	0.67	0.67	0.67	0.67
	TF-IDF		0.67	0.67	0.67	0.67
RF	n-grams	Char	0.68	0.69	0.68	0.68
		Word	0.63	0.63	0.63	0.63
	TF-IDF		0.64	0.64	0.64	0.64
DT	n-grams	Char	0.59	0.59	0.59	0.59
		Word	0.62	0.62	0.62	0.62
	TF-IDF		0.59	0.59	0.59	0.59
MLP	n-grams	Char	0.69	0.70	0.69	0.69
		Word	0.66	0.68	0.66	0.66
	TF-IDF		0.66	0.66	0.66	0.66

such as word n-grams, character n-grams and TF-IDF. These extracted features allowed us to capture pertinent information from the text. Regarding word n-grams, we specified an n-gram range of (1,3), including unigrams, bigrams, and trigrams, and we used a range of (2,5) for character n-grams. We proceeded then to train a diverse set of machine learning models, namely Support Vector Machines (SVM), Logistic Regression (LR), Random Forest, Decision Trees, and the Multi-Layer Perceptron (MLP), in order to identify the most effective model for our classification task. The experiments were carried out using Google Colab[1] and we used the *pandas* package for data manipulation and analysis, while *nltk* was used for tokenization and stop word removal during pre-processing. Additionally, the *sklearn* package was used for the training and evaluation of all machine learning classifiers.

3.2 Results and Discussion

The results obtained with various classifiers for irony detection using our dataset are presented in Table 4. The evaluation of these classifiers is based on three distinct sets of features: Tf-IDF, n-grams, and character-level features. Each row corresponds to a different classifier, and the columns provide metrics for accuracy, precision, recall, and F1-Score considering the different feature types. Among the tested classifiers, Logistic Regression stands out as the top performer, achieving an accuracy and F1-score of 0.70 when using character n-gram features.

[1] https://colab.research.google.com/.

Besides, the evaluation results indicate that the character n-gram feature consistently outperformed both word n-grams and TF-IDF across the majority of classifiers.

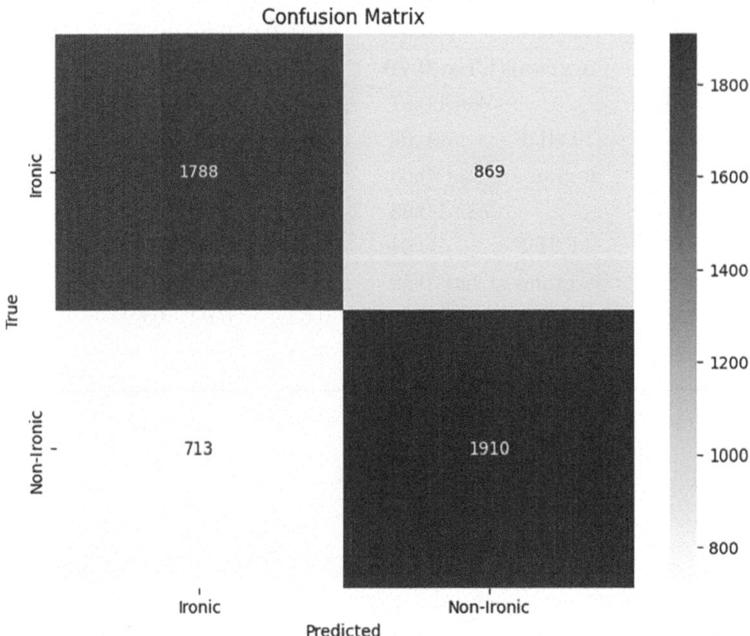

Fig. 1. Confusion Matrix for Irony Detection Model ARAP-Irony corpus

Figure 1 displays the confusion matrix, providing a comprehensive evaluation of the Logistic Regression model with character n-grams on our corpus ARAP-Irony. This matrix offers an in-depth description of true and false instances for both 'Ironic' and 'Non-Ironic' labels, providing crucial insights into the model's accuracy and effectiveness in discriminating between these categories. Our testing set comprises a total of 5280 instances. Out of the 2623 instances labeled as 'Non-Ironic', the model correctly identified 1910 instances. Likewise, for the 2657 instances labeled as 'Ironic', the model accurately predicted 1788 of them. These results demonstrate a good level of accuracy and effectiveness, which can be attributed, in part, to the balanced distribution of 'Ironic' and 'Non-Ironic' instances, as well as the diverse representation of different regions in our dataset.

The column chart presented in Fig. 2 visually illustrates this balance. It provides a representation of the distribution of 'Ironic' and 'Non-Ironic' instances across different regions in our dataset. Each column corresponds to a specific region, and the height of the column indicates the number of instances.

Figure 3 presents the distribution of instances across different regions in our corpus. Each slice represents a region, and the size of the slice corresponds to the proportion of instances from that region. This further emphasizes the balanced distribution of tweet instances in our irony corpus.

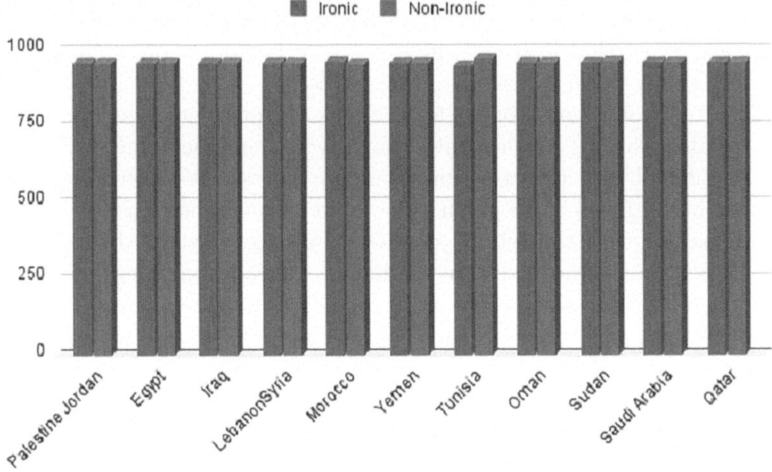

Fig. 2. Distribution of Ironic and Non-Ironic Instances Across Regions

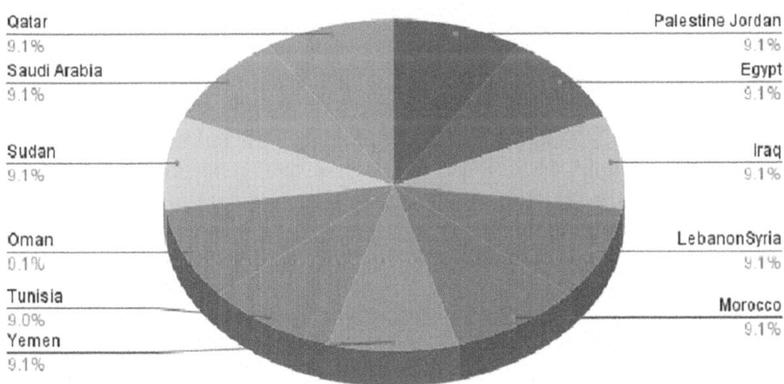

Fig. 3. Distribution of Tweets from Different Regions in our Dataset

4 Conclusion

In this paper, we presented ARAP-IRONY, which is a manually-annotated multi-dialectal Arabic irony corpus that includes 21.120 tweets and covers 11 Arabic dialects. Our proposed corpus is unique in its emphasis on Arabic dialects, which are quite diverse. For each of the 11 dialects, our corpus includes 40 tweets from 48 users that are balanced with respect to gender and three age groups (under 25, 25 to 34, 35 and above). For each user in our corpus, we have

20 ironic and 20 non-ironic tweets that were annotated independently by three annotators and we only included tweets that had at least an agreement of 2 annotators out of 3. 87% of the tweets in our corpus have an agreement of 3/3. We evaluated the quality of the annotation by inter-annotator agreements using Fleiss' kappa and got a value an overall Kappa score of 0.83, which we believe is good considering that irony is a highly subjective and is often challenging to identify, especially when considering text only.

In order to evaluate our corpus for the task of irony detection, we conducted several machine learning experiments using diverse classifiers, including Support Vector Machine, Logistic Regression, Random Forest, Decision Tree, Random Forest, and Multi-Layer Perceptron. The input to our models comprises Arabic text data, paired with the related dialect, resulting in either 'Ironic' or 'Non-ironic' classification. The inclusion of dialect information is critical since the interpretation of expressions might vary significantly depending on the specific dialect associated with the text. We achieved the highest accuracy and F1-score of 70% with Logistic Regression with character n-gram feature extraction.

Acknowledgements. This publication was made possible by NPRP 9-175-1-033 from the Qatar National Research Fund and by the generous support of the Qatar Foundation through Carnegie Mellon University in Qatar's Seed Research program. The contents herein reflect the work and are solely the authors' responsibility.

References

1. Dews, S., et al.: Children's understanding of the meaning and functions of verbal irony. Child Dev. **67**(6), 3071–3085 (1996)
2. Bosco, C., Patti, V., Bolioli, A.: Developing corpora for sentiment analysis: the case of irony and senti-TUT. IEEE Intell. Syst. **28**(2), 55–63 (2013)
3. Barbieri, F., Saggion, H., Ronzano, F.: Modelling sarcasm in twitter, a novel approach. In: Proceedings of the 5th Workshop on Computational Approaches to Subjectivity, Sentiment and Social Media Analysis, pp. 50–58 (2014)
4. Hernández-Farías, I., Benedí, J.-M., Rosso, P.: Applying basic features from sentiment analysis for automatic irony detection. In: Iberian Conference on Pattern Recognition and Image Analysis, pp. 337–344 (2015). Springer
5. Joshi, A., Sharma, V., Bhattacharyya, P.: Harnessing context incongruity for sarcasm detection. In: Proceedings of the 53rd Annual Meeting of the Association for Computational Linguistics and the 7th International Joint Conference on Natural Language Processing (Volume 2: Short Papers), pp. 757–762 (2015)
6. Reyes, A., Rosso, P., Veale, T.: A multidimensional approach for detecting irony in twitter. Lang. Resour. Eval. **47**(1), 239–268 (2013)
7. Rosso, P., Rangel, F., Farías, I.H., Cagnina, L., Zaghouani, W., Charfi, A.: A survey on author profiling, deception, and irony detection for the Arabic language. Lang. Linguist. Compass **12**(4), 12275 (2018)
8. Karoui, J., Zitoune, F.B., Moriceau, V.: SOUKHRIA: towards an irony detection system for Arabic in social media. Procedia Comput. Sci. **117**, 161–168 (2017)
9. Al-Ghadhban, D., Alnkhilan, E., Tatwany, L., Alrazgan, M.: Arabic sarcasm detection in twitter. In: 2017 International Conference on Engineering & MIS (ICEMIS), pp. 1–7 (2017). IEEE

10. IDAT: https://www.irit.fr/IDAT2019/ (2019)
11. Rosso, P., Pardo, F.M.R., Hernandez-Farias, I., Cagnina, L.C., Zaghouani, W., Charfi, A.: A survey on author profiling, deception, and irony detection for the Arabic language. Lang. Linguist. Compass **12**(4) (2018). https://doi.org/10.1111/lnc3.12275
12. Ghanem, B., Karoui, J., Benamara, F., Rosso, P., Moriceau, V.: Irony detection in a multilingual context. In: Advances in Information Retrieval: 42nd European Conference on IR Research, ECIR 2020, Lisbon, Portugal, April 14–17, 2020, Proceedings, Part II 42, pp. 141–149 (2020). Springer
13. Abbes, I., Zaghouani, W., El-Hardlo, O., Ashour, F.: DAICT: a dialectal Arabic irony corpus extracted from twitter. In: Proceedings of the Twelfth Language Resources and Evaluation Conference, pp. 6265–6271 (2020)
14. Alhaidari, L., Alyoubi, K., Alotaibi, F.: Detecting irony in Arabic microblogs using deep convolutional neural networks. Int. J. Adv. Comput. Sci. Appl. **13**(1) (2022)
15. Charfi, A., Zaghouani, W., Mehdi, S.H., Mohamed, E.: A fine-grained annotated multi-dialectal Arabic corpus. Proc. Recent Adv. Nat. Lang. Process. 190–204 (2019)
16. Fleiss, J.L.: Measuring nominal scale agreement among many raters. Psychol. Bull. **76**(5), 378 (1971)

Context-Aware Arabic Diacritization Using Transformers

Ruba Kharsa and Ashraf Elnagar(✉)

Department of Computer Science, University of Sharjah, 27272 Sharjah, UAE
{u21103616,ashraf}@sharjah.ac.ae

Abstract. The presence of diacritics plays a crucial role in representing the meaning and pronunciation of Arabic words and sentences accurately. Over the years, researchers have dedicated considerable efforts to enhance automated diacritization systems. However, to our knowledge, Bidirectional Encoder Representations from Transformers (BERT) models were not yet investigated for the full diacritization approach. This study introduces a novel approach that utilizes transfer learning and BERT for diacritizing Arabic sentences. To show the effectiveness of the proposed approach, this research paper utilizes the Arabic Diacritization (AD) benchmark dataset to compare the constructed BERT model with the most recent research using error metrics. The research findings demonstrate the significance of the proposed approach in improving the accuracy of diacritization. The trained model outperformed all previous techniques and achieved state-of-the-art (SOTA) results in all error metrics. The resulting syntactic DER and WER are 1.14% and 3.35%, respectively. In morphological diacritization, the best results showed a DER of 0.92% and a WER of 1.91%. These results represent a significant relative error reduction of 35% on average compared to previous research.

Keywords: automated diacritization system · word error rate · diacritic error rate · BERT Arabic contextualized models

1 Introduction

The process of adding short vowels and other symbols to letters is referred to as *tashkl* in Arabic, which translates as 'diacritization'. Diacritics hold a significant role in Arabic, they help the reader distinguish between words that have different meanings but are spelled with the same consonants (i.e., homographs). For example, the word *lm* consists of three consonants; with the insertion of different diacritics it could be read as *ilm* 'knowledge' or *alam* 'flag'. This makes diacritics essential for supporting non-natives and improving the results of Natural Language Processing (NLP) tasks.

R. Kharsa—Contributing author

B. Hdioud and S. L. Aouragh (Eds.): ICALP 2024, CCIS 2339, pp. 230–241, 2025.
https://doi.org/10.1007/978-3-031-79164-2_20

Table 1 presents a list of the eight main diacritics in Arabic. It shows each diacritic name, sound, position, an example using the letter R, and the sound it gives to the letter. However, each Arabic letter can have one of 15 possible options, because each character in a word can have zero, one, or two diacritics. Zero means the character does not require a diacritic. One indicates that the character has one of the main eight diacritics. Two means that the character has the shadda plus one diacritic (i.e., Shadda& Fatha, Shadda& Damma, Shadda& Kasra, Shadda& Tanween Fath, Shadda& Tanween Damm, or Shadda& Tanween Kasr)

Table 1. Arabic main diacritics on the Ra' letter.

Arabic Name	English Name	Sound	Location	Diacritized Ra'
فتحة	Fatha	a	above	رَ
ضمة	Damma	u	above	رُ
كسرة	Kasra	i	bellow	رِ
سكون	Sukun	No voice	above	رْ
تنوين فتح	Tanween Fath	un	above	رً
تنوين ضم	Tanween Damm	un	above	رٌ
تنوين كسر	Tanween Kasr	in	bellow	رٍ
شدة	Shadda	duplicate sound	above	رّ

Table 2 highlights the effect of diacritization on the pronunciation of words in an anonymous line of poetry, which means "A pain struck! Wasnt his illness managed!".

The table demonstrates how the use of diacritics carries considerable significance to the Arabic language because they can specify the exact pronunciation of the words and uncover more information about their meanings in different contexts. Moreover, the table shows that using diacritics greatly improves the results of NLP tasks, such as text-to-speech systems, which can aid blind and visually impaired communities.

Table 2. Effect of diacritization on the pronunciation of words.

Diacritized	Example	Transliteration
No	ألم ألم ألم ألم بدائه	ālm ālm ālm ālm bdā'h
Yes	أَلَمٌ أَلَمَّ أَلَمْ أُلِمَّ بِدائِهِ	alamun alamma alam ulimma bidā'ihi

Diacritics are often left out in Arabic scripts. However, the absence of these diacritics poses a challenge for Machine Learning (ML) and Deep Learning (DL) algorithms. The manual restoration of diacritics is time-consuming and complicated. This inspired NLP specialists to develop tools that automatically add diacritical marks to sentences. However, up to our knowledge, context-aware diacritization with transformers has not yet been investigated for full diacritization using the token classification method. Therefore, the primary contributions of this study are as follows:

- Utilizing transfer learning for the task of Arabic diacritization.
- Achieving context-aware diacritization
- Employing transformers (i.e., the BERT model) to perform sub-word Arabic diacritization using token-level classification. [1]
- Outperforming the previous research by achieving the lowest error rates on a widely recognized benchmark dataset: the Arabic Diacritization (AD) dataset [2].

The rest of the paper proceeds as follows, Sect. 2 reviews the Arabic diacritization literature, then Sect. 3 details the methodology of our approach and the used dataset. Section 4 presents the results and compares the findings with the literature. Finally, Sect. 5 summarizes our research outcomes and future work.

2 Literature Review

The topic of Arabic diacritization has seen a lot of research and studies over the years [3]. The diacritization approaches have ranged from rule-based methods and statistical methods to more advanced ML and DL techniques, which were used successfully in a variety of Arabic NLP tasks on text [4–9] and audio [10–12]. This section focuses on the recent research that specifically uses ML and DL for Arabic diacritization.

Sallab et al. [13] were the first to utilize deep learning for automatic Arabic diacritization. They employed the Confused Subset Resolution (CSR) technique along with POS tagging to improve syntactic diacritization. The CSR starts with a global Deep Neural Network (DNN), and then it identifies the error based on the confusion matrix analysis of the DNN prediction. The error is used to train multiple sub-classifiers. The final predictions are then decided using both the original DNN and the sub-classifiers. Sallab et al. [13] compared their results with previous work using the Arabic Tree Bank (ATB) [14], and the RDI dataset [15–17]. They decreased the classification error by 22% and achieved a syntactic and morphological classification error of 9.9% and 3%, respectively.

Darwish et al. [18] developed an automated diacritizer (Farasa) by combining rule-based methods with the Support Vector Machine (SVM) ML algorithm for Modern Standard Arabic (MSA) diacritization. They obtained the RDI closed-source dataset with 10 million tokens to train their model because they believed the ATB dataset with only 570 thousand tokens was insufficient. To evaluate their system, Darwish et al. [18] created a new dataset with 70 articles on various topics from Wikinews. They reported a DER of 3.54% and a WER of 12.76%.

Mubarak et al. [19] developed a sequence-to-sequence model and evaluated their system using the testing corpus from [18]. They significantly reduced the error of Darwish et al. [18] by achieving a WER of 4.49%.

Fadel et al. [20] employed three distinct Forward Neural Networks (FNN) and Recurrent Neural Networks (RNN) models, with different configurations. Notably, their most successful model was the RNN Block-Normalized Gradient (BNG), yielding a DER of 1.69% and a WER of 5.09%.

A recent study by Darwish et al. [21] utilized a feature-rich Long Short Memory (LSTM) model to perform diacritization on both MSA and Classical Arabic (CA). The authors used the RDI dataset for MSA and created a new dataset of 3 million tokens from CA books. The best configuration of their model produced a WER of 4.3% and 6% for CA and MSA, respectively.

In their study, AlKhamissi et al. [22] trained a deep neural sequence labeling model and evaluated it using the AD dataset [2]. This resulted in a DER of 1.94% and a WER of 5.34%.

Abbad & Xiong [23] used a multi-component approach to construct their model by combining DL (i.e., RNN with LSTM), rule-based, and context statistics methods. Moreover, they created a new open-source benchmark dataset called the TP dataset, which is a cleaned and processed version of the Tashkeela corpus [24]. Their experiments on the TP dataset resulted in a DER of 2.61% and a WER of 5.83% when excluding the CE characters.

In another study, Abbad & Xiong [25] used a BiLSTM deep learning network on a subset of the TP dataset [23]. They achieved a 2.45% DER and 5.42% WER when excluding the CE characters. However, when including the CE letters, the DER and WER increased to 3% and 8.99%, respectively.

Hifny [26] employed an ensemble of hybrid BiLSTM taggers with maximum entropy connection between input and output, effectively reducing the time and memory complexity of the ensemble. To address the high Out-Of-Vocabulary (OOV) rate in Arabic, they incorporated character-level and word embeddings. Their approach was evaluated using the ATB dataset, yielding a 4.3% syntactic WER, demonstrating the effectiveness of their proposed strategy.

Thompson & Alshehri [27] adopted a multitasking approach, including English translation, to enhance Arabic diacritization. They performed experiments on the ATB dataset and achieved a WER of 4.97%.

Masmoudi et al. [28] focused on the Tunisian dialect (TD) diacritization. They created a corpus for TD called TDTACHKIL and then proposed an automatic diacritization model based on statistical machine translation (SMT). The undiacritized text was the source language and the diacritized version was the target language. However, the resulting error rates were high (8.89% DER and 16.7% WER). Masmoudi and Maalej suggested utilizing a rule-based system along with their SMT, as well as increasing the size of their proposed corpus.

Abandah et al. [29] employed a transfer learning approach to enhance the diacritization process of Arabic poetry, which has a higher error rate than regular Arabic text. They experimented with a two-stage model that utilizes two classifiers, one for poetry meter classification and the other for verse diacritization.

Moreover, three transfer learning architectures with BiLSTM-based layers were investigated. The findings of Abandah et al. [29] showed that the transfer learning model with two-stacked BiLSTM components achieved the highest results in Arabic poetry diacritization with a DER of 3.54%. However, all of the proposed systems required an already-built classifier for poetry meter identification, which introduces a challenge and can greatly increase the difficulty of constructing the system.

Although there have been several attempts to improve Arabic diacritization using machine learning (ML) and deep learning (DL) techniques, there are still significant limitations and gaps in previous studies that need to be addressed. One major gap is the under-utilization of transfer learning approaches. Most previous research on Arabic diacritization trains models from scratch and does not exploit the benefits of pre-trained large language models. Another improvement can be achieved by adopting sub-word (token) classification instead of character-level classification. This approach takes advantage of the BERT model's ability to capture dependencies between tokens, where a token can represent a whole word or sub-word. Furthermore, most previous models rely on LSTM or RNN as base models, which are computationally expensive and require extensive training time due to their sequential nature. In contrast, transformer-based models with self-attention layers offer advantages in terms of computational complexity and parallelization capabilities. The self-attention mechanism reduces both the complexity of sequential operations and the maximum path length, improving efficiency compared to RNN-based models [30]. Moreover, the BERT model differs from previous models because it is context-aware, processing all input sequences simultaneously and capturing bidirectional relationships between tokens [31]. Lastly, despite previous efforts to minimize errors, there is still room for improvement. This research aims to propose a model that surpasses the performance of previous techniques and an extension of our ongoing work [32].

3 Proposed Methodology

3.1 Datasets

This research focuses on the diacritization of CA because the main MSA datasets which are the ATB dataset and RDI dataset [15–17] are closed-source with a high cost or a strict license.

The Tashkeela dataset is a famous open-source corpus and it is considered as the main dataset for CA [24]. It consists of 75M tokens from Islamic books and a small portion (1%) of MSA. The main problems with the Tashkeela corpus are that it is not processed and cleaned, has many undiacritized files, and is not divided into training, validation, and testing datasets. Thus, researchers could not use it as a benchmark dataset.

Fadel et al. [2] extracted the AD dataset from the Tashkeela corpus. They pre-process and clean a few fully diacritized files by dividing long lines and deleting English characters, HTML, and XML tags. Subsequently, they split the extracted files into three datasets (i.e., training with 24.5M tokens, validation with 102K tokens, and testing with 107K tokens).

This divided dataset is helpful because utilizing the same training and testing sets for evaluating different models ensures fair comparison between researchers. Therefore, this research uses the AD dataset to train and test the constructed model.

3.2 Error Metrics

The main Error metrics for evaluating the performance and effectiveness of the model predictions are the Diacritic Error Rate (DER) and Word Error Rate (WER). The DER is the proportion of characters with erroneous diacritics to the whole number of characters. The WER is the proportion of the words that have any errors in their diacritics to the total number of words. Each of the DER and WER is measured by including the Case-ending character of each word (+CE) that represents the syntactic evaluation and by excluding it (-CE) to assess the model on the morphological level. Another consideration in error metric calculation is whether to include or exclude undiacritized Letters (IUL or EUL). Fadel et al. [2] highlighted the issues of using the previous error metrics presented in Zitouni & Sarikaya's work. [33] that take into account the punctuation and non-Arabic characters resulting in decreasing the error. This research adopts the metrics that [2] presented because they are stricter and more accurate.

3.3 The BERT Model

BERT, introduced by [31], is a language representation model that outperforms previous unidirectional models by considering the entire context of a text sequence. It utilizes a stack of identical Transformer encoders that read the sequence bidirectionally, from both left to right and right to left simultaneously. BERT uses transfer learning, where the model is pre-trained on large amounts of unlabeled data and then fine-tuned on smaller labeled datasets for specific tasks. The pre-training stage creates a source model with learned parameters. The fine-tuning stage involves using the source parameters to initialize the model, and only adjusting the parameters in the output layer, which are learned in a supervised manner using labeled data for the target task. BERT uses WordPiece embeddings which is a subword-based tokenization method [34]. It segments words into smaller subword units by considering the trained model's language knowledge. It uses a special boundary character (#) to separate the subwords and to allow for the reconstruction of the original words. The WordPiece tokenization method provides a balance between the flexibility of character-based tokenization and the efficiency of word-based tokenization.

BERT input representation is a combination of token embeddings, segmentation embeddings, and position embeddings.

- Token Embeddings: Words are split into WordPiece tokens and each token is embedded into a d dimensional space ($d = 768$ for BERT-base, and $d = 1024$ for BERT-large).
- Segmentation Embeddings: BERT can take two sentences as input for tasks (like Question Answering). Sentence A and Sentence B are differentiated using segmentation embeddings.
- Position Embeddings: BERT uses position embeddings to capture the order of words in a sentence. If E_t represents the token embedding, E_s represents the segment embedding, and E_p represents the position embedding for a token at position i, the final embedding E_i for the token would be $E_i = E_t + E_s + E_p$.

3.4 Data Preprocessing

The preprocessing involves splitting the lines if they exceed 1000 characters over the following punctuation (،,؛,.,:,(,),{,}, [,] (,),{,}, [,]), removing the Arabic (taṭwīl) character, punctuation marks, small Arabic characters, and non-Arabic characters. One challenge in extracting diacritics from characters is that Arabic characters could be marked with zero, one, or two diacritics, meaning that the number of diacritics could be higher or lower than the number of characters, leading to a non-one-to-one mapping of diacritics to characters. To address this, the diacritics were recoded so that each character would have a single label as shown in Table 3 that illustrates the mapping technique. As the table shows, there are fifteen possible representations.

Table 3. Diacritic representation.

Diacritic	Representation	Count
No diacritic	c	0
Shadda	s	1
Sukoun	o	1
Kasra	k	1
Damma	d	1
Fatha	f	1
Tanween Kasr	r	1
Tanween Damm	m	1
Tanween Fath	h	1
Shadda + Kasra	K	2
Shadda + Damma	D	2
Shadda + Fatha	F	2
Shadda + Tanween Kasr	R	2
Shadda + Tanween Damm	M	2
Shadda + Tanween Fath	H	2

Table 4 summarizes the main preprocessing steps that are needed to extract diacritic representation from each sentence. For example, the word بِكَ is represented as بك in the second-to-last row and its diacritics are extracted into the code sequence “kf” (representing kasra and fatha) in the last row.

Table 4. Preprocessing the training file.

Preprocessing Step	Example Sentence
None	1 : بِكَ أَسْتَجِيـــــــــرُ، وَمَنْ يُجِيْـرُ سِوَاكَ.
Removing Stretching and Superscripts	1 : بِكَ أَسْتَجِيرُ، وَمَنْ يُجِيْرُ سِوَاكَ.
Removing the numerals, non-Arabic, and punctuation characters	بِكَ أَسْتَجِيرُ وَمَنْ يُجِيْرُ سِوَاكَ
Stripping diacritics	بك أستجير ومن يجير سواك
Preparing Diacritic representation	kf fofkcd ffo dkod kfcf

Then, each line is tokenized with the pre-trained Bert tokenizer. Each input token is then aligned with the corresponding diacritic representation of its characters. This is done to design the diacrtization as a token classification problem using the BERT model by having a set of input tokens and their corresponding classes. Following is an example of the final aligned tokens.

[[‘بك’, ‘kf’], [‘أست’, ‘fof’], ‘##جير’, ‘##kcd’], [‘ومن’, ‘ffo’], [‘يحي’, ‘dko’], [‘##ر’, ‘##d’], [‘سواك’, ‘kfcf’]]

The target space of the model is considered as all token’s diacritic combinations of the training dataset. After the preprocessing, tokenizing, and preparing the aligned tokens of the dataset. The number of different combinations of diacritics is 11594 possible classes (i.e., the target space labels)

3.5 Model Architecture

Figure 1, shows the abstract architecture of the model. Each sequence begins with the special $[CLS]$ token and ends with the $[SEP]$ token. If the input sequence is shorter than the maximum length, tokens get padded with the $[PAD]$ token to reach that length. After the tokens are inputted into the Bert model, each output from the BERT model (i.e., BERT contextualized representation) is connected to a Feed Forward Neural Network (FFNN) with the Softmax activation function, that assigns a probability to each class in the target domain. Subsequently, the class with the maximum probability is found and assigned to each input token. The model is trained to minimize the cross-entropy error to reach the best diacritization.

4 Experiments and Results

This section summarizes the experiments, results, and findings of using the Bert architecture with the task of Arabic diacritization.

The AraBERTv0.2-base model is chosen and acquired from the Hugging Face library. The model has a size of 77GB and its vocabulary size is 60k. It was pre-trained on a large Arabic-specific corpus (e.g., "OSCAR unshuffled and filtered, Arabic Wikipedia, The 1.5B words Arabic Corpus, The OSIAN Corpus, Assafir news article").

AraBERT has 12 encoder layers with 12 attention heads. The model's trainable parameters are 136M. The AraBERT model was trained with a batch size of 64, a max length of 128, and a learning rate of 5e-5. The experiments were carried out using Tesla K80 GPUs. To prevent overfitting, early stopping was used with the validation dataset. The model continued training for 10 epochs and 77 h.

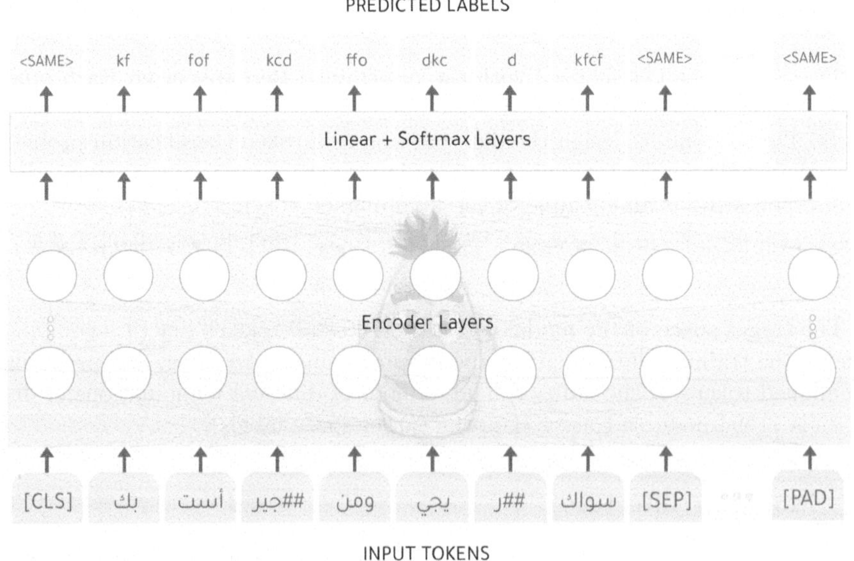

Fig. 1. The Bert model Architecture

As Table 5 demonstrates, our proposed BERT model showed a significant improvement and achieved the SOTA results on all metrics compared to four popular diacritic models on the AD dataset. The shown results were taken from [20] paper for systems trained on the same training set and tested on the same testing set to ensure fair and precise comparison. The proposed model introduced an average of 35% error reduction to [20] results that had the lowest errors on the AD dataset. Our proposed model has achieved a DER of 1.14% and a WER of 3.35% on the most challenging metric that includes the CE characters and undiacritized letters (+CE IUL) implying that the model is reliable even for grammar and syntax.

Table 5. Comparison between the proposed model and the existing best models on the AD testing dataset.

DER/WER %	IUL +CE	IUL -CE	EUL +CE	EUL -CE
Barqawi & Zerrouki [35]	3.73/11.19	2.88/6.53	4.36/10.89	3.33/6.37
Abbad & Xiong [23]	3.39/9.94	2.61/5.83	3.34/7.98	2.43/3.98
Alkhamissi et al. [22]	1.83/5.34	1.48/3.11	2.09/5.08	1.69/3.00
Fadel et al. [20]	1.78/5.38	1.39/3.04	2.05/5.17	1.60/2.96
AraBERT (Ours)	**1.14/3.35**	**0.92/1.91**	**1.28/3.12**	**1.03/1.79**

To calculate the required execution time of the model, 1000 sentences are inputted for prediction and an average of 3 runs is taken. The average execution time per sentence is 0.1 s, which is deemed reasonable for a diacritization system.

The following are examples of the model performance on five sentences. These examples vary from poetry to prose and from CA to MSA to show the notable potential and effectiveness of the proposed technique.

عَلَى قَدْرِ أَهْلِ الْعَزْمِ تَأْتِي الْعَزَائِمُ.

وَنَحْنُ نُحِبُّ الْحَيَاةَ، إِذَا مَا اسْتَطَعْنَا إِلَيْهَا سَبِيلًا.

الْأُمُّ مَدْرَسَةٌ إِذَا أَعْدَدْتَهَا، أَعْدَدْت شَعَبًا طَيِّبَ الْأَعْرَاقِ.

وَمَنْ لَا يُحِبُّ صُعُودَ الْجِبَالِ، يَعِشْ أَبَدَ الدَّهْرِ بَيْنَ الْحُفَرِ.

عَلَامَةُ التَّشْكِيلِ هِيَ شَكْلَةٌ تُوضَعُ أَعْلَى الْحَرْفِ الْعَرَبِيِّ أَوْ تَحْتَهُ لِتَوْضِيحِ نُطْقِ الْحَرْفِ.

5 Conclusion and Future Work

This research demonstrated the power of using Bert for Arabic diacritization, as the result signified, the proposed fine-tuned AraBERT model outperformed the previous ones with a large margin on all error metrics and achieved on average a 35% relative error improvement of the best existing model. The main challenge faced is the lack of open-source MSA datasets, therefore collecting a diacritized MSA dataset is considered a potential future work. Another future research would be developing a model for minimal diacritization where only the essential diacritics that affect the word's meaning are added. Moreover, experimenting with Large Language Models (LLMs) and Generative Pre-trained Transformer (GPT) architectures for the task of Arabic diacritization is another direction of this research.

References

1. Náplava, J., Straka, M., Strakova, J.: Diacritics restoration using bert with analysis on czech language. arXiv preprint arXiv:2105.11408 (2021)
2. Fadel, A., Tuffaha, I., Al-Ayyoub, M., *et al.*: Arabic text diacritization using deep neural networks. In: 2019 2nd International Conference on Computer Applications and Information Security (ICCAIS), pp. 1–7 (2019). IEEE
3. Azmi, A.M., Almajed, R.S.: A survey of automatic arabic diacritization techniques. Nat. Lang. Eng. **21**(3), 477–495 (2015)
4. Nassif, A.B., Darya, A.M., Elnagar, A.: Empirical evaluation of shallow and deep learning classifiers for Arabic sentiment analysis. Trans. Asian LowResource Lang. Inform. Process. **21**(1), 1–25 (2021)
5. Elnagar, A., Yagi, S.M., Nassif, A.B., Shahin, I., Salloum, S.A.: Systematic literature review of dialectal Arabic: identification and detection. IEEE Access **9**, 31010–31042 (2021)
6. Nassif, A.B., Elnagar, A., Elgendy, O., Afadar, Y.: Arabic fake news detection based on deep contextualized embedding models. Neural Comput. Appl. **34**(18), 16019–16032 (2022)
7. Elnagar, A., Yagi, S., Mansour, Y., Lulu, L., Fareh, S.: A benchmark for evaluating Arabic contextualized word embedding models. Inform. Process. Manage. **60**(5), 103452 (2023)
8. Yagi, S., Elnagar, A., Fareh, S.: A benchmark for evaluating Arabic word embedding models. Nat. Lang. Eng. **29**(4), 978–1003 (2023)
9. Yagi, S., Fareh, S., Elnagar, A., Balajeed, M., Mneizel, A., Al-Badawi, M.: Is Arabic punctuation rule-governed? Cogent Arts Human. **11**(1), 2303818 (2024)
10. Lataifeh, M., Elnagar, A., Shahin, I., Nassif, A.B.: Arabic audio clips: identification and discrimination of authentic cantillations from imitations. Neurocomputing **418**, 162–177 (2020)
11. Shahin, I., Nassif, A.B., Nemmour, N., Elnagar, A., Alhudhaif, A., Polat, K.: Novel hybrid dnn approaches for speaker verification in emotional and stressful talking environments. Neural Comput. Appl. **33**(23), 16033–16055 (2021)
12. Nassif, A.B., Shahin, I., Elnagar, A., Velayudhan, D., Alhudhaif, A., Polat, K.: Emotional speaker identification using a novel capsule nets model. Expert Syst. Appl. **193**, 116469 (2022)
13. Al Sallab, A., Rashwan, M., Raafat, H., Rafea, A.: Automatic arabic diacritics restoration based on deep nets. In: Proceedings of the EMNLP 2014 Workshop on Arabic Natural Language Processing (ANLP), pp. 65–72 (2014)
14. Maamouri, M., Bies, A., Buckwalter, T., Mekki, W.: The penn Arabic treebank: Building a large-scale annotated arabic corpus. In: NEMLAR Conference on Arabic Language Resources and Tools, vol. 27, pp. 466–467 (2004). Cairo
15. Diab, M., Habash, N., Rambow, O., Roth, R.: Ldc arabic treebanks and associated corpora: Data divisions manual. arXiv preprint arXiv:1309.5652 (2013)
16. Rashwan, M., Al-Badrashiny, M., Attia, M., Abdou, S.: A hybrid system for automatic arabic diacritization. In: The 2nd International Conference on Arabic Language Resources and Tools, pp. 54–60 (2009)
17. Rashwan, M.A., Al-Badrashiny, M.A., Attia, M., Abdou, S.M., Rafea, A.: A stochastic arabic diacritizer based on a hybrid of factorized and unfactorized textual features. IEEE Trans. Audio Speech Lang. Process. **19**(1), 166–175 (2010)
18. Darwish, K., Mubarak, H., Abdelali, A.: Arabic diacritization: Stats, rules, and hacks. In: Proceedings of the Third Arabic Natural Language Processing Workshop, pp. 9–17 (2017)

19. Mubarak, H., Abdelali, A., Sajjad, H., Samih, Y., Darwish, K.: Highly effective arabic diacritization using sequence to sequence modeling. In: Proceedings of the 2019 Conference of the North American Chapter of the Association for Computational Linguistics: Human Language Technologies, Volume 1 (Long and Short Papers), pp. 2390–2395 (2019)
20. Fadel, A., Tuffaha, I., Al-Ayyoub, M.: Neural arabic text diacritization: State-ofthe-art results and a novel approach for arabic nlp downstream tasks. Transactions on Asian and Low-Resource Language Information Processing **21**(1), 1–25 (2021)
21. Darwish, K., Abdelali, A., Mubarak, H., Eldesouki, M.: Arabic diacritic recovery using a feature-rich bilstm model. Trans. Asian Low-Resour. Lang. Inform. Process. **20**(2), 1–18 (2021)
22. AlKhamissi, B., ElNokrashy, M.N., Gabr, M.: Deep diacritization: Efficient hierarchical recurrence for improved arabic diacritization. arXiv preprint arXiv:2011.00538 (2020)
23. Abbad, H., Xiong, S.: Multi-components System for Automatic Arabic Diacritization. In: Jose, J.M., Yilmaz, E., Magalhães, J., Castells, P., Ferro, N., Silva, M.J., Martins, F. (eds.) Advances in Information Retrieval: 42nd European Conference on IR Research, ECIR 2020, Lisbon, Portugal, April 14–17, 2020, Proceedings, Part I, pp. 341–355. Springer International Publishing, Cham (2020). https://doi.org/10.1007/978-3-030-45439-5_23
24. Zerrouki, T., Balla, A.: Tashkeela: Novel corpus of arabic vocalized texts, data for auto-diacritization systems. Data Brief **11**, 147–151 (2017)
25. Abbad, H., Xiong, S.: Simple extensible deep learning model for automatic Arabic diacritization. Trans. Asian Low-Resour. Lang. Inform. Process. **21**(2), 1–16 (2021)
26. Hifny, Y.: Recent advances in arabic syntactic diacritics restoration. In: ICASSP 2021 - 2021 IEEE International Conference on Acoustics, Speech and Signal Processing (ICASSP), pp. 7768–7772 (2021). https://doi.org/10.1109/ICASSP39728.2021.9414500
27. Thompson, B., Alshehri, A.: Improving Arabic diacritization by learning to diacritize and translate. arXiv preprint arXiv:2109.14150 (2021)
28. Masmoudi, A., Aloulou, C., Abdellahi, A.G.S., Belguith, L.H.: Automatic diacritization of tunisian dialect text using smt model. Int. J. Speech Technol. 1–16 (2022)
29. Abandah, G.A., Suyyagh, A.E., Abdel-Majeed, M.R.: Transfer learning and multi-phase training for accurate diacritization of arabic poetry. J. King Saud Univ. - Comput. Inform. Sci. **34**(6, Part B), 3744–3757 (2022). https://doi.org/10.1016/j.jksuci.2022.04.005
30. Vaswani, A., et al.: Attention is all you need. In: Advances in Neural Information Processing Systems, vol. 30 (2017)
31. Devlin, J., Chang, M.-W., Lee, K., Toutanova, K.: Bert: Pre-training of deep bidirectional transformers for language understanding. arXiv preprint arXiv:1810.04805 (2018)
32. Kharsa, R., Elnagar, A., Yagi, S.: Bert-based arabic diacritization: A state-ofthe-art approach for improving text accuracy and pronunciation. Expert Systems with Applications **(to appear)** (2024)
33. Zitouni, I., Sarikaya, R.: Arabic diacritic restoration approach based on maximum entropy models. Comput. Speech Lang. **23**(3), 257–276 (2009)
34. Wu, Y., et al.: Google's neural machine translation system: Bridging the gap between human and machine translation. arXiv preprint arXiv:1609.08144 (2016)
35. Barqawi, Z.: Shakkala, Arabic text vocalization (2017). https://github.com/Barqawiz/Shakkala

Classifying Persuasion Modes in Arabic Debates: A Preliminary Language Model-Based Analysis

Ali Al-Zawqari[1(✉)], Abdul Gabbar Al-Sharafi[2], Mohamed Ahmed[3], Mohammad Majed Khader[3], and Gerd Vandersteen[1]

[1] Department of Fundamental Electricity and Instrumentation, Vrije Universiteit Brussel, Brussels, Belgium
{aalzawqa,gerd.vandersteen}@vub.be

[2] Department of English Language and Literature, Sultan Qaboos University, Muscat, Oman
alsharaf@squ.edu.om

[3] QatarDebate Center, Doha, Qatar
{mahmed,mkhader}@qatardebate.org

Abstract. In this study, we focus on competitive Arabic debates and employ language models to classify debaters' persuasion modes. Specifically, we aim to identify and categorize ethos, pathos, and logos-the foundational rhetorical strategies underpinning persuasive discourse. We propose two distinct approaches for persuasion mode classification to achieve these objectives. Firstly, we train a baseline language model using the ULMFiT method with an LSTM model. Secondly, we explore the fine-tuning of Language Models pre-trained on Arabic texts to leverage the contextual knowledge captured by pre-trained models. In the early stages of this research, we present preliminary results from each approach, outlining their respective strengths and limitations. Our findings demonstrate that CAMeLBERT outperforms other language models in the accuracy of classification and fairness. The CAMeLBERT reaches 91.7% accuracy, 90% f1-score, and less than 3.6% and 1.4% in demographic parity and equal opportunity differences, respectively.

Keywords: Debate analysis · Persuasion mode classification · Fairness in language models

1 Introduction

Arabic, ranked the sixth most widely spoken language globally, is a Semitic language that possesses unique linguistic characteristics, making it structurally different from other non-Semitic languages. Consequently, the development and exploration of Arabic natural language processing (NLP) applications encounter many challenges stemming from its distinctive linguistic structure [1]. Furthermore, the Arabic language presents an additional complexity due to its existence in three distinct forms: classical Arabic, modern standard Arabic (MSA),

B. Hdioud and S. L. Aouragh (Eds.): ICALP 2024, CCIS 2339, pp. 242–252, 2025.
https://doi.org/10.1007/978-3-031-79164-2_21

and several dialectical Arabic varieties, each representing a geographical region. Twenty-two countries recognize Arabic as an official language, where MSA is used in official settings such as education, publishing and broadcasting [2]. As a result, MSA attracts more study compared to the classical and dialectical forms [3].

This paper uses a unique dataset of spoken MSA, namely competitive debating tournaments. Competitive debating is an intellectually rigorous oral argumentative discourse activity governed by specific rules and regulations. Thousands of university and school students from different geographical regions participate in local and international Arabic debating tournaments that follow a modified format of the World Schools Debating Championship [4]. In this format, a motion is presented for every debate, and two teams compete against one another, representing a proposition and an opposition side of the motion. Every team consists of three speakers, each allowed to talk for 6–7 min. At the end of each debate, an adjudication panel selects one team as a winner based on each team's ability to persuade the panel using argumentation and refutation methods. These speeches are rich in argumentative elements for three reasons: 1) the definition of the motion is tailored to a specific problem, 2) the time for each speaker is limited, and 3) the specific evaluation criteria are focused on argumentation and persuasion abilities. In this work, we explore the possibility of having a language model-based classifier that can categorize the persuasion mode from different components of debating speech.

The remainder of this paper is organized as follows. We briefly introduced related work in Sect. 2. Section 3 introduces the dataset, the selected classification/language models, and performance metrics. The results are presented and discussed in Sect. 4. Finally, Sect. 5 concludes the work and the possibility of future research.

2 Related Work

NLP techniques have been used extensively to analyze persuasion modes in different settings. The authors in [5] proposed a cascade transformers system that relies on persuasive techniques detection to identify media bias using the Ukrainian crisis news dataset. Authors in [6] also used NLP techniques, specifically topic modeling with semantic attributes, to analyze the persuasion strategies implemented by Mental health apps.

In addition to analyzing persuasion methods, several papers discussed using NLP in argumentation mining. The authors in [7] proposed a transformer-based model for evidence-based medicine and argument mining in the medical literature. The authors also proposed an argument relation classification model in conjunction with the models used to predict the entities. Classifying arguments has also been used to analyze opinions and argumentative speeches. The authors in [8] used the conversational RuBERT model to classify opinions on social media platforms. Authors in [9] developed a transformer-based model to classify fallacious arguments from a corpus of 31 political debates from the US presidential campaigns. Authors in [10] compared a CNN-based model with an RRN-based model in character and word level in the classification of argument components in classroom discussions and ruled the advantage of using a CNN approach in both cases.

In the domain of Arabic NLP, the authors in [11] used a supervised learning approach to analyze the components of arguments in a corpus of 90 legal cassation decision documents of the Iraq Federal Court of Cassation. In another project, the authors in [12] pre-trained a bilingual BERT model called GigsBERT. They studied the model's performance for Arabic information extraction tasks: named-entity recognition, POS tagging, argument-role labeling, and relation extraction. Authors in [13] benchmarked a deep learning approach against a feature engineering approach in Arabic opinion mining and showed that using a deep learning approach is better than implementing a feature engineering approach.

3 Methodology

In this section, we describe the dataset used in this study and the preprocessing stage, the motivation behind selecting some language models to tackle this classification problem, and the chosen metrics to evaluate the different performances of the proposed solutions.

3.1 Dataset Description

Munazarat 1.0 is a real-world corpus representing a collection of over 70 competitive Arabic debates between 2013 and 2023, recorded and transcribed by authors in [14]. This corpus includes the main Arabic debate competitions at universities and schools. The corpus is highly diverse, including native and non-native Arabic speakers from over 25 countries. In addition, it is highly gender balanced, where the male-female distribution of speakers is 223 to 215. Authors in [15] proposed a new framework to annotate Munazarat 1.0. This framework presents a novel argumentation model integrating Aristotle's three main appeals with Toulmin's argument model [16]. In this annotation scheme, debate entities are classified into three main categories: Syllogistic Argumentation (Logos), Expressive Argumentation (Ethos), and Appellative Argumentation (Pathos). The Logos entities are categorized into sub-categories representing a modified version of Toulmin's model [16]. The authors in [15] selected 40 debates from Munazarat 1.0 at the first stage of the work, focusing on university-level competitions and native speakers. As described in the introduction 1, the following competitive debate format was with two debate teams (three speakers in proposition and three in opposition) per debate, resulting in 80 different teams in the annotated dataset and 240 speeches. The total number of words in these speeches is 204K. Figure 1 shows a snippet of one of the speeches in the dataset.

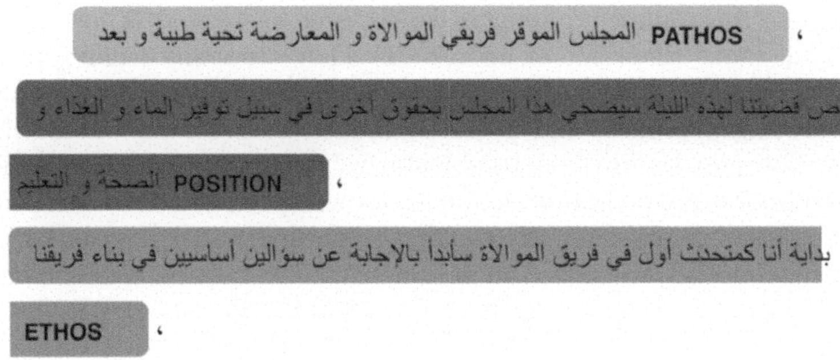

Fig. 1. Example of an annotated part of a debate speech.

3.2 Dataset Preprocessing

The first preprocessing step is to split each debate text into six samples, representing the debater's role: First, second, and third in both proposition and opposition. So, each speech will have two identifiers: the speaker's position and a specific debate tag. Then, we merge Toulmin's argumentative elements under the syllogistic argumentation category, resulting in three main classes: Ethos, Pathos, and Logos. Finally, the 240 speeches are split into training (including validation) and testing sets. The splitting considers two rules: 1) No speeches of the same debate should be presented in both training and testing, and 2) Representation of genders, years, and debate topics should be guaranteed in the testing set. The first concept is to prevent data leakage between training and testing sets, and the second is to evaluate whether the classifiers are not biased to specific topics or genders. The training sets include 34 debates. The testing sets include six debates on the following topics: two in politics and one debate on ethics & philosophy, human rights, technology, and sports. Table 1 summarizes the distribution of classes and genders in training and testing sets.

Table 1. The distribution of labels and genders in training and testing sets.

	Label			Gender	
	Ethos	Pathos	Logos	Male	Female
Training set	2106	1157	5741	111	93
Testing set	506	212	1147	20	16

3.3 Classification Models

This work falls under an Arabic text classification problem. Since the available data is relatively small, the most straightforward approach is to fine-tune a pre-trained language model on a similar task. There are multiple language models pre-trained for the argument mining task. However, these models have two shortcomings that make them out of interest: 1) They are trained only on English language datasets, where the argumentation scheme differs from the competitive Arabic debating approach, and 2) These models consider that non-syllogistic argumentation entities are non-argumentative elements, which contradict the proposed framework in [15]. For these reasons, we opt to train and fine-tune four language model categories: ULMFiT [17] as a baseline model, CAMeLBERT [18] as a language model pre-trained in various Arabic data, the second version of ARBERT [19] as it is trained on the largest MSA text, and DeBERTa [20] as it represents an improved version of both BERT [21] and RoBERTa [22]. In the following subsection, we briefly describe the models used in each category.

3.3.1 ULMFiT

As our baseline model, we employed Universal Language Model Fine-tuning (ULMFiT) [17]. We started by pre-training AWD-LSTM [23] on Arabic Wikipedia and fine-tuned it using texts from the training set of Munazarat 1.0. This fine-tuned model is then applied to our multi-classification task.

3.3.2 CAMeLBERT

Introduced in [18], CAMeLBERT is a variant of the BERT model tailored explicitly for Arabic language processing. Unlike BERT-base, which is pre-trained on English text, CAMeLBERT undergoes pre-training on a diverse Arabic text corpus, encompassing MSA, dialectal Arabic, and classical Arabic. This diversity makes CAMeLBERT a candidate worth investigating, as the competitive debates are officially carried out using MSA. However, debaters still use dialectal and classical Arabic during the debate. Thus, different variants of CAMeLBERT should be studied, namely: CAMeLBERT-dialectal, CAMeLBERT-classical, CAMeLBERT-MSA, variants of CAMeLBERT which is trained on half and quarter of the full MSA data, and CAMeLBERT-mix which represents a model pre-trained on a mixture of dialectal, classical, and MSA.

3.3.3 ARBERT

As outlined in [19,24], ARBERT is a large-scale pre-trained language model focused on MSA. It uses the same architecture as the BERT-base. Compared to CAMeLBERT, ARBERT is focused only on MSA. In addition, ARBERT has a larger vocabulary size than CAMeLBERT. The overall CAMeLBERT number of tokens is 17.3B, of which 12.6B are MSA, whereas ARBERT's number of tokens is 27.8B of MSA.

3.3.4 DeBERTa

DeBERTa was proposed in [20] to improve BERT and RoBERTa models with two techniques: a disentangled attention mechanism and an enhanced mask decoder. DeBERTav3 [25] is an improved version based on combining DeBERTa and ELECTRA [26]. The main difference between DeBERTav3 and CamelBERT

& ARBERT is that DeBERTav3 is an enhanced version of DeBERTa. Both DeBERTav3-small (44 million parameters) and DeBERTav3-large (304 million parameters) will be fine-tuned for the classification task of this study.

3.4 Performance Metrics

Accuracy and f1-score are used to evaluate the fine-tuned language model-based classifiers. Since we are working on a multiclass classification problem (Ethos, Pathos, and Logos), a macro-average will be the computed metric for the f1-score. This choice is linked to the goal of this stage of classifying the persuasion mode and, hence, treating all three classes equally. Both metrics are shown in Eq. 1 and Eq. 2.

$$\text{Accuracy} = \frac{\text{TP} + \text{TN}}{\text{TP} + \text{TN} + \text{FP} + \text{FN}} \tag{1}$$

$$\begin{aligned} \text{F1-Score} &= \frac{2\text{TP}}{2\text{TP} + \text{FP} + \text{FN}} \\ \text{Macro F1-Score} &= \frac{\sum_{i=1}^{n} \text{F1-Score}_i}{n} \end{aligned} \tag{2}$$

Here, n is the number of classes.

In addition to these metrics, we are interested in evaluating the fairness of the language models, as competitive debates happen in non-formal educational setups [4]. Knowing that these models perform at comparable levels across different debaters' demographics is essential. In this work, we will consider the language models fair if they satisfy two metrics: demographic parity and equal opportunity [27,28]. In short, assuming Z are specific attributes (e.g., speaker's gender), Y are target classes, and X is the input text. A classifier $h(X)$ satisfies demographic parity if $h(X)$ and Z are independent. Equality of opportunity demands that a classifier $h(X)$ and Z are conditionally independent given $Y = 1$. Equation 3 shows the demographic parity constraint, and the equal opportunity constraint is formalized in Eq. 4.

$$\mathbb{E}[h(X) \mid Z = z] = \mathbb{E}[h(X)] \quad \forall z \tag{3}$$

$$\mathbb{E}[h(X) \mid Z = z, Y = 1] = \mathbb{E}[h(X) \mid Y = 1] \quad \forall z \tag{4}$$

4 Results and Discussion

The experimentation of this work and the obtained results can be summarized in two stages: 1) We select language models suitable for this text classification problem, and 2) We trained/fine-tuned these models using the debate speeches and evaluated the classification accuracy of the testing set. The first step is to split the texts from 40 debates and generate 240 new texts representing each debate

Table 2. Evaluation of the language models on validation and testing sets.

Model	Validation set		Testing set	
	Accuracy	F1-score	Accuracy	F1-score
ULMFiT-LSTM	0.8533	0.8040	0.8670	0.6298
CAMeLBERT-CA	0.8968	0.8646	0.9019	0.8838
CAMeLBERT-DA	0.9134	0.8895	0.9040	0.8848
CAMeLBERT-MSA	0.9145	0.8920	**0.9174**	**0.8999**
CAMeLBERT-MSA-half	0.9179	0.8872	0.9105	0.8887
CAMeLBERT-MSA-quarter	**0.9212**	**0.8998**	0.9142	0.8974
CAMeLBERT-MIX	0.9101	0.8830	0.9115	0.8916
ARBERTv2	0.9046	0.8744	0.9013	0.8777
DeBERTav3-small	0.8957	0.8610	0.8869	0.8710
DeBERTav3-large	0.8979	0.8610	0.8944	0.8631

speech. Then, we tokenize the speeches using each language model tokenizer. For the ULMFiT, we tokenize the speeches using the ARBERTv2 tokenizer since it has the largest vocabulary of MSA. The learning rate for ULMFiT is selected using the strategy proposed by [29], while it is done through an iterative process for the other language models. In all models, we unified the batch size selection to 32. Table 2 summarizes all language models' performance in the persuasion mode classification. The results show that CAMeLBERT models outperform all other models in validation and testing sets using accuracy and f1-score. CAMeLBERT pre-trained in classical Arabic (CAMeLBERT-CA) showed the worst performance among these models. In contrast, CAMeLBERT pre-trained in MSA (CAMeLBERT-MSA) showed the best results, with around 92% accuracy and 90% f1-score. ARBERTv2 is coming second with around 2% lower performance than CAMeLBERT. As both ARBERTv2 and CAMeLBERT-MSA are trained in BERT-base architecture, it will be hard to interpret the difference in performance without investigating the data used in pre-training both models and their relationship to competitive debating.

In addition, we observe performance differences between CAMeLBERT variants on validation and testing sets. Particularly regarding CAMeLBERT-MSA's having the best accuracy on the testing set compared to its quarter-sized counterpart, which gives the best performance in the validation set. This divergence needs a deeper investigation into the underlying factors that may contribute to such disparities. A potential explanation lies in the concept of overfitting, where models might learn noise specific to the validation set rather than generalizable patterns applicable to unseen data. Also, CAMeLBERT-MSA, trained on a full corpus, may have developed a more robust understanding of MSA's nuances, enabling better generalization to the testing set despite its larger and potentially more complex samples.

The evaluation of fairness in language models showed acceptable differences in performance in favor of male against female debaters. ARBERTv2 delivers the worst performance in statistical independence with a demographic parity difference of 5.4%. The same model performed poorly compared to other models in statistical separation with an equalization of opportunity difference of +4.6%. The fairness of language model-based classifiers is summarized in Table 3. While these differences are within reasonable percentages, it is essential to mention that the current dataset is less representative than the whole corpus, as it only focuses on university-level students and native speakers. Therefore, we expect these numbers to get worse once school debates and non-native speakers are added to the annotated dataset, which makes the fairness of these language model-based classifiers a critical issue to further investigate.

Table 3. Evaluation of models' fairness using demographic parity & equal opportunity.

Model	Demographic parity	Equal opportunity
ULMFiT-LSTM	0.0363	0.0309
CAMeLBERT-CA	0.0532	0.0368
CAMeLBERT-DA	0.0506	0.0224
CAMeLBERT-MSA	0.0434	0.0220
CAMeLBERT-MSA-half	**0.0355**	0.0319
CAMeLBERT-MSA-quarter	0.0524	0.0183
CAMeLBERT-MIX	0.0510	**0.0134**
ARBERTv2	0.0541	0.0464
DeBERTav3-small	0.0506	0.0404

5 Conclusion and Future Work

Classification of argumentation modes is a crucial part of understanding the process of persuading people. This work focuses on competitive debates in Arabic, which is unique compared to previous works as it tackles argumentation in a spoken language. Also, due to the time limitation in competitive debating, the speeches tend to be richer in arguments compared to other argumentation texts. The modes of persuasion in this work are categorized into three classes following Aristotle's rhetoric: Ethos, Pathos, and Logos. To classify different elements of the speeches into one of these three categories, we trained/fine-tuned ten language models. The CAMeLBERT-based classifier showed the best results in both accuracy and fairness metrics.

We aim by this work to build models that have potential applications in educational tools for Arabic debate training and automated content moderation, enriching the NLP field with resources for a linguistically diverse and underrepresented language. In addition to that, models that can analyze and classify the persuasion modes can serve as a tool for scientists who work on studying propaganda and misinformation/disinformation campaigns.

In future work, this study will expand to cover the total size of Munazarat 1.0. This expansion will make mitigating bias on pre-trained language models more challenging. The second level of classification will be carried out as more insights come from the argumentative elements in the modified Toulmin's model. Also, we aim to progress with the work from simple classification to argument segmentation.

Limitations

One limitation in this project at the current stage is the number of annotated debates so far, which is still only 40 out of the entire corpus. Munazarat 1.0 is still a growing corpus; a huge part of it has not been annotated. This limitation should be considered as far as the initial findings of this study are concerned. Also, the presented work is limited to university-level students and native speakers, which limits the findings to a specific age band and background. The classification of modes of persuasion here is limited to the spoken language and is mainly dominated by MSA. For the computation resources, we used a single P6000 GPU for all language models except for DeBERTav3-large, where we used a single A6000 GPU.

Acknowledgements. This work was made possible by two QD Fellowship awards [QDRF-2022-01-003] and [QDRF-2022-01-005] from QatarDebate Center. In addition, the work was supported in part by the Vrije Universiteit Brussel (VUB-SRP19 and SRP78).

References

1. Shaalan, K., Siddiqui, S., Alkhatib, M., Abdel Monem, A.: Challenges in Arabic natural language processing. In: Computational Linguistics, Speech and Image Processing for Arabic Language, pp. 59–83 (2019)
2. Boudjellal, N., et al.: Abioner: a Bert-based model for Arabic biomedical named-entity recognition. Complexity **2021**, 1–6 (2021)
3. Oueslati, O., Cambria, E., HajHmida, M.B., Ounelli, H.: A review of sentiment analysis research in Arabic language. Futur. Gener. Comput. Syst. **112**, 408–430 (2020)
4. Khader, M.M.: A digital study on public speaking: Nlp & arguments analysis of the first corpus of arabic debates. Master's thesis, Hamad Bin Khalifa University (Qatar) (2020)
5. Rodrigo-Ginés, F.-J., Carrillo-de-Albornoz, J., Plaza, L.: Identifying media bias beyond words: Using automatic identification of persuasive techniques for media bias detection. Procesamiento del Lenguaje Natural **71**, 179–190 (2023)

6. Oyebode, O., Orji, R.: Deconstructing persuasive strategies in mental health apps based on user reviews using natural language processing. In: BCSS@ PERSUASIVE (2020)
7. Stylianou, N., Vlahavas, I.: Transformed: End-to-end transformers for evidence based medicine and argument mining in medical literature. J. Biomed. Inform. **117**, 103767 (2021)
8. Kalabikhina, I., et al.: Identifying reproductive behavior arguments in social media content users' opinions through natural language processing techniques. Population Econom. **7**(2), 40–59 (2023)
9. Goffredo, P., Haddadan, S., Vorakitphan, V., Cabrio, E., Villata, S.: Fallacious argument classification in political debates. In: Proceedings of the Thirty-First International Joint Conference on Artificial Intelligence, IJCAI, pp. 4143–4149 (2022)
10. Lugini, L., Litman, D.: Argument component classification for classroom discussions. EMNLP **2018**, 57 (2018)
11. Jasim, K., Sadiq, A.T., Abdullah, H.S.: A framework for detection and identification the components of arguments in arabic legal texts. In: 2019 First International Conference of Computer and Applied Sciences (CAS), pp. 67–72 (2019). IEEE
12. Lan, W., Chen, Y., Xu, W., Ritter, A.: An empirical study of pre-trained transformers for arabic information extraction. In: Proceedings of the 2020 Conference on Empirical Methods in Natural Language Processing (EMNLP), pp. 4727–4734 (2020)
13. Baly, R., et al.: A characterization study of Arabic twitter data with a benchmarking for state-of-the-art opinion mining models. In: Proceedings of the Third Arabic Natural Language Processing Workshop, pp. 110–118 (2017)
14. Khader, M.M., Al-Sharafi, A.G., Sioufy, H., Zaghouani, W., Al-Zawqari, A.: Munazarat 1.0: A corpus of Arabic competitive debates. In: The 6th Workshop on Open-Source Arabic Corpora and Processing Tools with Shared Tasks on Arabic LLMs Hallucination and Dialect to MSA Machine Translation (OSACT 2024)@ LREC 2024 (accepted 2024). European Language Resources Association (ELRA)
15. Al-Sharafi, A.G., Khader, M.M., Al-Sioufy, M.H., Zaghouani, W., Al-Zawqari, A.: A hybrid annotation model for Arabic argumentative debate corpus. In: The Eighth International Conference on Arabic Language Processing, ICALP 2023, Rabat, Morocco, April 19–20, 2024 (accepted 2024). Springer
16. Toulmin, S.E.: The Uses of Argument. Cambridge University Press, Cambridge (2003)
17. Howard, J., Ruder, S.: Universal language model fine-tuning for text classification. arXiv preprint arXiv:1801.06146 (2018)
18. Inoue, G., Alhafni, B., Baimukan, N., Bouamor, H., Habash, N.: The interplay of variant, size, and task type in Arabic pre-trained language models. In: Proceedings of the Sixth Arabic Natural Language Processing Workshop. Association for Computational Linguistics, Kyiv, Ukraine (Online) (2021)
19. Elmadany, A., Nagoudi, E.M.B., Abdul-Mageed, M.: Orca: A challenging benchmark for arabic language understanding. arXiv preprint arXiv:2212.10758 (2022)
20. He, P., Liu, X., Gao, J., Chen, W.: Deberta: Decoding-enhanced bert with disentangled attention. In: International Conference on Learning Representations (2021). https://openreview.net/forum?id=XPZIaotutsD
21. Devlin, J., Chang, M.-W., Lee, K., Toutanova, K.: Bert: Pre-training of deep bidirectional transformers for language understanding. arXiv preprint arXiv:1810.04805 (2018)

22. Liu, Y., et al.: Roberta: A robustly optimized bert pretraining approach. arXiv preprint arXiv:1907.11692 (2019)
23. Merity, S., Keskar, N.S., Socher, R.: Regularizing and optimizing lstm language models. arXiv preprint arXiv:1708.02182 (2017)
24. Abdul-Mageed, M., Elmadany, A., Nagoudi, E.M.B.: Arbert & marbert: deep bidirectional transformers for arabic. arXiv preprint arXiv:2101.01785 (2020)
25. He, P., Gao, J., Chen, W.: DeBERTaV3: Improving DeBERTa using ELECTRAStyle Pre-Training with Gradient-Disentangled Embedding Sharing (2021)
26. Clark, K., Luong, M.-T., Le, Q.V., Manning, C.D.: Electra: Pre-training text encoders as discriminators rather than generators. arXiv preprint arXiv:2003.10555 (2020)
27. Zafar, M.B., Valera, I., Rogriguez, M.G., Gummadi, K.P.: Fairness constraints: Mechanisms for fair classification. In: Artificial Intelligence and Statistics, pp. 962–970 (2017). PMLR
28. Agarwal, A., Beygelzimer, A., Dudík, M., Langford, J., Wallach, H.: A reductions approach to fair classification. In: International Conference on Machine Learning, pp. 60–69 (2018). PMLR
29. Smith, L.N.: Cyclical learning rates for training neural networks. In: 2017 IEEE Winter Conference on Applications of Computer Vision (WACV), pp. 464–472 (2017). IEEE

Strengthening Deep Learning Through Morphological Analysis for an Arabic Lemmatizer Development

Samir Belayachi(✉) and Azzeddine Mazroui

Department of Computer Science, Faculty of Sciences, Mohammed First University, BV Mohammed VI, Oujda 60000, Morocco
samirbelayachi@gmail.com

Abstract. Morphological analysis is an essential step in many natural language processing applications. Indeed, information retrieval and processing algorithms often use a morphological analyzer as a text preprocessing step. The rich morphology of the Arabic language, combined with the frequent absence of diacritical marks in texts, make morphological analysis particularly complex. Numerous morphological analyzers have been developed for the Arabic language using machine learning techniques such as Hidden Markov Models and support vector machines. In this article, we present a new Arabic lemmatizer that combines deep learning and out-of-context morphological analysis using the Alkhalil Morpho Sys analyzer. The tests carried out demonstrate the effectiveness of this approach, and an accuracy of the order of 98% was achieved in the test set.

Keywords: Natural Language Processing · Arabic language · Morphological analysis · Lemmatizer · Deep learning

1 Introduction

Given the morphological richness of the Arabic language, the morphological analysis of this language is of crucial importance in the field of Natural Language Processing (NLP). This analysis focuses on identifying the basic morphological units of words, such as stems, lemmas and roots, commonly called canonical forms.

The stem is obtained by eliminating clitics attached to the word, and the lemma represents the uninflected form of the stem and corresponds to dictionary entries. The root is an abstract form of the word, usually consisting of three, four or, exceptionally, five letters. The stem, lemma and root of the word سيساعدونه /sysAEdwnhA[1] (they'll help him) are respectively يساعدون /ysAEdwn/ (they

A. Mazroui—These authors contributed equally to this work.

[1] Buckwalter transliteration http://www.qamus.org/transliteration.htm/.

B. Hdioud and S. L. Aouragh (Eds.): ICALP 2024, CCIS 2339, pp. 253–260, 2025.
https://doi.org/10.1007/978-3-031-79164-2_22

help), ساعد /sAEd/ (to help) and س ع د . The lemmas are generated from the (root, pattern) pairs by the derivation process.

Morphological analysis aims to identify the canonical forms of words, which are useful for several NLP applications. Indeed, search engines use one of these canonical forms to index words. Similarly, to alleviate the out-of-vocabulary problem in machine translation, several research studies have shown the value of using canonical forms [1]. Sentiment analysis, topic detection and text readability also use these canonical forms to improve their performance [2,3].

The lemmatizer is a morphological analyzer that extracts lemmas from words of a sentence. It takes into account the specific context of each word within the sentence. Previous approaches used for developing a lemmatizer rely on two modules. The first module performs a morphological analysis of words out of context, generating all potential lemmas for each word analyzed. The second module exploits the context of the word within the sentence to identify the correct lemma for each word among these potential lemmas. It often relies on machine learning techniques such as Hidden Markov Models (HMM) or Support Vector Machine (SVM).

In this research, we propose a new approach to the development of a lemmatizer. We have combined a recurrent neural network (RNN) with an out-of-context morphological analysis. The input of the RNN is the sequence of the sentence words, and the output is the sequence of their corresponding lemmas. We have implemented a filter that requires the RNN to select for each word a lemma among the potential lemmas obtained from its out-of-context morphological.

The remainder of the article is structured as follows. In the following section, we present a state-of-the-art relating to lemmatizers developed for the Arabic language. The third section is dedicated to the description of the adopted methodology which combines an out-of-context morphological analysis and a deep learning model. Subsequently, we present in the fourth section the test results obtained. Finally, we conclude the article by presenting some thoughts on future work.

2 State of Art

The main aim of a lemmatizer is to normalize the inflected forms of words to their basic form. This reduces vocabulary to fundamental units, facilitating information retrieval, text analysis, machine translation, document classification and other NLP applications. The development of lemmatizers is generally based on linguistic rules, lexical databases and machine learning algorithms. Below are some of the most widely cited morphological disambiguation analyzers in the literature.

- MADAMIRA [4] is a set of open source morphological analyzers including a lemmatizer, a stemmer, a segmenter, a POS tagger and a diacritization system. The lemmatization process is carried out in two phases. In the first phase, the SAMA analyzer [5] is used for an out-of-context morphological analysis, generating several potential lemmas for each word analyzed. In the second phase, the system uses an SVM classifier and language models to select the most probable lemma for each word from the potential lemmas obtained in the first phase.

- FARASA [6] is also a set of open source morphosyntactic disambiguation tools developed by Qatar Computing Research Institute (QCRI). It includes a segmentation module, a POS tagger, a diacritization system and a lemmatizer. To develop these tools, an SVM model [6] and the randomized greedy algorithm [7] were used.
- Alkhalil Lemmatizer [8] was developed in the computer science research laboratory of the Mohammed first University, Morocco. This morphological disambiguation system is open source and operates in two steps. First, it performs an out-of-context analysis using the Alkhalil Morpho Sys analyzer [9], generating several potential lemmas for each word analyzed. It then performs a disambiguation phase based on HMM or splines in addition to the Viterbi algorithm. The tests carried out show an accuracy of around 94%.
- Ibn-Ginni [10] is positioned as a linguistic analyzer dedicated to the Arabic language, taking advantage of the speed of Buckwalter's Arabic Morphological Analysis (BAMA) [11]. Although BAMA is recognized for its excellence in text analysis of standard Moderne Arabic, its limitations in covering Classical Arabic led to the development of Ibn-Ginni. The latter significantly extended the linguistic scope by analyzing three million words from various sources using the Alkhalil Morpho Sys analyzer. The results of this analysis phase were carefully refined manually and integrated into the BAMA system database, resulting in a significant improvement in the quality of the analysis. Ibn-Ginni supports around 78,000 lemmas and 397,000 stems in its morphological database, considerably extending linguistic coverage, particularly for Classical Arabic. The structure of this analyzer's morphological database follows a format similar to that of BAMA.

These various tools exploit linguistic morphology in the first stage and then use machine learning techniques in the second stage to perform disambiguation. Our aim in this work is to use a novel approach in which morphological information would be integrated more efficiently with deep learning methods. This reflection is part of a quest to optimize the performance of the lemmatizer, by taking advantage of the specific benefits offered by deep learning in resolving the morphological and semantic complexity of the Arabic language.

3 Description of the Methodology

3.1 Training Corpus

Deep learning requires the availability of a large training corpus. We have thus collected a corpus from several sources (websites and digital libraries) consisting of around 100 million words and covering a dozen topics [12]. To carry out the training and testing phases of our RNN model, we extracted from this corpus a sub-corpus of 900,971 words and asked two linguists to annotate it according to the lemma tag. And in order to build our RNN model, we need to define the vocabulary V, which contains the model input words, and the list L of lemmas linked to the model outputs. For the vocabulary V, we have considered the one corresponding to the corpus made up of 100 million words, and we have retained only the frequent words appearing in the corpus more than 60 times. This vocabulary is made up of 88,859 distinct words. We then applied the AlKhalil Morpho Sys [9] analyzer to the words in this vocabulary, and as the analysis is out-of-context, the analyzer proposes one or more lemmas for each analyzed word. Thus, the list L of adopted lemmas is made up of the 32,569 distinct lemmas obtained as a result of this analysis. Table 1 presents some statistics relating to this corpus.

Table 1. Statistics of the corpus and lexicons

Size of the labeled corpus	900,971
Size of the vocabulary V	88,859
Size of the lemma list L	32,569

3.2 Model Architecture

An RNN is a type of artificial neural network model designed to process sequential data [13]. Unlike conventional neural networks, RNNs have a structure that enables them to retain an internal memory, making them particularly suitable for processing temporal sequences such as sentences in natural language processing.

The main feature of RNNs is their ability to take into account previous contextual information when processing each element of a sequence. Indeed, an internal memory in the form of a hidden layer enables the model to capture long-term dependencies between sequence elements and to process variable-length sequences efficiently.

However, RNNs have limitations, including the difficulty of retaining long-term information due to the phenomenon of gradient disappearance. RNN variants, such as Long Short-Term Memory (LSTM) and Gated Recurrent Unit (GRU), have been developed to overcome these limitations and improve the ability of RNNs to process long sequences of data.

In our approach, we adopted a bidirectional LSTM (BLSTM) that takes into account both the right-hand and left-hand contexts of words. This BLSTM was then coupled with the AlKhalil Morpho Sys analyzer to perform selective lemma extraction. Indeed, for a given word, we forced the model to select a lemma from the potential lemmas obtained by the out-of-context analysis performed on the word by AlKhalil Morpho Sys. So, before applying the softmax activation function, whose purpose is to assign probabilities to the vector provided by the hidden layer, we added a filter that enables the model to only keep the components of the vector provided by the hidden layer and that correspond to the word's potential lemmas. This filter is in the form of a binary vector where the only non-zero values, equal to 1, correspond to the positions of the word's potential lemmas in the lemma list L. We then apply the softmax function σ to the result of this filtering. The filter enables us to focus the model's attention solely on the relevant information linked to the lemmas provided by the morphological analysis, thus favoring a more targeted and precise representation during the activation phase. Figure 1 below illustrates the architecture of this model.

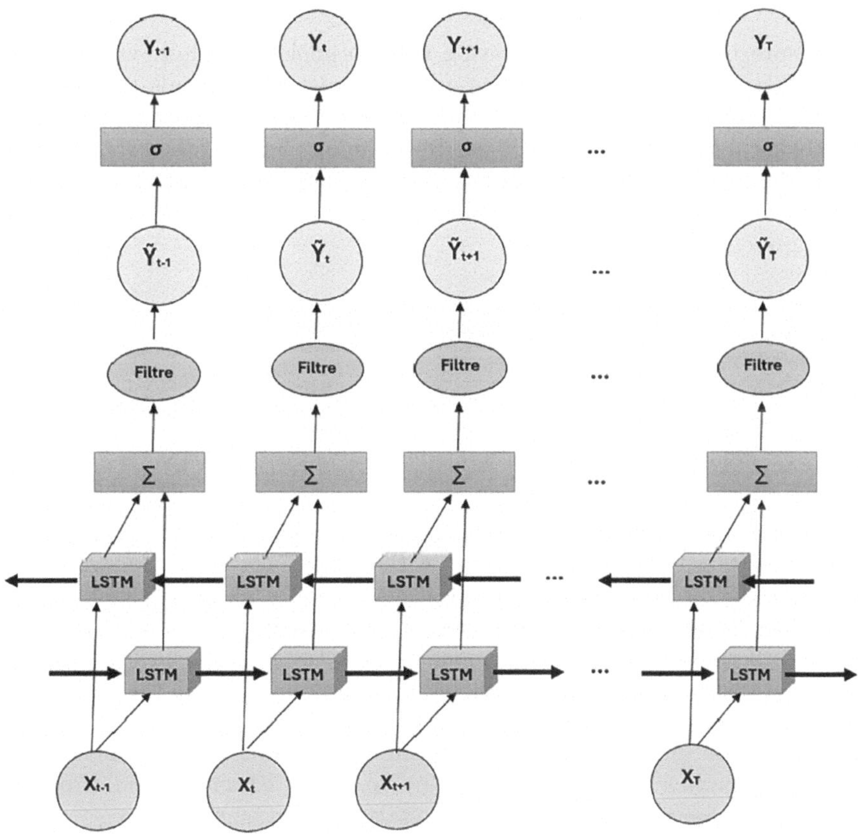

Fig. 1. Model architecture

This model adopts a bidirectional recurrent neural network architecture processing sequences of size 57 (representing the maximum sentence size). The embedding layer consists of 128 neurons, while the hidden layer consists of an

LSTM cell with 128 neurons. The Σ vectors are obtained only following a linear transformation and without applying an activation function. Their size is equal to the size of the lemma list L. The vector Σ is then multiplied by a morphological filter in the form of a vector of the same size as L. This filter corresponds to a binary vector where the only non-zero values are equal to 1 and correspond to the positions of the potential lemmas of the word in L. The softmax activation function is then applied to the result obtained to transform this result into a probability vector adapted to the specific morphological context of the lemmatization task. During the training phase, we set a batch size of 32 and ran the algorithm for 10 epochs.

4 Model Evaluation

To measure the impact of integrating the morphological filter, we evaluated two models. The first, considered as a basic model, corresponds to the model without morphological filtering in Fig. 1, and the second is the one that applies morphological filtering. We carried out the training phases of the two models on 80% of the labeled corpus extracted randomly. Then we tested the models on the remaining 20%. The accuracy results on the training set E_A and the test set E_T are presented in Table 2.

Table 2. The accuracies of the two models

	Corpus E_A	Corpus E_T
Model without morphological filtering	99.89%	93.50%
Model with morphological filtering	98.12%	98.08%

The results obtained by the model without morphological filtering on the test corpus E_T are equivalent to those using state-of-the-art machine learning approaches. In addition, the integration of morphological filtering significantly improved the performance of the model. Indeed, the model achieved very high levels of precision by recording an increase in accuracy of more than 3.5 points compared to the base model to reach 98.08% on the test set E_T. These results demonstrate the robustness of our approach, thus offering a promising solution for this specific linguistic task. Finally, by analyzing lemmatization errors, we noted that a large part is due to the out-of-vocabulary phenomenon.

5 Conclusion

In this paper, we developed a new hybrid lemmatizer that combines the advantages of deep learning with the integration of out-of-context morphological analysis of words. We thus required the neural network to choose its solution only among the potential solutions provided by an out-of-context morphological analysis of the word. This integration of morphological analysis into the neural network made it possible to considerably improve the performance of our model by increasing the accuracy by more than 3.5 points compared to the basic model not integrating morphological analysis.

In the future, we plan to analyze approaches to mitigate the effect of the out-of-vocabulary phenomenon. We also plan to apply this same approach to other morphological analyzers such as the stemmer, the root extractor, and the POS tagger.

References

1. Berrichi, S., Mazroui, A.: The impact of word segmentation techniques on neural and statistical machine translation: English-arabic case. In: Kacprzyk, J., Balas, V.E., Ezziyyani, M. (eds.) Advanced Intelligent Systems for Sustainable Development (AI2SD'2020), pp. 454–462. Springer, Cham (2022)
2. Koulali, R., El-Haj, M., Meziane, A.: Arabic topic detection using automatic text summarisation. In: 2013 ACS International Conference on Computer Systems and Applications (AICCSA), pp. 1–4 (2013). https://doi.org/10.1109/AICCSA.2013.6616460
3. Berrichi, S., Nassiri, N., Mazroui, A., Lakhouaja, A.: Interpreting the relevance of readability prediction features. Jordanian J. Comput. Inform. Technol. **9**(1) (2023)
4. Pasha, A., et al.: MADAMIRA: A fast, comprehensive tool for morphological analysis and disambiguation of Arabic. In: Proceedings of the Ninth International Conference on Language Resources and Evaluation (LREC'14), pp. 1094–1101. European Language Resources Association (ELRA), Reykjavik, Iceland (2014). http://www.lrec-conf.org/proceedings/lrec2014/pdf/593Paper.pdf
5. Maamouri, M., Graff, D., Bouziri, B., Krouna, S., Bies, A., Kulick, S.: Ldc standard arabic morphological analyzer (sama) version 3.1 ldc2010l01. Web Download. Philadelphia: Linguistic Data Consortium (2010)
6. Abdelali, A., Darwish, K., Durrani, N., Mubarak, H.: Farasa: A fast and furious segmenter for Arabic. (2016). https://doi.org/10.18653/v1/N16-3003
7. Zhang, Y., Li, C., Barzilay, R., Darwish, K.: Randomized greedy inference for joint segmentation, pos tagging and dependency parsing. In: Proceedings of the 2015 Conference North American Chapter Association Computer Linguistics Human Language Technologies, pp. 42–52 (2015). https://doi.org/10.3115/v1/N15-1005
8. Boudchiche, M., Mazroui, A.: A hybrid approach for Arabic lemmatization. Int. J. Speech Technol. **22**(3), 563–573 (2019). https://doi.org/10.1007/s10772-018-9528-3
9. Boudchiche, M., Mazroui, A., Bebah, M.O.A.O., Lakhouaja, A., Boudlal, A.: Alkhalil morpho sys 2: A robust arabic morpho-syntactic analyzer. J. King Saud Univ.-Comput. Inform. Sci. **29**(2), 141–146 (2017)
10. Nazih, W., Fashwan, A., El-Gendy, A., Hifny, Y.: Ibn-ginni: An improved morphological analyzer for arabic. ACM Trans. Asian Low-Resour. Lang. Inform. Process. **23**(2), 1–22 (2023)
11. Buckwalter, T.: Buckwalter arabic morphological analyzer (bama) version 2.0. linguistic data consortium (ldc) catalogue number ldc2004l02. Technical report, ISBN1-58563-324-0 (2004)

12. Belayachi, S., Mazroui, A.: Comparison of the lexicons of contemporary and the classical arabic language. 4ème édition des Journées Doctorales de l'Ingénierie de la Langue Arabe, Mohammed V University Rabat (2021)
13. Schuster, M., Paliwal, K.K.: Bidirectional recurrent neural networks. IEEE Trans. Signal Process. **45**(11), 2673–2681 (1997). https://doi.org/10.1109/78.650093

Enhancing Arabic Word Sense Disambiguation with Ensemble BERT-Based Models

Asma Djaidri[1,2](✉), Hassina Aliane[2], and Hamid Azzoune[1]

[1] Laboratory of Research in Artificial Intelligence (LRIA), USTHB, BP 32, Bab Ezzouar, 16111 Algiers, Algeria
{adjaidri,hazzoune}@usthb.dz

[2] Research Center for Scientific and Technical Information, CERIST, Rue Des 3 Freres Aissou Ben Aknoun, 16028 Algiers, Algeria
haliane@cerist.dz

Abstract. Word Sense Disambiguation (WSD) is a pivotal challenge in natural language processing (NLP), especially for languages with rich morphological features such as Arabic. In this paper, we introduce a novel approach for Arabic WSD by leveraging the power of stacked ensemble models of BERT-based models. Given the scarcity of sense-annotated resources for Arabic, we first created a new dataset consisting of 51,161 context-gloss pair instances for Arabic verb senses and their context of use, derived from the Arramooz Alwaseet dictionary. Then, we fine-tune four pre-trained models-AraBERT, CAMeLBERT, ArBERTv2, and Arabic ALBERT- on our dataset for the task of binary text classification in WSD. After that, we apply a stacked ensemble technique that combines the strengths of these individual models to achieve superior disambiguation performance. The obtained results demonstrate the superiority of our ensemble strategy over individual baseline models, showcasing its superiority in Arabic WSD. This comprehensive study highlights the importance of advanced ensemble methods in NLP, marking a significant progress in Arabic language understanding and paving the way for further investigations in this crucial area.

Keywords: WSD · Context-gloss pair · Arabic language · BERT · Binary text classification

1 Introduction

Word sense disambiguation (WSD) is a natural language processing (NLP) task that aims to automatically identify the correct meaning of a word within a specific context [1]. For example, the word "run" as a verb, can mean different meanings. In the sentence "She runs every morning," "run" means she is physically running. But in "She runs the dishwasher," "run" means she starts the machine. Understanding the different meanings of polysemous words depending on the context is challenging and crucial for various NLP tasks.

B. Hdioud and S. L. Aouragh (Eds.): ICALP 2024, CCIS 2339, pp. 261–272, 2025.
https://doi.org/10.1007/978-3-031-79164-2_23

Recent advances in deep learning and pre-trained models such as BERT (Bidirectional Encoder Representations from Transformers) [2], and ELMO (Embeddings from Language Models) [3], have improved the state-of-the-art for WSD tasks by enhancing the ability to capture contextual information and represent the meanings of words within sentences. The main challenge of fine-tuning pre-trained models for Arabic WSD is the lack of sense-annotated resources for the Arabic language [4]. To address this challenge, we created a new dataset of context-gloss pairs for Arabic verbs, extracted from the Arramooz Alwaseet dictionary[1] [5]. Subsequently, we extracted glosses and contexts, following a methodology close to previous studies: [4,6,7], to form context-gloss pairs. As a result, the dataset we built consists of 51,161 context-gloss pair instances, 50.27% of them are labeled as *True* and 49.73% are labeled as *False*.

Al-Hajj and Jarrar in their study [4] fine-tuned three pretrained Arabic BERT models separately: AraBERT [8], QARiB [9], and CAMeLBERT [10]. In recent studies, such as [11,12], ensembling Methods to BERT demonstrated superior performance over traditional single models. Ensemble methods have been shown to reduce overfitting and improve generalization by combining the strengths and mitigating the weaknesses of individual models, leading to improved performance [13]. In this work, we explore the efficacy of stacked ensemble models utilizing BERT-based architectures for Arabic word sense disambiguation. Our focus is on disambiguating verbs, a critical element for accurate understanding of Arabic sentences. We fine-tune four pre-trained models; AraBERT [8], CAMeLBERT [10], ArBERTv2 [14] and Arabic ALBERT [15] on our created dataset for the task of word sense disambiguation as binary text classification.

The key contributions of this paper can be outlined as follows:

- Introduction of a novel dataset of context-gloss pairs for Arabic verbs, addressing the scarcity of sense-annotated resources for Arabic in WSD research.
- Application of stacked ensemble models utilizing BERT-based architectures to Arabic WSD, a novel approach aimed at improving disambiguation performance for Arabic verbs.
- Comparative analysis of model performance, offering insights into the efficacy of different pre-trained models and ensemble strategies for Arabic WSD.

The rest of this paper is organized as follows: Sect. 2 reviews related work. Section 3 details our dataset creation and model fine-tuning methods. The experimental setup, evaluation metrics, and the discussion of results are presented in Sect. 4. Section 5 concludes the paper with final remarks and directions for future research.

2 Related Works

Word Sense Disambiguation approaches can be categorized into three main groups based on the extent of knowledge resources utilized in the WSD

[1] Taha Zerrouki. 2011. Arramooz Alwaseet: Arabic Dictionary for Morphological Analysis. http://arramooz.sourceforge.net/.

process [1]. Supervised approaches require the use of completely labeled training datasets, while unsupervised approaches use unlabeled datasets [1]. When a system relies on external knowledge resources, it is considered a knowledge-based approach [1]. Due to the limited availability of annotated Arabic training corpora, the majority of existing Arabic word sense disambiguation methods are of the unsupervised variety [16]. On the other hand, since the emergence of transformers and large language modeling, such as BERT [2] and Flair [17], the performance of WSD models has seen significant improvement.

More recent research has generated Arabic context-gloss pairs for assessing Arabic word sense disambiguation as a binary classification task using BERT, such as [4,6]. Authors in [6] constructed an Arabic context-gloss pairs dataset, composed of 5347 unique words, about 15K true senses, and about 15K false senses. They proposed two different models to tackle the WSD problem with BERT, with the most successful model achieving an F1 score of 89%.

In [4], a similar approach was applied, with an additional contribution that involved identifying, locating, and tagging target words and investigating the use of different signals to highlight the target words in context. Furthermore, the author divided the dataset into training and testing datasets with criteria to avoid repeated context in training and test sets that might introduce bias to the results. The dataset in [4] is composed of 26169 unique words, 60323 true senses, and 106884 false senses. The authors in [4] fine-tuned three pre-trained models- AraBERT [8], QARiB [9], and CAMeLBERT [10]-, and the best performance was achieved using AraBertv2 [8], resulting an accuracy of 84%.

In this work, we aim to explore the effectiveness of ensemble methods applied to BERT-based models for the Arabic WSD task, employing a supervised approach that utilizes labeled context-gloss pairs for over 5,000 Arabic verbs.

3 Method

In this section, we present our approach to addressing the challenge of word sense disambiguation (WSD) for Arabic verbs, leveraging an ensemble of BERT-based models. Considering the subtleties and complexity of Arabic, we fine-tune multiple BERT-based models for binary text classification using context-gloss pairs of Arabic verbs that we have constructed. Our proposed approach aims to improve the accuracy of Arabic WSD by employing four different BERT-based models: AraBERT [8], CAMeLBERT [10], ArBERTv2 [14] and Arabic ALBERT [15].

The motivation behind selecting these models stems from their pre-training on fill-mask tasks with modern standard Arabic texts. This specialization makes them highly adaptable to specific NLP tasks, such as text classification. The following subsections provide an overview of the data preparation, the architecture of the models, and the training process for each model, as well as our ensemble strategy and the training of the meta-model.

3.1 Dataset Building

We extracted the context-gloss pairs from the Arramooz Alwaseet dictionary[1] [5]. This dictionary consists of three parts: nouns, verbs, and particles for the Arabic language. We are interested in verbs; therefore, we selected the dictionary of transitive verbs with one preposition from the Arramoz Alwaseet. This dictionary retrieves 5,976 verbs. We performed a pre-treatment process on the Arramoz dictionary to get a dataset labeled and ready for training. The different steps of this process are described in the following subsections.

3.1.1 Context-Gloss Pairs

The selected dictionary is composed of different columns. We have selected two interesting columns for our work: "verbs" and "definitions.". The texts in this dictionary are written with diacritics. We observed that the definitions are written in a specific format:

< 1. "Context example 1": definition 1. 2. "Context example 2": definition 2. 3. "context example 3": definition 3.....>

To create context-gloss pairs for our dataset, we followed the following procedure:

- Definitions were divided into separate parts based on numerical indicators (e.g., 1., 2.), where each part represents a specific context-definition pair. Single-context senses were kept as is.
- We reformatted the data, which was structured with multiple senses per verb in a single row, into a format where each row represents a specific verb-sense pair. To achieve this, we broke down the list of senses into individual rows, ensuring each verb was correctly associated.
- We segmented the context-definition pair into two parts: "Context" and "Sense". As a result, the new data format comprises three columns ['verb', 'context', 'definition'].
- We remove any row with missing data.
- We apply Arabic text pre-processing to all the data: remove the Arabic punctuation, remove numerical digits, remove diacritics (ex: shadda اّ , fatha اَ , kasra اِ . normalize [إأآا] to ا , normalize گ to ك , and remove any non-Arabic letter.
- We remove duplicated data to ensure a proper split into training and test datasets later.
- We keep only polysemous verbs, those with at least two senses.
- We removed specific instances where the same verb within identical contexts could have multiple senses. This was necessary because it produced different labels for the same verb-context-sense combination.

As a result, we have identified 5728 unique verbs and generated 25,721 pairs of context- glosses for those verbs. Each record in the dataset is a tuple of three elements (the verb, a context example, and a definition (gloss) of that verb in the context example). The generated dataset is ordered alphabetically by Arabic verbs.

3.1.2 Annotating Context-Gloss Pairs

The pairs generated in the previous step are labeled with " 1 ". Then, similarly to [4,6], we generated new pairs labeled with " 0 " as follows: for each verb, we associated each definition with another context example of a different definition for the same verb. Table 1 illustrates examples of records from the generated labeled dataset. In Table 2, we present statistics about our generated dataset. Our created dataset, is accessible online[2].

Table 1. Example from our generated verb labeled context-gloss pairs.

verb	sense	context	label
ائتكل	اكلت بعضها بعضا	ائتكلت الديدان	1
ائتكل	اشتد لهيبها	ائتكلت الديدان	0
ائتكل	اكلت بعضها بعضا	ائتكلت النار	0
ائتكل	اشتد لهيبها	ائتكلت النار	1

Table 2. Statistics about our generated Arabic verb context-gloss pairs.

	count
# Unique verbs (diacritic-free)	5728
# Average sense per verb	6.26
# Max sense per verb	57
# Total number of pairs	51,161
% of pairs label with 1	50.27%
% of pairs label with 0	49.73%

We fine-tune BERT-based models by training them with a sentence-pair classification objective, where the model learns to determine the relationship between two sentences. To align our dataset with this objective while keeping the target verb's information, we concatenate the " verb " and " context " columns, separated by a comma ','. Consequently, the inputs to our BERT-based models are pairs of sentences, consisting of ["verb+context", "sense"], where the output labels indicate whether the given sense of the verb in the context is correct (1) or not (0). In Table 3, we provide an illustration of preprocessed sentence pairs for fine-tuning the BERT model for the verb ائتكل .

We divided the dataset into training, validation, and test sets. The training set is 80%, validation set is 10%, and test set is 10% of the dataset. We shuffled

[2] https://figshare.com/s/9c558f732bf5afb08217.

Table 3. Example of a preprocessed sentence pair for fine-tuning the BERT model.

verb+context	definition	label
ائتكل ، ائتكلت الديدان	اكلت بعضها بعضا	1
ائتكل ، ائتكلت الديدان	اشتد لهيبها	0

training and validation sets for randomness. We obtained 40,928 sentence pairs for training, 5,116 sentence pairs for validation, and 5,117 for test.

In order to explore the effects of input data formatting on the performance models, we created two variation datasets. In Variation 1, the input dataset comprised two sentences: the verb followed by a comma and its context, concatenated to form a single 'verb+context' column. Variation 2 introduced a more structured format:الفعل (the verb) + [verb] + في المثال (in the example) + [context] + معناه (means), also consolidated into the " verb+context " column. This nuanced manipulation of the input data was aimed at assessing whether a more explicit contextual framing could enhance the model's ability to disambiguate verb meanings.

Table 4. Illustration of the two context-gloss pairs variations.

Variation	verb+context	definition	label
Variation 1	ائتكل ، ائتكلت الديدان	اكلت بعضها بعضا	1
Variation 2	الفعل ائتكل في المثال ائتكلت الديدان معناه	اكلت بعضها بعضا	1

3.2 Modelization

In this part, we present our proposed approach to Arabic WSD. As mentioned earlier, we combined four pre-trained BERT-based models to create one meta-model using the stacking method. In machine learning, stacking is a strong ensemble learning technique that combines the predictions of multiple base models to get a final prediction with improved performance [18]. It involves training a variety of base models on the same dataset. Their predictions are then used as inputs for a higher-level model, known as the meta-model or second-level model, which makes the final decision [19]. The core concept of stacking is to combine the predictions of different base models to get more predictive performance than utilizing a single model [19].

We fine-tuned four pre-trained BERT-based models: AraBERT [8], CAMeLBERT-MSA [10], ArBERTv2 [14] and Arabic Albert [15]. Recognizing the unique linguistic characteristics of Arabic, it was crucial to fine-tune these models using our training dataset to adapt their comprehension to the subtleties of Arabic verb senses.

- **AraBERT**[3] is a pretrained language model based on Google's BERT architecture, utilizing the same BERT-Base configuration. In this work, we employed the model "bert-base-arabertv02". Unlike "bert-base-arabertv2", which processes pre-segmented text where prefixes and suffixes are split using the Farasa Segmenter [20], AraBERTv02 does not use pre-segmented text. It is trained on 77GB of Modern Standard Arabic (MSA) data, comprising 8.6 billion tokens.
- **CAMeLBERT-MSA**[4] is a collection of BERT models pre-trained on Arabic texts with different sizes and variants. We used the pretrained "bert-base-arabic-camelbert-msa" for Modern Standard Arabic (MSA). CAMeLBERT-MSA is trained on MSA data 107GB of text and 12.6 billion tokens.
- **ArBERTv2**[5] is the updated version of ARBERT model described in [21]. ARBERTv2 is trained on MSA data 243 GB of text and 27.8 billion tokens.
- **Arabic-ALBERT**[6] is a variant of the ALBERT [22] (A Lite BERT) model that has been specifically pre-trained on Arabic text. The models were pre-trained on 4.4 Billion words from the Arabic version of OSCAR[7] dataset and Arabic Wikipedia. The corpus and vocabulary set are not restricted to Modern Standard Arabic, they contain some dialectical Arabic too.

Table 5. Hyperparameters used during the fine-tuning process.

Hyperparameter	Value
learning rate(lr)	2e-5
batch size	16
number of epochs	4
Weight decay	0.01
lr scheduler type	linear
warmup ratio	0.1

The hyperparameters used in the fine-tuning process are identical across all models. These parameters are detailed in Table 5.

To enhance the overall accuracy of our system, we integrated the unique advantages of each BERT-based model through an ensemble technique. This approach assumes that combining the knowledge from four different models-AraBERT, CAMeLBERT, ArBERT, and Arabic ALBERT -will increase the accuracy of the results. To be more precise, we used a stacking architecture in which the outputs of these models feed into a logistic regression meta-model,

[3] https://huggingface.co/aubmindlab/bert-base-arabertv2.
[4] https://huggingface.co/CAMeL-Lab/bert-base-arabic-camelbert-msa.
[5] https://huggingface.co/UBC-NLP/ARBERTv2.
[6] https://huggingface.co/asafaya/albert-base-arabic.
[7] https://oscar-project.org/.

Algorithm 1. Stacking Ensemble Bert-based models with Linear Regression Meta-Model.

Require: Training set X_{train}, Validation set X_{val}, Test set X_{test}
Ensure: Ensemble predictions Y_{pred}
Train base models (AraBERT, CAMeLBERT, ArBERTv2,A-ALBERT) on X_{train}
Predict on X_{val} using each base model to create new features:
for each base model **do**
    $X_{val}^{model} \leftarrow$ predictions of base model on X_{val}
end for
Combine X_{val}^{model} for all base models to form X_{meta}
Train Linear Regression meta-model on X_{meta}
Predict on X_{test} using base models to create test features:
for each base model **do**
    $X_{test}^{model} \leftarrow$ predictions of base model on X_{test}
end for
Combine X_{test}^{model} for all base models to form X_{meta_test}
$Y_{pred} \leftarrow$ Linear Regression meta-model predictions on X_{meta_test}
return Y_{pred}

carefully integrating their advantages to achieve enhanced predictive performance. Importantly, we utilized the same validation set for training the logistic regression meta-model that was used in the training of the four individual BERT models. Furthermore, we evaluated the performance of the meta-model on the same test dataset to ensure consistency and comparability across our experiments. Algorithm 1 outlines our stacking ensemble BERT-based models method for improving prediction performance.

4 Results and Discussion

In this section, we present the results of our study about the efficacy of a stacked ensemble of BERT-based models for the task of Arabic Word Sense Disambiguation. Our proposed approach combines the strengths of AraBERT, CAMeLBERT-MSA, ArBERTv2, and Arabic-ALBERT (A-ALBERT) to predict the correct sense of ambiguous verbs in Arabic text. Performances were assessed based on accuracy and F1-score metrics under varying conditions, including changes in *SEED* values for dataset splitting and modifications in input format for the models.

Initial experiments illustrated in Table 6, focused on evaluating individual model performances with a fixed *SEED* of 9 and 42, to ensure consistency in training, validation, and test splits across all models. This approach ensures that each model is trained and validated on the identical dataset, allowing for a fair comparison of their capabilities. Among the individual models, AraBERT demonstrated the highest performance, achieving an accuracy and F1-score of 81.53% and 81.47%, respectively with a *SEED* of 9. This suggests that AraBERT is particularly well-suited for the Arabic WSD task among the models tested.

Notably, fine-tuning each of these BERT-based models required approximately 4 h.

Table 6. Performance comparison of individual and ensemble BERT-based models for Arabic word sense disambiguation across different initialization SEEDs.

Model	SEED	Accuracy	F1 Score
AraBERT	42	80.61%	80.59%
CAMelBERT	42	79.49%	79.47%
ArBERTv2	42	77.83%	77.53%
A-ALBERT	42	75.35%	75.32%
AraBERT	**9**	**81.53%**	**81.47%**
CAMelBERT	9	79.46%	79.45%
ArBERTv2	9	79.28%	79.22%
A-ALBERT	9	75.25%	75.23%
AraBERT+CAMelBERT+ArBERTv2	42	81.27%	82.08%
AraBERT+CAMelBERT+ArBERTv2	**9**	**81.88%**	**82.69%**
AraBERT+CAMelBERT+ArBERTv2	**No SEED**	**93.64%**	**93.79%**

Table 7. Performance comparison of two AraBERT model variations on Arabic Word Sense Disambiguation task.

Model	SEED	accuracy	F1-score
AraBERT Variation 1	9	**81.53%**	**81.47%**
AraBERT Variation 2	9	80.84%	80.83%

Furthermore, two variations of AraBERT were explored to assess the impact of input formatting on model performance, as discussed in Sect. 3.1.2. Variation 1 utilized a straightforward concatenation of the verb and its context, resulting in the highest observed accuracy and F1-score of 81.53% and 81.47%, respectively (Table 7). This suggests a slight advantage in maintaining the semantic integrity of the input without additional structuring. In contrast, Variation 2 employed a more structured format by embedding the verb within a descriptive sentence, which yielded slightly lower performance, with an accuracy of 80.84% and an F1-score of 80.83%. These findings indicate that while structured input formats may aid in certain NLP tasks, for Arabic Word Sense Disambiguation, a more direct presentation of the verb and its context could be more effective. Based on these results, subsequent experiments will utilize Variation 1 of the dataset.

The ensemble approach, which combines the strengths of different models, shows small but notable performance improvements (Table 8). Notably, the combination of AraBERT and ArBERTv2 emerges as the most effective, achieving

Table 8. Comparative performance of individual and ensemble BERT-based models for Arabic Word Sense Disambiguation with SEED of 9.

Model	Accuracy	F1-score	Precision	Recall
AraBERT	81.53%	81.47%	–	–
CAMelBERT	79.46%	79.45%	–	–
ArBERTv2	80.19%	80.15%	–	–
A-ALBET	75.25%	75.23%	–	–
AraBERT+CAMelBERT	81.61%	82.41%	79.11%	85.99%
AraBERT+ARBERTv2	**82.11%**	**82.97%**	79.35%	86.93%
AraBERT+A-ALBERT	81.75%	82.56%	79.19%	86.23%
CAMelBERT+ARBERTv2	79.91%	80.61%	78.02%	83.38%
CAMelBERT+A-ALBERT	79.63%	80.09%	78.71%	81.35%
ARBERTv2+A-ALBERT	79.48%	80.27%	77.42%	83.35%
AraBERT+CAMelBERT+ARBERTv2	81.88%	82.69%	79.30%	86.38%
AraBERT+CAMelBERT+ARBERTv2+A-ALBERT	81.94%	82.76%	79.32%	86.51%

an accuracy of 82.11% and an F1-score of 82.97%. This suggests that the complementary strengths of these two models are particularly well-suited for the Arabic WSD task. The superior performance of the AraBERT and ArBERTv2 ensemble highlights the potential of leveraging multiple models to enhance WSD tasks. This method enables a deeper comprehension of semantic subtleties and context, likely due to methodologies and training data variations inherent in each model. It's essential to recognize that adding more models to an ensemble does not guarantee improved results, as illustrated by the specific instance where AraBERT+CAMeLBERT+ArBERTv2's performance did not surpass AraBERT+ArBERTv2.

Some models show a mix of outcomes: their accuracy might drop slightly, but their F1-scores tend to improve. For instance, while CAMeLBERT+ArBERTv2 exhibited a slight decrease in accuracy (79.91%) compared to ArBERTv2 alone (80.19%), the F1-score for this ensemble (80.61%) surpassed that of both individual models (ArBERTv2's 80.15% and CAMeLBERT's 79.45%). This enhancement in F1-score indicates a refined balance between precision and recall, indicating a deeper understanding of the Arabic WSD task.

It's important to note that while the "No SEED" results showed remarkably high performance, the decision to work with a fixed *SEED*, is critical for ensuring consistency and reproducibility across training and validation datasets. This method ensures that the improvements observed are attributable to the model's capabilities and not variations in dataset composition.

5 Conslusion

In conclusion, we presented a new dataset of context-gloss pairs for Arabic verbs, that we extracted from the Arramooz Alwaseet dictionary. Each pair of context and gloss is labeled with 0 or 1. This dataset is used in our exploration into the effectiveness of ensemble methods involving four pre-trained BERT-based models: AraBERT, CAMelBERT, ARBERTv2, and Arabic ALBERT, each fine-tuned for the task of Arabic WSD. We investigated how these separate models' could be used by stacked ensemble method to improve the performance of polysemous Arabic verb sense disambiguation. The results from our experiments underscore the value of ensemble methods in achieving superior accuracy and F1-scores compared to individual model performances. This highlights the efficacy of ensemble approaches in leveraging the complementary strengths of different models to better tackle the complexities of Arabic WSD. In future works, it would be beneficial to explore the application of advanced ensemble techniques to further improve disambiguation accuracy.

References

1. Navigli, R.: Word sense disambiguation: a survey. ACM Comput. Surv. **41**(2) (2009). https://doi.org/10.1145/1459352.1459355
2. Devlin, J., Chang, M., Lee, K., Toutanova, K.: BERT: pre-training of deep bidirectional transformers for language understanding. CoRR **abs/1810.04805** (2018)
3. Peters, M.E., Neumann, M., Iyyer, M., Gardner, M., Clark, C., Lee, K., Zettlemoyer, L.: Deep contextualized word representations. In: Walker, M., Ji, H., Stent, A. (eds.) Proceedings of the 2018 Conference of the North American Chapter of the Association for Computational Linguistics: Human Language Technologies, Volume 1 (Long Papers), pp. 2227–2237. Association for Computational Linguistics, New Orleans, Louisiana (2018). https://doi.org/10.18653/v1/N18-1202
4. Al-Hajj, M., Jarrar, M.: ArabGlossBERT: fine-tuning BERT on context-gloss pairs for WSD. In: Proceedings of the Conference Recent Advances in Natural Language Processing - Deep Learning for Natural Language Processing Methods and Applications. INCOMA Ltd., Shoumen, Bulgaria(2021). https://doi.org/10.26615/978-954-452-072-4_005
5. Zerrouki, T.: Towards an open platform for arabic language processing. PhD thesis (2020). https://doi.org/10.13140/RG.2.2.29882.82881
6. El-Razzaz, M., Fakhr, M.W., Maghraby, F.A.: Arabic gloss WSD using BERT. Appl. Sci. **11**(6) (2021). https://doi.org/10.3390/app11062567
7. Yap, B.P., Koh, A., Chng, E.S.: Adapting BERT for word sense disambiguation with gloss selection objective and example sentences. In: Findings of the Association for Computational Linguistics: EMNLP 2020, pp. 41–46. Association for Computational Linguistics, Online (2020). https://doi.org/10.18653/v1/2020.findings-emnlp.4
8. Antoun, W., Baly, F., Hajj, H.: Arabert: transformer-based model for Arabic language understanding. In: LREC 2020 Workshop Language Resources and Evaluation Conference 11-16, pp. 9 (2020)
9. Abdelali, A., Hassan, S., Mubarak, H., Darwish, K., Samih, Y.: Pre-training BERT on Arabic tweets: Practical considerations (2021). arXiv:2102.10684 [cs.CL]
10. Inoue, G., Alhafni, B., Baimukan, N., Bouamor, H., Habash, N.: The interplay of variant, size, and task type in Arabic pre-trained language models. In: Proceedings of the Sixth Arabic Natural Language Processing Workshop. Association for Computational Linguistics, Kyiv, Ukraine (Online) (2021)

11. Xu, C., Barth, S., Solis, Z.: Applying ensembling methods to BERT to boost model performance. (2019). https://api.semanticscholar.org/CorpusID:204830597
12. Wu, Z., Liang, J., Zhang, Z., Lei, J.: Exploration of text matching methods in Chinese disease qa systems: a method using ensemble based on BERT and boosted tree models. J. Biomed. Inform. **115**, 103683 (2021). https://doi.org/10.1016/j.jbi.2021.103683
13. Dietterich, T.G.: Ensemble methods in machine learning. In: Multiple Classifier Systems, pp. 1–15. Springer, Berlin, Heidelberg (2000)
14. Elmadany, A., Nagoudi, E.M.B., Abdul-Mageed, M.: ORCA: A Challenging Benchmark for Arabic Language Understanding (2023)
15. Safaya, A.: Arabic-ALBERT. https://doi.org/10.5281/zenodo.4718724
16. Elayeb, B.: Arabic word sense disambiguation: a review. Artif. Intell. Rev. **52**(4), 2475–2532 (2019). https://doi.org/10.1007/s10462-018-9622-6
17. Akbik, A., Bergmann, T., Blythe, D., Rasul, K., Schweter, S., Vollgraf, R.: FLAIR: an easy-to-use framework for state-of-the-art NLP. In: Proceedings of the 2019 Conference of the North American Chapter of the Association for Computational Linguistics (Demonstrations), pp. 54–59. Association for Computational Linguistics, Minneapolis, Minnesota (2019). https://doi.org/10.18653/v1/N19-4010
18. Džeroski, S., Panov, P., Ženko, B.: In: Meyers, R.A. (ed.) Machine Learning, Ensemble Methods in, pp. 5317–5325. Springer, New York, NY (2009). https://doi.org/10.1007/978-0-387-30440-3_315
19. Soni, B.: Stacking to Improve Model Performance: A Comprehensive Guide on Ensemble Learning in Python. URL (2023). https://medium.com/@brijesh_soni/stacking-to-improve-model-performance-a-comprehensive-guide-on-ensemblelearning-in-python-9ed53c93ce28
20. Darwish, K., Mubarak, H.: Farasa: A new fast and accurate Arabic word segmenter. In: Calzolari, N., (eds.) Proceedings of the Tenth International Conference on Language Resources and Evaluation (LREC'16), pp. 1070–1074. European Language Resources Association (ELRA), Portorož, Slovenia (2016). https://aclanthology.org/L16-1170
21. Abdul-Mageed, M., Elmadany, A., Nagoudi, E.M.B.: ARBERT & MARBERT: Deep bidirectional transformers for Arabic. In: Proceedings of the 59th Annual Meeting of the Association for Computational Linguistics and the 11th International Joint Conference on Natural Language Processing (Volume 1: Long Papers), pp. 7088–7105. Association for Computational Linguistics, Online (2021). https://doi.org/10.18653/v1/2021.acl-long.551
22. Lan, Z., Chen, M., Goodman, S., Gimpel, K., Sharma, P., Soricut, R.: ALBERT: A lite BERT for self-supervised learning of language representations. CoRR **abs/1909.11942** (2019)

Author Index

B. Hdioud and S. L. Aouragh (Eds.): ICALP 2024, CCIS 2339, pp. 273–274, 2025.
https://doi.org/10.1007/978-3-031-79164-2